Doug Frank studied at Wheaton College and received the Ph.D. degree in history at the State University of New York (Buffalo).

He has been on the teaching faculty of several Christian liberal arts colleges, and is the author of the recently reissued *Less Than Conquerors: The Evangelical Quest for Power in the Early Twentieth Century* (Wipf and Stock Publishers, 2009).

Since 1975, he has taught in an undergraduate study center in the mountains near Ashland, OR, where students are invited to pursue their own intellectual and religious questions in a community of supportive peers and mentors.

www.dougfrankbooks.com

This is a beautiful piece of work, extraordinary for its spiritual and theo-logical—as well as its psychological and sociological—insight. In the first half of the book, I thought, "This is the best and deepest diagnosis of what's wrong with American evangelicalism I've ever read." In the second half of the book, I thought, "This is one of the best and most moving accounts of Jesus' humanity and death that I've ever read."

This book will stay with me for a long time, and I will recommend it to many friends. In fact, I've already started making a list.

– BRIAN McLAREN
Speaker (www.brianmclaren.net)
Author of *The Secret Message of Jesus* and
Finding Our Way Again—and other titles

●　　●　　●

A Gentler God is a fascinating insight into the psychology of evangelicalism and the men who gave shape to it. Doug Frank carefully, lovingly uncovers the emotional damage that can result from clinging to an "immaculate-magical-almighty" deity, when our souls might be saved by the messy and merciful Jesus.

The author beautifully articulates a Savior who might break our hearts open—truly "save us" in a profound way not just from some deadly fate after we die, but from the "deathliness" and "hell" of living now, locked up in false pretenses, loveless fear and damning shame.

I wish everyone (I'm not exaggerating) would read this book.

– DEBBIE BLUE
Pastor, House of Mercy, St. Paul, MN
Author of *Sensual Orthodoxy* and
From Stone to Living Word

●　　●　　●

I have encountered many within the Christian community whose souls have been crippled by a distant, majestic, untouchable God. In *A Gentler God*, Doug Frank tenderly traces our destructive attraction to this false God while uncovering the earthy, vulnerable, shameless person of Jesus as the true revelator of unconditional Love.

If read as openly as it is written, this book has the capacity to release a kind of human freedom and vitality that each of us aches to embody. Doug Frank is a healer and this book a much-needed balm.

– MARK YACONELLI
Author of *Wonder, Fear, and Longing* and
Contemplative Youth Ministry

•   •   •

Reading *A Gentler God* is like listening to someone telling truths in a house filled with family secrets. Frank leaves no corner of evangelical theology and practice un-probed and un-narrated. His dogged pursuit of a genuine salvation event sends him back to the Bible to discover the good news of an authentically human Jesus and a God who treasures, rather than condemns, the "beautiful mystery of the self."

Frank touches a nerve so deep that evangelicals—both professed and disaffected—will *feel* something while reading this book. And this is precisely what Frank aims to do: to attend to the yearnings, betrayals and lost-loves of evangelicals. No other book has so aptly named, and met, the deep longings and deeper disappointments of wayward evangelicals.

– SHELLY RAMBO
Assistant Professor of Theology
Boston University

•   •   •

Doug Frank is kind and gracious and dangerous and fearless and honest—all at the same time. This is a book I'm convinced is going to help lots of people find liberation from the malevolent Being they never believed in in the first place.

These pages contain a lifetime of experience, wisdom, pain, healing—and, of course, resurrection. Deeply moving, extraordinarily insightful—this is a rare book.

– ROB BELL
Founding Pastor, Mars Hill Bible Church
Grand Rapids, MI
Author of *Velvet Elvis* and *Sex God*

．　　．　　．

Doug Frank finds his model for a gentler God in the unpredictable, but welcoming Jesus of the Gospels. His exploration arises from his fundamentalist childhood, including his evangelical college years, but leads on to an examination of the evangelical tradition itself.

Frank questions a loving God who tolerates eternal torture for those who fail. Instead, he points to the hospitality of Jesus, who confronts the "godly" and redeems life's failures. Frank's personal story makes his argument accessible, but he is also knowledgeable in the Bible and psychology. This is a book you don't want to miss.

– MARGARET G. ALTER
Author of *Resurrection Psychology:*
An Understanding of Human Personality Based on the
Life and Teachings of Jesus

．　　．　　．

Jesus welcomed all to the table. Unclean outcasts and respected religious professionals alike were held in the grace of the God he knew. Doug Frank knows this God. And he knows this God through Jesus.

It was a painful journey. Raised and educated in American evangelical Christianity, Frank has experienced the soul-chilling terror of a God both condemning and cold. He knows the shame that festers before a capricious judge, and the self-doubt from the crazy-making insistence that such a Being is benevolent.

But Frank knows more. He knows a God who loves and feels. He reveals, through careful theology and stories from his soulful experience, how this God is at odds with the God too often proclaimed in evangelical communities, even though this "gentler" God is the very one these communities so deeply yearn for.

This book is a feast for all who have been touched by evangelical Christianity, whether traumatized or transformed. It welcomes the child scarred by condemnation and the dogmatic convert clutching after theological certainty. Indeed, like Jesus, it welcomes the scarred child and dogmatic convert in each of us.

– FRANK ROGERS JR.
Muriel Bernice Roberts Associate Professor of
Spiritual Formation, Claremont School of Theology
Author of *The God of Shattered Glass*

⬤　　⬤　　⬤

A Gentler God is a labor of love, aimed at healing *the* common wound of Protestant and Catholic evangelicals. It's hard to explain "love" to veiled "hate" without sounding mean, but this book pulls it off. The gentleness with which Doug Frank deconstructs the Almighty of popular preaching and the schizoid salvation story of America's patriarchs could not be more respectful of the God of infinite love, the forgiveness of Jesus and evangelical tradition itself.

Nowhere does Frank take the tone of "educated and freed authority" who "knows better." With the improvisational humility of a teacher/healer who's worked with hundreds of wounded faithful—and suffered faith-wounds himself—Frank applies salves and bandages as soothing as the touch of a truly loving parent, the mercy of the Gospels, the wind on the plain of Mamre.

Welcome to the masterwork of a huge-hearted, evangelical son.

– DAVID JAMES DUNCAN
Author of *The Brother K* and *God Laughs and Plays*

. . .

No one has shaped my understanding of the gospel more profoundly over the years than Doug Frank. He writes with passion, clarity and uncommon insight. The Jesus who emerges in these pages offers true rest to those wearied of the triumphalist God of American evangelicalism.

A wonderful, troubling book that offers a gospel for the disenchanted, for whom the church is just another dead building and God a nagging presence or a painful absence.

– RANDALL BALMER
Episcopal Priest
Professor of American Religious History
Barnard College, Columbia University

A GENTLER GOD

A GENTLER GOD

Breaking free of the Almighty in the company of the human Jesus

DOUG FRANK

WIPF & STOCK · Eugene, Oregon

Wipf and Stock Publishers
199 W 8th Ave, Suite 3
Eugene, OR 97401

A Gentler God
Breaking free of the Almighty in the company of the human Jesus
By Frank, Doug
Copyright © 2010 by Frank, Doug All rights reserved.
Softcover ISBN-13: 978-1-7252-8372-5
Publication date 6/29/2020
Previously published by Albatross Books, 2010

*Religion can hide us as nothing else
from the face of God.*
Martin Buber[1]

Your face, God, do I seek.
Psalm 27:8

*The God of curved space, the dry
God, is not going to help us, but the
son whose blood spattered
the hem of his mother's robe.*
Jane Kenyon[2]

Jesus has me in his grasp.
Otsu[3]

---

1   Quoted in Nicholas Lash, *Easter in Ordinary: Reflections on Human Experience and the Knowledge of God* (Charlottesville: University Press of Virginia, 1988), 178.

2   Jane Kenyon, "Looking at Stars," in *Otherwise: New and Selected Poems* (St. Paul, MN: Graywolf Press, 1996), 175.

3   Otsu is a character in Shusaku Endo's novel, *Deep River*, Van C. Gessel, trans. (New York: New Directions Books, 1994), 191.

CONTENTS

•   •   •

PART TWO

IN THE COMPANY OF THE HUMAN JESUS

ACKNOWLEDGMENTS

I BEGAN WRITING THIS BOOK IN the early 1990s. Countless conversations, many now forgotten, contributed to the intellectual and emotional ferment that gave birth to the convictions expressed here.

Many friends have done me the favor of thinking with me about the issues explored in this book and offering me constructive feedback to successive versions of the manuscript. Others have generously offered their technical help.

To all of the following, and any I have inadvertently overlooked, I offer heartfelt thanks:

Sam Alvord, Lynn and Mark Baker, Randall Balmer, Thomas Becknell, Debbie Blue, Bev Byrnes, John Caputo, Tim Copeland, Carole Cragg, Doug Davidson, David James Duncan, Bob Ekblad, Kristin Fast, Brenda Martin Hurst, Michael Hyrniuk, Kenn Inskeep, Julia Janeway, Grey Jensen, Del Jones, Steven Jungkeit, Alison Kling, Bill Lawton, Nancy Linton, Diane McArdel, Barbara McClure, Robert MacKenzie, Daniel Marsh, Jeremy Myers, Jen Ledford Miatke, Rudy and Shirley Nelson, Brett Nicholls, Kris Pikaart, Shelly Rambo, Frank Rogers, Ross and Ruth Roskamp, David Sheagley, Jamie Skillen, John Stackhouse, Heather Hillstrom Starbird, Mike Van Eerden, Dave Willis, Jon Witt, Mark Yaconelli, Philip Yancey.

Thirty years ago, my colleague, John Linton, persuaded me that the Bible is the source of unadulterated good news. He has been unwavering in that conviction. I have read the Bible in the light of his interpretive insight ever since. *Part Two* of this book, in particular, has his mark on it from beginning to end. I am deeply grateful for his guidance, and his very good friendship.

Special thanks to the hundreds of college students who, since 1975, have ventured to our mountain hamlet near Ashland, Oregon, to read and think and talk with us at the Oregon Extension. They have been a source of life to me. Their questions and challenges, their honesty and forgiveness have nurtured my evolving understanding of God and of myself.

Without the stimulating conversation, incessant prodding and perceptive editing of John Waterhouse, this book would not have been published. He is a fine friend.

My mother and father, Ethel and Walter Frank, have always stood by me, even when I raised questions about what is nearest and dearest to their hearts. In my sixty-eight years, I have never had occasion to question their unconditional and unrelenting love for me. Their faithfulness to me is a parable of the God I portray in *Part Two* of this book.

My wife, Marjorie, and my daughter, Sara, have taught me that being a mess does not disqualify me for love. Their love has made tangible the presence of Jesus in my life. With gratitude, I dedicate this book to them.

INTRODUCTION

TRUST JESUS!

This command leaps out at unsuspecting drivers from a giant billboard that sits beside an interstate highway near my home. The words, in large black letters, are superimposed over a gaunt hand with a spike driven through it. The hand belongs to Jesus. It drips bright red blood from jagged wounds. In all probability, the sign—a one-size-fits-all directive to an endless stream of passing strangers—is the brainchild of an "evangelical" Christian.[1] It broadcasts the belief that has reinforced brand loyalty among this variety of Christians for many generations: that, as far as God is concerned, there is only one way to heaven.

I know the overtones these words are intended to carry. It would not surprise me to see a second billboard, a mile down the road, spelling out the implications of the first: *OR ELSE!*

I know the tone because I am an evangelical Christian myself. I grew up in a pastor's home, had a "born-again" experience in my childhood, spent most of my discretionary time as a teenager in Christian youth programs, graduated from a well-known evangelical college, and, after a brief time-out in a university graduate school, have spent my life as a history professor in evangelical colleges. I love the Bible, and my students will tell you I can't stop talking about

---

1 Evangelicalism, as I will use the term, describes a loose coalition of believers from many Christian denominations who accept the Bible as their final authority, who believe they are "saved from sin" and "born again" to eternal life only if they accept the death of Jesus on the cross as payment for their sins, who cultivate a "personal relationship" with God as the path to a transformed life, and who believe it is important to spread the gospel to all the world. Estimates vary widely on how many Americans are evangelicals, depending on how the pollsters ask the question. Most estimates fall between 30% and 40%.

Jesus. If the Apostle Paul could say, "Brothers, I am a Pharisee, a son of Pharisees" (Acts 23:6), I can say, "Dear Reader, I am an evangelical, a son of evangelicals."

But I have a bone to pick with my fellow Christians, and it has something to do with that gruesome highway sign. The word *evangelical* is derived from an ancient term meaning *good news*. Whenever I pass that sign, I feel a familiar twisting in my guts that translates as *bad news*. The potential good news represented by a sympathetic figure like Jesus is out-shouted by the sign's unspoken threat. The threat can remain unspoken—although, of course, in many religious circles it does not—because it automatically triggers a voice planted firmly, by long conditioning, in my evangelical heart. That voice *says*, "God will love you forever." But it *means*, "In the end, it'll be God's way—or the highway!"

Evangelical Christians are most often distinguished from "mainline Protestants"—not to mention Roman Catholics, the Eastern Orthodox and other historic expressions of Christianity—by reference to their doctrinal statements or theological perspectives.[2] I have no quarrel with these attempts at definition. But I believe they represent a surface reality. What is most interesting to me is not what we evangelicals *think*, but how we evangelicals *feel*—specifically, how we feel about ourselves and God. Since evangelicals are taught that what we feel isn't very important, this deeper reality is sometimes hidden, even from ourselves. Often, the only way we know it's there is when we pass a highway sign, or read a Bible verse, or hear a line from a preacher's sermon, and take the time to notice that we've just felt a twisting in our guts.

---

2 I followed conventional practice when I described evangelicalism in a previous footnote. George Marsden, the dean of the historians of American evangelicalism, offers a short-cut definition: "anyone who likes Billy Graham." *Understanding Fundamentalism and Evangelicalism* (Grand Rapids, MI: William B. Eerdmans Publishing Company, 1991), 4–6.

This book is an attempt to understand the source of the twisting in my guts, and to offer hope to those who share this condition with me.[3] I believe the condition is widespread. Many religious traditions are authoritarian and punitive. Invariably, God is called on to play the role of enforcer. So mention of the word "God" can engender ambivalent feelings—including that wrenching in the gut—in people from many religious backgrounds. It can be distasteful even to those who did not encounter religion in their childhood families, but who soaked up the commonly used "God language" in the surrounding culture, or who have had to fend off the advances of well-meaning, religious zealots.

I am eager to speak to anyone for whom the word "God" has become distasteful, but who still yearns for an encounter with a divine Spirit whose essence is love—genuine, unfettered love.

This book will focus on the God I have known since earliest childhood. I will put him under the microscope, as it were, and ask: does he look like Jesus, or like the God Jesus spoke of? Does he look like the divine Spirit whom Jesus called his "Father"?[4] If not—and now you know my conclusion before I begin—where in the world has he come from?

Over the years, I have reached a few conclusions as to the source of the evangelical God. These have been eye-opening and liberating for me. I'd like to share with you those conclusions—and hopefully that liberation. I have also heard authentically good news in the

3   A text often quoted by evangelical youth leaders, to motivate teens to "evangelize"—meaning, tell their "unsaved" friends about Jesus—is I Peter 3:15: "Always be prepared to make a defense to any one who calls you to account for the hope that is in you, yet do it with gentleness and reverence." I hope my childhood youth leaders will take some credit for the spirit and purpose of this book.

4   Although careful evangelical scholars insist that God is without gender, evangelicals commonly think of God as masculine. I will use masculine personal pronouns when referring to the God of my childhood—the God of twentieth-century evangelicalism. I will avoid those pronouns when I speak about the God I meet in Jesus.

life and words of Jesus—a different Jesus than I first met in Sunday school. This news has worked very deep changes in my *feelings*—both about God and about me. I would like my evangelical sisters and brothers—and anyone wounded, angered or alienated by their experience with a threatening God—to hear that news too.

If you are a Christian reader, particularly an evangelical, you may wish to take exception to my suggestion that there is truly good news about Jesus that you haven't yet heard. And perhaps you are right. But I hope you will give me a chance to explain fully what I mean by "good news." I want you to know that I believe the spirit of Jesus is continually present in every human heart, and thus the good news is always somewhere inside all of us. And yet, its voice can easily be drowned out by the bad news associated with the conventional evangelical God. This book is an attempt to clear some of the static in the religious air around us, in hope that a clearer signal will beam through.

●   ●   ●

I know there are readers of this book who are products of a Christian upbringing and who will not be surprised to hear me describe the evangelical God as a bringer of bad news. These are evangelical-ism's "walking wounded." Many continue to attend church services, hoping to hear good news, but often leave feeling worse than when they entered. They still try to read the Bible, but they encounter in its pages only God's absence—and in some cases, God's condemna-tion. They know something is not so "good" about the "good news." Two of these people are friends of mine: Steven and Bev.

I mentioned to Steven, then in his mid-twenties, that I was writing a book I hoped would be of use to "disaffected evangelicals" like him. In a return email, he described these people from personal experience:

I know many people, and I am one of them, who have who stopped hearing good news in the nostrums and shibboleths of the evangelical subculture. They have struck out on a different path (often with cynicism, rage and irony as traveling companions), hoping to find a life-giving word elsewhere: in mainline churches, books, even coffee shops.

But although they left in a fit of pique, most of them are still, from time to time, haunted by the specter of the "old neighborhood." They wonder what went wrong with them—or with it—and why. They wonder where they will ever hear good news, now that the meanings of the Bible have been exhausted by insipid Sunday school lessons, and their first impulse is to hurl the holy book across a room rather than read it. Still, in their heart of hearts, they want to believe that there is something that will cut through the veneer of piety and give real food to their souls. They feel a little schizophrenic, repulsed by and yet vaguely attracted to Jesus and his gospel—almost in spite of themselves.

Another friend, Bev, then in her thirties, described her experience of being a "disaffected evangelical" this way:

Faith seemed to be about swallowing the teaching of the church. When that teaching began to rumble in my gut, I was told to "deny myself"—to ignore the rumblings and pray, sometimes desperately, that God would please make the turmoil go away so I could be "right in God's eyes." I now see that these were the church's eyes. What drove me away was this constant need to measure up, to be "in" and not "out" in this divisive, judgmental, rule-based system. Of course, the "words" are always about love and forgiveness and mercy. But they don't describe the reality.

I'm talking about an enormous system of conditions and demands, a *rigid* model of what it means to be "right with God."

Many Christians protest when I talk like this; but maybe—when one is part of the system—one has trouble seeing the wood for the trees.

At any rate, there are many like me. Right now, we're all wandering around, searching for a spiritual community and having a hard time finding one.

Neither Steven nor Bev uses the word "pain." Like many "disaffected evangelicals," they may feel it is overly dramatic to believe that their despair, disappointment, confusion, sadness or anger qualify as pain. But pain is what their stories, and many similar stories, convey.

I hope this book will help readers who are evangelicals and former evangelicals like Steven and Bev, as well as readers from other restrictive religious traditions, to honor their pain. I will try to show that their pain, although very real, was inflicted by a false God. I hope they will allow themselves to believe in a truer God, one who was present in Jesus and whose news is unabashedly good. Like them, Jesus was tormented—and ultimately hounded to his death—by the false God of institutional religion. But he is alive, and he has experienced their pain.

*   *   *

I've organized this book in two parts—one for the bad news, the other for the good. Each part may be read separately. Although each makes occasional reference to the other, neither requires that you read the other in order for it to be understood.

Part One takes a long, hard look at the God who hides within and maintains the institutional structure of evangelical Christianity. Evangelicals do not have a "lock" on this God—"he" has appeared, in one guise or another, in many times and places throughout the history of Christianity,[5] and he shows up in non-Christian religions as well. But evangelicals have put a particular spin on him, and that spin has shaped my life and my religious experience for over sixty years.

In order to know myself, I have had to become more familiar with this God, and try to understand him from the inside. I will show that this God does not give evidence of a truly loving heart, and this makes it hard for his children to love him, as Jesus urged, "with all our heart" (Mark 12:30). Once we can admit we *don't* love this unlovable God "with all our heart"—a very painful admission, to be sure—I believe we will have passed an important milestone on the journey to find and love a truer, better God.

Part Two is about this truer, better God. I hear this God's liberating word in the living spirit and the dying gasps of the shabby human being who was nailed, two thousand years ago, to a splintered pole in Palestine.[6] Unlike the "bad-news God" of evangelicalism, this human God feels genuine warmth for me—in the words of the familiar hymn, "just as I am"—and my heart instinctively reciprocates. In the embrace of this human God, my fear of God and my religiously-inspired enmity toward myself begin to find relief.

•   •   •

I would like to address, briefly, a few specific concerns I can imagine naturally arising in my readers.

Many evangelicals, including a good many close friends, are abidingly loyal to their local churches—and rightly so. These churches

---

5 A rich and disturbing portrait of a "bad God" can be found in Jean Delumeau, *Sin the Fear: The Emergence of a Western Guilt Culture 13th-18th Centuries* (New York: St. Martin's Press, 1991).

6 Which is why the highway billboard, with its blaring command, usually brings a wry smile to my face. I actually do trust Jesus. It's just not the sign-maker's Jesus.

are often the richest experience of "community" available in our secularized and individualized twenty-first century. For many, our deepest friendships, our times of fun and recreation, the nurture of our children, our support in times of suffering all occur within the context of the local church. Nothing that I write is meant to trivialize or deny these gifts, or minimize the importance of the local church.

It is my experience that individual evangelicals, including church members, are often kinder, wiser, far more tolerant and accepting than the God who seeps like a poison gas through their church's language and teaching. I believe that an encounter with the God who comes to us in Jesus—of whom I will speak in *Part Two*—has the potential to open floodgates of honesty in our church lives, permitting us to confess more openly to one another the burdensome ambivalence that we have carried secretly in our hearts. Such honesty, and such a Jesus, can only deepen the undeniable graces of our church experience.

From time to time I will offer brief vignettes from my own spiritual journey and I will use them to illustrate the character of evangelical Christianity. Your experience—even if you are an evangelical—may be very different from mine. I hope you will bring your own experience to this text and prioritize its truths over mine.

The winding narrative of my life has, of course, brought me to deep convictions. At times, my enthusiasm for these convictions may imply that I consider them to be true in some absolute or timeless way. In fact, however, they are the considered conclusions of my own lived experience. They have no greater claim to absolute truth than the evangelicalism I critique. I hope that putting them into book form will encourage you to take your own experience more seriously and bring it to the ongoing human conversation about God.

Because I still consider myself to be part of the evangelical "family," I will often use the pronoun "we" when generalizing about evangelical attitudes, viewpoints, beliefs or spiritual experience. But my views are a minority position within that family. When it would be awkward, and/or untrue to include myself in these generalizations, I will use the personal pronoun "they."

I do not mean by this to distance myself from evangelicals as my community of faith, but to be honest about the fact that I no longer share certain theological perspectives that the evangelical gatekeepers consider, at this moment at least, to be non-negotiable. Of course, time and human experience have a strange way of re-negotiating what was once considered non-negotiable.

Several women who read early drafts of this book alerted me to passages in which, in their opinion, my explorations of Christian faith and my models of personal development speak more pointedly to the experiences of males than of females. I am grateful for their candor, and I see their point. Where I could, I worked to minimize the effect of my gender-bias. But I cannot completely escape the undertow of my own experience, and am continually surprised by how deeply and unconsciously my voice is implicated within and distorted by a masculinist bias.[7] I therefore have tried even more assiduously to speak in the first person, so as to avoid implying that everyone shares my experience. I am gratified that a number of women readers have not felt excluded from the broader contours of my account, and am eager to hear from any who do.

Lastly, to improve the book's flow, I have put technical theological comments, and related but not critical material, into footnotes. I also provide there a sampling of the source materials with which I have been in conversation.

---

7   Observations by my teaching colleague, Nancy Linton, and conversations with another friend, Dr. Shelly Rambo, have been particularly helpful here. Both have shared with me their enthusiasm for Grace M. Jantzen's book, *Becoming Divine: Towards a Feminist Philosophy of Religion*, which analyzes the conventional Christian God quite like I do, but proposes a different way forward. Had I read her book earlier in my own writing process, I am sure her mark would have been seen more frequently in these pages.

*　　　*　　　*

I see signs of healthy ferment in evangelical circles these days, which lead me to believe that the bad-news God of evangelicalism may be undergoing a crisis of credibility. Younger evangelicals seem more willing than their parents to admit how they feel about God. They seem less interested in wooden, literalistic readings of the Bible and are less attracted to logical nitpicking. They listen with greater freedom to the spirit of a biblical text. They seem more willing to trust what their hearts *do* believe, less interested in hearing what others think they *should* believe.

I am also heartened by the popularity, among evangelicals of all ages, of voices courageous enough to entertain the possibility that God's love may be truly unconditional and never-ending.[8] I trust that these presage an historic shift toward a more truly freeing and nurturing God.

These signs may, however, only imply another wave of the cosmetic changes that evangelicalism accommodates so readily and co-opts so deftly without altering its underlying allegiance to the same old bad news. I agree with Brian McLaren's assessment, summarized in the title of his recent book, that the good news that Jesus brings means *Everything Must Change.*

In evangelicalism, however, nothing truly important—nothing that touches the deepest levels of our being—can possibly change until we bring our most destructive perceptions of the character of God out of the darkened corners of our own spirits and allow them to dissolve in the strange light cast by Jesus. Once they do dissolve,

---

8　Among these are books by Kathleen Norris, Henri J. M. Nouwen, David James Duncan, Brennan Manning, Jean Vanier, Frederick Buechner, Virginia Hampl, Brian McLaren, Shane Claiborne, Debbie Blue, Donald Miller, Rob Bell, Russell Rathbun, Anne Lamott, Jan Bonda, Mary Oliver, Jalal Al-Din Rumi, Hafiz, William P. Young, Thomas Merton, Simone Weil, Richard Rohr, Philip Gulley, James Mulholland, Cynthia Bourgeault and Gerald May.

the word "evangelical" itself will require an historic redefinition, if not a well-deserved retirement. I hope this book can make a small contribution to that long-awaited dissolution.

PART ONE
BREAKING FREE OF THE ALMIGHTY

"*The Newtonian God [is] that tasking and antiquated figure who haunts children and repels strays, who sits on the throne of judgment frowning and figuring, and who with the strength of his arm dishes out human fates, in the form of cancer or cash, to 5.9 billion people—to teach, dazzle, rebuke, or try us, one by one, and to punish or reward us, day by day, for our thoughts, words, and deeds.*"
Annie Dillard*

---

* *For the Time Being* (New York: Alfred A. Knopf, 1999), 165.

CHAPTER 1
Born Again. . . and Again
Getting right with a punitive deity

The pastor said
every time you breathe in, breathe out
eight people go to hell.
Gina Bergamino[1]

EVERYONE KNOWS HOW you get to be an evangelical Christian. You're "born again." You have a personal meeting with God. He "saves" you and welcomes you into his family. He promises you an eternity in heaven. You are "in the fold."

And once you are "in the fold," you have a personal relationship with Jesus Christ or with God—these are interchangeable. If you don't have this personal relationship, you're not an evangelical. Evangelicals know that, although God definitely wants you to hold the right beliefs and live the right kind of life and attend a "Bible-believing church," none of this matters unless you have been "born again" and enjoy a personal relationship with God.

Evangelicals usually have a story about when and where they were "born-again." The impact of this experience lingers deep inside us, silently shaping our understanding of the God we met in that dramatic moment. I had a "born-again" experience when I was

---

1 "In Missouri," *Christian Century*, 107 (#19), June 13–20, 1990, 588.

seven years old. Perhaps because I was encouraged to repeat the story from time to time, it is one of the few childhood experiences I remember well.

·   ·   ·

SOFTLY AND TENDERLY

My story is in two acts. In the first, a slight boy in a brown suit stands in a church pew with his head bowed and his eyes closed. Although he is motionless, a fierce battle rages inside him. The hundred or so members of his father's congregation are also standing. The "invitation" is being issued—a nightly ritual, during this annual week of "revival services." As the congregation sings the sweet, pleading hymns they know so well—"Softly and tenderly, Jesus is calling"— the visiting evangelist invites reluctant sinners to raise their hands and accept Jesus as their personal Savior.

The sermon this night, as every night, is calibrated to reap a harvest of souls. Its touch-point is the tale of a man who waited too long to say yes to Jesus. He refused to raise his hand in answer to the pastor's invitation. He walked out of the church doors and into the night. As he crossed the street, he was struck and killed by a passing car. Now it is too late—his soul will burn forever in the lake of fire.

This story has riveted the boy. He is suddenly and acutely aware that death stalks him, ready to pounce as he plays in the schoolyard or sleeps in his bed. The boy's heart is leaden in his chest. He sees with utter clarity and deep terror what death will mean: never again will he see his mother and father, his brothers, his warm, simple-hearted grandmother, his Aunt Clara, who calls him her "favorite oldest nephew," his wry Uncle Jimmy, his beloved cousins. If he does not summon the courage to raise his hand, he will spend eternity in hell. The prospect of unspeakable pain doesn't terrorize him nearly as much as the knowledge that he will be utterly alone.

The boy yearns to settle his eternal destiny. But first, he must overcome his intense shyness. Finally he manages, for a brief instant, to raise a hand into the air. The preacher notices—"Yes, I see that hand"—and relief washes over the boy. He is "saved."

But just as he begins to relax, the preacher raises the ante. Now he wants anyone who raised a hand to step out from the pew, walk to the front of the church, and kneel at the altar. It takes a bold public gesture like this to confirm the "sincerity" of such a momentous decision.

The boy is small for his age. He feels dwarfed by the phalanx of adults to his right and to his left, blocking his exit from the pew. He can't imagine pushing past them all—they seem lost in prayer— and he winces to think of treading the long red carpet alone. Fear freezes him in place until, finally, it is too late. The haunting pleas of the final invitation hymn—"Come home, come home, ye who are weary come home"—give way to what seems an eternal silence. The service ends, and, with a heavy heart, the boy joins his family as they walk down the block to their home.

·   ·   ·

ONCE AND FOR ALL

The second act opens later that same night in the boy's bedroom. His mother is kneeling next to him, on the cold, hard floor, as he says his nightly bedtime prayer. "Now I lay me down to sleep. I pray the Lord my soul to keep. If I should die before I wake. . ." His voice falters. . .

Ever since leaving the church, he has been looking for the courage to tell his parents he isn't sure he's really saved. He didn't go forward—isn't that a necessary part of the deal? He doesn't want to die and go to hell. But his tongue seems frozen. Now, at the last line of the prayer—"I pray the Lord my soul to take"—the dam bursts and he breaks into a sob. His mother asks what's wrong, but no words come out. She calls his father, who kneels beside him, laying his arm gently across the boy's shoulders.

The boy's head is buried in his crossed arms, his tears drip into the bedspread. He manages a few muffled words: "I raised my hand... but I didn't go forward... I want to be saved." His father says that's good; there's no need to worry, it's not too late. Now is a good time to make sure. He leads the boy, line by line, in a short prayer. The boy hears his own thin, wavering voice telling Jesus he is sorry for his sins and wants to be saved. Then his father prays, his deep preacher's voice filling the room with authority and certainty.

His father says "amen," and the boy smiles through his tears. He knows everything is settled, once and for all. His father tells him he will never again be in danger of going to hell. An unbelievable happiness floods him. He is exhausted, but in a good way. He feels clean and fresh and light. He crawls into bed, a brand new person.

•   •   •

I'VE GOT THE JOY

I did not know it then, of course, but the battle between life and death that had been waged in my worried little heart on that night in 1949 was at that very moment energizing Christians all across America, and the rest of the English-speaking world, with headline-grabbing results.

Many Christians believed they were witnessing an unprecedented religious revival.[2] Fiery young preachers like Jack Wyrtzen in New York City, Charles Templeton in Toronto, Torrey Johnson

---

2 The best recent account of this revival, of the talented "band of brothers" whose energy fueled it, and of the evangelical movement that it inspired, is Garth M. Rosell, *The Surprising Work of God: Harold John Ockenga, Billy Graham, and the Rebirth of Evangelicalism* (Grand Rapids, MI: Baker Academic, 2008).

in Chicago, and Billy Graham in many cities across the country were packing stadiums and convention halls with cheering crowds of young people and their parents. They were masterful showmen who shared an identical formula for success: give teenagers a jolly good time, and then scare the hell out of them. These young men—some of them barely out of their twenties—shaped evangelical Christianity's understanding of God for the next half-century.

The most dynamic young preacher in my hometown of Philadelphia was Percy Crawford. His name figured large in our household pantheon. Crawford was a pioneer of Christian radio and television, and even though my parents heroically refused to admit television into our home until I was in high school, that wondrous little box did beam its flickering black-and-white images into my grandfather's home. During occasional visits, so long as it didn't compete with the exhilarating carnage of the Friday Night Fights, we kids were permitted to watch Percy Crawford's television program. On one occasion, we actually attended a Crawford rally in downtown Philadelphia.

Everybody familiar with Crawford's meetings knew he had fathered four handsome sons: Don, Dick, Dan and Dean. They sang as a quartet in his weekly rallies, and their names tripped as one word from the tongues of Philadelphia's evangelicals: *dondickdanandean*. My parents had four sons as well—I was the eldest—and showed a similar affection for the letter "D": *dougdavedaleandon*.[3]

When I was about ten, this mysterious connection between our family and the Crawfords suddenly dawned on me. I took pride in our resemblance to a Christian celebrity family, and began to think of Percy Crawford as a famous distant uncle. The connection soured after my parents stood the four of us up in matching sweaters in front of the church, one Sunday evening, to sing as a quartet. The effect

---

3 Years later, they named our serendipitous sister "Dawn."

was not pleasing. Our parents took mercy on us and quietly terminated our musical career.

What I remember about Crawford's rallies was their electric intensity. Song-leaders whipped the throngs of mostly young people into a frenzy and got them stomping their feet, leaping into the air, and shouting gospel choruses like "I've Got the Joy, Joy, Joy, Joy Down in My Heart." Christian athletes and other celebrities, whose public successes and healthy demeanors gave proof of the happiness found in Jesus, gave inspiring personal testimonies. And then, without skipping a beat, the fun-and-games atmosphere would give way to the deadly seriousness of the sermon.

Serious did not mean boring. Percy Crawford, like all those fresh-faced young evangelists, knew how to funnel an atmosphere buzzing with youthful adrenalin into a moment of great drama—and then turn up the heat. He contrived entertaining mixtures of biblical texts re-cast in the vernacular of youth, spellbinding stories of young people at the brink of salvation or doom, and a powerful rhetoric of personal intimacy. He riveted his youthful audiences to their seats. And then, at the climactic moment, he wrenched them up out of their seats and lured them down the aisles to "accept Jesus as their personal Savior."

At which point his voice took on an alluring intimacy. To the accompaniment of sentimental invitation hymns, he implored each listener, as if that person alone were the object of his deepest concern, to accept God's offer of salvation. Even his warnings of the dire penalties reserved for those who stayed in their seats were issued in pleading tones of almost irresistible tenderness.[4] The emotion in the hall was palpable, and the effect cathartic.

---

4 I do not doubt the sincerity of this tenderness. If you have been convinced that God will damn every unbeliever to eternal hell, and you know the way of escape, your heart may well break at the thought that a single one of these beautiful young people might reject God's offer of salvation.

. . .

ISN'T HE WONDERFUL?

The gentleness that crept into the voices of preachers like Crawford, Wyrtzen and Graham in the climactic moments of their sermons worked so effectively in part because their tones, up to that point, had *not* been gentle. The topic of many of these sermons, a favorite for its dramatic possibilities, was the horrifying reality of hell. The business of the evening was rescuing sinners from the certain prospect of eternal torment, while convincing them that the God who would readily send them to the lake of fire still loved them with an everlasting love.

If you are an evangelical Christian and you were born in the 1930s or '40s, you may already have an adequate collection of riveting lines from sermons like Percy Crawford's stored in the dim recesses of your brain. If not, you may not really "get" how persistently preachers like Crawford banged away on the subject of death and hell, how eloquently they depicted life on earth as "a grand rush into the jaws of death" where we are awaited by "an awful judge, a severe judge" who seems eager to serve up, to those who turn away from his love, an infinity of torture.

Here is a Percy Crawford sampler. Try "listening" through the ears of an impressionable fourteen-year-old:

- I tell you, if I were not trusting Jesus, if I were not a Christian, I would be afraid to live a day without Christ, lest I should drop into hell. I would be afraid to go to sleep, knowing as I do what the Bible says about hell.
- He who hesitates is lost. That is true and that is why I cry out to you, "Escape for thy life." Flee to the arms of the Son of God for forgiveness while there is still time, lest you go to the place where Jesus said, "There shall be weeping and wailing and gnashing of teeth,"

a hell from which you cannot escape.

- A man once said to me, "Well, how can God burn the body of a sinner, if that body is destroyed by fire, or scattered on the sea?" This problem is not beyond God's ingenuity. . . God is going to give the sinner a new immortal body, as it pleases him, which will be capable of burning and burning and never being consumed, so that "they gnawed their tongues with pain" and "suffered and cried out in their agony."

- Death in hell. . . is unending, continual agony, and it is the destination of all who spurn the love of the Savior. Do you wonder then why I am so anxious to get you to thank God for Jesus, for hell lasts a long time. Hell is more than a swear word. It is a reality. [5]

Often, the terror was intensified by way of a dramatic story of some dying soul who missed heaven by just a hair's breadth:

> I was preaching at a young people's rally, and as usual, at the close, I gave an invitation for any who cared to accept Christ. A girl at the back of the church leaned over to her chum beside her and urged her to accept Christ. The chum said, "Not now." Again the girl spoke to her chum and asked, "Why don't you make sure?" But the chum said, "Not tonight." She spoke to the chum a third time and urged, "Your mother and father would like to see you make sure," but the reply was, "Don't bother me. I'm not taking him tonight." And the meeting was over.
>
> She was introduced to me at the close of the service, a beautiful girl, just seventeen, the picture of health. She went back to her dormitory at school, she went to sleep, she got up in the morning,

---

[5] Percy Crawford, *Whither Goest Thou: A Series of Radio Messages Preached on 250 Stations over the Mutual Network* (East Stroudsburg, PA: The Pinebrook Book Club, 1946), 42, 24, 81, 57, 114. By my reading, all but one of the twenty sermons in this book specialize in terror.

had breakfast, and twenty minutes after breakfast, she fell over dead. She was almost a Christian. And they had a lovely funeral for her. The preacher spoke of her fine influence on those around her, but no one said anything about her spitting in the face of the Son of God. But you cannot do that and go to heaven.[6]

I did not hear this sermon when it was delivered. But I can feel the dissonance just below its surface. A few moments before Crawford spoke these lines, his organist, Norman Clayton, would have played one of his intimate compositions, like "He holds my hand" or "Now I belong to Jesus."[7] The audience might have sung "Isn't he wonderful, wonderful, wonderful?" But then, this "wonderful" Jesus becomes the sort of person who interprets a young girl's reluctance to walk forward in a crowded arena as a spit in his face. And this loving God is portrayed as someone who will go to the trouble of resurrecting a dead body—just to make sure that person will suffer eternal pain.

When I heard sermons like these as a child, I was not attuned to their emotional ambiguity—at least not consciously. I had heard sermons like them so often that the terror had been normalized. I suspect the same was true for Percy Crawford, and for the vast majority of his audiences.

●　　　●　　　●

RUNNING SCARED TO JESUS

Of course, this conversion ritual has a long history in conservative Protestantism. After the Second Great Awakening, in the first half of the nineteenth century, evangelicalism emerged as the most

---

6 Crawford, *Whither Goest Thou*, 69–70.

7 Joel Carpenter, *Revive Us Again: The Re-Awakening of American Fundamentalism* (New York: Oxford University Press, 1997), 165.

boldly entrepreneurial expression of worldwide Christianity. It adapted with lightning speed to the opportunities for religious innovation offered by a pluralistic, secularizing society and the shrinking monopoly power of traditional religious institutions. It understood that, when people felt free to "choose" a religion rather than settle for the one they were born into, the rewards of church growth and cultural influence, and ultimately even political power, would go to the winner of the competition for souls.

By the late nineteenth century, American evangelicals had become very effective in this competition. They borrowed, from the business world, the newest technologies for persuading and mobilizing people *en masse*. They excelled in inventive, crowd-pleasing oratory that traded heavily on personal appeal and celebrity status.

If one genealogy best describes the central dynamic of American evangelicalism in the free enterprise arena, it is the lineage, not of thoughtful theologians, but of charismatic mass evangelists. The greatest of these are just four: Charles Finney, Dwight L. Moody, Billy Sunday and Billy Graham.

Along with dozens of lesser figures, these four have helped fix the ritual of individual conversion at the center of evangelicalism's competitive strategy. Whatever your conscious motives may be, if you can incite hundreds of people to stand up, walk to the front of the church (tent, auditorium, amphitheater) and sign the bottom line (quite literally, in modern times), you can lay claim to the leadership of American evangelicalism. Naturally, you will generate vast sums of money and build a corporate structure, which will help your name generate even bigger headlines. It will be obvious that God is putting his stamp of approval on your work.[8]

Powerful incentives are needed to get this ball rolling. For

---

[8] Roger Finke and Rodney Stark describe the free market or entrepreneurial model of church growth in *The Churching of America, 1776–1990: Winners and Losers in Our Religious Economy* (Piscataway, NJ: Rutgers University Press, 1992).

evangelical Christianity, these incentives have focused on the two most emotionally charged of human experiences: our yearning for love and our susceptibility to fear. Virtually every evangelistic sermon relies on this two-pronged formula: God so *loves you* that he graciously offers you eternal life; God is so *angry with you* that he will punish you for ever and ever if you refuse his gracious offer. The carrot is never more than a few sentences removed from the stick.

The great revivalists in American history have applied this arguably self-contradictory formula with rigid consistency. The gentle D. L. Moody, a former shoe salesman, leaned toward heart-felt descriptions of God's love for the sinner, while the uncouth and comical Billy Sunday, a former baseball player, issued dire warnings in the tough language of the streets.[9] But both of them, and their imitators, made it abundantly clear that the *limits* of God's love are reached at the moment of death. The God who today offers sinners his love will tomorrow, as a matter of course, turn his back on them if they reject his offer, and will consign them to eternal torture.

These mass evangelists seemed to know that, for some things, fear is a more powerful motivator than love—that portraits of a reject-ing God are more effective than portraits of a loving God in getting sinners out of their seats and down the aisles. Almost without excep-tion, evangelical preachers have specialized in evoking fear. It is impossible to imagine their sermons without this component.

9　Billy Sunday said America was under the influence of "damnable, hell-born, whisky-soaked, hog-jowled, rum-soaked moral assassins." Parents allowed their children to "gad about the streets with every Tom, Dick and Harry, or keep company with some little jack rabbit whose character would make a black mark on some piece of tar paper." America was "fast hastening to the judgment that overtook Pompeii, . . .when God Almighty made old Mount Vesuvius vomit and puke in a hemorrhage of lava."

For these and many other examples, see Doug Frank, *Less Than Conquerors: The Evangelical Quest for Power in the Early Twentieth Century* (Eugene, OR: Wipf and Stock Publishers, 2009), 184–195. Originally published as *Less Than Conquerors: How Evangelicals Entered the Twentieth Century* (Grand Rapids, MI: William B. Eerdmans Publishing Company, 1986).

Naturally, an outsider might be excused for wondering: "Are you trying to scare us into loving God?" Jack Wyrtzen, the leading New York City youth evangelist from the 1930s through the 1950s (and a beloved evangelical leader well into the 1990s), had obviously heard the question, and had an answer: "Yes, I am."

In a model sermon reprinted in his biography, death and hell appear about two minutes after his sermon begins, and they re-surface about once a minute to the very end. Here is a typical passage:

> You must face death. . . You can't buy your way out of that appointment with God. . . You might have loved ones who will weep tears over you in your dying moments. But all their entreaties cannot stave off that dreaded moment, or stop the sword of death from one day plunging into your very being. . . You're going to spend that eternity in a wonderful Heaven or in an awful Hell. . . Every unconverted person in this world has death, judgment, and the Lake of Fire before him, and every throb of your pulse will bring you nearer and nearer to these awful realities. . .[10]

In the middle of this sermon, Wyrtzen poses rhetorically the all-too-obvious question: "Jack, what are you trying to do—scare me into getting converted?" He answers:

> Yes, I would to God that I could scare you into getting converted. If you're still unconverted, then it's quite evident that the "love of God" hasn't interested you very much, has it? Maybe what you need is to be scared a little, and if you're bound for hell, it's something to be scared about.[11]

---

10 George Sweeting, *The Jack Wyrtzen Story* (Grand Rapids, MI: Zondervan Publishing House, 1960), 50–57.
11 Sweeting, 56.

Like Wyrtzen, most preachers have defended such tactics by saying, simply: "They work." It may be true that they increase the number of adherents to their movement. But they do not work to enhance a trusting relationship with a loving God.

* * *

"THE WORLD OF THE DAMNED"

Someone living most of his or her life within the evangelical Christian world is unlikely to notice what may strike non-evangelicals, or non-Christians, as immediately obvious: that the God who presides over the conversion ritual is not acting like someone who really loves people. He acts like someone who is mostly interested in "sticking to the plan" and "closing the deal." He is like the vacuum cleaner salesman who gushes with good will and acts like your best friend—until you decide not to buy a vacuum cleaner. Then, he's not your best friend anymore—although, to be fair, vacuum cleaner salesmen don't ordinarily incinerate you forever.

The "conversion formula" insists, of course, that God devised his plan of salvation because he loves us and wants us to be with him forever. It also assures us that God continues to love us *even after* we reject his plan of salvation. But if we happen to die before we've changed our minds, then he sends us to a hell of constant, unbearable pain. This translates as: God shows us his eternal and unconditional love by rejecting us if we reject him—by sentencing us to unspeakable agony and declaring that he has no further interest in us.

To anyone not conditioned to accept the conversion ritual at face value, this is emotionally incoherent. It sounds like the behavior of a damaged human being with a sentimental, distorted or immature understanding of love. It defies what human beings know *instinctively* about the feelings of a parent for a child. It makes a mockery of the word "love."[12]

The most successful evangelists are the ones who make this incoherence seem plausible. Billy Graham has been very good at that. He is the embodiment of evangelical Christianity. Graham's effectiveness in the pulpit, to a large degree, has rested on his ability to project deep personal interest—a genuine interest, I believe—in the eternal soul of every individual in his vast audiences. People seem to know that Graham has a good and gentle heart, and they trust him instinctively. Caught up in this trust, they rarely step back and notice the emotional contradictions in the "God" Graham proclaims—a God whose supposedly infinite love makes room for abrupt, irreversible, eternal abandonment.[13]

In the late 1940s, Billy Graham was the hottest young evangelist on the religious landscape, and publishers were quick to put his sermons into print. Graham's first two published sermon collections closed with a sermon on hell.[14] One of them paints this picture:

> Two worlds are swinging in space throughout eternity. One is the world of the saved—paradise; salvation; glory; splendor; brilliant and dazzling beyond human comprehension or description; a place of joy and laughter, with gates of pearl, walls of jasper, palaces of ivory, streets of transparent gold, a river of life. The dwellers—who? All those who have been washed in the blood of the Lamb, those who have accepted Christ as Savior. . .
>
> The other is the world of the damned. In that world through

---

12 Evangelicals excuse God's behavior by saying God is required by his "holiness" to punish us forever, so God really has no choice. I will question this interpretation of God's character in Chapter 3.

13 In later years, Graham softened some of his rhetoric about fire and brimstone without ever denying that they are still the bottom line for those who, in life, turn away from Jesus.

14 Graham citations taken from Billy Graham, *Calling Youth to Christ* (Grand Rapids, MI: Zondervan Publishing House, 1947), 130, 43–47, 65–76, 91, 116–129, 106–109.

time without end, eternity, there will be weeping, wailing and gnashing of teeth. There is no love there because men by rejecting Christ have slain their own power ever again to feel his presence. Hell will be a place of tormenting memories.

My friend, you must make a choice. Life is but a vapor. . . it will soon be over. What you do with Christ here and now decides where you shall spend eternity. . .

Young man, young woman, father, mother; [it just takes] a heart attack, an atomic bomb, an automobile crash, a hotel fire, and perhaps you will start your long journey. Have you made preparation?

Graham traced his own Christian faith back to a sermon he heard as a teenager about the terrors of hell. Perhaps for him, as for many evangelicals, the stories of a God who stops forgiving people when they die became firmly fixed in his consciousness before he had lived his way into a more mature understanding of the meaning of love. Or perhaps he was trapped by his success as master practitioner of the conversion ritual—a ritual which "worked" with mind-numbing efficiency—and unable to get the emotional distance required to recognize the bizarre nature of the "love" his "two-worlds" story conveyed.

If we listen to his story with fresh ears, however, certain anomalies become apparent. While the people in hell are crying, the people in heaven are laughing, as if they are not touched by the agony of the lost—a group that surely includes personal friends or family members. The people in hell are tormented by their memories, but the people in heaven seem to have no such memories, as if they are taking no responsibility for people whose torture they might have prevented had they been more faithful in speaking to them about Jesus.

And the Jesus in Graham's story seems willing to accept the victory of death over life, of pain over healing. We do not know that it ever occurred to the most prominent evangelist in Christendom that Jesus might love people enough to go to hell to rescue them.

·   ·   ·

"YOU ARE A FREE MORAL AGENT"

Billy Graham's early sermons are full of mixed messages about God's love.[15] In one, he responds to the Christian young people who tell him they live in continual despair. First, he offers the standard evangelical remedies—read your Bible, pray more often, tithe faithfully, commit your life to God. Then he tells them about God's love for them:

> He is interested in every detail of your life. The little heartaches, burdens and troubles that nobody else knows about—in these he is keenly interested. He has numbered the hairs of your head. He wants to help you with even the most simple things that you would ordinarily not bother anyone about.

Graham then concludes with the story of a father who asked his son to put firewood into the woodstove. When the son, "absorbed in a novel," didn't respond, the father "lost his temper and said angrily, Son, if you don't get that stick of wood and bring it in and put it on the fire, you can leave this house." The son "stalked out and slammed the door." Two weeks later, the son returned, begging for forgiveness. The father "softened for a moment. Then he grew stern and, pointing to the woodshed, said, Son, that same stick of wood

---

15 I am using Graham's early sermons to explore the roots of today's evangelicalism. But his sermons during the succeeding half-century have continued to display these mixed messages. The evening after I wrote this section of the book, a local television station carried a recent Billy Graham meeting. He ended his sermon with this refrain: "We need to make sure before it's too late."

is in the woodshed. Get it, bring it in, put it on the fire, and you can come in."

Graham believes God is this kind of father. But this father is impatient, quick-tempered, rigid and rejecting—is he the kind of God to whom we would take our "little heartaches"? And isn't he quite different from the father in Jesus' story about the prodigal son, who does not start out by ordering his son around, but who welcomes his returning son with open arms and invites him to a party (Luke 15: 11–32)?[16]

In another early sermon, Graham speaks to the "hundreds of young people" who feel constant anxiety about whether or not they are saved. He tells them there is no reason to be anxious: God is a "Heavenly Lover" who feels a "tender, longing love" for them. God "suffers and is kind." He "endures everything."

But his conclusion sends a different message: we will all take a "final exam" when we die. If we fail the exam, we will "never go to heaven." But would a "tender, longing" God give such an exam, passing summary judgment on those who fail? In sermon after sermon, throughout a sixty-year preaching career, Billy Graham painted these emotionally jarring portraits of God. To my knowledge, if he noticed the inbuilt contradictions, he did not mention them from the pulpit.

Occasionally, however, his listeners noticed. One young woman suggested that "future anguish seems incompatible with the fatherly love of God." Graham admitted the "awfulness and horribleness of spending age after age without God, without hope, without light,

---

16 The father in Graham's story is, in some respects, much like Frank Graham, Billy's own father. Graham remembered the feel of his father's hands against him: "they were like rawhide, bony, rough. He had such hard hands." See Chapter 2, footnote 65 (page 96). *Billy Graham: A Parable of American Righteousness* (New York: Little, Brown, 1979), 30, 49. This childhood experience might explain why Graham doesn't notice how unlovable the father in his story is. It might also reveal a yearning to be known and loved by such a father.

where the fire is never quenched. . ." But if we go there, he said, we cannot blame God:

> God will never send anyone to hell. If you go to hell, it will be because of your own deliberate choice. Hell was never prepared for man but for the devil and his angels. If you choose to follow Satan you will follow him to his ultimate destiny, but you will do it in spite of all that God has done to stop you.
>
> He sent his prophets. He gave you his Word. He has given you a faithful pastor and the prayers of a godly mother. He sent his only Son. The Holy Spirit is constantly warning you. What more can a God of love do? You are a free moral agent! God did not create you as a machine to be compelled to love him! You can choose either to obey or to disobey him. You have the power of free choice.
>
> Never forget that God is a God of love. Only those who reject or neglect Christ will be in hell. . . Men go to hell because they reject God's plan of salvation in Christ.

Billy Graham does not say whether his answer satisfied the young woman. But I have the same question, and Graham's answer doesn't feel altogether satisfying to me. I might have wanted to ask a few follow-up questions:

- God says I have the power of free choice, but does God have the power of free choice? If so, why does he make rules like these?
- Why, unlike most loving human parents, does God decide that disobedience is simply a lack of love?
- Why does God decide that the proportionate punishment for a finite disobedience is an infinite agony, in a place originally prepared for Satan?
- Why does God decide that the moment of death is our final deadline?

- Why does God doggedly stick to his "plan of salvation" as if he has no choice, even though it will separate him forever from many of his beloved children?

Many evangelicals will answer: God really has no choice—he is forced by his nature to set these ground rules. But then God is not as free as we are. He is not free to love.

•   •   •

"I WISH WE'D ALL BEEN READY"

Fear sells well in pop culture, as any devotee of horror or suspense movies knows. So it was inevitable that the evangelical expertise in fear-mongering would escape its institutional confines and make its way into the pop-culture market. Books like Hal Lindsey's *Late Great Planet Earth* and Frank Peretti's *This Present Darkness* have sold millions of copies.

The mother of all evangelical horror stories, of course, is the multi-volume *Left Behind* book and film series by Tim LaHaye and Jerry Jenkins, which has enjoyed long runs on the best-seller lists. These books blithely—even joyfully—perpetuate the common assumption that the God of "love" is more importantly the God of wrath, torture, destruction and abandonment.

An excellent example of the religious horror genre is the 1972 movie *Thief in the Night*.[17] During its first two decades, an estimated fifty million people viewed it. It is still shown to young people in churches across America. It depicts a world in which Jesus has suddenly removed all his true followers to a safe place in the heavens, leaving the rest to endure a reign of terror here below.

---

17 For a colorful commentary on the film, see Randall Balmer, *Mine Eyes Have Seen the Glory: A Journey into the Evangelical Subculture in America* (New York: Oxford University Press, 1989), 48–70.

It turns out they should have listened to the preacher, who had warned them in these words:

> Any minute, any second, could be the last chance that anyone has to give himself to Jesus, because when he returns it will happen. . . in the twinkling of an eye. Millions of people will suddenly disappear. . . and a shocked world will discover suddenly that what the Bible said is true. This is no joke. . . So Christian, be alert. And, friend, if you haven't given your life to Christ, do it and do it now. . .

Patty, the movie's lead character, neglects her soul's salvation an instant too long. She awakens to find her new husband gone (he is in heaven with Jesus). Denied food and shelter and hunted down by the helicoptered agents of a repressive world government, Patty cries: "I would rather have been scared into heaven than have to go through this!" One of the film-makers agrees: "If they get into the kingdom through being scared, that's better than not making it at all."

A friend of mine first saw the film when she was in high school. Without any prompting, I ask her whether she remembers anything about it. "It was frightening," she says, and then she recalls the scene in which Patty wakes up in an empty house and finds her husband's razor buzzing in the bathroom sink, interrupted by Jesus' return.

Twenty-four years after she first viewed the film, my friend repeats the lyrics of the sound-track song as she remembers them: "A man and wife asleep in bed, she hears a noise and zap, he's dead."[18] She wonders why we were all so "gung ho" for Jesus after seeing that movie, when "what stayed with me was the terror of sudden separation from everyone I loved—and the fear of God's revenge."

---

18 The official lyrics: "A man and wife asleep in bed, she hears a voice and turns her head"—followed by: "He's gone. I wish we'd all been ready."

She pauses for a few moments and then says, "I mean, if that just wouldn't make you *hate* God, I don't know what would."

I was talking with a small group of college students when one of them said it was this movie that shaped her image of God. Others chimed in excitedly, some sardonically, recalling specific scenes. Six of the seven students had seen the movie at least once as teenagers. They admitted it had been a thrilling as well as a scary experience, comparable to horror films they saw at the local theater. Several recalled having nightmares about the movie weeks thereafter.

My seven students were typical American evangelical youth. Their homes were sprinkled from east to west coasts. They represented five different Christian colleges and a variety of Protestant denominations, not all of them revivalist-oriented or evangelical. (Some of them had seen the movie while accompanying a friend to a church youth group not approved by their parents.) They were coming of age in the late-1990s, and this twenty-five-year-old film was an emotionally-charged part of their inner lives.

It would not be a stretch to say that this Christian horror movie, penetrating the imaginations of young people with its stark visual images and verbal warnings, has been one of the most effective pieces of religious propaganda produced by twentieth-century Christians. It has offered our young people a memorable, pseudo-religious thrill: a bone-rattling experience of the fear of God in the name of the love of God. Yes, it "works"—it gets evangelical kids, and some of their friends, to "make sure their hearts are right with God."

But what sort of God? Its legacy in our young people's spirits is the conviction of a God who will abandon them unless they love him—and love him in the nick of time.

●　　　●　　　●

LURKING IN THE EVANGELICAL HEART

Most evangelical preachers still affirm the doctrine of eternal punishment as it has been traditionally taught.

Many—heirs to heavy conditioning on this subject from early childhood—seem to think they are trapped by the biblical text into the wooden interpretation of wrath and hell that Billy Graham represents. They worry that any move to explore these images as more subtle and complicated metaphors—as I will try to do in *Part Two*—will stigmatize them as mushy-headed liberals who want to evade the clear meaning of the Bible.

Understandably, they do not want to awaken the barking dogs that guard evangelicalism's institutional gates and viciously attack anyone they suspect of departing from what they have defined as a more "literal" interpretation of the Bible.[19] Out of a fear deeply conditioned into them, and the yearning to be pleasing to the only "Father" they know, these guardians enforce a deadening conformity to lifeless teachings in many evangelical denominations. Many evangelical—and formerly evangelical—pastors and scholars, who have dared to raise honest questions, know their bites can be fatal.

But although most evangelical pastors still affirm the standard view of hell, increasing numbers of them are joining "mainline" Christian pastors in leaving it out of their sermons. In a society that gives so much attention to understanding and repairing human relationships—and that seems to know, sometimes more clearly than

---

19 Of course, such "literalists"—like everyone else—select which portions of the Bible they will interpret literally, and which they won't. Most "literalists" do not follow the Old Testament's dietary restrictions, such as its proscription of pork (Deuteronomy 14:8); they do not avoid clothes that mix wool and linen together (Deuteronomy 22:11); they do not support capital punishment for adultery (Deuteronomy 22:22); they do not require the brother of a man who dies to take the deceased's widow as his wife (Deuteronomy 25:5–6). It is the rare "literalist," also, who takes literally Jesus' instruction: "But if anyone strikes you on the right cheek, turn the other also" (Matthew 5:39).

the church, what it means when we say the word "love"—conventional teachings on hell sound an increasingly discordant note.

For many Christians, hellfire-and-brimstone sermons have been replaced by more gentle invitations to faith on the basis of God's love. A few courageous evangelical theologians are even beginning to suggest that we may have had these fire-and-brimstone teachings wrong all along.[20]

By the same token, many sensitive and thoughtful evangelical parents are increasingly reluctant to threaten their children with eternal damnation, even when the sentimental appeals to a warm, loving God do not control their children's behavior as well as they might wish. They seem to know, somewhere deep in their hearts, that fear never motivates genuine love.

But the evangelical community has not outright rejected, or transformed, its doctrine of hell. So hell continues to hold silent sway over the evangelical heart.[21] Many conversations over the years have convinced me that—for all our denials—a hard-hearted God, confusingly defined as loving, still resides inside most evangelicals. Although God's tender love is often proclaimed, God's wrath is alive and well behind the scenes. Evangelicals might avert their eyes, but a callous and demanding God still has the power to cast his shadow and, at a level of which they may be only dimly aware, pluck the strings of our fears. As he does so, this God confirms himself as someone not to be trusted.

Hell remains the silent linchpin of evangelical belief. Its implications for genuine trust in a loving God are palpable, but rarely

---

20 Two examples: Clark H. Pinnock and Robert C. Brow, *Unbounded Love: A Good News Theology for the 21st Century* (1994) and Brian D. McLaren, *The Last Word and the Word After That: A Tale of Faith, Doubt, and a New Kind of Christianity* (2005). I will add my voice to theirs in later chapters.

21 A recent academic survey of evangelical beliefs lists "the reality of heaven and hell" among the top four. Christian Smith et al., *American Evangelicalism: Embattled and Thriving* (Chicago: University of Chicago Press, 1998), 25.

acknowledged. While it may be too much to say that the language of the popular "praise and worship" music belies a secret distaste for this God, it does work very hard to cover over the emotional ambivalence that I believe most evangelicals feel toward him.[22] And that ambivalence—particularly when unadmitted—stands in the way of the call to freedom that might otherwise be heard from Jesus: the freedom to be completely human, completely oneself, in a relationship with a God whose love knows no end.

* * *

MAKING SURE

For many years, when someone asked me when I had been saved—"when was your 'second birthday', Doug?"—the scene beside my childhood bed flashed before my eyes. I thought of it as the moment when my fate was settled, once and for all.

But my behavior during the following ten years did not give credibility to the "once and for all." Like many evangelical children, then and now, I became a "serial conversionist." I raised my hand or walked forward, accepting Jesus and settling my soul's salvation "once and for all" at least a dozen times in church and revival services—as well as in the youth rallies, summer camps and weekend retreats that constituted my social life. I had to "make sure" that I was saved—over and over again.[23]

As I got older, the routine got easier, the emotions less palpable, the aftermath more predictable. I would resolve afresh to maintain my

---

22 Distaste is actually a mild word. Hatred is what many of my "recovering" evangelical students, as well as some of today's more outspoken anti-religious figures (many of whom share narrow religious upbringings), feel for the evangelical God.

23 Julia Scheeres captures this uncertainty: "'Where will YOU spend ETERNITY?. . . Endless BLISS or Endless TORTURE?' We are haunted by these questions. If we die tomorrow, will we join the choir of angels or slow roast in HELL? We're not sure of the answer." *Jesus Land: A Memoir* (Berkeley, CA: Counterpoint, 2005), 4.

"personal relationship with God" by daily Bible reading and prayer. I would launch programs for monitoring my feelings, thoughts and deeds in order to be "perfectly pleasing" to God. These initiatives worked well for a day or two, not so well for another week or two, and then not at all.

Invariably, I drifted into long seasons of something that, with a little help from the pulpit, I came to think of as "back-sliding" and hardheartedness. Then a charismatic youth speaker or a dramatic sermon would hook me one more time, tripping me into an emotional meeting with God, another confession of my hard-heartedness, another "come to Jesus" moment.

I was stubbornly—perhaps self-protectively—unreflective about all this. If you had asked me what the God was like with whom I was engaged in these ceaseless rounds of approach and avoidance, I would have said something like: "He's big and holy and he loves me and wants the best for me, which is to do his will. When I don't, he's very disappointed with me. He may have to be hard on me from time to time, but it's for my own good." If you had asked me whether I knew I would go to heaven when I died, I would have answered: "Yes, I've accepted Jesus as my personal Savior, although I don't always live a life that's pleasing to him."

These affirmations would have been sincere reflections of what one part of me believed. But other parts of me clearly did not believe them. Despite my church's teaching that after the very first "decision for Christ" the saved were "eternally secure," these other parts of me were insecure. So I was a sitting duck for the next speaker gifted at awakening my guilt and pleading with me to make sure.

"Making sure" has been an evangelical cottage industry for as long as the conversion ritual has dominated our understanding of the Christian experience, and the cause is not hard to find. Can we really trust a God whose wrath is terrible and whose love seems fickle? Can we feel connected to a God who seems so disconnected from those he "loves"? Oft-repeated phrases reinforce the unspoken suspicion that God's love cannot be trusted:

- God is not someone to be "trifled with."
- God "cannot look on sin."
- At the last judgment, God will pronounce the horrifying words, "I never knew you; depart from me."
- Then it will be "too late." God will "spew us out of his mouth" and consign us to "eternal torment."

Each of these phrases re-confirms what God is like beneath the surface. He is a seething pool of wrath. No wonder I needed constantly to make sure. In my gut, God's wrath was far more believable, emotionally charged, and palpable than God's love.[24]

It seems obvious to me now that to have a caring, mutual relationship is difficult when one party is threatening the other with death. I smile as I write this: does something so plain need to be said? But, for decades, it was not plain to me at all. I never questioned God's suitability as a relationship partner. I accepted as uncontroversial God's prerogative to structure human salvation however he wanted, and my responsibility to knuckle under if I wanted a relationship.

My failed relationship with God was always, unquestionably, my own fault. By definition, it was always *I*, never God, who drifted away; always *my* heart, never God's, which was hardened. These defining assumptions operated automatically and powerfully for me, closing off any chance that I would ask the simplest questions:

---

24 I am interpreting the "making sure" ritual as animated, at least in part, by the distrust we feel in the presence of a demanding and wrathful God. But human destiny is shrouded in uncertainty, and each human heart yearns to know what cannot be known: that we are safe in life and in death. The "making sure" ritual also taps into this more generic human yearning, and it deserves the respect we owe to every human longing.

- Is God really like that? Is this the way love works?
- Who's the hardhearted one here?
- Is my off-again, on-again relationship with God really my fault, or is it God's?

Because the conditioning of my religious upbringing had worked so effectively to shut off any openness to self-exploration or genuine self-awareness, I could not—and did not—ask these obvious questions or make these relatively simple discoveries.

In my twenties, however, I became acutely aware that God felt distant, and that I had nothing resembling a genuine feeling of love for him. Occasionally, this troubled me. Over the succeeding decade or two, I tried various ways to escape the contradiction—most of them one stab or another at shutting off my feelings.

For a while, one preacher's eloquent weekly sermons on God's transcendent majesty and power left me with an exalted and breathless sense of awe that I misidentified as love. At another time, I decided that our fate after death isn't what Christian faith is about—it's about acting justly and mercifully in this life. I told myself that love for other human beings is the only real evidence of love for God, which meant that my personal feelings toward God were irrelevant.

For a few years, I tried on the idea that all our talk about a "relationship with God" was just a ritualized rhetorical style—there was no such thing as a "relationship with God," and we misunderstood the Bible if we made this our priority. At one point, I comforted myself with the thought that I probably did love God, except I just did it in a more rational, less emotional way than other people did.

These and other valiant efforts carried me along for brief periods of time. But they didn't satisfy my heart, where I sensed not simply the absence of loving feelings for God, but the absence of God altogether. Throughout these years, I did not gain the freedom to question the portrait of God I had been given. I never considered the possibility that my hardheartedness was perhaps a healthy human defense against a hardhearted God.

When, as a boy of seven, by my bedside, I settled my soul's salvation "once and for all," I felt washed with relief. But—although it is difficult to be sure at the distance of sixty years—that relief came because I was now feeling approved by God, not loved. And my relief was only a temporary soothing of my panic. I had been scared half to death by visions of eternal aloneness and physical torture.

The God I took with me from that sermon and that bedside was easy to fear, but impossible to love. My spiritual experience, for many years thereafter, could be characterized simply as a struggle to be approved by, and to make myself love, this unlovable "God." My strategy, in this struggle, always focused on changing my behavior or my feelings. It took many years, and an experience with Jesus of which I will later speak, before I could see that it was God that needed to be changed.

As for that seven-year-old boy, I am certain he knew in his heart that genuine love—the love for which he inwardly yearned—does not threaten its beloved with pain and death.

And I trust that little boy's heart more than ever.

CHAPTER 2

The God that Shame Built
Yearning for a respectable father

After the very long period during which the theologian has been confronted in the picture of Christ with the "unmoving, unemotional countenance of the God of Plato. . ." the time has finally come for differentiating the Father of Jesus Christ from the God of the pagans and the philosophers in the interest of Christian faith.
Jurgen Moltmann[1]

I DID NOT OFTEN HEAR the word "evangelical" during my childhood. Our little denomination recognized the term as applying to us, but we preferred the label "fundamentalist."[2] We built our faith on the

---

1 *The Crucified God* (New York: Harper and Row, Publishers, 1973), 215.

2 Fundamentalism emerged in the 1920s as the conservative wing of evangelical Christianity in America. It came to the defense of what it believed to be biblical doctrines lately threatened by "modernism" or "liberalism," which downplayed the supernatural, prioritized ethical living (known by some as "the social gospel") over personal salvation through the blood of Christ, and emphasized the love, and not the wrath, of God. The definitive study of fundamentalism is George M. Marsden, *Fundamentalism and American Culture: The Shaping of Twentieth-Century Evangelicalism, 1870–1925* (New York: Oxford University Press, 1980).

The word "fundamentalism" has since been broadened to include intolerant, hyperorthodox factions within many religions. In that context, George Marsden's definition of a fundamentalist as "an evangelical who is angry about something"—if you replace "evangelical" with "Muslim" or "Hindu"—still applies (*Understanding Fundamentalism and Evangelicalism*, 1). In this wider context, as well, one might hypothesize that fundamentalists are angry about something because their God is angry about something—or vice versa.

"fundamentals" of scripture. We believed every story in the Bible to be historically accurate and literally true: the Red Sea actually parted, the sun actually stood still, and the four young Hebrews came out of Nebuchadnezzar's howling furnace without even the scent of fire on their robes. We believed the Bible revealed God's "plan for the ages," a schedule of future events available to anyone who cared to consult the relevant texts.

The Bible told us we were living in the "last times." Soon, Jesus would appear in the clouds to take his people—Christians, not Jews—away from this earth.[3] This "rapture" would set in motion the "tribulation"—seven long years of social upheaval and bloody tyranny—which Jesus would bring to an end when he descended with a mighty force to wage the Battle of Armageddon and begin his millennial reign on earth.[4]

The certainty, imminence and finality of these events remained my father's lodestar throughout his long life. They prodded him to tell every willing stranger about God's "plan of salvation." They also required that the Sunday morning and evening church services—both of which our family, and most church families, attended each week—focus entirely on the necessity of getting right with God.

We called these "evangelistic," not "worship" services. Invariably, they ended with an opportunity for sinners to raise their hands and accept Jesus as their Savior. These "invitations" were often less

---

3 A colorful, airborne Jesus—surrounded by fluffy, white clouds—was painted on the front wall of our small sanctuary, high above the pulpit, keeping our eyes fixed on eternity.

4 This "plan for the ages" was a feature of dispensationalism, a system of biblical interpretation formulated in the nineteenth century to help explain why good morals and godliness seemed to be in decline. Its "premillennialism" (predicting that Jesus' second coming would occur before the establishment of his millennial kingdom) replaced "postmillennialism," the reigning interpretive grid at the time, which predicted the imminent arrival of God's kingdom on earth.

Fundamentalism was almost exclusively dispensationalist. For an extensive survey and detailed critique of dispensationalism, see my *Less Than Conquerors: The Evangelical Quest for Power in the Early Twentieth Century*, 60–102.

drawn out in the morning than in the evening, but no service ended without one. My father did not want anyone's eternal damnation to be laid to his account.

My father was the minister of the Salem Mennonite Brethren in Christ Church, located in a cramped, working-class neighborhood just off Broad Street, North Philadelphia's major artery.[5] In my mind's eye, the diminutive brick building hunkers down in a self-protective posture, trying to ignore the worldly bustle passing by just a few steps from its front entrance. Even as a boy, I had vague inklings of the dissonance between the picture we had of ourselves and the picture others seemed to have of us. Most people in the world—the "unsaved," who streamed along Broad Street on weekdays—didn't give our little church a passing glance. They seemed entirely unaware that we had the monopoly on God's plan for the ages.

Summer mornings, as a ten-year-old, I would sit on my red wagon for hours, watching traffic flow up and down Broad Street. I was fascinated by the men and women traversing that busy thoroughfare on foot or in their cars. They were an alien species, different—in a way I could not name—from the people who met to sing and pray in our little church each Sunday. Some hidden part of me mourned the distance I felt between us. The mystery of their otherness, whose texture I can still faintly touch after these many years, betrayed some primal yearning to know them. To a little boy's eyes, they seemed important, purposeful, confident—unconcerned about the fate that a severe God had prepared for them. My heart felt their unconcern.

In hindsight, I would say these strangers beckoned me to a kind of freedom. The freedom of a life carried out beyond the gaze of an enraged and threatening God. The freedom to be comfortable with the world as it is. The freedom to be fully, confidently, here and now.

---

5 We were keenly aware that Jesus had designated the "broad" way as the one leading to destruction (Matthew 7:13).

• • •

"THIS WORLD IS NOT MY HOME"

The people who met within the walls of the Salem Church did not seem particularly happy about the here and now or pleased with their place on the planet. Our favorite gospel chorus said it plainly: "This world is not my home, I'm just-a passin' through. My treasures are laid up somewhere beyond the blue."

In our own way, we took Thoreau's dictum to heart: "Read not the Times. Read the Eternities."[6] We took little interest in the world beyond our doors. We didn't talk about politics or vote. We didn't attend "secular" concerts or visit art galleries. Occasionally, we ventured to the ballpark for a Phillies game, but we didn't feel comfortable with the language used by the people seated around us. We didn't darken the doors of theaters or taverns or dance halls. A Bible institute, not university, was the proper schooling for our young people, and missionary work was their highest calling. Our pastors were recruited from the ranks of our most devout young men and sent off to work in a city mission under the tutelage of an older minister. They did not study theology—the Bible was sufficient.

One of our heroes, the revivalist Dwight L. Moody, had said half a century earlier: "I look on this world as a wrecked vessel. God has given me a life-boat and said to me: '. . .save all you can.'"[7] We recognized this same mandate, and bent our energies to the task. But we did not expect marked success—Jesus had warned us that only a few would find the narrow gate (Matthew 7:14).

So our forays beyond Salem's walls took on an air of tokenism. On Saturday nights, rain or shine, my family and a few church members

---

6 Henry David Thoreau, "Life without Principle" in Joseph Wood Krutch, ed., *Thoreau: Walden and Other Writings* (New York: Bantam Books, 1962), 369.

7 Quoted in James F. Findlay, Jr., *Dwight L. Moody: American Evangelist, 1837–1899* (Chicago: University of Chicago Press, 1969), 253.

would set up a portable pump organ and a small public address system on a busy Philadelphia street corner. We sang and gave our "testimonies," extended gospel tracts toward wary passersby, and told Bible stories to small clutches of children. We tried, gently, to divert the attention of passing drunks. We inured ourselves to the patronizing smiles of the rich and powerful.

I can still see my parents standing bravely on that street corner. . . *My mother*, barely five feet tall, erect and proper in her navy dress with its white collar, her hand occasionally reaching up to reverse the effects of a stiff breeze on her prim dark hair, those deep, beautiful eyes and that absolutely believable smile leaving no question that she *cared* about the fate of each passing soul.

My father, tall, gaunt, Lincolnesque jaw and brow, dark-rimmed glasses—his trouser legs a bit too short, revealing bright yellow socks. And his singing—I remember this best—his deep, lusty baritone voice erupting out of the heart of an unshakeable conviction. He just stood back on that street corner and belted it out as if auditioning for the opera—and he gave us all the courage to do our best under these awkward circumstances and offer our comparatively feeble voices to the gospel cause.

If my parents and the other adults huddled on those bustling corners felt any embarrassment or shame in the presence of those condescending smiles, they didn't mention it. I feel it for them now—the pathos of these simple souls ignored by all but dogs and children, carrying the weight of their humble, broken beginnings and their equally humble attainments, bravely looking into the eyes of their social betters and saying: we love you, we care about your eternal destiny, we have an answer for your soul's distress.

But perhaps they did not feel the shame. Or, perhaps they did not allow themselves to feel it. But I felt it—the ache to be invisible, to sink into the sidewalk; the dead weight of some obvious truth about us, a truth I could not name.

I think I can name it now. We were nobodies yearning to be somebodies. Our footing on this planet and in our time felt precarious. Our only claim to fame was a heavenly Father who had no real power in this world except the power to destroy it and replace it with another. We were hoping against hope for the dawning of this other world—a world in which we would really matter.

•   •   •

BEING FUNDAMENTALIST

In the fall of 1959, I began my freshman year at Wheaton College, a Christian liberal arts college in a suburb west of Chicago.[8] I had to overcome the misgivings of my father, who favored Moody Bible Institute, the proudly fundamentalist stronghold in Chicago's city center.

During my high school years, I had several times, under the influence of a revival sermon, committed myself to "full-time Christian service." My dad thought Moody offered the finest training available for a future pastor or missionary. I chose Wheaton College instead, attracted by its verdant campus—well-insulated from the grime of Chicago—and vaguely aware of its reputation as the premier "evangelical" college. I was still not entirely comfortable with the word "evangelical," but I sensed that Wheaton might offer a slightly less controlling climate than Moody—or the one in which I had been raised.

My enlightenment about the meaning of the word "evangelical" began immediately. Not long after my parents helped me move into Saint Hall—the optimistically-named freshman dorm[9]—and said

---

8 Wheaton students, I was soon to learn, joked that the campus was "thirty miles from the nearest source of sin."

9 In actuality, the dorm was named for a Wheaton College alumnus, Nate Saint, who had, with several fellow-missionaries, been killed in 1956 by native tribes in the Ecuadorian

their awkward farewells, my roommate and I heard excited voices across the hall. Timidly, we stuck our heads in and introduced ourselves.

A few of our classmates were deep into a "bull-session," and we were invited to join in. The subject was eschatology, a word I didn't recognize. I listened long enough to figure out that it had to do with the "end times." I recognized that term. All those charts, plastered across the front wall of my home church every year during the "prophecy" conference, displaying the precise pattern of future events—all that, it turned out, was eschatology. I began to relax. I knew this stuff cold.

The specific question under discussion had to do with the "millennium," Christ's thousand year reign. Did it occur before or after Christ's "second coming"? I knew only one way to think about these events, so I laid them out in their proper order. I may have been a bit smug.

The others (excluding my silent roommate) glanced at one another. They seemed slightly amused. "So you're pre-trib and pre-mil," one of them said. "You must be a dispensationalist. That's fundamentalism. A lot of evangelicals don't believe that any longer."

I remember the shame that flooded me, and not much more.

* * *

THIS WORLD *IS* MY HOME

At Wheaton in the early 1960s, fundamentalists were called "fundies."[10] Sometimes the term was a simple descriptor, as in "my

rain forest. They became overnight fundamentalist heroes. Their story was often used on campus to illustrate the costs of true Christian discipleship. Their story is told by Elisabeth Elliot, wife of one of the deceased, in *Through Gates of Splendor* (New York: Harper and Brothers, 1957).

10 It would not surprise me to hear that this word is still used by Wheaton students today.

grandparents are fundies, but they don't really push it on me." More often, it was a term of derision: "You know why fundies don't believe in sex? Because it leads to dancing."

No one I knew wanted to be called a fundy. Fundies were moral prudes, so they weren't any fun. Fundies were socially awkward, so they weren't cool. Fundies were religious zealots, who made you uncomfortable with their incessant God-talk: "The Lord this, the Lord that." Fundies were culturally backward—"Ingmar who?"—so they were uninteresting. Fundies were anti-intellectual—they were afraid of new ideas, preferred to reaffirm the old ones—so you couldn't have a real discussion with them. And fundies were dogmatic. They thought they owned the franchise on God's eternal truth.[11]

Stereotypes, all of them, but if you came from a fundamentalist background as I did, you knew plenty of people who fit the bill. My father and mother came uncomfortably close. So the stereotypes, however overstated, helped shaped what many of us saw when we looked in a mirror. I would guess that, during those years, Wheaton's campus was chock-full of fundies trying hard not to let anybody know.[12]

---

[11] By the late-1950s, fundamentalists were most identified with their belief in "separatism." They refused, as true believers, to worship, cooperate with, or remain in the same denominations with, those who had turned against the true faith, narrowly defined. It was on this basis that Jack Wyrtzen and other fundamentalists refused to endorse Billy Graham's mass meetings in New York City in 1957, because Graham had invited "liberals" to participate in the planning and sit on his platform. About that time, Graham stopped calling himself a fundamentalist, and fundamentalists began to think of Graham as apostate.

Garth Rosell summarizes this growing split in *The Surprising Work of God: Harold John Ockenga, Billy Graham, and the Rebirth of Evangelicalism* (Grand Rapids, MI: Baker Academic, 2008), 157–159. A wonderful example of the fundamentalist perception of Graham can be found online at www.sharperiron.org/attachment.php?attachmentid=176.

[12] The most prominent local example of a fundy was John R. Rice, whose newspaper, *The Sword of the Lord*, circulated nationally. Rice was still famous for his 1941 book, *Bobbed Hair, Bossy Wives, and Women Preachers*. He was not a friend of Billy Graham.

The alternative to being a fundy was being an evangelical.[13] Many of the differences seemed trivial. An evangelical might break the college rule against going to the movies; a fundy probably would not.[14] An evangelical might read the Revised Standard Version of the Bible; a fundy preferred the "Authorized" or King James Version. An evangelical was more likely than a fundy to take a philosophy course. An evangelical was less likely than a fundy to attend chapel on the day Jack Wyrtzen preached the sermon. If one of the storied "Wheaton revivals" broke out, the fundies stayed in the chapel through the night crying to God for forgiveness, while the evangelicals went to the library to study and then slept soundly in their beds.

Campus leadership, by and large, seemed to be in the hands of evangelicals. The students I would have identified as evangelicals were the campus movers and shakers; it was easy to imagine a political future for them after college. Evangelicals were the creative writers and artists who made no secret of their aspirations to success in the world of "secular"—not just Christian—art. In fact, they argued there was no real difference between secular and Christian art.

Evangelicals were the intellectuals on campus—they talked about Descartes and Heidegger, Allen Ginsburg and Herman Hesse, as if they were old family friends. Evangelicals edited the student newspapers. Evangelicals read the books that were hot on university campuses. You knew one day they would be writing books and teaching in the universities.

But evangelicals seemed most distinguished from fundies by an

---

No one I knew would admit to attending Rice's Baptist church in downtown Wheaton.

13 I am neatening up here, for purposes of discussion, two categories that were often intermixed, loosely defined, and shifting in meaning depending on context.

14 Wheaton students joked that, when the movie *Ben Hur* opened in Chicago's downtown theaters in 1959, Wheaton's president bought a ticket just so he could sit in the back row and take attendance.

attitude or ethos—a way of being in the world. It was a way of being that I found alien and intimidating, but also enviable. I'm not sure that at the time I brought this way of being to consciousness, and I certainly never named it.

Had I done so, I might have used words like "sophisticated," "cool" or perhaps "worldly." I would have meant that evangelicals were interested in the ideas and activities of the wider cultural world—a sinful predilection, in my home church, which probably accounts for my impression that they were living a bit dangerously. But "worldly" also in the sense that they seemed at home on the planet, as if the planet belonged to them as much as to anyone. They exuded a sense of entitlement. They expected to matter in this world.

I was slightly in awe of these people. A part of me yearned for membership in their ranks. They reminded me of the strangers I watched as a boy, making their way along Broad Street, embracing the world as it was, certain of their own importance. Or the self-possessed men and women who rushed past our little band of street-corner fundamentalists, unimpressed by our ownership of the eternal truths. They reminded me of the people I wished to be rather than the person I knew I was.

But a part of me knew I would never qualify. That part— fearful and full of shame—silently governed my behavior during my four years at Wheaton College.

•   •   •

GOING TO SEE THE CIRCUS

I suspect the line separating fundamentalists and evangelicals at Wheaton College—to borrow from Solzhenitsyn—actually cut right through the heart of the majority of Wheaton students in those days.[15]

Most of us grew up in fundamentalist homes and churches. Throughout childhood, we had all been force-fed fire-and-brimstone sermons and dispensationalist predictions of doom. Many of us had participated in Bible club programs that browbeat us into carrying our Bibles to school and witnessing to our classmates about Jesus. I was not the only one who had stood on street-corners handing out tracts and enduring the taunts of the unregenerate. The pool of shame among Wheaton's students, I now believe, was deep and wide.

We did not talk about it, of course. Shame is something humans experience as shameful. But it showed itself in the contempt clinging to the word "fundy," and the ridicule heaped on those who showed "fundy" characteristics. Contempt and ridicule are two of the most reliable indicators of shame. They allow us to dump the shame we feel on someone else, and thus lighten our own loads—at least temporarily.[16]

This dynamic surfaced most visibly when a fundamentalist speaker appeared in chapel, or when one of the aforementioned "revivals" broke out on campus, as seemed to occur every few years. Those revivals traded on fundamentalist logic: were we ready for the second coming? Would Jesus find us faithful when he returned? Guilt and fear were thick on the campus. Chapel services extended for hours, sometimes late into the night, as sinners prayed and wept and found forgiveness and started over.

Some of the "spiritually callous" students who were not caught

---

15 "The line separating good and evil passes. . . right through every human heart—and through all human hearts. . . Inside us it oscillates with the years." Aleksandr I. Solzhenitsyn, *Gulag Archipelago 1918–1956: An Experiment in Literary Investigation* (New York: Harper and Row, 1974), IV, 615.

16 Of course, we were unconsciously also dumping it on the fundy part of ourselves, intensifying our own shame and stoking the fires of self-enmity.

up in the emotionality of these events—I was occasionally among them—did not repair to the library or snuggle in their beds. They crept into the back rows of the chapel to listen, nudging and grinning, rolling their eyes and commenting sarcastically to one another as their classmates took turns spilling their shameful secrets into a microphone, confessing their spiritual coldness and anger and selfishness and lust—the lust, particularly, in all its lurid detail.

Later, over pizza, we would recount for one another each tearful confession. Something about this outbreak of fundamentalist spirituality was endlessly fascinating, and endlessly disturbing, to those— like myself—who chose to observe it from afar. It mirrored the fundamentalist conflicts in our own souls, triggering shame and the palliative of contempt.

Most Wheaton faculty members were conspicuously absent during these overheated affairs. They were at least a generation older than we, so their fundamentalist roots ran deeper than ours. They tried to be discreet in commenting on these religious outbreaks, but you could tell they were not enthusiastic. They distrusted the anti-intellectual, emotionally-charged spirituality that revival speakers used to rouse our slumbering spirits. The "circus" in Edman Chapel—as some of us called it—was an embarrassment to them.[17]

---

17 Daily chapels offered additional opportunities for faculty discomfort. In one, a famous street minister urged us to sell everything, drop out of college and join him as an ambassador of Christ to Amsterdam's prostitutes. In class, later that day, a professor hazarded a guess that a college degree might be a better investment in our futures than a one-way ticket to Amsterdam.

A famous youth evangelist told us our academic studies were enhancing our minds, but starving our hungry hearts. By the time the podium's warning light came on to tell him his time was up, he had worked up quite a head of steam; he ignored the light and kept preaching, assuring us our professors would be eager to delay the start of classes so as not to "quench the spirit."

Our professors, it turned out, didn't agree. They considered their lectures more important than this fellow's shallow rantings, and questioned the merits of a religious fervor that disrupted class attendance and interfered with students completing their assignments. I thank those professors. They were the first serious Christians I met who

• • •

BEARING THE STIGMATA

I entered college at the end of a decade of rapid transition for conservative Christians in the United States. One of these transitions
involved self-definition: were we going to call ourselves fundamentalists or evangelicals. Preachers who had risen to prominence
in the 1930s—Jack Wyrtzen, Percy Crawford, John R. Rice, Carl
McIntire—wore proudly their reputation as "fightin' fundamentalists." But the preachers and other leaders who came to fame after
World War II—Harold John Ockenga, Bob Cook, Billy Graham—
gradually adopted the label "evangelical." Among many conservative Christians—especially those outside the South—this label
seemed to be carrying the day.

The appeal of the "evangelical" label was greatly augmented by
a talented group of young scholars that moved into leadership in
Christian higher education at the very same time. Rudolph Nelson
wrote a thoughtful study of one of them, Edward Carnell, a philosophy professor and widely published Christian apologist who
also served briefly as president of Fuller Theological Seminary in
Pasadena, California.[18] Nelson offers a group portrait of Carnell's
scholarly colleagues in the immediate post-war years.[19] He considers them "an honor roll of mid- to late-twentieth-century American
evangelicalism." Among others, they include Kenneth Kantzer,

---

were not afraid—or only a little afraid—to caution me about the foolishness that comes
cloaked in the robes of hyper-spirituality.

[18] Fuller Theological Seminary was the nerve center for the movement to replace
"fundamentalism" with "evangelicalism." See George Marsden, *Reforming Fundamentalism:
Fuller Seminary and the New Evangelicalism* (Grand Rapids, MI: William B. Eerdmans
Publishing Company, 1987), 146–147, 165–171.

[19] *The Making and Unmaking of an Evangelical Mind: The Case of Edward Carnell*
(Cambridge University Press, 1987), 54–60.

Merrill Tenney, George Eldon Ladd, Bernard Ramm, Harold Lindsell and Carl F. H. Henry.[20]

Many of these scholars began their academic careers during the 1930s, as undergraduates in staunchly fundamentalist colleges. In contrast to their immediate forebears, however, who shunned non-sectarian learning as apostate, these men pursued graduate degrees at Harvard Divinity School and other leading universities. With their newly-minted Ph.D.s, they migrated back into conservative Christian colleges and seminaries. From their professorial posts, they wrote the books and trained the scholars that shaped the conservative Christian agenda in America for the next fifty years.

This agenda was fueled by a sense of crisis. Carl Henry, one of their leading voices, believed American civilization was foundering on the shoals of godlessness and craved fresh leadership. He urged evangelicals to supply that leadership by building "a new world mind for the forthcoming era."[21] He was not satisfied, as my fundamentalist parents were, with a God who reigned in heaven. He wanted one who mattered on this earth. He imagined himself and his peers at the head of a conservative theological and philosophical movement that would return God to public life in America and spark the revival of a "truly Christian culture."[22]

---

20 Kantzer was president of Trinity Evangelical Divinity School and editor of *Christianity Today* magazine. Tenney was dean of Wheaton College Graduate School. Ladd was theology professor at Fuller Theological Seminary. Ramm was a widely-read professor of systematic theology at the American Baptist Seminary of the West. Harold Lindsell and Carl F. H. Henry were both, for a time, professors at Fuller Theological Seminary and prominent evangelical spokespersons. Nelson also names other commonly-recognized stalwarts like Gleason Archer, Everett Harrison, Paul King Jewett, Glenn Barker and Samuel Schultz.

21 George Marsden, *Reforming Fundamentalism,* 78. Marsden describes Henry and his colleagues at Fuller Seminary as "determined to produce a body of Christian writing that by force of argument would gain an audience even in the greatest intellectual centers of civilization." They believed that "modern culture is not beyond hope, and Christians have the task of transforming culture to bring it more in conformity with God's law and will" (8, 76).

22 *Remaking the Modern Mind* (Grand Rapids, MI: Wm. B. Eerdmans Publishing Company, 1946), 199.

But beneath their confident spirits, Nelson tells us, many of them bore a deep wound of the spirit: the stigma of fundamentalism. Most of them grew up in fundamentalist homes and/or fundamentalist churches. Their tender young spirits were well acquainted with the shame that I and many others carried into Wheaton College, the shame that fueled the campus-wide contempt for fundies. The label "evangelical," which they did so much to popularize, was generated and constituted by this shame. It announced to the world: we are not fundamentalists. We do not deserve your ridicule. We will show you. We will *matter*.

·   ·   ·

"THICK IN THE MEAN STREETS"

It is impossible to imagine intellectually gifted fundamentalist young people growing up in the 1930s and '40s untouched—unscarred— by the opprobrium routinely heaped on "fundamentalists." That opprobrium focused primarily on fundamentalist disdain for the world of learning. It ridiculed fundamentalists as unsophisticated, uneducated, unintelligent rubes.

The iconic example of this ridicule is the popular reaction to the Scopes trial in 1925. Scopes had run afoul of a Tennessee law prohibiting the teaching of evolution in the public schools. During his trial, Scopes' lawyer, William Jennings Bryan, took the stand and defended a fundamentalist interpretation of the Bible's creation account. Opposing attorney Clarence Darrow made a fool of him,

---

A recent observer of religion in America summarizes the view which Carl Henry shared with most conservative Christians of his time: "The history of American evangelicals goes something like this: In the beginning they controlled everything, and suddenly they didn't. And ever since, they've been beating their heads against their stone tablets, wondering why." Hanna Rosin, *God's Harvard*, 53.

labeling him one of the "bigots and ignoramuses" who preferred ancient myths to modern science.

H. L. Mencken, a popular national columnist, cemented the fundamentalist in the American mind as the embodiment of backwardness and stupidity. He traveled to Dayton and published dispatches that one historian calls a "masterpiece of ridicule."

Fundamentalists, Mencken wrote, evoke the scent of "greasy victuals [in] the farmhouse kitchen" and "the tune of cocks crowing on the dunghill." "Heave an egg out of a Pullman window," he wrote, "and you will hit a fundamentalist almost anywhere in the United States today. . . [They] are thick in the mean streets behind the gas-works. They are everywhere where learning is too heavy a burden for mortal minds to carry, even the vague, pathetic learning on tap in the little red schoolhouse."[23]

Mencken's portrayal of fundamentalism was a caricature. Most fundamentalists at the time lived in urban, not rural settings, and came from the middle class. Many were well-educated. Some fundamentalist scholars, like Princeton's J. Gresham Machen, had achieved high acclaim in the non-fundamentalist world. But fundamentalism's reputation was not susceptible to statistical analysis or counter-examples.[24] During the 1920s and '30s, the word only deepened its association in the public mind with ignorance, crudeness, backwardness, intolerance, resentment.

The bright young scholars, emerging from respected graduate schools in the post-war years, preparing to lead a renaissance of conservative Christian scholarship, were keenly aware of this reputation. Kenneth Kantzer, one of the most respected and kind-spirited

---

23 George Marsden, *Fundamentalism and American Culture,* 187–188.

24 Most caricatures like this have staying power because the fear that the characteristics they are describing are true of us—that we are "backward" or "dumb"—is nearly universal in the human psyche.

THE GOD THAT SHAME BUILT

of them, put it succinctly: the term "fundamentalist" had become "an embarrassment instead of a badge of honor."[25]

.   .   .

MENTAL INCOMPETENTS

The fundamentalist scholar of this generation who came closest to confessing his shame in print was Carl F. H. Henry. Henry was a newspaper reporter who became a Christian and decided he needed a Christian education. He enrolled at Wheaton College and then went on to study for two doctorates simultaneously. As a graduate student, in 1947, he published *The Uneasy Conscience of Modern Fundamentalism.*[26] The book became a founding document of the modern "evangelical" movement.

In *Uneasy Conscience,* Henry set out to "perform surgery" on fundamentalism.[27] He accused fundamentalism of being obsessed with saving and perfecting individual souls in preparation for the next world, while it ignored the wider needs of this present world. Fundamentalists loved to rail against movies, dancing, card-playing and smoking, he wrote, but they ignored "admitted social evils" like "warfare, racial hatred and intolerance, the liquor traffic, and exploitation of labor or management." Henry thought this made fundamentalism essentially un-Christian. Historic Christianity, he wrote, always challenged "the predominant culture of its generation" in order to re-shape it as a "divinely related social order."

Decades before Jerry Falwell and other leaders of the religious right allied with despised enemies like Roman Catholics to battle gay

---

25 This line is widely quoted on the internet. I have not been able to find an original citation.

26 (Grand Rapids, MI: William B. Eerdmans Publishing Co., 1947). It was re-issued in 2003 with an introduction by Fuller Seminary president, Richard J. Mouw.

27 Carl F. H. Henry, *Confessions a Theologian* (Waco, TX: Word Books, 1986), 112.

rights and abortion, Henry urged evangelicals to ally with non-fundamentalists to launch a "vigorous assault against evils." Through vigorous social action, Henry believed, Christians could bring the entire globe to "the judgment seat of Christ."[28] God intends to reign over the world in the here-and-now, he said, not just the sweet-bye-and-bye.[29] And we are God's instruments for that reign.

Henry wrote in a sober, objective style, proceeding by calm, logical argumentation. But emotional energy—and the layer of pain beneath it—seeps out from between his lines. His attacks on fundamentalism contrast sharply with the book's rational tone and irenic spirit. The words "embarrassed" and "embarrassment" appear repeatedly in this short book: embarrassment that fundamentalists are world-denying; that they indulge in "prophetic extravagances;" that they are "anti-ecumenical," or isolationist, or theologically "uncritical," or "overly-emotional."

Henry's embarrassment even included the peripheral issue of fundamentalist church music—it reminded him, he said, of barn-dances or "spiritualized juke boxes." Henry's shame made some of his judgments appear angry and severe: he labeled fundamentalist thinking "unintelligible," fit only for "a mental incompetent."[30]

Henry's burden of shame was not unique to him. Rudy Nelson's study of the young men of Henry's cohort offers evidence that the stigma of fundamentalism bore down on many of their spirits. Since they were intellectually gifted young men, popular assumptions that fundamentalists were uneducated and intellectually mediocre—

---

28 The religious right has until recently shown little interest in issues like war, racism or labor exploitation. In bringing these issues to the attention of conservative Christians, Henry was not just ahead of *his* time; he was ahead of *our* time as well. As of this writing, a small cadre of progressive evangelicals—led by Jim Wallis, Tony Campolo, Rich Cizik and Joel Hunter—are renewing Henry's call for more balanced social engagement by evangelicals, and some conservative voices are awakening to the evils of racism and poverty.

29 *Uneasy Conscience,* 17–20, 38, 84–88.

30 *Uneasy Conscience,* 10, 16–17, 19, 23–24, 36, 43, 50, 61.

"mental incompetents"—cut especially deep. They sought relief for these wounds by dedicating themselves tirelessly to academic achievement. They wrote tracts and gave speeches urging Christians to bring a godly perspective to every aspect of life, including the political, and thus to become fully-engaged citizens of this world. They became the leading advocates in the (successful) campaign to replace the term "fundamentalist" with the more respectable label "evangelical."[31]

And in their theological scholarship, they went about replacing the fundamentalist God with a more reputable God, a God designed to relieve their shame.

•   •   •

FEELING RIDICULOUS

What sort of God might shame construct? If we understand how shame works, the answer might be relatively straightforward.[32]

Shame is an internal voice, often triggered by external events, that says to us: "You are irremediably deficient. You are weak, or small, or stupid, or incompetent, or clumsy, or ugly, or broken. You are thus ridiculous, fit only for contempt. In sum, you are *unlovable*." For human beings, these words comprise a sentence of death. We

---

31 The term "evangelicalism" came into currency after the founding of the National Association of Evangelicals in 1942. Later in the 1940s, Harold John Ockenga, pastor of Boston's Park Street Church and first president of Fuller Theological Seminary, proposed displacing fundamentalism with the "new evangelicalism." By the mid-1950s, most conservative Christians had made the switch. Marsden, *Reforming Fundamentalism*, covers this ground very thoroughly (10, 153–171).

32 Gershen Kaufman, whose *Shame: The Power of Caring* (Rochester, VT: Schenkman Books, Inc., 1980) revolutionized my understanding of shame when I first read it, spells out shame's origin and nature, and enumerates the standard psychological strategies for defending against shame: blaming, scapegoating, contempt, rage, striving for success, striving for power, striving for perfection, internal withdrawal.

are made in and for relationships; when love is threatened, we are destabilized at our very core.

As humans, we are comprised of many disparate internal parts.[33] Each part has its job: to carry our wounds, to manage our worldly affairs, to extinguish pain when it is triggered from within or from without. Shame is deeply painful. When we experience it—which everyone does, in varying degrees, as subjects of criticism or humiliation or laughter, beginning early in childhood—specific protective parts of us are born. These internal "sub-personalities" have a job to do: to prevent this pain from ever happening again.

Let's say you are an intellectually gifted and perceptive fundamentalist young person, growing up in an era when fundamentalism is the butt of jokes. Every mention of this caricature reawakens an awareness of your own deficiencies, and the wounds inside you begin to bleed. A part of you will come to life. Its job is to stop the internal bleeding. This part of you will try in various ways to show—both to yourself and to other people—that this painful caricature is not true. It will help you distance yourself in every way possible from

---

33 My understanding of human psychological development has been fed from many sources, including most prominently Elizabeth O'Connor, Rollo May, Carl Rogers, Frederick Perls, D. W. Winnicott, Mikhail Bakhtin, Etty Hillesum, Del Jones, Gerald May, Alice Miller, Melanie Klein, Richard Rohr. Throughout this book, however, I lean most heavily on the model elaborated by Richard C. Schwartz in *Internal Family Systems Therapy* (New York: The Guilford Press, 1997).

Schwartz argues convincingly that the human personality is inherently multiple—it is made up of a number of sub-personalities that jostle and argue among themselves constantly, each vying for control of the whole system. He calls these sub-personalities "parts," since that's what his clients call them when they begin revealing themselves to him, as in: "A part of me is feeling hopeful today, but another part feels really scared." The key to healthy functioning, and the goal of psychotherapy, is the fostering of friendly relationships among the parts, and between the parts and the deepest essence of a person, which Schwartz calls the Self.

Every time I speak of a "part" or "parts" of a person, in this book, I am operating within the parameters of Schwartz's model. For a full, and convincing, description of the "multiple self," see *Internal Family Systems Therapy*, 8–17.

the shameful aspects of fundamentalism: by getting the best possible education; by writing respectable books and becoming recognized as a leading scholar; by attacking fundamentalism publicly for its backwardness, its social irrelevance, its other-worldliness, its anti-intellectualism; by striving for prominence and power in social and political spheres.

This part of you might proclaim that it's time for Christians to return America to the good old days of the nineteenth century, when evangelicals held coveted places of honor in American life. It might propose that Christians revive that older, more respectable name—"evangelicals"—and get rid of the embarrassing association with fundamentalism altogether. If this part has a strong enough voice in you, you will listen to it and do what it says.

None of these measures will seem adequate, however, if you are still stuck with the ridiculous, fundamentalist God. So the theologian in you will begin to imagine the lineaments of a new God. Unlike the old, fundamentalist God, he will have to be intellectually respectable, so you'll need to use philosophical language, high-sounding abstractions—not images or stories—to describe him. Unlike the fundamentalist God, who seems stifled as an actor in the social and political realm, the God created by your shame will need to be free of any taint of inadequacy; so you'll emphasize his power and majesty (and gain a bit of that power and majesty by association with him).

Where the fundamentalist God has adopted an apocalyptic stance toward his world, giving up any ongoing relevancy on the larger world stage, you'll make sure your God is perceived as truly sovereign, as deeply implicated in and fully in charge of the affairs of civilization. Where the fundamentalist God is driven by his punitive fury, you will make your God controlled, cerebral, and without feelings—as you yourself, a person torn by the feelings shame unleashes, might wish to be. You will do all this out of sheer desperation, yes, but also as a heartfelt quest for the kind of God you imagine you need in order to heal your wounds.

The God you end up with will escape the stigma of fundamentalism. By association with this new, more amenable God, the shame-drenched picture of your own diminished self might soon be forgotten.[34]

•   •   •

SELF-SUFFICIENT DEITY

Carl F. H. Henry was a tireless scholar with a flair for public relations. He quickly rose to prominence as the spokesperson for a rising evangelical Christianity. When he died in 2003 at age ninety, an evangelical journalist said: "If we see Billy Graham as the great

---

34 A healthier way of relating to my shame, according to Richard Schwartz (*Internal Family Systems Therapy*), and one that yields a more constructive theology, would be to confess, understand, and ultimately learn to love my shame. If I could see it as a part of me that has been working long and hard to earn me the love it knows I need, I might feel compassion for that part of me and, in the warm light of compassion, it might loosen its grip on me. Loving it doesn't mean overlooking the harm it has inadvertently done me.

My shame is essentially a voice of self-accusation and self-ridicule planted deep inside me, unsettling my inner world, poisoning me with the venom of self-hatred. Its presence makes my inner world a place of hostility rather than of hospitality. Before it will relax its hold on me, however, and learn to play a more constructive role inside me, I will need to go on a healing journey toward a fuller self-understanding.

I will need to identify the sources of my self-enmity in the critical and shaming responses of others toward me during my childhood. I will need to learn compassion for the more vulnerable, small, scared, weak-feeling parts of me that my shamed part urges me to keep hidden away. I will have to embrace those small and weak-feeling parts as essential aspects of my humanity, sources of my gentleness and compassion for others who are also small and weak. I will have to see my shame as holding within itself a yearning for unconditional love.

In *Part Two*, I will show how the crucified Jesus accompanies us on exactly this kind of healing journey.

public face and generous spirit of the evangelical movement, Carl Henry was the brains."[35]

Billy Graham himself labeled Henry "the most eminent of conservative theologians."[36] Henry was among the prime movers in Fuller Theological Seminary's early years. In the mid-1950s, Henry joined Graham to launch the flagship evangelical periodical, *Christianity Today*, which he edited until 1968. During his lifetime, he produced a flood of scholarship aimed at the evangelical public as well as academic readers.[37] Well into the 1990s, Henry helped define how evangelicals would think about God. But his own life offers a case study in the theological implications of shame.

Henry started his academic career with a bang. Between 1946 and 1948, while writing two doctoral dissertations, he published three scholarly books.[38] Each of them is replete with references to God. Here is a representative sampling of the words and phrases Henry used in these books to describe God:

> Creator, Supporter and End of all things
> almighty, holy Lord of the universe
> conserving cause of the universe
> maker and judge of man
> powerful world-maker
> maker and Lord of life
> master molder

---

35 David Neff, quoted in Laurie Goodstein, "Rev. Dr. Carl F. H. Henry, 90, Brain of Evangelical Movement," *The New York Times*, December 13, 2003.

36 Quoted in Henry, *Confessions,* 291. Henry also notes that *Time,* in its January 15, 1968 issue, considered him "the arbiter in defining and defending conservative Protestantism."

37 His *magnum opus* is *God, Revelation and Authority*, 6 vols., (Waco: Word, 1976–1983).

38 References to Henry's work in this section come from these three books: *Remaking the Modern Mind,* 82–83, 119, 137, 146, 149, 193–196, 202, 207, 245, 293; *Notes on the Doctrine of God* (Boston: W. A. Wilde, 1948), 11, 22, 33, 39, 43, 54, 61, 68, 78, 92–93, 100; *The Uneasy Conscience of Modern Fundamentalism*, 76, 84, 39.

sovereign ruler

holy living, omnipotent, loving God

true Lord of the universe

omnipotent Creator

architect of the world of nature

self-contained God

self-sufficient deity

all-perfect

supernatural

immanent as well as transcendent

personal, sovereign first cause

previous prime cause

personal, holy, merciful God

sovereign Father

sovereign God of the universe

sovereign Lord of history

almighty, holy God

If you have been raised in the Reformed or Calvinist wing of Protestantism—which was introduced to Henry at Wheaton College—or if you have studied in one of the many evangelical colleges where the spirit of Henry's theology has made inroads since the 1940s, these words and phrases may not make much of an impression on you. You might be tempted to put them into the "been there, done that" category. "Of course God is sovereign," you might say. "Of course God is the Creator, Supporter and End of all things. What's the big deal?"

But contrast these words, for a moment, with words and images used to describe God in a 1940s-era fundamentalist sermon by Percy Crawford, Jack Wyrtzen or Billy Graham:

patient

forgiving

warning

pleading

hater of sin

loving Father

demanding judge

closer than a brother

wrathful

punisher

avenger

These descriptors are not entirely pleasant. But neither are they cerebral or bland. They draw on concrete human images and human feelings to portray God as a recognizable, personal entity. Their language is relational, implying a connection and interaction—again, not always pleasant—between God and ourselves. Whatever else you can say for him, fundamentalism's God seems real—frighteningly real, wonderfully real, but definitely *real*.

Henry's list, by contrast, is not alive enough to be either pleasant or unpleasant. Although, in one of his books, Henry insisted that God is not an "abstract deity," his portrait of God is uniformly abstract.[39] His language describes an inconceivably large being, so

---

[39] *Remaking*, 194–196. Edward J. Carnell, the philosopher of religion and later president at Fuller Seminary, was often mentioned in the same breath as Carl Henry during my years at Wheaton. His *Introduction to Christian Apologetics: A Philosophical Defense of Trinitarian-Theistic Faith* (Grand Rapids, MI: Wm. B. Eerdmans Publishing Company, 1948) offers characterizations of God that have a very similar ring: absolute Being, sovereign Lawgiver, sovereign Creator, sovereign Sustainer, sovereign Consummator, Deity, Author and Judge of the Universe, Almighty, personal, triune. He also describes human beings as "God's property" that God has the right to "dispose of" as he sees fit.

Carnell's God has no emotions and his love for humans flows from a "divine volition." Being "Almighty" means God is "independent" and "free to do what he wants without being called into account." He is "responsible to no one but himself." Oddly, Carnell thought his

super-human as to be un-human. It portrays God as a far-off controller—"sovereign" was one of Henry's favorite terms, and it has become one of the most common descriptors of God in evangelical church language today.

Unlike the fundamentalist God, this God is not tempted to throw in the towel on his sinful creation. In his sovereignty, he rules and molds, conserves and creates. God is so all-competent, so sovereign, that human beings seem but interchangeable parts in his cosmic machinery.

Moreover, Henry's God is neither warm, nor person-like. Admittedly, the fundamentalist God is angry and punitive, so you might want to stay out of his way. But he does have feelings, and he evokes a wide range of feelings in return. He touches the human heart.

By contrast, Henry's God doesn't have feelings—in fact, Henry thought giving God feelings made him seem *too* human.[40] So his God has a palpably distant, cold, objective feel. He is "self-sufficient" and "self-contained"—meaning, he exists in splendid isolation, and has no need for anything beyond himself. He is walled-off from us, and so is his heart. Even when he describes his conversion experience, Henry calls the God he met in a moment of profound emotion "the Great Archer" and "the transcendent Tetragrammaton."[41] It's

---

own descriptions of God bore little resemblance to "the gods of the ancients" who were "too near abstract principles of impersonal intelligence to be of service to man in worship." These characterizations and others like them can be found on pp. 56, 61, 91, 142, 159, 166, 168, 176, 215, 234, 251, 260, 271, 292, 294, 296, 304, 319, 323, 329.

In his later works, Carnell struggled to conceptualize a warmer, more relational God. These later works did not get much favorable attention from evangelical scholars.

40 Recently, the ancient doctrine, heavily influenced by Greek thought—that God is without feelings and cannot suffer—has come under fire from a few brave evangelicals. See for example John Sanders, *The God Who Risks: A Theology of Providence* (Downers Grove, IL: InterVarsity Press, 1998) and Clark H. Pinnock, *Most Moved Mover: A Theology of God's Openness* (Grand Rapids, MI: Baker Academic, 2001).

41 *Confessions of a Theologian*, 46. The term "tetragrammaton" refers to the Hebrew

hard to feel anything toward such a God, hard to imagine what it would mean to love him. But "love"—which I believe Henry, like every human being, yearned for—is a word that appears only rarely in Henry's writing, and when it does, it looks lost and lonely.

The same is true of the word "personal." Henry did use the term from time to time, but invariably it appears in tandem with another word—like "sovereign" or "holy"—and that other word drains "personal" of any recognizably personal meaning.[42] In his books, Henry utilized the word "sovereign" again and again, elaborating on it at length, but he generally passed by the word "personal" without comment. The only counter-examples I can find seem to highlight the rejecting or punitive side of the personal: God shows he's personal by giving us moral laws that we must obey, by warning us against trying to save ourselves, by demanding repentance and punishing the unrepentant.[43]

In one of his more intriguing sentences, Henry wrote: "God is self-sufficient deity, having social relations within his own nature, yet not treating impersonally his creatures."[44] The final clause tries feebly to assure us of what the sentence as a whole denies. Henry's God doesn't seem much interested in a relationship with us. He has more cosmic fish to fry.

So Henry's God does not remind me of Jesus—the human being whom Christians through the ages have identified as God's presence among us.[45] The sort of deity who might eat, drink or answer a question with a riddle—or teach by telling a story—does not show

---

Bible's practice of referring to God by the letters "YHWH."

42 *Remaking the Modern Mind*, 202, 277, 16, 18.

43 *Notes on the Doctrine of God*, 56, 35–36, 64.

44 *Remaking the Modern Mind*, 195–196.

45 The fundamentalist preachers tended to do much better with this. You can find stories about or by Jesus that point to almost all of the terms on their list—although I believe that many of those stories, when they are carefully interpreted, point to a much better God than the one fundamentalists preached.

up in Henry's writing. There is no weeping, scolding, celebrating—no feel for the texture of suffering and dying. There is no hint of the melancholy, homeless human who seemed content to wander the countryside in an imperial backwater, stopping to look suffering individuals in the eye and whisper an intimate word of healing.

On very rare occasions, Henry refers to Jesus. But his Jesus bears little resemblance to the one we meet in the Gospel narratives, and the name itself—"Jesus"—is not often used. Instead, Henry speaks of the "second person of the Trinity" or "Christ"—accentuating his divinity rather than his flesh and blood humanity. Henry describes Jesus as "perfection." He is the one coming "in power and great glory." Jesus embodies "the highest values of world culture." He is the source of the "Hebrew-Christian world-life view."[46] He is, in other words, a rational principle and not a human being like we are.[47] He is not the sort of being Jesus might have called his Father, or even more endearingly, his "Abba."[48]

And yet, evangelicalism is well-known for its tendency to measure the genuineness of a person's faith by the degree to which they have achieved a "warm, personal relationship with God." How can Carl Henry not notice?

·   ·   ·

[46] *Re-Making the Modern Mind*, 159, 209, 33, 56, 258, 295, 299.

[47] Henry's colleague, E. J. Carnell, wrote similarly about Jesus: "Christ, as Creator, is the Author of the many, and, as Logos, is the principle of the One. . . Christ is the truth, for he is the Logos, the synthesizing principle and the true meaning of reality."

To have faith in such a Christ is necessarily a rational matter: "And when a man sees and embraces this truth with a cordial trust, he has proper faith, for generic faith is but a resting of the heart in the sufficiency of the evidence. . . The better our propositions stick together, the more truth we have; the more truth we have, the more faith we have; the more faith we have, the more coherence we have." *Christian Apologetics*, 354, 107.

[48] "Abba" is an Aramaic term of endearment for a father, often translated "daddy." See, for example, Mark 14:36.

A FATHER ANOMALY

Historically, Christians have understood God as a "Trinity"—three persons in one. The "first person" of the Trinity is God the Father. When Carl Henry offered evangelicals a new, less shameful God, he focused on God the Father. How did it escape Henry's attention—and the attention of evangelicals generally—that this "father" was not a warm, relational being as one might wish a father to be?

I have been suggesting that the young men who gave us the new evangelicalism were shaped by deep wounds of shame, generated in them by their association with fundamentalism. But I suspect these wounds did not begin with fundamentalism. The foundation for debilitating shame—the raw wounds later re-sensitized by shameful encounters—is originally laid in one's childhood family.

Every theologian was once a child, of course. The experiences of a little child are hidden away within the psyche of every scholar laboring at a desk to write the truth about God. The childhoods of the young men who fashioned evangelical Christianity's God in mid-century America, to a startling degree, are littered with broken father-son relationships.

In my opinion, that is where their shame was born. It was their *father-generated* shame, as much as their fundamentalism-generated shame, which accounts for this anomaly in their theology: that they yearned for a warm, accepting "father" and at the same time seemed intent on portraying God as a uniquely cold and distant father.[49]

Psychologist Gershen Kaufman offers a story to illustrate the genesis of shame in childhood. A man arrives home from work. His young son greets him excitedly at the door—he has been waiting all day for his father to come home and play with him. The father is

---

49 Of course, the word "father" has resonated deeply in humans throughout the ages, shaping all manner of gods in its image, not least because human society has been typically patriarchal, and human fathers have thus been powerful figures in the lives of their children.

weary. He wants to relax and read the paper. The son pleads. At first the father puts him off gently. But the son persists. The father loses his patience and snaps: "Leave me alone, will you? Can't you see I'm not interested in playing right now?" The boy is deflated, and slinks off to his bedroom.[50]

How does this incident generate shame in the boy? Kaufman explains that shame occurs when the interpersonal bridge connecting two people is abruptly broken. The logic of this incident, for the boy, goes like this: "My father is the most important person to me. His anger shows he doesn't love me. The fault must be mine. There is something wrong with my need for him. I am deficient. I deserve abandonment. Now I am radically alone and bereft of love."

If this wound cuts deep enough into the boy's spirit, it will be reactivated many times during his life. It will bring a surge of unbearable pain every time the boy feels criticized, rejected or scorned. The boy, or man, will even be able to activate it himself, just by listening to the part of him to which this incident has given birth, the part which criticizes, rejects or scorns him. Ironically, that part will try to "protect" him from further shame by shaming him internally, in hope that he will avoid whatever behaviors threaten to shame him externally.

How might this boy, now a grown-up theologian, imagine and describe a "heavenly Father"? Much would depend on the larger pattern of his own father's behavior. Was this early shaming incident the only one like it, and was it followed up by the father acknowledging his injury and begging his son's forgiveness? Or was it part of a pattern of fathering—quite common in twentieth-century America—in which the father is silent, withdrawn, unfeeling and inaccessible for long periods, coming alive only in moments of rage? If the son knows no other than this father, might he be forgiven for

---

50 *Shame*, 14.

imagining a heavenly father who is a "better," but not altogether different, version of his own father—his own father with some of the harder edges knocked off?

.   .   .

A TERRIFYING FRACAS

Carl Henry's childhood shame fairly leaps from the pages of his autobiography.[51] He was born in 1913 to recent German immigrants living in a neighborhood derisively called "Chickentown." During these years of the Great War, when it was shameful to be German in America, his father changed the family name from "Heinrich" to "Henry." Still, Carl remembers that his own name had "an uncomfortably Prussian ring: Carl Ferdinand Howard Henry."

Carl writes that his father was humiliated for being German, often arriving home "too breathless and fearful to eat." Once, his father was denounced as a "scab," chased, caught and "hurled over a fence"; he "reached home several hours late, his clothing in tatters." Henry carried these pictures in his heart to the end of his life.

Carl does not describe his father as a strong, self-sufficient man. As a six-year-old, he saw his mother "pummeling" his father with a broomstick for coming home late from work, and drunk. He says the incident "left lingering scars." His father botched a pig slaughter and accidentally set fire to their family home. He stole apples from a

---

51 Here I am focusing on instances of Henry's shame in his relationship with his father. His autobiography offers many additional vignettes of his sensitivity to shame. On the first day of school, he wet his pants. (I did the same, which helps me feel great warmth for the young Henry.) He was "uncontrollably overweight" in high school and had rheumatism, so that he "shuffled awkwardly" among his classmates. He was known as "a country boob." A classmate publicly accused him of cheating, and he felt stigmatized for coming "from the other side of the tracks." When he was a journalist, a rival writer called him "the fat school graduate." On one occasion, when asked in public to talk about "God's plan for his life," Henry says he was "embarrassed" and "felt threatened by a sense of public exposure and nakedness. . ." *Confessions*, 16, 26, 28, 32, 50–51, 45.

local orchard—making Carl stand guard—and, during Prohibition, made mash whiskey in the family kitchen and served it to his neighbors, turning the family home into an "alcoholic spa." Carl recalls how his father raged at other drivers on the road: "G— d— kike, so I'm not going fast enough for him!"

One can imagine a son being embarrassed by, and wanting to distance himself from, this kind of father. In fact, he began doing so, he says, as a "young teenager." When his father began writing bad checks to cover his gambling debts, Carl added his "middle and differentiating initials" to his name, becoming Carl F. H. Henry.[52]

What was Carl's relationship with his father? A yawning distance seems to have separated them. Carl's stories offer no instances of a father's humor or playfulness; no vacations; no warm encounters or fatherly chats; no advice for a boy becoming a man; no counsel about education or occupation. During the family's weekly "fun-time," his father took his Sunday nap. Weekdays, he worked hard, leaving on the train before sunrise and returning after sunset. He expected his children to work hard, too—perhaps, especially, Carl, the oldest of eight.

Carl writes: "Father had a violent temper (some of which he showered on me)." Once, after his father cursed and threatened to beat him for neglecting his chores, Carl became "infuriated." He threw a rock through the kitchen window and ran off. His mother went after him, and "in tears," took his hand and led him home. The episode was never mentioned again.

But the tension between father and son worsened. Carl tells this story:

> Late one night, after everyone had retired, I heard my father shouting for my mother, apparently determined to shoot her, and

---

52 *Confessions*, 16.

presumably carrying a loaded gun. He demanded that she come out of hiding. I knew that now and then, although he was not a persistent drunkard, Father drank too much and altercations ensued. But never had I heard anything like this. I froze in my bed as the commotion continued. . . I do not know to this day how as a young lad I then had the temerity to do what I did. I swung open my bedroom door to the central hallway and. . . called out in the darkness to my father and asked if he needed help. Next I walked out boldly, wrested the gun from his hand, ran back into my room and hurled the weapon [out an open window] into the snow-covered night.

After this "terrifying fracas," the teenage Carl "trembled sleeplessly until dawn."[53]

•   •   •

A SURROGATE FATHER

People who, as children, experience shame and alienation in their relationship with a parent often spend their lives looking for a substitute parent, someone with whom they can symbolically revisit and heal their inner wounds. For Carl Henry, a Christian philosopher and theologian, God might become such a surrogate father—a "heavenly" father who, unlike his earthly father, would be sovereign, universally respectable and all-sufficient. With such a father, Carl might hope to forge the relationship he never had with his earthly father—a relationship to quiet the voice inside that told him he was irremediably deficient and unlovable.

Whether or not a surrogate relationship turns out to be truly healing, however, depends on the degree of self-awareness in the

---

53 *Confessions*, 16–25.

person seeking the relationship. Very often, the search for a sur-rogate parent is not carried out with self-understanding, and the results are disappointing. On the surface, a satisfactory surrogate father must *appear* to be the polar opposite of the real father, and thus to promise a more satisfying father-son relationship, along with an alternative model of manhood for the son to imitate. Unconsciously, however, the surrogate father will not have emotional appeal for the surrogate son unless he is also quite *like* the real father.

It is this instinctive "familiarity," emanating from the surrogate father's underlying emotional or relational style, which uncon-sciously draws the surrogate son to him. This familiarity is at first unnoticed, even vociferously denied, by the surrogate son. He is sure that he has found a very different father than his own, a father who will finally give him what he needs. But if he has not grown in self-awareness, the surrogate father will be more like his real father than he knows, and he will find himself reliving, with the surrogate father, the relational frustrations of his childhood.

I would not be quite so convinced that Carl Henry's God func-tioned as his surrogate father if that God did not bear an uncanny resemblance to an actual, human surrogate father in Henry's life—the philosopher, Gordon Clark. Clark was the sole philosophy professor and one of the very few Calvinists at Wheaton College when Henry enrolled in the 1930s.[54] Many of the brightest young men who came to Wheaton during his tenure, and who would rise to prominence as evangelical scholars, studied under Clark. It was Clark who first introduced them to a more respectable God—the super-sized, sovereign God of Reformed theology.[55] Through these

---

54 For a helpful portrait of Clark and assessment of his influence on the young evangelical scholars of the 1930s, see Nelson, *Making and Unmaking*, 36–39. Carl Henry also describes Clark in *Confessions*, 66–67.

55 John Calvin and the Reformed tradition since him have made the sovereignty, holiness and majesty of God their grounding principle. A recent spokesperson for this viewpoint is R. C. Sproul, Jr., *Almighty Over All: Understanding the Sovereignty of God*

gifted students, Clark put his mark on late twentieth-century evangelical theology.

Gordon Clark was an "unabashed rationalist," according to those who knew him. He saw his lifelong task as making Christianity intellectually respectable.[56] Carl Henry said that Clark believed "Christianity satisfies the intellect because it is true, and truth is the only everlasting satisfaction."[57] Clark believed he could bolster the existence of the Christian God—a God much like the one later popularized by Henry—by the use of iron-clad logic. Henry was one of the many young men who fell under Clark's spell.[58] He later dedicated his first philosophical book to Clark.[59]

On the surface, as one would expect, Gordon Clark appeared to be the opposite of Carl Henry's father. He was a morally principled, sophisticated, "dapper" man, smoothly articulate, intellectually masterful and emotionally controlled. His personality gave

---

(Grand Rapids, MI: Baker Books, 1999).

John Piper is also a vigorous defender of God's sovereignty, particularly its necessary corollary: that God predestines some people to heaven and others to hell, without regard to their merit. He does some fancy stepping to show, to his satisfaction, that sentencing people to hell is not inconsistent with God's loving nature. His argument is on-line at http://www.desiringgod.org/ResourceLibrary/TopicIndex/43/1582_How_Does_a_Sovereign_God_Love?

Douglas John Hall identifies two primary theological traditions in the history of Christianity: the "thin" tradition, with the suffering Jesus at its center, and the "thick" tradition, with a sovereign potentate at its center. The thick tradition is most congenial to Christians who possess or crave cultural power. Which is why it is called "thick"—it has dominated Christian theological thinking for sixteen centuries. *Lighten Our Darkness: Toward an Indigenous Theology of the Cross* (Philadelphia: Westminster, 1976).

56 *Making and Unmaking*, 37.

57 *Confessions*, 67.

58 In an appreciative introductory essay to a Clark Festschrift, Carl F. H. Henry states that, at Wheaton, Gordon Clark "made a lasting contribution to a score of young scholars who were to articulate Christian theism aggressively in the contemporary milieu. Among these were Edward John Carnell. . . , Billy Graham. . . , and the present writer." Quoted in Nelson, *Making and Unmaking*, 36.

59 Edward Carnell did the same.

the impression of a kind of "sovereignty." He was the very paragon of respectable, educated Christian manhood. Because he looked so different from their own fathers, Clark was powerfully attractive to young men like Carl Henry.

Outside his cadre of "protégés," however, many considered Clark arrogant, disagreeable, a prima donna. He could be combative, stubborn, and cold—in other words, he resembled Henry's father. With his rapier logic, he intimidated many of his colleagues and, it seems, most of his students.[60]

Henry says Clark "followed logic more devotedly than he followed Dale Carnegie,"[61] a circuitous way of indicating that he was imperious and unfriendly. Clark was particularly uncomfortable with matters of the heart. He was suspicious of feelings—it is "stupidity," he wrote, to believe in a "non-intellectual, emotional religion."[62] He was the sort of man who could not show human weakness or vulnerability, would not let anyone see what was broken inside him. He was not gifted in relating to others in warm or personal ways. In emotional style, he was Carl's father's twin.

Gordon Clark was thus equipped to do double duty for Carl Henry and the other young protégés whom he trained for the leadership of the new evangelicalism. He was the shiny, sovereign, surrogate father Henry could look to in the quest to escape, or heal, the wounds of his childhood relationship with his own father. He was also a persuasive propagandist for a shiny, sovereign, surrogate God, a God of whom Henry and his colleagues need not feel ashamed—a God Henry could recommend to evangelicals as less shameful, more respectable, than the shabby, angry, disengaged, ignorant old God of fundamentalism.

And because this professor, and this God, were so attractive on

---

60 Nelson, *Making and Unmaking*, 37.

61 *Confessions*, 66–67.

62 "Faith and Reason," *Christianity Today*, February 18, 1957, 9; March 4, 1957, 11, 15.

the surface, it is possible that even as bright a man as Carl Henry never noticed that neither one offered the openness of heart, the warmth of personal disclosure, the deep human connection that his heart yearned for.

•   •   •

MYSTERIOUS AND REMOTE

Carl Henry's autobiography does little to reveal what was buried inside its author.[63] Like many males of his time, and many of ours as well, he kept his feelings and his suffering to himself. That he tells us as much as he does is a remarkable gift, allowing us to sense some of the pain he carried in his heart for a lifetime. I thank him for this gift.

I have explored Carl Henry's story because I suspect it is not the exception but the rule. If we surveyed the life stories of other evangelical scholars who came to prominence at mid-century, I believe we might find hints that their relationships with their fathers were at least as troubled and unsatisfying as Henry's.[64] Such stories suggest

---

[63] This temperamental style, shared by so many of the progenitors of the "new evangelicalism" rising at mid-century, has been written into evangelical theology and spiritual practice, as I will argue throughout this book, and accounts at least in part for the ability of evangelicals to "believe" a system of dogma that is emotionally incoherent, as I illustrated in the first chapter. Most of the leading evangelical models of spirituality and maturity do not trust emotion and show no curiosity about what is going on at the deeper places inside themselves. So they can glibly say things that make no sense to self-aware individuals.

[64] It is beyond the scope of this study to survey these relationships. The official biographies offer tiny hints—there is a lot of work to be done to fill out this picture. The best information available is for Edward Carnell, particularly Rudy Nelson's *Making and Unmaking* (16–25, 112).

Carnell once wrote: "Our adult anxieties trace to the persistence of feelings that are conditioned in childhood. . . by the harsh or unpredictable behavior of parents." Edward John Carnell, *The Case for Biblical Christianity*, ed. Ronald H. Nash (Grand Rapids, MI: Wm. B. Eerdmans Publishing Co., 1969), 137.

that the natural urge to overcome shame—shame inflicted in childhood and reinforced by their association with fundamentalism—helps explain the attraction of many evangelical scholars to an abstract and distant God, a surrogate "Father" whose sovereignty camouflages an incapacity for warm connection.[65]

The God celebrated by Henry, and so many other evangelical thinkers, looks suspiciously like a cleaned-up, beefed-up version of a relationally-distant father. In fact, the sovereign deity bears an uncanny resemblance to the way many males of our own time speak about their fathers—as mysterious and remote figures unable to share their inner lives with their sons. American men often depict

---

He also wrote to a friend: "I am fully aware that the root of my anxieties goes back to childhood. I am a minister's son who was raised in a highly legalistic and emotionally erratic atmosphere. The scars of these early childhood experiences are still with me" (quoted in *Making and Unmaking,* 112).

Of all the early leaders of this movement, Carnell seems to have been the one most encouraged by severe emotional difficulties to break the mold and begin exploring his own internal landscape.

65 One could do a similar study of the relationships which the prominent youth evangelists had with their fathers, which might help explain why the youth evangelists could be oblivious to the emotional incoherence of a God who professed love but promised abandonment, and whose most palpable emotion is wrath.

Billy Graham's father was described as "absolutely straightbacked," a "surpassingly muted and unassertive soul" whose discipline was "implacably sustained," usually by means of a "wide leather belt"; who, according to Graham, "never could really understand anyone who wanted to do anything other than physical labor. . . never played a game in his life. . . never cared about fishing or hunting or baseball, anything like that." Graham and his father "inhabited two separate dimensions, were caught up on opposite sides of some invisible barrier like figures sealed behind plate glass, through which they only beheld each other soundlessly moving and grieving."

For these and other portraits of both Graham and his father, see Marshall Frady, *Billy Graham: A Parable of American Righteousness* (New York: Little, Brown, 1979), pp. 30, 25, 49, 33, 37, 40; and William Martin, *A Prophet with Honor: The Billy Graham Story* (New York: William Morrow and Company, Inc., 1991), 57–61.

Percy Crawford included in one his sermons these lines: "My dad was a blacksmith who ruled his home with an iron hand, or rather a raw-hide whip. When any of us did not appear in church, he used to march us down to the basement and flog us with that raw-hide whip." Percy admitted to feeling "in revolt" against his father. *Salvation Full and Free,* 7–8.

fathers as intimidating, forbidding, projecting a "distant, judgmental quality." They use landscape metaphors—"mountains or rocks or other mute objects of nature"—or they describe fathers as distant, or up high, looking down with disapproval. They remember their fathers either having an angry, threatening face or else withdrawing into silence.[66]

These characteristics, in their general tenor, call to mind the "sovereign father" that Carl Henry, and so many of the younger evangelical scholars, found in God. Were they drawn to this God—almighty, majestic, sovereign—as to a surrogate father with whom they hoped finally to enjoy the relationship their childhood never afforded them? Their God reflected the massive size and imagined capabilities of every infant's father. What father is not the "first principle" or controller of the universe, at least during early years of limited awareness?

But the cruel experience of a growing child can bring disappointment and embarrassment about the father's powers, as it must have for the young Carl Henry, whose father was quite visibly a bumbler, a tyrant and failure. Henry was not about to let this happen to God, whose superhuman capabilities were a constant emphasis in his texts.

But while Henry might secretly yearn for a God who possessed the warm, personal, vulnerable qualities his earthly father lacked, he had no experience to draw on that would allow him believably to elaborate such a picture. So he could cite "personal" and "loving" as attributes of God's, but he could offer no credible description of how such attributes might really work.

Henry's God—the God many evangelicals would become familiar with in Christian college religion classes—turned out to be very much better than his own father in terms of power and intellect

---

66 Samuel Osherson, *Finding Our Fathers: How a Man's Life Is Shaped by His Relationship with His Father* (New York: Fawcett Columbine, 1986), 20, 22, 29.

and respectability, but a mirror image of his own father in his ability to show real affection.

●   ●   ●

TRIUMPANT, BUT STRANGELY DISTANT

By 1959, when I entered Wheaton College, Carl Henry and Edward Carnell were two of the most celebrated thinkers in American evangelicalism. Their world-controlling sovereign had bested the world-denying fundamentalist tyrant in most conservative Christian colleges and seminaries. Both Henry and Carnell visited Wheaton as honored lecturers during my undergraduate years, and their ideas were discussed enthusiastically in Wheaton's religion and philosophy classes.

The text assigned in my freshman religion course, *Your God Is Too Small*, was one indication that Wheaton had embraced Henry's triumphalist spirit. Although it was written by a British scholar, J. B. Phillips, its title delivered a typically American message—one that Carl Henry would have been pleased to endorse.[67]

In *Your God Is Too Small*, Phillips scolded Christians for worshipping "a God who is really too small to command [our] adult loyalty and cooperation." Recent scientific discoveries, he said, suggested an "immeasurably bigger" and more "incredibly complex" being than we had imagined, one that was "big enough to account for life. . . big enough to command [our] highest admiration and respect."

Phillips admitted that this picture did not harmonize readily with the New Testament's portrait of a human-scale Jesus. It must have been very difficult for God to give up the trappings of deity and become human, he said. When he took the form of Jesus, God

---

67 Phillips was previously known for his graceful, paraphrased version of the New Testament: *The New Testament in Modern English* (New York: The Macmillan Company, 1960).

felt "a repugnance which we cannot begin to imagine." The "real" God, Phillips implied, is an awesome, outsized being very unlike the human Jesus.

Although, in other writings, Phillips parted ways with evangelical orthodoxy, his title conveniently encapsulated Henry's new evangelicalism.[68] The God of fundamentalism was too small. The God of Henry and of Wheaton College—the God of American evangelicalism—was definitely not. He mattered in this world, not simply the next, and he expected Christians—as his "vice-regents"—to matter, too.

Increasingly, over the next forty years, American evangelicalism lived up to the aspirations of Henry and his formidable sovereign God. Evangelical churches grew more rapidly than any other in American Protestantism.[69] Evangelical voices downplayed the

---

68 J. B. Phillips, *Your God Is Too Small* (New York: The Macmillan Company, 1961), 7, 106. Phillips didn't identify himself as an evangelical. His warm temperament did not sit easily beside Henry's cerebral theism, and at times he expressed opinions that Carl Henry—and most American evangelicals then and now—would reject. For example: "If it is true, as John declares, that 'God is love,' it would make sense that any action that sprang from love had its origin in God. It would also mean that those who did give themselves in love did in fact 'know God,' however loudly they might protest their agnosticism. I have never been happy with any ecclesiastical or theological system in which correctness of belief was of paramount importance." J. B. Phillips, *Ring of Truth: A Translator's Testimony* (London: Hodder & Stoughton, 1967), 50–51.

69 Christian Smith and his colleagues, cited earlier, identify evangelicalism as "the strongest of the major Christian traditions in the United States" (20–47). I am just as surprised as anyone by evangelicalism's success. Over twenty years ago, I wrote a book on evangelical theology's formative years—the period just before and after 1900. In the book's epilogue, I allowed myself to speculate on the future of American evangelicalism: "I do not look for conservative Christianity's current resurgence to be consummated in real political power" (*Less Than Conquerors: The Evangelical Quest for Power in the Early Twentieth Century*, 277). With the election of George W. Bush, it came closer than I had expected possible.

On the other hand, one should perhaps not make too much of this resurgence. Christian Smith and his colleagues located most of the signs of evangelicalism's vitality within the institutional network that evangelicalism spawned even *as* it continued to lose the battle for wider cultural hegemony. Most of its attempts to reclaim its cultural leadership—by outlawing abortion, returning prayer to the public schools, censoring the

gloomy escapism of fundamentalism and staked their claim to full participation—as foot-soldiers of a sovereign God—in the affairs of this world. Evangelicals built mega-churches where, surrounded by theme park amenities and smiling born-again baristas, tens of thousands could raise their voices in praise to Almighty God. They pulled down dispensationalism's severe "end times" charts from their church sanctuaries and replaced them with video screens, rock bands, sacred drama and dance.

Evangelicals learned to cheer their own pop music and television personalities, and lionize professional football players who, in after-game interviews, refused to answer reporters' questions until they had first credited Jesus with their victory. They redefined alcohol, social dancing, cinema and the arts as gifts from a sovereign God. They staked their claim to the airwaves—one cannot turn the radio dial without running a gauntlet of evangelical music, conversation, political commentary and sermonizing. They decided that "Christian service" meant more than just church and mission work—it included upward mobility in the business and professional world as well.

Over these years, evangelicals also began to consider their God—and themselves—as fully entitled to the leadership of American culture. They would support an evangelical president's impulsive and ill-planned military adventures as a manifestation of God's sovereignty in all the earth. They would embrace free-market capitalism as God's way of producing wealth, and give virtually uncritical support to the political party that served as spokesperson for the interests of the wealthy.[70]

---

media, teaching "creationism," keeping homosexuality in the closet—have failed. Even where it has succeeded, as within its own institutions, it has often done so by embracing the consumerist cultural styles of its foes.

[70] In a rich historical survey, *Thy Kingdom Come: How the Religious Right Distorts the Faith and Threatens America* (New York: Basic Books, 2006), Randall Balmer chronicles and laments the wholesale surrender of American evangelicalism to the Religious Right.

And evangelicals would build colleges and universities by the hundreds. In many of these, among both faculty and students, the severe God of fundamentalism continued to mix with the more genteel, world-transforming God of evangelicalism in ways difficult to untangle. Increasingly, however, these institutions aimed their sights at the wider scholarly world, providing faculty grants and release-time for scientific research, rewarding scholarly publication with public recognition and tenure. With a certain wearying repetitiveness, they articulated their mission as inculcating a "Christian world and life view" by teaching their students to "integrate faith and learning."[71] Under their auspices, several generations of evangelical students were trained to move into leadership in American life, with remarkable success.

He says he speaks as a jilted lover: "The evangelical faith that nurtured me as a child and sustains me as an adult has been hijacked by right-wing zealots who have distorted the gospel of Jesus Christ. . . They appear not to have read the same New Testament that I open before me every morning at the kitchen counter" (ix).

For John Caputo, an alliance between sovereign-God theology and conservative politics is no surprise: "Can one imagine any more sovereign power than God's? Can one imagine anything more supportive of the established order, anything more top-down, more entrenched in the status quo. . . than religion and religion's 'God'?. . . What has founded and grounded top-down orders of sovereign power more firmly than such a 'God'? . . .Is not the very idea of God as the sovereign lord of the universe the very model after which every terrestrial sovereignty is designed? Is not the sovereign Father Almighty, Creator of Heaven and Earth, the very model of every earthly patriarchy? How often has the 'reign of God' meant a sovereign reign of theocratic terror? What has been more violent than theocracy? What more patriarchal, more hierarchical? What more authoritarian, inquisitorial, misogynistic, colonialist, militaristic, terroristic?" *The Weakness of God: A Theology of the Event* (Bloomington, IN: Indiana University Press, 2006), 32–33.

71 This was a thoroughly rationalistic exercise: "faith" as a set of truthful propositions drawn from the Bible; "learning" as a set of truthful propositions espoused by a particular field of study; and "integration" as comparing and contrasting these two sets of propositions to see where they agreed and disagreed. The vulnerable, human Jesus did not fit comfortably into its logical confines, and its dry intellectualistic understanding of "faith" did not ignite the spirit. Douglas and Rhonda Jacobsen, in *Scholarship and Christian Faith: Enlarging the Conversation* (New York: Oxford University Press, 2004) offer a trenchant but generous-spirited critique of the "'integration of faith and learning" model.

So the God that Henry and others like him willed to American evangelicals may have been just the God they needed, if social respectability and political power were their goals.[72] This God's sovereignty entitled him—and his loyal followers—to the governance of his planet. But his sovereignty, and all the out-sized attributes and regal behaviors that went along with it, left him a cold and distant figure. He resembled the fathers many post-war Americans actually had, rather than the kind their hearts truly desired. He was less tyrannical and condemning than the fundamentalist God—we can thank Carl Henry and his colleagues for that. But he was also less human and less emotional than the God he was meant to replace, and that made having a "relationship" with him deeply problematic.

And in truth, he did not exactly kill off the fundamentalist God. Henry's God took up residence in the evangelical head, while his fundamentalist counterpart remained lodged in the evangelical heart.[73] Within many evangelicals, it seems, the personalities of these

---

72 When he published his autobiography, in 1986, Henry admitted he was disappointed with evangelical Christianity's achievements: "Fifty years ago I had, as a young Christian, grand visions of the world impact of evangelical Christianity; today, as a timeworn believer, I still dream at times of the movement's profound potential. Admittedly, it is difficult, especially in latter years, to distinguish dreams from hallucination." He believed evangelicals were "forfeiting" the "biggest opportunity since the Reformation" for the "penetration of the world."

Still the crusader, Henry called on evangelicals to "marshal their available resources of prayer and projection in order to initiate in 1990 a national impact to climax the twentieth century in its final decade with a massive outpouring of spiritual and moral energy." He hoped such a crusade would "advance an alternative to secular humanism's cultural domination." *Confessions*, 401–403.

73 Patrick Henry College, in Purcellville, VA, is an intriguing example of the commingling of the old fundamentalism and the new evangelicalism. Its God has not given up on this world: its purpose is to train evangelical young people to win high political office so they can "shape the culture and take back the nation." To be taken seriously in the political realm, students are encouraged to appear tolerant and reasonable and not to threaten people with hell or quote the Bible in defense of their cause.

On campus, however, a scrupulous moral conformity is enforced and faculty must teach that the Bible (as interpreted by the school's president) always trumps secular

two Gods are confusingly intermingled, first one surfacing, then the other, depending on the relative usefulness of the carrot and the stick. Rarely is it acknowledged that these are two different Gods, each with his distinct personality, and that neither sits comfortably beside the human Jesus.

The growing influence of the sovereign evangelical God is most evident in the changing tone and format of Sunday morning church services, where evangelism has taken a back seat to worship: "Come, let us worship him together" has all but squeezed out "Come forward, right now, and take Jesus as your Savior."[74] The evangelical God is also the one referenced in Christian college classrooms and faculty lounges. He is the default God of much of evangelical theological writing and academic discussion, and he dominates the Christian college "faith and learning" industry.

The old fundamentalist God, on the other hand, can be heard in the more conservative spokespersons for the "religious right"; in the language of mass evangelism and the theology of gospel tracts; among missionaries and youth ministers; in some college chapels, home Bible studies and prayer groups—and, of course, among the many who consider themselves part of the broader evangelical movement, but prefer the rock-solid tenor of the term "fundamentalist."

And yet, although in many ways these two Gods have distinct

---

learning. "Non-Christian" thinkers (like Catholics—St. Augustine would be one) are not to be trusted. Students must sign a "statement of faith" that reads, in part: "All who die outside of Christ shall be confined in conscious torment for eternity."

It's as if the fundamentalist God has decided he'll make a bid for power in this world after all, so he dresses up in evangelical clothing when he goes out in public, but he reverts to his old boorish habits when he's among friends. For an engaging look at Patrick Henry College, see Hanna Rosin, *God's Harvard: A Christian College on a Mission to Save America* (New York: Houghton Mifflin Harcourt, 2007).

74 When evangelicals worship God, they tend to start out by telling him he is the greatest, not in love, but in power and glory and majesty—all the things humans are not. Then they speak of his love, as if to right an imbalance known deep in their unconscious.

personalities, in one way they are quite the same. Both say they love you, but neither of them is very convincing. One of them, in his anger and abandonment, seems all too "human," but frighteningly so. The other, in his cold rationality and abstract sovereignty, seems entirely inhuman.

No wonder Jim Plueddeman, a Wheaton grad of 1965, could say in 1991: "God still seems strangely distant or irrelevant to many of my classmates, who began to doubt their faith at Wheaton during the 1960s."[75]

---

75 "Blanchard Hall Revisited," *Wheaton Alumni*, December 1990/January 1991, 8.

CHAPTER 3

Nothing but the Blood
Paying the price for forgiveness

> *This God of the logicians. . . knew neither love nor hate.*
> *He was a God without sorrow and without glory—an*
> *inhuman God. His very justice was only a mathematical,*
> *logical justice, and so really an injustice.*
> Miguel de Unamuno[1]

IN THE FIRST TWO CHAPTERS, I explored the pictures of God imprinted in my soul by the young heroes of resurgent evangelicalism. The "crusades" mounted by Wyrtzen, Graham and their peers re-packaged the old fundamentalist God in the slick new language of teen culture, allowing an incoherent mixture of love and terrorism to slip down more easily, but at the cost of lodging deep within me a silent distrust for a God who consigns his loved ones to eternal torture.

The rising scholars who anchored their "world-views" in an abstract, impersonal sovereign—a divine "first principle"—left me with a God who is more interested in social control and right ideas than in the genuine transformation that flows from the trusting encounter of two vulnerable hearts. The word "love"—if it implies

---

1 Quoted in Moltmann, *The Trinity and the Kingdom: The Doctrine of God* (Minneapolis: Fortress Press, 1993), 37.

the open, receptive, non-threatening presence of one spirit to one another—did not seem to apply to either God.

And yet, during those very years, evangelicals seemed to be winning adherents by the droves. If a convincing picture of a genuinely loving God was not winning them, what was?

One answer, I believe, lies in the mysterious power of evangelicalism's defining story. This story encapsulates evangelical Christianity. It is repeated, with only slight variations, whenever evangelicals want to explain—to the thousands packed into sports stadiums or simply to a friend over a cup of coffee—what it means to be "saved." The unique appeal of this story helps explain the persistence and spread of evangelicalism in the late twentieth-century world.

Here is one way to tell the story.

· · ·

"PLEASE DON'T DESTROY THOSE"

It is Sunday morning, well before church. Two little boys, six and four, are in their pajamas bouncing and squealing on the bed, trying to outdo each other in attracting the attention of their father. He's in his pajamas, too. Late the night before, he returned from his weekly travels as a salesman. Now he's come into their bedroom to visit with his boys and catch up on the week's excitement.

The older boy shoves a fistful of small papers at his father—wrinkled grocery-store receipts that mom had been stashing in a kitchen drawer. "Mom was going to throw them in the trash fire," the boy tells his dad. He explains that he had rescued them from destruction. When he plays "railroad conductor," he uses them for his passenger tickets. Does his father want to play?

A great idea, his father says. But there's something more important than playing "railroad conductor."

"You know," his father says, "that reminds me of what the Lord

Jesus did for us in saving us from our sins. We were all going to be burned up in hell, because that is what happens to sinners, but Jesus came and died on the cross for us and he could say to his Father, *Please don't destroy those. I have a use for them.*"

At this moment, by his own testimony, the older boy was "born again."[2]

This boy was Stephen Paine, a prominent evangelical of the post-war years. Paine was one of the founders of the National Association of Evangelicals and a long-time president of Houghton College. When he related this story to his biographer, it may not have occurred to him to wonder what he had learned, on the bed that day, about the kind of father God is. Nor, perhaps, was his father aware of the deeper message this story conveyed. Neither of them probably noticed how this kind of heavenly father felt inside them. They had not been schooled to pay attention to what was inside them.

But what might Stephen Paine—deep inside—have heard in his father's story?

The moment with his dad is special. The setting is warm and safe. Young Stephen is excited about the game he has invented, eager to share it. But suddenly the subject shifts. The game is forgotten. Dad is talking about sin and hell and death. Nothing "pretend" about this.

And another "father" has entered the conversation—a heavenly father. The heavenly father doesn't sound much like the earthly father. Since he thinks these little boys are sinners, he considers them useless. He has decided to throw them out, as if they were trash.[3] This father is going to throw two little boys into a fire that burns

---

2 Miriam Paine Lemcio, *Deo Volente: A Biography of Stephen W. Paine* (Houghton, NY: Houghton College, 1987), 24–25. I have paraphrased the story, but quoted Stephen's father exactly.

3 As Edward J. Carnell wrote, our heavenly Father has the right to "dispose of us" as he sees fit.

forever. He doesn't express remorse; he doesn't seem particularly interested in saving them from the fire. Luckily, Jesus comes along just in time to change the father's mind by dying on the cross.

Still, the father seems reluctant to abort his plans to burn these boys. Jesus has to say "please" and offer his father a good reason to save them. Jesus knows better than to ask his father to save them simply because they are his beloved children. Jesus has to come up with a different approach: "I have a use for them."

The adult Stephen later recounts his response to this story: "At that moment, I said, 'That is what I believe' and I made quite a definite commitment in my little boy's heart to that truth." Of course he did—a scared little boy would be foolish to disregard such horrific warnings. It would not occur to him to question the story's truthfulness. This is his father—why would his father tell an untrue tale? By the end of his father's narrative, this little boy would have only one thing in mind: how can I make sure that whatever Jesus did to satisfy this big, angry father, he will also do for me?

Is it possible that, by the end of this story, Stephen and his brother might have been thinking: "I have just met a heavenly father whom I can love and trust down to the center of my being"? When Paine describes his decision, many years later, he does not say his heart was filled with love for this heavenly father. He says his heart made a "commitment" to a "truth." Stephen had reached a logical conclusion: even if he did not feel drawn by love to such a father, he knew he must believe a terrible truth about this father if he had any chance of avoiding an awful fate.

By all accounts, Stephen Paine grew up to be a remarkably wise and good man. He became a careful thinker, a beloved college administrator and a lifelong Christian. Perhaps at some unrecorded moment, he experienced release from this terrible truth and the father who loomed behind it.

He did tell this story late in life, though, without taking note of the cruelty of the father. Did he continue to live his little boy's life and then his adult life, day after day, with the echoes of this story lodged deep inside him—a story that in simple, stark images depicts a God whose wrath is absolutely certain, but whose love is definitely not?

•   •   •

PAYMENT FIRST, FORGIVENESS LATER

I am certain that Stephen Paine's father told his sons this story, that morning on the bed, out of a fatherly love for them and an admirable zeal for their salvation. The story—to which he put his own creative twist—was deeply embedded in his mind. He did not think about its implications.

The story he told is deeply embedded in every evangelical heart. Evangelicals tell it because it seems the quickest way to explain to the people they care about how they can be saved and escape eternal fire.[4] They rarely notice its implications.

Nor do they generally notice that it's a *story*. They think of it as the "simple gospel" of Jesus Christ or "the gospel in a nutshell." To most evangelicals, it encapsulates everything they believe about God and humanity, life and death, heaven and hell. It's just "the truth."

Evangelical gate-keepers agree that this story says it all. They call the story "the penal substitutionary" theory of atonement or just "the substitutionary atonement." They doubt that someone can be a Christian without subscribing to this story's absolute truth.[5]

---

4 The defining version of the story does not draw attention to God's callousness the way Stephen's father did. But it is significant that this is the form in which Stephen remembered it. It may mean that the story's hidden callousness is not truly hidden from our hearts.

5 Carl Henry's conversion serves as an example. When Henry tells a saintly Christian woman how he has become a Christian at a friend's prodding, she is at first "overjoyed." Then she begins to probe for Henry's understanding of the event. Did his friend specifically mention evangelicalism's defining story—in her words, "Christ's substitutionary death"?

The fact that it's a story is what makes it so easy to remember—and repeat. It has a simple narrative structure—beginning, middle and end—and major and minor characters. It has a coherent plot-flow complete with dramatic suspense, a climactic scene and a (mostly) happy ending.

His friend did not. But Henry finesses the situation, assuring the woman that he has indeed accepted Christ "as the sinner's substitute."

Later, he wonders whether the friend who converted him was clear enough on this issue—if not, perhaps both his friend's and his own conversion are in question. Henry makes sure to clarify for himself and his readers that he did indeed become a Christian under the auspices of evangelicalism's defining story. Henry, *Confessions*, 45–48.

According to J. I. Packer, a much-loved evangelical scholar, the penal substitution theory of atonement "is a distinguishing mark of the world-wide evangelical fraternity" and "takes us to the very heart of the Christian gospel." "What Did the Cross Achieve? The Logic of Penal Substitution," *Tyndale Bulletin* 25 (1974), 3–45, quoted in Stott, *The Cross of Christ*, 7.

A recent summation of "what is primary and essential in the gospel as evangelicals understand it" puts it this way: "Jesus paid our penalty in our place on his cross, satisfying the retributive demands of divine justice. . . We affirm that the atonement of Christ by which, in his obedience, he offered a perfect sacrifice, propitiating the Father by paying for our sins and satisfying divine justice on our behalf according to God's eternal plan, is an essential element of the gospel. We deny that any view of the atonement that rejects the substitutionary satisfaction of divine justice, accomplished vicariously for believers, is compatible with the teaching of the gospel." David Neff, "The Gospel of Jesus Christ: An Evangelical Celebration," *Christianity Today*, June 14, 1999 (Vol. 43, #7) 49. Evangelicalism's immediate forebears, the fundamentalists, always included this story prominently when they listed the critical beliefs ("fundamentals") of every true Christian. Marsden, *Fundamentalism*, 117.

Atonement theory is, as of this writing, a very hot topic among evangelicals. A younger generation of theologians is producing a flood of scholarship to challenge the dominance of the "penal substitutionary" view and offer instead a paradigm that does not rely on a God who repays human violence with divine violence. An excellent introduction to this debate—including a history of "penal substitution," a critique of its assumptions, a survey of the relevant biblical texts, and a stimulating exploration of truly "good news" alternatives—may be found in Brad Jersak and Michael Hardin, eds., *Stricken by God: Nonviolent Identification and the Victory of Christ* (Abbotsford, BC: Fresh Wind Press, 2007). The hostility these theologians are receiving from the religious establishment discourages any hope that their alternative paradigms will soon receive a fair hearing or that "penal substitution" will go away quietly.

In Chapter 8, I will offer suggestions toward a less violent and more healing understanding of atonement.

The main character in evangelicalism's defining story is a father. His son appears in a supporting role. The human race serves largely as extras, although their fate hangs in the balance. As in most stories, the personality of the main character is conveyed in the greatest detail, controlling the ebb and flow of the story. The main character is an excellent composite of both the fundamentalist and the evangelical "Gods" we have explored so far.

The story's usefulness is apparent if we think about the logical structure of the "salvation" sermons that evangelicals typically preach. The preacher usually starts with the bad news: "You are a sinner, destined for hell." The listener naturally wonders: "How can I escape this fate?" The preacher answers: "By believing in the Lord Jesus Christ as your personal Savior." The listener wonders: "But exactly how does believing in Jesus save me?" The preacher answers: "Because he's the one who died on the cross for your sins." A thoughtful listener might then ask: "Why can't my sins be forgiven without somebody dying for them?"

At this point, the preacher tells the defining story, which makes the answer plain: "Because your sins are so serious that God cannot forgive you unless somebody pays a penalty for them—and payment can only be made by killing someone." If this makes sense to you, you are ready to be saved. It has made sense to millions upon millions of people over the past half-century.

This story achieves its power, in part, by sheer repetition. Mass evangelists and media preachers tell the story again and again—some as often as they preach. When throngs pour into the stadium aisles in a Billy Graham meeting, a "personal worker" meets them and tells the story once again, now labeled "the plan of salvation." When converts begin attending an evangelical church, they will hear this story over and over, and if they send their children to Sunday school, their children will hear it again and again. It doesn't take very long before the tiny voices inside them that want to whisper timid questions about this story have been safely locked away.

Although preachers tell this story often, they don't always tell it in full. They don't have to, because their listeners know it by heart. A quick reference to one component of it—"the cross," "the blood of Christ" or "he paid it all"—settles the whole of it into place in the listener's awareness. It is actually possible to summarize the defining story in a single sentence: "Christ died for your sins." Five simple words, easy to advertise on billboards.

Most evangelical Christians believe that this story is plainly spelled out in the Bible. This limits their freedom to really *listen* to it, hear its hidden messages, and ask hard questions about it. In reality, the term "penal substitutionary atonement" does not appear in the Bible, and the story itself does not appear in anything like the version preachers use today. The evangelical gate-keepers insist that it is the only possible interpretation of certain scattered Bible passages. In fact, they have heard this interpretation so unrelentingly that they cannot imagine any other. So it's hard for them to admit that there are other ways to read those biblical passages, and that the Christian church has never been unanimous in its thinking about the atonement.[6] They rarely notice that this view of the atonement was not prominent among Christians during the first one thousand years after Christ.

I am a great fan of stories—they are the most basic way humans make sense of human existence and convey this sense to one another and to the next generation. A good story is among the dearest of

---

6 In two very brave books, *Recovering the Scandal of the Cross: Atonement in New Testament and Contemporary Contexts* (Downers Grove, IL: InterVarsity Press, 2001) and *Proclaiming the Scandal of the Cross: Contemporary Images of the Atonement* (Grand Rapids, MI: Baker Academic, 2006), Joel B. Green and Mark D. Baker set the major theories of the atonement in their historical contexts, show the limitations of the "penal substitutionary" theory, and call on evangelicals to create fresh stories that speak to our own time.

treasures. Neither am I without respect for evangelicalism's defining story—at its heart is the cry of the human spirit for forgiveness, reconciliation and freedom. I will try to show that—as is true of many human devices—its satisfactions are appealing, but temporary. Its appeal is to a part of us—the part that feels ashamed and guilty and thinks we deserve punishment rather than love—but it never contemplates the possibility that there might be a God who does not think the way that part of us thinks. Thus its "good news" falls far short of the good news that Jesus brings.

Many evangelical Christians are not aware that Jesus, an incorrigible storyteller, never told this particular story. In fact, this story is quite unlike the stories Jesus told. His stories were not so tightly outlined, so logical. They were metaphorical and often puzzling. They could be read in many different ways, so they freed the listeners' imaginations. Often they did not have conventional endings that brought true closure.[7]

Evangelicalism's defining story can only be read in one way. Its closure is dramatic and unmistakable.

•   •   •

WHY GOD DEMANDS BLOOD

Evangelicalism's defining story comes in many versions.[8] Here is

---

7 James Breech explores the meaning of Jesus' open-ended stories in *Jesus and Postmodernism* (Minneapolis: Fortress Press, 1989).

8 The website of "Got Questions Ministries" explains it this way:

The "substitutionary atonement" refers to the fact that Jesus Christ dies on behalf of all sinners. The Scriptures teach that all men are sinners. The penalty for our sinfulness is death. Romans 6:23 reads, "For the wages of sin is death, but the gift of God is eternal life in Christ Jesus our Lord." That verse teaches us several things. Without Christ, we are going to die and spend an eternity in hell as payment for our sins. Death in the scriptures refers to a "separation." Everyone of course will die, but some will live in heaven with the Lord for eternity, while others will live a life in hell for eternity.

The death spoken of here refers to the life in hell. However, the second thing this verse

Billy Graham's version, excerpted from an early sermon titled "A Scarlet Thread." Graham believed it would answer the questions young people asked him about "why God demands blood" and "why God had to die for me."[9]

> *The holiness of God is the message of the entire Old Testament* [his italics]. To the prophets God was absolutely the Holy One, the One with eyes too pure to behold evil, the One swift to punish iniquity. It is his holiness by which God desires to be remembered, as that is the attribute that glorifies him... God hates sin... Sin is vile and detestable in the sight of God... The sinner and God are at opposite poles of the moral universe...
>
> Go back with me in your imagination to Eden for a moment. God said, "In the day that thou eatest of this particular tree, thou shalt surely die." Man ate it. He died. Suppose that God had said, "Adam, you just made a mistake! That was a slight error on your part! You are forgiven, but please don't do it again." Reverently speaking, I say that God would have been a liar. He would have not been holy; neither would he have been just. He was forced by his very nature to keep his word. God's justice was at stake. Man had to die spiritually and physically... He had to pay for his own sins...

---

teaches us is that eternal life is available through Jesus Christ. This is his substitutionary atonement. Jesus Christ died in our place when he was crucified on the cross. We deserved to be the ones placed on that cross to die because we are the ones who live sinful lives. But Christ took the punishment on himself in our place—he substituted himself for us and took what we rightly deserved... We can only pay the price of sin on our own by being punished and placed in hell for all eternity. But God's Son, Jesus Christ, came to earth to pay the price of our sins. Because he did this for us, we now have the opportunity to not only have our sins forgiven, but to spend eternity with him. In order to do this, we must place our faith in what Christ did on the cross. We cannot save ourselves; we need a substitute to take our place.

For full text, including Bible references, see http://www.gotquestions.org.

9 Graham, *Calling Youth*, 100–115.

How can God be "just," that is, true to himself in nature and true to himself in holiness, and yet justify the sinner?. . . The only solution to the problem was for an innocent party voluntarily to give his blood, an act which would be followed by death as a substitution before God for the death that was every man's due. Where was such an individual?. . . There was only one possibility! God's own Son was the only personality in the universe who had the capacity to bear in his own body the sins of the world.

But would he? If he did, he would have to come to earth, live as a man, be despised and rejected of men, a man of sorrows and acquainted with grief. He would have to bear our griefs and carry our sorrows. Then he would have to be smitten of God and separated from God. . . Then, in a dark moment, God would lay on him the iniquity of us all. . . He would have to buy sinners out of the slave market of sin. . . [The] price would be his own blood. . .

Hallelujah! That is exactly what happened!. . . He came to have his blood extracted. . . The blood was extracted! God demanded death, either for the sinner or a substitute! Christ was the substitute!

Graham's version of the story ends on an oddly joyful note, considering the brutality of the language. Still, it emphasizes God keeping his word and honoring justice instead of venting his wrath.

Here is a harsher, more recent version written by an evangelical scholar:

We are prisoners of death because we are inherently rebellious to God. . . Our rejection of God was not simply unfortunate. We did something tragically wrong. Thus we owed a debt to justice. Since the injustice and wrongness of our choice angered God, he would not impart life to us until justice was satisfied. That is the bad news. The solution involved appeasing God's wrath by removing the source of his anger.

This is where we get to the good news. In the midst of his wrath, God was merciful enough to do for us what we could never do for ourselves. He provided a way to satisfy justice through Jesus' death on the cross. Though Jesus' death paid our debt to justice, it did not grant across the board justification. Justification is conditional on placing our trust in God, and believing that Jesus' death was adequate and necessary.[10]

Another theologian elaborates on this so-called "satisfaction theory"—an alternate name for the defining story. He wonders how God the Father can really be satisfied by just one death for sins so revolting that they require eternal punishment. "After a thousand years," he writes, "a sinner will not have been punished enough to satisfy the wrath of God and thus be allowed into heaven. Ten thousand years will not be enough; nor will a million, or even an eternity." So how can just one death satisfy God? Only because God pours his wrath on Jesus with unmitigated fury:

> Who can even begin to grasp the "width and length and depth and height" of the true spiritual suffering of our Lord and our God as his Father turned his back upon him. Who can begin to comprehend the love that drove a Father to pour out his unmitigated wrath upon his dearly beloved Son for such rebellious worms and wretches as us?
>
> Perhaps now we can begin to understand why God had to die for man. Surely only God the Son could bear the unmitigated wrath of God the Father. . . Why did Christ have to die? It was for you; it was for me; and above all, it was for his own glory.[11]

---

10 Jack Crabtree in McKenzie Study Center newsletter, copyright 1986.
11 David Clark, "Why Did Christ Have to Die?" *New England Reformed Journal*, Autumn 1996.

These lines exemplify an odd feature of some evangelical preaching—the thrill it seems to derive from the vision of an "out-of-control" Father venting his wrath on an innocent Son in order to bring "glory" to himself.

•   •   •

GOD'S LOVE IS NOT AN ORDINARY LOVE

John R. W. Stott's *The Cross of Christ* is a popular study of the atonement.[12] Stott was the leading British evangelical preacher of his generation, a man beloved by American evangelicals. In 2005, *Time* listed him as one of the "100 most influential" people in the world today.

For several decades, John Stott has symbolized for me an intelligent, compassionate and broad-minded evangelicalism. Recently, to his great credit, he has dared to question the evangelical understanding of hell as a place of God-sponsored eternal torture. I hold him in the highest respect. Stott's understanding of evangelicalism's defining story offers me a chance to question it in its most reputable form. My questions may take us into more tangled theological territory than you have a taste for. If so, I encourage you to skip over this section and the next two. You can recommence at page 124 with the section titled *Evading Jesus*.

On the first page of his book, Stott sets out the view he is going to defend:

> Evangelical Christians believe that in and through Christ crucified God substituted himself for us and bore our sins, dying in our place the death we deserved to die, in order that we might be restored to his favor and adopted into his family.

---

12 (Downers Grove, IL: InterVarsity Press, 1986). Material taken from 7, 87–90, 106–108, 124, 128, 131–132, 150–151, 158–159.

From the start, Stott is aware that this defining story raises a question in anyone who hears it critically, or for the first time: why can't God just forgive us, without requiring the cross? "If we sin against one another," Stott writes, "we are required to forgive one another. We are even warned of dire consequences if we refuse. Why can't God practice what he preaches and be equally generous without requiring blood?"

Stott's answer lays the necessary foundation for the whole story: our sins are so serious, and the majesty of God is so pure, that death is a fitting penalty. We must not draw parallels between *our forgiving others* and *God forgiving us*, because God is not "a private individual" and sin is not just a "personal injury." God is author of the laws we break, so "sin is rebellion against him." Forgiving sins actually constitutes a "profound problem" for a holy God. It is amazing that God can find any way at all to forgive us.

Of course, this reasoning rests on two assumptions: that an offense against the maker of a law is more serious than an offense against someone whom the law is meant to protect; and that truly serious offenses do not qualify for forgiveness. But if I break a law and harm a fellow-citizen, have I offended the legislator who made the law more than I am offending my fellow-citizen? If I have done so, can that legislator not still forgive me? And if we are made in God's image, is God not in some way very like a private individual? And why would God's "majesty" intensify the need for punishment instead of heightening the possibility of forgiveness? Is God not majestic in love?

John Stott answers: God's love is a particular kind of love—a "holy love." *Holy love* is a love that "yearns over sinners" and yet cannot risk doing anything to "condone their sin."[13] So God's problem is

---

13 This raises a question, of course: When we forgive someone for offending us, are we condoning their behavior? Why then would Jesus ask his followers to forgive "seventy times seven" (Matthew 18:21–22)? Why would he want God to forgive those who crucified

how to "express. . . his love. . . without compromising his holiness," and how to express "his holiness. . . without frustrating his love." Stott believes God solved this problem at the cross, where "God through Christ paid the full penalty of our disobedience himself. He bore the judgment we deserve in order to bring us the forgiveness we do not deserve. On the cross divine mercy and justice were equally expressed and eternally reconciled. God's holy love was 'satisfied'."

•   •   •

TRAPPED BY HIS HOLINESS

I'd like to take a closer look at this strange contrivance: "holy love." It rests on an assumption—unquestioned among evangelicals—that there is a profound distance between humanity and God: God is infinitely holy, humans are infinitely unholy. Although Dr. Stott is known as a kind and gentle man, his depiction of humanity in these pages feels surprisingly uncompassionate. The tone I imagine in Jesus' voice when he speaks of humans as "sheep without a shepherd" seems absent.

In order to distinguish "holy love" from human love, and thus make a "death penalty" plausible, Stott must treat sin as infinitely disgusting. So humans are "godless," "haughty" and "self-centered." Stott does not look more empathically into the human soul—as I am sure he does in his daily encounters with real human beings—to find deeper explanations for human sinfulness than a "spirit of revolt against God," an easy formula which does not begin to explain the real causes of human behavior. We hear in Stott the same disgust at human sinfulness that we hear in the preaching of Billy Graham and his fellow evangelists, or in J. B. Phillips' suggestion that becoming human was "repugnant" for God.

---

him (Luke 23:34)?

Once he has heightened our sense of human sinfulness, Stott thinks it will be easier for us to understand God's wrath. God's wrath isn't like human wrath—"arbitrary and uninhibited"; it's "always principled and controlled." It's simply an expression of the biblical truth that "sin cannot approach God, and God cannot tolerate sin." When the Bible tells us God is holy, it is evoking great "height" (thus putting God far above us), and also great "distance" (thus putting God far away from us). This explains why "God cannot tolerate or 'digest' sin and hypocrisy... They are so repulsive... that he must rid himself of them. He must spit or vomit them out."[14]

This distance between God's infinite holiness and humanity's disgusting sinfulness essentially *traps* God into requiring a penalty. He cannot do otherwise—a part of God's own character needs to be "satisfied." God needs to "satisfy himself;" he must be his "true self" and "act according to the perfection of his nature." He "cannot repudiate any part of himself, because he is perfect. He cannot contradict himself. This is his integrity... God... never deviates one iota, even one tiny hair's breadth, from being entirely himself." The only satisfaction for this "part of himself" is retribution.

But Stott seems to be overlooking a key biblical text: that "God is *love*" (1 John 4:8).[15] This is the only statement of God's very essence, as distinct from God's attributes, that we find in the Bible. Nowhere does the Bible say, "God *is* holiness" or "God *is* justice." In his essence, God is just one thing: *love*. To defend the defining story, Stott must add "holiness" and "justice" to love, and in turn use these phrases to re-define love. He treats "love" like Carl Henry treats

---

14 My friend Bob Ekblad reminds me that "holy" can also mean "different, other or strange." When Stott and other evangelicals use the word "holy," they seem unwittingly to be depicting God as just like themselves—as sharing their own moralistic attractions and repulsions, not as warmly accepting sinners in the "strange" or "different" way that Jesus did.

15 This biblical writer makes love so central to God's character that he can write: "*everyone who loves is born of God and knows God*" (I John 4:7).

"personal": he couples it with another word, and then so *prioritizes* the other word that the original word loses its meaning.

For Stott, the core meaning of "holy love" is found in the word "holy." To support that meaning, he quotes an earlier British writer, P. T. Forsyth: "Christianity is concerned with God's holiness before all else. . . [We should speak] less about God's love and more about his holiness." This is convenient for Stott's argument, but it does not strike me as the message of Jesus.

Forsyth wrote: "Without a holy God, there would be no problem of atonement. It is the holiness of God's love that necessitates the atoning cross." If we are the ones who prioritize holiness, defining it as a self-protective purity caught in its own need to condemn and unable to forgive, then we are the ones making a problem out of atonement, not God.[16]

.   .   .

FORGIVENESS *IS* A PROBLEM FOR GOD

Because God's "holy love" forces him to "come to terms with the unholy lovelessness of man," Stott writes, God *came in Jesus* to die for our sins.

---

16 God's holiness continues to be the theological linchpin for many evangelical thinkers today. An example is David F. Wells who, in *No Place for Truth: Or Whatever Happened to Evangelical Theology?* (Grand Rapids, MI: Wm. B. Eerdmans Publishing Company, 1993) bemoans the interest that evangelical churches are showing in "relationships," "wholeness" and "the therapeutic" rather than in "truth"—the business of theology. Like Stott, he portrays God's holiness as "fundamental to who he is and what he has done" and sees Jesus as witnessing first and foremost to God's holiness.

Wells interprets Jesus' death on the cross as "the holiness of God [coming] into its full and awful expression" as Jesus [bore] "the consequences of [God's] wrath. . ." and he portrays the suffering of the lost in hell as "God's judgment [vindicating] for all eternity his holiness." His prescription is to recapture a sense of God's holiness as "the very cornerstone of Christian faith, for it is the foundation of reality" (299–301). God's love receives only passing notice.

Here Stott makes a welcome advance over much evangelical preaching. God doesn't *send* Jesus, but *comes* in Jesus, so that he *himself* can pay the penalty for our sins. Stott knows the offensiveness of a Father-God who effects a "grudging salvation" by torturing his innocent son. Such "caricatures," Stott admits, divide God from Jesus and "denigrate the Father," depicting him as "a pitiless ogre whose wrath has to be assuaged. . . by the loving self-sacrifice of Jesus." Stott regrets the fact that, all too often, evangelical sermons still propagate "crude interpretations" like these.

Given this clarification, it is clear that Jesus was not the *object* of God's punishment. Instead, both "God and Christ were subjects and objects, taking the initiative together to save sinners." Here Stott brings Jesus and God very close, allowing him to say that in Jesus, God gave himself for us. He quotes St. Paul with approval: "God was *in Christ*, reconciling the world to himself." If God's "holy love" is one leg of Stott's argument, God's *self*-sacrifice, in Jesus, is the other. Once they are understood, he writes, "the objections to a penal substitutionary atonement evaporate."

But do they? These twin foundations actually work at cross-purposes to one another: while the second *identifies* God with Jesus, the first seems to *distinguish* God from Jesus. It is hard to find in Jesus anything like the "holy love" Stott finds in God. Jesus forgives sins freely. God cannot. Jesus doesn't worry that forgiving sins means condoning sins. Jesus doesn't treat forgiveness as if it is a "problem." When Jesus forgives sins, he simply says: "Your sins are forgiven" (Mark 2:1–12). Is he speaking *for* God at this point, or *against* God?

Stott's Jesus would have to say: "I am identified with a holy God, so forgiveness is a real a problem for me. I'm only able to forgive you if someone dies in your place. But not to worry—the Father is here inside me and together we're going to punish us on the cross. I'm saying this because I'm afraid my forgiving you implies that I condone sin, which I don't. I want to make sure you know how revolting your sins are, and understand that God isn't going to let you get away with them. You can only actually be forgiven by my retroactively applying my future death on the cross to your sins."

This is what "holy love" might say. Of course, it's *not* what Jesus says.

I notice another difference between Stott's God and Jesus. Jesus doesn't vomit at the sight of sinful humanity. His enemies know him precisely for this—that he eats and drinks with the "vermin" of Palestine's social hierarchy. Jesus never belabors the holiness or majesty of God. Although he considers himself one with the Father, he does not tout his own holiness or majesty. Nothing about Jesus makes us want to say: "Ah, this is not just love he is expressing—this is a *holy* love whose wrath must be satisfied by making someone pay."

Some form of "penalty" often does occur in Jesus' stories, sometimes with great "wailing and gnashing of teeth."[17] But, as I will try to show later, it comes in the natural course of events, not as a punishment designed to make us pay.

Stott's rendition of the penal substitutionary atonement, like the standard evangelical version, distorts the Bible's portrait of Jesus and evades the tender vulnerability of love. Perhaps, instead of using words like "holiness" and "justice" to strip love of its meaning, we need to move in the opposite direction: to re-imagine the meaning of a "holiness" and a "justice" that are so infused with the spirit of an infinitely forgiving love that they require no penalty at all. After we see Jesus, the apostle Paul wrote, *all* things become new (2 Corinthians 5:17). Perhaps this includes our favorite theological terms. Perhaps, it includes evangelicalism's tried and true defining story.

---

17 An example is Matthew 8:12. All references to this phrase, with one exception, are in Matthew, which may indicate that he felt especially energized by the possibility that our actions have consequences.

•　　•　　•

EVADING JESUS

Stott's elaboration of the defining story is the most painstaking, gentle-spirited and carefully-nuanced version that I can find among evangelicals. And yet, ask it a few simple questions—"does God's holiness confine God's love?" or "did Jesus have a problem with forgiveness?"—and the house of cards begins to tumble down. At the same time, *The Cross of Christ* is a helpful book to read if one is trying to understand the way one must think if one is to be a card-carrying evangelical.

Two features of evangelical thinking jump out at me.

First, Stott's rendition of the defining story resembles both the preaching of the young evangelists we met in Chapter 1 and the teaching of the young scholars we met in Chapter 2, in this respect: it evades the actual way and words of Jesus.

The young scholars—Carl Henry and his colleagues—paid little attention to the flesh-and-blood Jesus. His day-to-day life, his actual teachings, his humanity were useless in their campaign to construct a sovereign and almighty God. They treated Jesus as a principle, not a person.

The young evangelists, on the other hand, mentioned Jesus often. But usually he was simply the one who threatened people with hell and then died at the hands of his wrathful father. They showed no interest in the mystery of Jesus' internal world: the radically new way of being and seeing that his stories pointed to, his intentional con-frontations with the most intensely religious people of his day. To them, he was the "Son of God" sent to tell us we are displeasing to God, and then to suffer and die in order to pay the penalty for our sins.

These preachers often illustrated the meaning of the cross by reference to the Old Testament sacrificial system: Jesus is like the spotless lamb, killed on the altar for the sins of the people. Perhaps they treated Jesus' concrete life as they would have treated the lamb's concrete life: as irrelevant to the role that each had to play. For evangelicals in general, I believe, Jesus is a convenient instrumentality of salvation, and little more. We do not show much interest in hearing what he had to say, or in learning to listen to the Spirit the way he did.[18]

Second, Stott's rendition of the defining story gives me a clue as to why this story has such deep appeal: it matches the logic of our (mostly) unconscious inner world. It confirms a judgment we humans seem driven to make about ourselves: that we are very bad (so bad that God "vomits" when he thinks about us) and we need to pay for it (or else we'll find ourselves condoning it, and we'll keep doing it). This is the logic of the universal condition of shame.

It is also the logic of obedience training, equally effective when used on children and dogs. "Bad dog!" we say. "Shame on you!" and we whack it with a newspaper. This logic is planted deep inside us in childhood by well-meaning parents and other authorities, who worry that love is not enough. They are afraid that punishment is the only way to make us good people.

The defining story of evangelicalism confirms this logic of obedience, so it "feels right" in a primal place deep inside us. The story says: "You are very bad!" and a self-hating voice inside us says "Yes! I am!" The story says: "Your badness is so unacceptable that it disqualifies you from life and love! You deserve to die!" and a self-hating voice inside us says: "Yes! That's true! I deserve death, not love!" And then the story, having raised our shame, guilt and dread

---

18 In my experience, most evangelical sermons use texts from St. Paul, who did not know Jesus during his lifetime, so could not tell stories about him. St. Paul's epistles are mostly didactic, not narrative. They lend themselves to answers, while the Gospel narratives lend themselves to questions.

to a fever pitch, says: "Good news! God is going to kill somebody else instead!" And we melt in relief. We feel "saved."

But are we saved? We are certainly not saved from the voice inside us that hates us—that voice has simply been reinforced by a condemning God. But would a truly loving God, any more than a truly loving parent, tell us: "Your badness is so unacceptable that it disqualifies you from life and love! You deserve to die!" If a loving God wished to save us, would that God not help us recognize that perhaps it is a part of us—not God—who cannot tolerate sin? Wouldn't a loving God want to point out that it is an accuser inside us, and not God, who—with good intentions, but limited understanding—is making us feel unlovable? Wouldn't a loving God wish to lighten our burden of guilt?

Perhaps evangelicalism's defining story simply puts into the mouth of God a voice we hear inside ourselves, many times a day—the voice that hates who we are and constantly accuses us of falling short. A loving, saving God would want to give us some distance from that voice so that we could understand it and ultimately heal it—not affirm it and reinforce its power to alienate us from ourselves.

If salvation only "heals" our enmity with God at the cost of confirming our enmity with ourselves, it is a poor salvation indeed. It uses the logic of obedience training to keep us from loving and trusting ourselves. It doesn't free us to become mature and whole human beings.

These two features of evangelicalism—a superficial understanding both of Jesus and of our own inner world—go hand in hand. Because evangelicals don't pay attention to the flesh-and-blood Jesus, we don't wonder why "sinners" were drawn to him. We don't ask: is it because he confirmed the worst they believed about themselves? Or is it because the voice inside them that hated and accused them found absolutely no echo in him?

•   •   •

"I CANNOT SIMPLY FORGIVE YOU"

One of Jesus' most familiar parables is the story of the "Prodigal Son." Although Jesus told the story in order to challenge the social and religious exclusivism of the Pharisees and scribes, it also has startling implications for our understanding of what it might mean to be genuinely "saved."[19]

A son deserts his father with departing words that, for people in Jesus' time, mean he wishes his father were dead. When he finds himself hungry, lost and alone, he returns, hoping his father will accept him as a servant. His father sees him from afar, and a wave of compassion washes over him. He runs to his son, embraces him, kisses him. He calls for a celebration because, as he says, "this my son was dead, and is alive again; he was lost, and is found." No concern that he is condoning the son's behavior. Not a whisper of the exacting demands of "holy love."

Two evangelical scholars, Rebecca Adams and Robin Collins, have re-written this story to illustrate how Jesus might have told it if he had wanted it to express the defining story of evangelicalism.[20] Here is their version:

> In desperation, the prodigal son returns home, armed with a little speech that begs his father to welcome him not as a son but as a hired servant. As he rounds the far bend, the father sees his son, and waits patiently for him to arrive.
>
> The son falls on his knees and launches into his speech, but his father pulls him to his feet. He says to his son: "I cannot simply

19 Luke 15:11–33.

20 "Understanding Atonement: A New and Orthodox Theory" (1996). It can be found at http://home.messiah.edu/~rcollins/AT7.HTM. With their permission, I have altered their text slightly.

forgive you for what you have done, not even so much as to make you one of my hired men. In your wild living, you have broken my law, insulted my majesty, and offended my holiness. Simply to forgive you would be to trivialize sin; it would make a laughing-stock of my sense of justice and overturn the moral order of the entire universe."

The father insists that the son must pay a penalty: he must die. The son says, "But father, is this penalty not a bit extreme?" The father replies: "My wrath burns hot against you, and it must be satisfied."

"But father, please. . ." the son begins to plead.

"No," the father says, "the price must be paid." And he looks in the direction of the elder brother, whose heart suffers for his little brother.

Then the elder brother says: "I will offer my life if you will forgive this son and welcome him back into your love. With your permission, I will hand myself over to my enemies, in the neighboring city, who will kill me. Will you accept my death as a sacrifice?"

The father agrees. The older son goes off to his death. The younger son feels grateful. Father and son live happily ever after.[21]

·   ·   ·

A BETTER FATHER

My own father, Walter Frank, believes firmly that evangelicalism's defining story is plainly taught in the Bible. For him, it is the "gospel in a nutshell," the logic of salvation, the bedrock of the faith. It is

---

21 In their story, Adams and Collins do not take into account Stott's insistence that the Father came to die in and with Jesus. To add that wrinkle to their story, however, would not make the logic of it less nonsensical.

also a very personal story for him. It explains how God could forgive him when, as a boy of sixteen, he accepted Jesus as his personal Savior. My father's mission in life has been to share evangelicalism's defining story with everyone he meets.

When my father was younger and more vigorous,[22] we often discussed our theological differences—sometimes with fireworks, usually with grace. Dad would quote Bible texts to me. I would re-interpret those texts, giving them a different meaning.[23] Dad would reiterate his interpretation, presenting it as the "plain meaning" of the text. I would say his meaning wasn't plain at all—it's just the way he first heard it, and always read it, so now it seemed plain. Dad would shift ground a bit and tell me God is love, which is why he sent his Son to die. And the conversation would drop down into familiar grooves.

Doug: "I don't see love in a punitive, bloodthirsty God."

Dad: "God isn't really bloodthirsty—he's simply bound by his holiness and his justice."

Doug: "This makes God sound like he's not really free to love us as a genuinely loving human being would."

Dad: "We need to believe what the Bible plainly says, whether it makes sense to us or not. . ."

And we would be off on another round.

Neither of us was easily shaken. Usually, we re-traced the deep ruts of every previous argument and finally agreed to disagree. I knew my father would pray for me before he retired for the night, and usually I would be comforted by that knowledge.

Occasionally, however, our set pieces were punctuated by moments of true puzzlement. Usually, I was the puzzled one—Dad

22 As of this writing, he is ninety-five years old.

23 I will explore how I am hearing many biblical texts in *Part Two.*

had thrown a Bible text at me that seemed to clinch his side of the argument, and in the moment I couldn't come up with an alternative reading. Only once do I recall Dad looking stumped.

This happened during one of our last theological discussions. We were walking along a logging road near my home. I said, "You know, Dad, you're a much better father than the Father who requires Jesus to die." And I reminded him of the "pinball episode."

When I was in eighth grade, I fell in love with pinball machines. My early-morning newspaper delivery route was putting serious money—a few dollars—in my pocket for the first time. They were hard-earned dollars: long, cold walks under heavy loads at five in the morning, blowing snow, frozen fingers, snarling dogs—sometimes snarling people. By the time I headed home, I felt I had earned a treat. I began stopping at the corner soda fountain, a few blocks from my home, for hot chocolate and a doughnut. Eventually, I was drawn to the pinball machines in the back of the store.

At seven in the morning, the pinball machines sat silent. I was often the only person in the place, so I could try them out without drawing attention to myself. Soon, to my surprise, I got very good at knowing just how much bouncing around the machines could take before the "tilt" sign ended a game prematurely. Most mornings, I racked up more free games than I could play before I had to head home for breakfast and then to school. By the time I left, other kids were stopping in on their way to school. With understated gallantry, I would bequeath them my free games. My reputation grew.

How did my father find out? He never told me. Perhaps he noticed how much time my paper route was taking. Perhaps he was just out for a morning walk, passed the store, and caught the rear profile of his son, bouncing that machine around with such remarkable confidence. If so, he did me the favor of not coming in and humiliating me. He waited until I came home from school one afternoon, and asked if I would come talk to him in his bedroom.

"Was that you I saw playing a pinball machine at the Liberty Café this morning?" I knew my father disapproved of pinball machines, and of hanging out in disreputable places with disreputable people, and of spending money foolishly. I told him no, it must have been somebody else. A silence settled over the room.

Then, with as much nonchalance as I could muster, I fled. Down the hall, I shut the door to my bedroom and sat on my bed. I knew I was caught. Just beneath my skin, my whole being was shriveling up and draining out. My lying words were out there in the air; they had become material reality. They had slipped out of my mouth in the merest instant. There was no way to get them back in. I waited for my father to pass my door on his way down the stairs, but I heard nothing.

After an eternity, I went back to his bedroom. He was sitting where I had left him, looking sadder than I had ever seen him look.

"I lied," I said.

"Yes, I know."

"I'm sorry."

"I forgive you, Doug."

Then we talked about why I had lied, how I was spending my money, and what he thought was so harmful about pinball machines. He said it wasn't the pinball machines that hurt him, but the lie. He was quiet and very tender—and so was I. It was one of the most profound moments of connection that I have ever shared him.

Those many years later, as we walked along the road and I recounted this story, my eyes welled with tears—and so did his. I told him that, at the time, he had surprised me by not requiring some sort of punishment. But now that I was a father, I understood. Love doesn't require punishment. It yearns to forgive, and be forgiven. The incident had hurt both of us, and we both had known it. For me, that was punishment enough. Healing would not come by way of further penalty, but by reconnection.

"You knew this, Dad," I said. "Don't you think God knows it, too?"

He looked me in the eye as if seeing me for the first time that day. We walked quietly for a few moments. Then he said: "All that really matters, Doug, is that we love the Lord."

That seemed a good enough place to stop.

CHAPTER 4

Caught in the Cross-Hairs

*Squirming beneath the gaze of
an all-seeing potentate*

*I like Santa and God, but I like Santa the best.
I only like God a teeny weeny bit, because he wants us
to be good every day and that's really hard.*
Jonathan Nicholls[1]

IT IS A WARM SUMMER EVENING in 1954. The sun's last light is fading and the bulbs strung on wires from tree to tree at Mizpah Grove are coming on. Mizpah Grove is the camp meeting that my family attends for up to six weeks each summer. It occupies a few dozen thinly-wooded acres upslope from the railroad switchyard, a brick factory building and a block of row-houses in a working-class neighborhood at the edge of Allentown, Pennsylvania.[2]

Summers at Mizpah bring the excitement of living in walled tents, carrying water in buckets from outdoor faucets, washing your face

---

1 Jonathan was four years old when he said this. He is the son of Brett Nicholls, a friend from New Zealand. Quoted with permission.

2 When I visited Mizpah Grove a few years ago, I found an unkempt abandoned lot that looks barely large enough for a church picnic, much less a gathering of hundreds of tents and thousands of the faithful. Quarter-pounder-with-cheese wrappers drifted lazily among the weeds where once the Spirit of God blew, knocking a good many saints clean off their feet.

in porcelain basins, sleeping in pungent, straw-filled bunks, chasing friends up and down the dusty "avenues" between groups of gossiping adults on their little camp stools, watching in mute admiration as teenage boys prove their manhood by drinking Moxie—a horrible soft drink potion in an ominously dark bottle. I look forward to these hot July weeks with great anticipation.

Summers at Mizpah also mean training in endurance. Every morning, we sit through an hour of Bible study and another of missionary reports. Every evening, we sit interminably in the long slatted pews of a cement-floored, outdoor tabernacle, sheltered from the elements by a slanted roof resting on massive steel girders.

We young teen-aged boys sit together as close to the escape routes at the back as our parents will let us, talking among ourselves (if we aren't being watched) or reading Christian adventure stories (the only permitted diversion) while the featured preacher goes on and on. His sermon is always followed by a spate of invitation hymns— "Just as I am without one plea" or "Almost persuaded"—that beckon young and old down the aisle to kneel in the thick sawdust and pray for salvation.

Many nights after the service, as the faithful amble off to the snack shop or chat in little groups outside their tents, we boys—many of us preachers' sons—return to the darkened tabernacle with flash-lights and sift through the sawdust for coins and other treasures that drop unnoticed from the pockets of disheveled sinners.

But this particular night, the coin patrol is forgotten. It is my own slight figure kneeling in the sawdust. My life has been in the sermon's cross-hairs. The preacher has delivered a serious warning to young people: take care of your eternal destiny now, before the cares of the world harden your tender spirits. The preacher knows there are young people in his audience whom God is bringing "under conviction."

I am one of them. A question mark is raised over my life. I am unsettled, scared. I want all questions removed. Several of my friends are going forward, so this seems a good time to "make sure." I am braver than I was at seven. I step into the aisle and walk down to the front.

·   ·   ·

HARDENED SINNER

But why the question mark on this particular night? Because earlier this very day, on the wooded slopes above the tenting grounds, I have for the first time touched the magical lips of the lovely Sandra. Sandra is a pretty, bespectacled thirteen-year-old from my home church. A few party kissing games hadn't prepared me for *this* kiss, this first *real* kiss: the trembling it brings to every part of my body, the sheer unspeakable ecstasy of it. I know I have met the love of my life.

But those childhood kissing games hadn't prepared me, either, for the guilt and panic that settle over me as Sandra and I descend the wooded slope, answering the call of the dinner bell, separating as we reach the circle of tents, nonchalantly joining our families at the cafeteria, letting on quite visibly that nothing at all has happened. Of course, something has happened. I have felt forbidden desire, known forbidden pleasure.

And a part of me is already scheming to do it again. It occurs to me that I must be what the preachers refer to as a "hardened sinner."

Another part of me is worried about being caught. My friend Keith, who has been conducting his own explorations with one of Sandra's friends on a nearby bench, loves to recount his exploits in lurid detail. Can I rely on him to leave me and Sandra out of his stories? And is it possible that my father—or another minister—

walking with God in the heat of the afternoon, spotted me through the trees? And speaking of God, what was *he* thinking?

The evening service in the tabernacle features a sermon just for me. "Even when you're alone, God sees you. He knows your heart. He hears your deepest thoughts." The thrill is fading fast.

So here I am, kneeling in the sawdust, feeling conspicuous and alone. Someone's arm is once again draped across my shoulder, a voice is intoning a prayer for me to repeat after him—comforting me, assuring me that God is very close, God is forgiving.

A few tears roll down my cheeks. Familiar feelings course through me—relief, cleanness, freedom. This is, once again, the first moment of a brand new life. I have a chance to start over. Gratitude floods me, and a new resolve. I will stay far away from Sandra. I will never again risk the terrible panic that gripped me in the aftermath of that encounter with the enchanted Sandra and her irresistible lips.

But something goes terribly wrong. By the next afternoon, the terrors of the night have lost their immediacy. Sandra and I are nuzzling again, this time a bit less tentatively. We're down in the thin grass, deep into the trees, out of sight of the nearest tents. My father and the other ministers never range this far. I have ditched my good friend Keith. We're absolutely alone. I am tasting ecstasy.

But it will only take a slight breeze fluttering the leaves overhead to remind me, for the briefest instant, that Sandra and I are not truly alone. And later that night, as I lie next to my brothers on the straw, and contemplate my eternal fate, only a thin canvas roof will separate me from an all-seeing God.

●　　●　　●

IS HE LORD OF YOUR CAR?

When I tell stories like this to adult evangelicals, many will say: "Yes, of course, I had these experiences, too. But I always knew that God loved me. I knew that once I was saved I was 'eternally secure.' I knew I would go to heaven when I died."

Well yes, I "knew" that, too—but that "knowing" was only skin deep. So, I re-frame my question: "That's what you *thought*, what you told yourself, what you wanted to be true. But is it how you *felt*? Did you feel safe knowing that a holy, righteous and powerful God was hearing your every thought, examining your every move? Did you feel affirmed and supported, exactly as you are?"

Since the Reformation, evangelical theology's touchstone has been the free grace of God. Salvation does not depend on our doing good works, but on the unmerited favor of a God who loves and freely forgives.[3]

The church, however—an institution which, like every institution, from time to time relies on coercive tactics—has quickly appended a cautionary message: those who *are* saved by grace will *necessarily* testify to their gratitude and love for God by living clean lives and doing good works. This formula invites the twin-humped camel of moralism and perfectionism to stick its nose between the flaps. Today, that camel has made itself very comfortable in the evangelical tent and most evangelicals have accepted its rights as proprietary.[4]

One of the manifestations of this perfectionism—and a staple of the spiritual guidance evangelicals give teenagers—is "Lordship teaching." "Lord" is one of those words I believe the New Testament actually intends as a kind of inside joke—or, more conventionally put, as a paradox: "See this un-Lordly Jesus? See him washing his disciples' feet? See him going like a lamb to the slaughter? Funny kind of 'Lord', isn't he?"

---

3 The oft-used phrase "freely forgives" appears to contradict evangelicalism's defining story, as explored in the previous chapter.

4 An exception is Philip Yancey in *What's So Amazing About Grace* (Grand Rapids, MI: Zondervan Publishing House, 1997).

In evangelical sermons, unfortunately, the word "Lord" does not often bring the human Jesus readily to mind. Instead, it connotes a God, or "Christ," who expects total (sovereign) control over each thought, each action—even each feeling—of our daily existence. A common evangelical trope is: "Jesus does not want just to be our Savior. He wants to be our Lord." That means he wants to take control of "every room in our spiritual house," fill every moment of our consciousness, dictate every decision. "If he is not Lord of all, he is not Lord at all."

An example of this teaching appeared as late as 1999 in *Decision*, a monthly publication of the Billy Graham Evangelistic Association. The sermon, reprinted from a 1953 book by Francis W. Dixon, is entitled "Is Jesus Lord of Your. . . ?"[5] It begins like this:

Is Jesus Lord of your home? Is he Lord of your job? Is he Lord of your friendships? Is he Lord of your car? Is he Lord of your library? Is he Lord of your relationships with the opposite sex? Is he Lord of your service? Is he Lord of your time?

If Jesus is Lord in our lives, it means that in all these realms of life, he holds absolute sway. He is on the throne of our lives, and there is no rival. He is there at our invitation, with our willing and glad consent.

If Jesus is Lord of your life, Dixon continues, he expects "unquestioning obedience." Jesus' "Lordship" implies "an unquestioning bowing down to his will and an unhesitating and unquestioning doing of his will." Clearly, Dixon's Jesus is not interested in what we may think about his will. Instead of inviting questions because he takes us seriously as thoughtful human beings, is interested in knowing us better, and wishes to have our informed consent, he hears questions as signs of insubordination. Dixon's God sounds like an impatient parent dealing with a sassy child: "Shut up and do as

---

5 Francis W. Dixon, "Is Jesus Lord of Your. . . ?" *Decision* 40:6 (June 1999), 26–27.

you're told." Is he taking his cue from earthly fathers, instead of the heavenly Father?

Dixon goes on to say that God "has the right to send you where he wants to send you." Our only response should be: "You are my Lord, and if you want me in Africa, or in India, or if you want me to stay in the office until the end of my days, by your grace I will do it!" If we do submit to Jesus' "Lordship," we will earn a "certain reward." Jesus will one day say to us, "Well done, thou good and faithful servant: enter thou into the joy of thy Lord."

But didn't Jesus promise to make us free (John 8:32)?

Dixon's sermon does not spell out what happens if we do not grant Jesus minute-by-minute control of our lives. But the same biblical text that promises rewards to good and faithful servants promises "outer darkness," where "men weep and gnash their teeth" (Matthew 25:30).[6] Most preachers make the implication of this teaching more ominously clear: if Jesus is not Lord of all, then serious questions must be raised as to whether we were sincere in taking him as our Savior in the first place. And if he is not our Savior, then eternal punishment awaits us. Once again, the shadow of a threat passes over our spirits—a disguised "spiritual terrorism" enforcing a disguised "spiritual totalitarianism."

I believe "Lordship talk" rises out of a genuine human yearning to be just one thing and to speak with just one voice. And it reflects what may be the deepest human thirst: a thirst for undivided, unselfconscious union with the divine. In practice, however, it works against those legitimate human desires. By heightening and dramatizing the all-seeing critical eye of an intrusive, all-knowing God, it deepens our sense of guilt and shame. This has certain institutional benefits: it encourages church attendance and keeps tithes and

---

6 In Chapters 10 and 11, below, I suggest more hopeful meanings for "darkness" and the weeping and gnashing of teeth that occur there. Francis W. Dixon, and Billy Graham who published his sermon, take it to describe a place of eternal torture.

offerings flowing. It cultivates a habit of obedience to whomever we are told represents God's will. In a pluralistic society, where church attendance is voluntary and each church competes for market share with its counterpart down the block, "Lordship talk" helps reinforce brand loyalty.

There were times, during my teenage years, when I felt my internal disorder keenly and longed for relief. I wished "the Lord" would move into every room of my house and sweep it clean. Today, this language sounds like a prescription for constant self-judgment, relieved only by denial and repression. That is the way it was for me.

My daughter, Sara, once gave me a glimpse of the implications of this view of a God who peers, with critical concern, into our souls all hours of the day and night. As an eight-year-old, she said: "I wish God didn't see everything. I'd like to have some privacy." She knew instinctively that she could not explore and grow in her understanding and acceptance of herself—her whole self in its human ebb and flow—so long as she lived with a nosy, perfection-seeking God.

My daughter didn't hear this "Lordship teaching" in our home. Her perception of a seeing-eye God probably reflected common childhood images of God, mixed up with the part of herself that watched and disapproved of her, and reinforced by the God-talk she heard from schoolmates who belonged to the local "Good News Club." With a little "Lordship teaching," my wife and I could easily have heightened her self-consciousness and self-condemnation. The result might have been a more outwardly compliant child. Like most parents, I wished for this on occasion. But any compliance secured by "Lordship teaching" would only have reinforced her natural resentment towards an intrusive and coercive God, and alienated her from the parents who insisted that she love this God.

And if she had felt such resentment, she would have had to keep it hidden—even from herself—since the all-seeing God dislikes resentment and regularly scrutinizes people's lives, looking for some trace of it.[7]

•   •   •

THE EYE THAT SEES ALL

In *Discipline and Punish*, social historian Michel Foucault explores a popular nineteenth-century design for prison architecture in England and America.[8] In the center of the prison stands a tall, multi-storied tower surrounded by a circular courtyard. At the outer edge of the courtyard is a circular, multi-storied prison building. Each story comprises a single ring of cells facing the courtyard and tower.

The internal wall of each cell, facing the courtyard and tower, is a phalanx of steel bars. In the opposite wall, facing the world beyond the prison, is a barred window, allowing plenty of light into the cell. From each level of the central tower, a prison guard can watch the many-leveled ring of cells. The inmate's figure is visible through the bars at all times. There is no privacy and no escape.

The prison's architect called this design a *panopticon*. Visibility is its governing purpose. The cells, writes Foucault, "are like so many cages, so many small theaters, in which each actor is alone, perfectly individualized and constantly visible." Visibility operates continually, even in the absence of a watching eye. The central tower has

---

7 Thomas Matthews testified to the difficulty of getting rid of this seeing-eye God: "I still think of God—no, not think, but apprehend, as I was trained as a child to envision him—as a watchful, vengeful, enormous, omniscient policeman, instantly aware of the slightest tinge of irreverence in my innermost thought, always ready to pounce if I curse, if I mention him in anger, fun or mere habit (though with ominous patience he might hold his hand for a time). . ." *Under the Influence* (New York: Macmillan, 1977), 343, quoted in Terence E. Fretheim, *The Suffering of God: An Old Testament Perspective* (Philadelphia: Fortress Press, 1984), 1.

8 Michel Foucault, *Discipline and Punish: The Birth of the Prison* (New York: Vintage Books, 1979), 200–202.

interior partitions that keep its interior dark so that the prisoners in the cells can never know whether, at any moment, an observer actually inhabits the tower. It is visibility alone, not the guard, which governs the inmate's behavior, and thus it is visibility that punishes.

In Foucault's words, "the inmate will constantly have before his eyes the tall outline of the central tower from which he is spied upon." But the inmate "must never know whether he is being looked at at any one moment." He must simply be aware that he *may* be being seen. The visibility goes only one way: in the ring of cells, "one is *totally seen*, without ever *seeing*; in the central tower, one *sees everything* without ever *being seen*."

The panopticon's designer considered it a humane alternative to the heavy-handed controls of the dark, subterranean dungeon. The control it exerts is so light-handed it is barely felt. And yet the control is utterly pervasive.

For Foucault, the panopticon is a metaphor for life in modern society where human subjectivity is shaped by ever more efficient and intrusive modern technologies of surveillance (testing, measuring, evaluating, record-keeping), which constitute, in effect, a tiny moving theater in which each individual is the sole actor and in which each is perfectly controlled. We are prisoners of an unseen but highly effective control mechanism: the anxiety of being scrutinized by an unseen authority who holds all the cards.

Foucault's narrative offers an intriguing (and disheartening) possibility: that the intrusive, demanding God of American evangelicalism, functioning through the medium of its "Lordship" language, serves a wider purpose: social control in a mass society. It serves the purposes of the hidden network of powers that conspire to shape a docile and pliable citizenry. If so, this casts an ironic light on evangelicalism's self-styled image as a counter-culture, actively resisting "the world" and offering a radical alternative to the secular society. In effect, the evangelical God cooperates with the wider society as a mechanism for shaping compliance and exerting velvet-gloved control.

This hypothesis is suggestive. Widespread evangelical support for an American president who approved investigative torture, instituted domestic surveillance and trampled civil liberties like no American president before him may offer this hypothesis some credibility.[9] But for my purposes, it is enough to notice the effect of this endlessly scrutinizing God on evangelical individuals. The panopticon offers a glimpse of evangelicals living out their spiritual lives under the all-seeing eye of a powerful figure they cannot see. This eye is alert to their slightest failing, real or imagined.

What combination of conscious compliance and unconscious anger might be the fruit of such a life? How could such "Lordship" permit a person ever to feel truly free? How authentic a relationship with God will a Christian develop under such an all-seeing gaze? How wearying might the Christian life become?[10]

In one vital respect the inmate of Foucault's panopticon is better off than the beleaguered evangelical. The inmate feels no pressure to summon from within his heart a deep, abiding *love* for the observer in the tower.

●   ●   ●

---

9 Evangelicals believe in a God who uses torture as a matter of necessity. Perhaps this inures them to the torture of prisoners held without benefit of *habeas corpus* at Guantanamo Bay, which American officials defend as necessary for the protection of American citizens. On the other hand, if they brought this portrait of God into full awareness, and felt its implications in their hearts, would they be able to better empathize with the human beings subjected to "enhanced interrogation techniques" like water-boarding?

10 Patrick Henry College is a current example of the panopticon at work. But it does not rely exclusively on the eye of God to enforce moral conformity. Its students are obliged to do God's work for him by reporting their peers' moral failures to the school staff. Rosin, *God's Harvard*, 167–182.

KEEPING THE KIDS IN THE FOLD

Why has this intrusive God been so readily accepted as the mainspring of evangelical spirituality?

The fundamentalist founders of what became contemporary evangelicalism, as we saw, were young people speaking to young people. Percy Crawford named his radio and television programs "The Young People's Church of the Air" and "Youth on the March." Billy Graham preached under the auspices of "Youth for Christ." The evangelicalism that now bids for social and political power first sprouted in halls full of teenagers singing, "Christ for me, yes, it's Christ for me!"

These rallies were fantastically successful.[11] Naturally, church workers across America began paying attention. Percy Crawford's "distinctive style"—his sporty clothes, practical jokes, fast cars, jazzed-up gospel tunes, high-voltage staccato preaching—became "the norm for youth evangelists."[12] Local churches quickly joined the parade. "Youth programs" became the cutting edge for congregational life: Friday night youth socials, Saturday night rallies, Sunday night "youth groups," week-end youth retreats, week-long youth-oriented revival crusades, "fun-packed" summer camping programs, all built on the excitement of youth as a way to spearhead the numerical growth of local congregations.

All this responded beautifully to the deepening—and

---

11 During the mid-1940s, over 300 rallies occurred weekly, in venues like Madison Square Garden and Carnegie Hall. On Memorial Day, 1945, seventy thousand people filled Chicago's Soldier's Field for an open-air celebration of God and country, complete with a flag ceremony featuring high school cadets and four hundred marching nurses. George Beverly Shea sang with a five-thousand-voice choir. Billy Graham and Percy Crawford preached. Then "a spotlight circled the darkened stadium while a huge neon sign blazed *Jesus Saves* and the choir sang *We Shall Shine as Stars in the Morning*." Joel Carpenter, *Revive Us Again*, 161, 166. Much of this section draws on Carpenter's definitive account of evangelicalism's rise out of the ashes of Depression-era fundamentalism.
12 Carpenter, *Revive Us Again,* 164.

understandable—anxieties of American parents during the rapid social change of the postwar years. Growing affluence and the explosion of consumerism were beginning to chip away at the old Protestant work ethic; advertising was luring Americans toward more readily available pleasures; new entertainment media were flashing hitherto unknown lifestyle possibilities before the eyes of young and old alike.

Christian parents sensed that, without their permission, these forces were gaining access to their children, enticing their children toward values and interests that seemed dangerous and un-Christian. They sensed that capitalism and the consumer culture thrive on what is new, denigrating more traditional ways of thinking and acting, enticing children to become culturally, intellectually, socially, spiritually *different* from their parents. For parents, these differences threatened to tear their children away from them. Teen religion promised to reverse that process.

So it was the *parents* of those jubilant crowds of young people who endorsed, organized and funded the rallies, the retreats, the camps and the clubs. It was the parents who breathed a sigh of relief when their children chose Jesus over jazz or rock 'n roll, and the parents who embraced any bright young star with a talent for making Jesus look enough like jazz and "rock 'n' roll" to attract their kids' attention. And no doubt it was the parents who sighed with relief every time a light-hearted "singspiration" segued into grim descriptions of death and hell and the severe Judge who was bound by his nature to send his beloved children—and theirs—straight into the flames if they didn't behave. It was the parents, filling the side bleachers, who thrilled to the sight of their children walking down the aisles.

A God who loves us conditionally can seem quite useful to the part of a parent that worries about losing a secure connection with their children. It's tempting to want to plant at the center of our child's consciousness the image of a God who never sleeps because he's interested in everything you do, and who can send you to hell if he doesn't like what he sees.[13] More subtle truths about the mystery of God, invitations to lives of genuine trust, growing compassion or deeper self-awareness, or even careful exegesis of biblical texts in all their complexity, are easily overlooked when fearful parts of us take over.

But if keeping the kids in the fold is the church's primary task, the portable God who keeps watch on you from the center of your being soon becomes the only God the church is preaching, and not just to the kids. In those postwar years, the adolescent tail was soon wagging the entire evangelical dog. New musical and preaching techniques seeped from Saturday night rallies into Sunday morning worship. Exemplary young people took the pulpit to give testimonies or perform music in the adult services. Gradually, the language of teen enthusiasm became the common language of adult spirituality.

Occasionally, adults sensed that teen language didn't match their mature experience of God. According to one historian, some evangelical adults noticed the "frothy" and "sickening shallowness" of it

---

13 Christian Smith and his fellow sociologists (*American Evangelicalism*, 50–51) tell us that evangelicals "do the best possible job raising and training their children to grow up to be good (meaning evangelical) Christians." One mother they interviewed described her parenting strategy this way: "I buy my kids Christian music, and I buy it for myself. I have Sandy Patti and other Christian artists. If I go to a Christian concert, I buy all their tapes, and we play a lot of that in the car when we're traveling. I also have the Bible on tape, and we listen to that—the whole Bible on tape while traveling." Smith believes evangelicals do a better job than any other religious group in generating programs to help "make sure that high-school and college-age evangelicals do not stray from the evangelical fold."

A wide array of publishing houses, non-profits and educational institutions labor ceaselessly, churning out slick program materials, handbooks, curricula and conferences attended by thousands, to provide over-worked local youth ministers with the tools to carry out this mandate. A prominent component of this network is Youth Specialties, Inc., founded by Mike Yaconelli and Wayne Rice in 1969, conducting three giant conventions each year and claiming to serve 100,000 youth ministers. (www.youthspecialties.com)

I understand, completely, the desire of Christian parents to raise their children "in the faith." Perhaps we should be more careful to ask ourselves exactly what sort of God we hope our children will have "faith" in.

all. But the train had left the station. American evangelicalism was firmly in the grip of an adolescent spirituality.[14]

Today, this adolescentization is most evident in the way in which evangelicalism has adapted pop culture's primary themes—the infinite joys of adolescent romance and sexual fulfillment—to its own purposes, moving them from the register of carnal love into the register of spiritual devotion. God has become the heart-throb next door: a beautiful, exciting, intimate friend who is perfectly matched to my romantic needs, who will love me forever.

The "praise and worship choruses" that—with their plaintive crooning and repetitive lyrics—occupy twenty minutes or more of many Sunday services are filled with this imagery. Their themes are remarkably uniform: "Our" God is glorious and perfect, holy, righteous and just. Yet this amazingly "awesome" God is closer to me than a lover:

There's no place I'd rather be
Than in your arms of love,
In your arms of love,
Holding me still,
Holding me near,
In your arms of love.[15]

These are the sentiments of teen romance, as one might find them expressed in a diary toward a warm, idealized father, an intimate

---

14 Carpenter, *Revive Us Again*, 172, 175–176.

15 Rosin, *God's Harvard*, 82. These songs display a legitimate human yearning for a God who understands and loves each of us in our unique individuality. Two aspects of them concern me: that they are unconsciously given their energy by the unspoken belief that the same God who "holds" us is also willing to condemn us; and that, like the language of teen romance, they presume a superficial understanding of love that evades its invitation to a deeper self-awareness and an embrace of suffering.

I will explore these latter themes in *Part Two*.

new "best friend," or the girl or boy who is meant just for me. As in Crawford's rallies, these lyrics concentrate on the "good" God, implicating him deeply into our affections, while the "bad" God—who scrutinizes us each moment of the day and night—waits to show up later, during the sermon.

This is now the language of evangelicalism at large. It pervades the thinly "Christianized" media environment that constitutes the life-world of many adult evangelicals. It depicts a God who loves us infinitely, but who watches to see if we are obeying his commands. When we fail, the wonderful, warm, loving God of the worship choruses silently morphs into the frowning, disappointed or angry Father who can turn his back on us, bring misfortune into our lives and finally send us to hell.

Overt reminders of this God are not nearly so ubiquitous in twenty-first century evangelical youth ministry as they were at its inception, sixty years before. Pop culture tends toward the "cool," so the overt fear-mongering of those 1940s youth rallies has been toned down. But this demanding, disapproving and ultimately abandoning God is an unshakeable substratum of evangelical spirituality. It's the very big, very attentive elephant—or better, saber-toothed tiger—that everyone knows sits in the corner, even though no one mentions it out loud.[16]

The "carrot" of a warm loving God may be what evangelicals sing about, but the "stick" of a demanding God who has high expectations for their lives still enforces the silent regime of fear in their hearts.

●   ●   ●

---

16 Christian Smith (*American Evangelicalism*, 25) finds that evangelicals are more confident of their essential beliefs than any other grouping of American Christians.

A TRIP DOWN MEMORY LANE

During a recent visit to a nearby city, I walked one Sunday morning to the local Baptist church. Friendly handshakes and an elegantly-printed program met me at the door. I slipped into a back row next to an older couple—probably in their eighties. His eyes were closed in prayer or sleep, but she greeted me with a warm smile.

By the time the choir called us to worship, most of the pews were filled. I looked out over a sea of white- and gray-heads. A few middle-aged singles and couples were sprinkled throughout, along with a handful of young families. This was the "traditional" service—the "contemporary service" had taken place earlier. At the pastor's suggestion, I signed a little card and greeted the folks nearby. We sang several hymns and the choir performed a medley.

The hymns were stately and triumphant—their subject, the majesty and power of God. One implored us to "glorify God's name." The next hailed God as King and Lord, and anticipated the day when we will all reign with him in heaven. The next scrolled through a long list of God's various names. All but one were lofty and imposing.

The exception was "Emmanuel," which means, of course, "God with us." (My mind drifted to a squalling child born to a slightly confused couple in a manure-laden stable. The unvarnished humanity of it felt out of place in this hymn, whose soaring tones reached for a realm infinitely above and beyond us.) The next hymn was about God's "righteous, omnipotent hand." We finished on a slightly warmer note: "Love divine, all loves excelling."

Announcements were next, the offering plate was passed, the pastor prayed, and we settled in for the sermon. Its topic was printed in the bulletin: "The Lordship of Christ." I looked twice to make sure I had read correctly. On this random Sunday, in this random church, I had stumbled into an iconic sermon topic, one about which I had been writing that very week. I wondered whether these people had heard it as many times as I. I began scribbling madly on the back of the bulletin.

From the start, I noticed a familiar tone in the pastor's voice—the tone of a loving but weary parent, gently scolding a mildly mischievous child. Why have we again forgotten what the pastor has told us so many times before: that we "cannot count Jesus as Savior without crowning him as Lord"? Why have we once again snatched the reins of our lives out of the hands of a loving God? Why do we insist on running our own lives? The pastor seemed genuinely to care about these questions. I felt a bit ashamed for treating his sermon as a case study, instead of stopping to ask these questions of myself.

I knew some kind of warning would likely follow this gentle scolding. We didn't have long to wait. About five minutes into his sermon, the pastor said: "People will be rejected at the gates of heaven because they received Jesus as their Savior, but didn't make him their Lord." He said it twice, in a slightly plaintive, "you know this is true" tone of voice.

The sanctuary was full of people I took to be lifelong Christians. This wasn't a rescue mission on Skid Row or a revival service for rowdy teens. These aging Baptists knew all too well the stakes of the game—they had been playing it for many years. One gentle reminder on a sunny July morning—"rejected at the gates of heaven"—was surely enough.

My mind went back to the hymn we had just sung: "Jesus, thou art all compassion, pure, unbounded love thou art." The pastor had just beckoned into the room something that didn't feel at all like unbounded love—the looming reality of eternal retribution. This reality had certainly been dramatized for these people again and again by far more lurid sermons than this. It took only one understated sentence—a sentence probably chosen out of habit by a preacher who meant no harm by it—to tap into that deep pool of barely suppressed though thoroughly normalized horror.

The pastor spent most of his remaining time illustrating the "Lordship of Christ." He likened it to the thirty-foot dinosaur at Minnesota's "Mall of America"—it's "built up piece by piece out of Lego blocks," making us more and more "strengthened in him." He likened it to a giant antenna held to the ground by steel wires, making us "secure." The pastor spelled out these and other illustrations at some length.

I was listening very carefully—the whole sermon seemed a wonderful gift to my writing project—but it was hard to know what to make of his illustrations. The image of a giant plastic dinosaur wasn't connecting with anything real in my day-to-day life. The towering antenna with its steel wires brought Gulliver to mind, pinned to the ground by the Lilliputians—not a very joyful or freeing prospect.

A surreal "Monty Python" image popped into my head: the pastor releasing his words, like weightless little party balloons, up into the rafters of the sanctuary, where they drifted noiselessly about before slipping out a skylight and dissipating harmlessly into the universe. These illustrations touched nothing real, nothing of flesh and blood. They sounded pleasing, but stirred none of the troublesome stew of our lived experience.

The pastor moved toward his conclusion. These were not his own ideas, he said, but God's. As if to add weight to God's endorsement, he said they were also Billy Graham's. I scribbled down the Graham quote: "No man can be said to be truly converted to Christ, who has not bent his will to Christ." To me, bending our will sounds like trying to make ourselves do what we don't want to do. Does Christ want such disciples?[17]

The pastor now stepped out from behind the podium, and knelt down on the carpet. I felt a surge of affection for him—he seemed good-hearted, humble and sincere. He told us this position—down

---

[17] Will-power is also what parents hope will make a mysterious appearance in our teenagers when they're being tempted, by evil friends, to take that first sip of beer.

on our knees—is the only one that acknowledges the Lordship of Christ. Still on his knees, he prayed, promising God that we were ready to give him total control of our lives. We want to settle this "once and for all," he said.

The senior citizens around me sat still and listened politely. They could have been wax dummies—that is the way their generation sits in church. But I am not far removed from them in years, and I know they are not really made of wax. They are alive to the exigencies of age, and carry with them a catalog of worries.

Will their money run out before their lives run out? Will some dreaded illness snatch away the quality of their lives, robbing them of their faculties, making them forget their grandchildren's names and birthdays? Will they die alone in an institution—perhaps that high-rise retirement home I noticed just across the street? Will they lose the power to decide their own fate, have their independence wrested away by well-meaning relatives or health professionals, be attacked on the street or robbed in the middle of the night? Will their spouse die, leaving them lonely? Or will they die, leaving their spouse to fend without them?

I know they wonder who they have been, how they got to where they are, and what their lives have meant. And whether they did right by their children and their friends. And what, perhaps, they might have done differently.

I wondered whether the pastor had read his audience quite right. Did these senior citizens really need to hear a sermon on obedience? Was it helpful to treat them like recalcitrant teenagers, reminding them of the God who feels he has to threaten them to make them believe or behave—who is always disappointed, never truly pleased, with them? Did they need to hear about the God who wants them to suppress their own will, knuckle under and do his—a God who, in effect, wants to make their decisions for them rather than draw them inward toward themselves and their own deepest sense of how to live their lives?

I wished, for a moment, that this was a Quaker meeting, so I could venture a few words to my fellow-seekers. I wanted to remind them that there is One who knows what it means to be human, who like them has suffered abandonment and loss. One who promises to be present to them in their declining years—not as an insecure, intrusive Lord, but as one who looks on them fondly, without expectation or accusation. I wanted to tell them that God actually *likes* them, just as they are. That God invites them not to be afraid of the chaos of feeling inside them, but rather to understand that everything inside is important and has something of value to say to them.

I might have said it would be okay if they couldn't imagine themselves as giant dinosaurs or electric pylons, and assured them that God's love is really warm and safe—safe enough to make it possible for them to embrace themselves, after all these years, as they really are. I would have smiled and suggested we all take more seriously the old invitation hymn: "Just as I am, without one plea."

The service ended. The elderly woman to my right invited me to come again. I thanked her and headed out into the street. I wondered where she had filed the latest sermon. She seemed unfazed by it. Perhaps she knew better than I that these anthems are just window-dressing, that the pastor's vague threats are well-intended boiler-plate, and that the man from Nazareth can be trusted to go with her on each step of her uncertain journey.

•   •   •

AWAKENING FROM THE DREAM

If evangelicalism's spiritual style—its language about God and about our relationship with God—has been shaped by the unac-knowledged fears of parents into a tool for keeping their kids in the fold, it will not promote Christian adulthood. It can only promote an indefinitely prolonged adolescence.

To be an adolescent, as I understand it, is to be enchanted by the "dream of integrity"—the beautiful dream that one day the unruly riot of inner voices pushing us toward the good, the bad and everything in-between will die out, and in their place will be only one voice, a voice of truth and goodness and absolute certainty, and this voice will guide us to our proper success, even perhaps heroism, in the world. "Growing up," in the prototypical adolescent mind, means expelling everything inside that seems childish, grasping, anti-social, violent, self-serving, needy, destructive or unattractive—in other words, becoming internally unified around the one right voice, the voice that we imagine will bring us the approval, and the affection, that we need.

Acquiring this sort of "integrity," of course, necessitates tireless inner scrutiny. We cultivate an inner climate of self-accusation and self-disapproval, and engage in daily inner combat. We close ourselves to any honest curiosity about what really is (instead of what we hope or dread is) inside us. Much of what is inside us in adolescence we experience as an enemy. We are not gentle with enemies—Lordship teaching, unlike the teaching of Jesus, urges us to be quite brutal toward our inner enemies—and thus we are not gentle with ourselves. Our inner world is not a welcoming or hospitable place.

A more genuine maturity dawns as we awaken from this "dream of integrity." Mature adulthood, it becomes clear, is not the consequence of successfully combating and extinguishing every disapproved part of ourselves. It consists, rather, in gradually learning to accept all of what we are in our marvelous discord and complexity. This means welcoming and respecting each internal voice—no matter how unsociable or troublesome; cultivating its friendship, inviting it to speak, helping it trust the inner dialogue and the self who conducts that dialogue, encouraging it to relax and take up the more constructive roles that it has always wanted to play in the intricate system we call the person.

To be mature is to know that every part of us, no matter how troublesome, has been born in us for a reason and needs our embrace. To the adolescent, "wholeness" may mean an artificially created, willpower-enforced "unity" or "unanimity." But to the mature, "wholeness" means throwing our arms around the variegated whole of us, accepting our multiplicity and inviting every part of us into a peaceful inner dialogue. The inner climate of the mature, in contrast to the adolescent, is warm and hospitable.

It is tempting for anxious adults to promote the dream of integrity among adolescents—to identify for them the one approved voice of truth, goodness and absolute certainty (the "Lord's" voice) and urge them to begin right now, once and for all, living resolutely in obedience only to that voice, turning away from—actually, expunging from their internal worlds—the entire chorus of competing voices. If this dream is packaged religiously and promoted as entertainment by charismatic young men or women, themselves in thrall to this dream and purporting to represent its finest accomplishments, compliant adolescents may be the temporary result. Parents will breathe a sigh of relief.

But this program will backfire. Over time, a sense of falseness and futility will accompany that "good" behavior, and the parts of us that we expunge will turn up in other forms, fueling outbursts of internal misery or external "bad" behavior. And that will send us back to church, or to the local Christian bookstore's shelf of spiritual self-help books, where unfortunately we will once again be admonished to embrace the adolescent dream and guide our lives by its illusory appeal which, because it is illusory, will need to be reinforced by continual repetition, endless warning.

An evangelicalism shaped by and for the young will doom both young and old to a lifelong spiritual adolescence.

CHAPTER 5

You Must Not Be Yourself

Guarding the evangelical family secret

We make ourselves real by telling the truth.
Thomas Merton[1]

AT WHEATON COLLEGE IN THE 1960s, chapel services occurred daily and student attendance was required. The usual format called for an organ prelude, a hymn, a prayer, and a sermon by a visiting pastor, scholar, businessman or "missionary statesman." These sermons often recounted inspiring stories of miraculous events in the lives of dedicated Christians who had resolved to "make every moment count for the Lord."

A steady diet of this could be demoralizing. It was easy to feel like a failure, mucking around in the detritus of our own mediocre lives while a mighty God moved mountains for the kinds of people who "gave him their all."

One way to block out the self-denigration these chapels fueled was to hone our cynicism to a fine point. Cynical or sarcastic talk was called "mocking" by Wheaton students. My friends and I thought we were very good at it. It was our characteristic mode of expression. But it seemed to peak, daily, in the half hour after chapel as we

---

1   *No Man Is An Island* (New York: Image Books, 1967), 145.

walked to the student center to check our mailboxes and visit for a few minutes in the nearby lounge.

During chapel, however, a different part of my internal repertoire kicked in—a part that simply shut the whole thing out. Chapel reminded me of church and Sunday school, Bible camp and youth retreat, missionary conference and revival service. I had heard it all. Midway through my freshman year, a door slammed shut inside me. Most mornings, by the time the organist had finished his majestic prelude, I was slumped down in my seat studying for my next class or reading Newsweek magazine. Many chapels flew by as I mentally cheered Fidel Castro, debated Nixon and Kennedy, banged my shoe with Khrushchev, protested at a Greensboro lunch counter, and hoped against hope that Vietnam would not invade my life after graduation. Thanks to required chapel, I acquired a Newsweek habit that endured for decades.

I still attend college chapels from time to time, sometimes as a guest speaker. My eye is immediately drawn to the slackers and latecomers who slink into the back and slide down in their seats until they can barely see me; and to the seemingly oblivious "airheads" who carry on running conversations with their friends throughout my talk; and to the current affairs junkies who, in deference to a long, honorable tradition, pull out a Newsweek the moment I step to the podium; and to those I know will mock me over lunch. My heart salutes each and every one of them. I know exactly what they're up to.

At the same time, I do my best to attract their attention just long enough to tell them that the God they have heard too much about is, indeed, a burdensome fellow—enough to make you want to run from the building screaming if he comes at you one more time. I'd like to tell them that they are on to something important—that the God they are passively resisting is purely fictional—an evangelical shibboleth and little more.

I believe these students are right to dislike and distrust this God. He's not the real God—the humble child who cries to us from a cattle stall. I am hopeful that if their hearts hear that baby's cry—or if they can for one moment glimpse the human being who hangs on the cross, without the distorting lens of evangelicalism's official story—they might just catch themselves feeling curious about God. Perhaps even drawn to God. It is the powerful, demanding and punitive things that we admire or fear, but the small things that we love.

. . .

LISTENING TO THE SCAPEGOAT

Most families have secrets—truths about the family system that cannot be spoken aloud. Naming the secret would raise embarrassing questions about that happy family photograph beaming from its hallowed spot on the mantle, smiling parents surrounded by smiling children. Naming the secret would break a family's code of silence. It's not a code anyone acknowledges, but it's one that everyone obeys.

This code of silence helps maintain a slightly uncomfortable stability—a stability that benefits, primarily, the family members with the most power in the family system. It keeps surface conflict to a minimum, or at least confined within well-worn tracks. It guards the family's reputation. It helps—or tries to help—the family avoid its all-too-real pain. The family—like many individuals—operates on the principle that fully encountering its own pain will destroy it, and then love—or what passes for love—will be lost. The "code of silence" is not a sign of confidence, but of despair. It signifies that the family does not believe its pain can be healed and the genuine love it yearns for achieved.

Family secrets take their toll. In most families the toll is paid in unequal amounts. Often, one child pays for all the rest.[2] Some pay more passively: loneliness, aimlessness, sarcasm, withdrawal, depression. Some pay more actively: tantrums, truancy, drugs, promiscuity, suicide. People shake their heads: How can such a bad kid come from such a fine family? Often, the bad kids themselves do not know the answer. They would like to be more "normal" and feel "happier," but they can't seem to make it happen. Their families try to help—advising, encouraging, pressuring, taking the "problem child" to treatment. Anything that doesn't involve confessing the family secret.

The students whose body language spells passive resistance to required chapel—and those who never show up, even though threatened with disciplinary action—are sending a message to the evangelical family. They know the family secret—they suffer it daily. They may not quite know that they know it, or as yet have words for it. But if they did find words, here is what I think they would say, in a vernacular more permissible in their day than in mine: "All this talk about a loving heavenly Father is bullshit. He doesn't love me, and I don't love him. I'm tired of trying to love a distant, unfeeling bastard. I want a break from the lies this family tells. I want a break from this family."

I wish we evangelicals could listen to these young people instead of scolding them, praying for them, witnessing to them or shunning them. If we could help them find words for what their hearts know, they might help us find words for what our hearts know. Together, we might find the courage to explore the contours and the costs of this family secret. We might find the freedom to shout it from the housetops.

•   •   •

2   Perhaps this is another reason why the penal substitutionary theory of the atonement makes so much sense to so many people.

SPILLING THE SECRET

I hope it's clear by now that the first four chapters of this book constitute my attempt to bring the evangelical family secret into the open. The confusing emotional mixture of love and condemnation that we hear in the young evangelists' God; the strange attachment of those bright evangelical scholars to a super-sized, distant and relationally-crippled God; the toxic appeal, for the countless champions of evangelicalism's defining story, of a God whose love is so hardened and ultimately defeated by his own holiness and justice that he must kill his son; and the invasive presence of a scrutinizing God that "Lordship" teaching plants inside us, preventing us from outgrowing our spiritual adolescence—each of these contributes a unique component to the construction of the evangelical family secret.

In this chapter, I would like to spell that secret out in bold letters. What might we say about our heavenly Father—our *evangelical* heavenly Father, not the "Abba" of Jesus—if the truth that is buried in our hearts could make its way out of our mouths?

I think we might say:

> Our heavenly Father is very big. He wants us to feel very small.
> He wants us, in our hymns and prayers, to remind him that he
> is big and we are small. He is obsessed with his own holiness
> and acts like he does not want it stained by the deficiencies of his
> wayward children.
>
> He says he wants a relationship with us, but we often experi-
> ence him as distant and inaccessible. Since he is unchangeable,
> he has no feelings and doesn't suffer, so it is hard to feel connected
> to him. He does not seem to need us. If we do not have a warm
> and trusting relationship with him, it is always our fault.[3] The

---

3 My friend Lynn Baker remembers hearing this maxim: "If you are not feeling close to

kind of relationship he wants with us seems to require that we stay children all our lives—that we never really grow up.[4]

Our heavenly Father scrutinizes us obsessively. He is never happy with what he finds. He wants us to focus on becoming what he has decided we ought to be—his "will" or "plan" for us—rather than who we really are. We get the feeling that he doesn't much like or trust us as we really are. His revulsion against sin increases that feeling, particularly since he has told us it is in our very nature to sin.

Since our heavenly Father does not really like who we are independently of his plan for us, it is hard to understand what it means to say he loves us. The bottom line seems to be that he loves us *only if* we obey him. His need to threaten us with punishment seems to indicate that he does not trust love, freely given, to draw us to him. His insistence on punishing a substitute for our sin before he can forgive our sin is the expression of a bitter and vengeful man trapped in his own wrath.

Our heavenly Father is willing to give us a lifetime to comply with his requirements, but then he says "Time's up!" If we haven't accepted his Son as our Savior, he abandons us forever. He turns toward his "good" children, with whom he enjoys eternal bliss, while he torments his "bad" children eternally in hell. In apparent contradiction to the Bible's portrait of God, his mercy is strictly circumscribed, while the consequences of his anger go on forever (Psalm 30:5).

God today, guess who moved?" It has been widely seen in car window transfers and on church billboards. It keeps us from appreciating that moving away from an unloving God might be a means of emotional survival.

4 Roberta Bondi believes the story in John 11 about Mary's and Martha's responses to Jesus after the death of Lazarus suggests that God does not want people to relate to God as "passive, obedient, little children" but as "adult friends." *Memories of God: Theological Reflections on a Life* (Nashville: Abingdon Press, 1995), 41–44.

Is this the same heavenly Father who promises to take away our hearts of stone and give us hearts of flesh (Ezekiel 36:26)? How can he possibly keep this promise, when he, himself, seems not to have undergone that blessed transformation?

•   •   •

"HELP ME TO LOVE YOU MORE"

I have drawn here the portrait of a big bad God. It's a harsh portrait, grating to my own ears. Few evangelicals would be comfortable subscribing to it. Just reading lines like these can make many evangelicals feel guilty. Agreeing with them, saying them aloud, is even more dangerous: if such a heavenly Father exists, he will not take these charges lying down. Most evangelicals, I imagine, would reject this portrait out of hand—and some quite angrily.[5]

But I have not conjured the portrait out of thin air. In forty years of college teaching, I have had countless conversations with evangelical students—and occasionally with their parents. I've also spent many hours with college professors, counselors and administrators.

In moments of honesty, especially when stories of personal difficulty are being shared, the specter of a stony-hearted Father often makes its appearance. At one time or another, each of the components of this harsh portrait has been articulated in my presence by a hurt, scared or angry human being. Invariably, this human being is from an evangelical family or an evangelical church.

Often, people are surprised when, in the middle of an intense conversation, they hear such descriptions coming inadvertently from their own lips. They have been so completely taken in by their own ritualistic repetitions of the approved language about a loving God that the injuries they felt at the hands of the harsher God

---

5 This anger, which I have witnessed, may be one clue that a seam of truth has been uncovered.

living deep within them have been kept secret, even from themselves. The shock they feel on articulating these injuries, however, is often accompanied by a wave of relief and sense of freedom. For many of them, the discovery of this harsher God has, after a period of mourning, launched their journey toward a better God, a truer Father revealed in the human Jesus.[6]

The dissonance between the "doctrinally correct" God that many evangelicals carry in their heads and the harsher God living in many an evangelical heart shows up in a variety of ways in evangelical language and practice, revealing the silent ubiquity of the family secret. Here are a few examples.

- "Christian apologetics" is an evangelical cottage industry. Until recently, most evangelical colleges required a Christian apologetics course for graduation. Some of evangelicalism's most popular speakers and authors are "defenders of the faith." For a long time, Josh McDowell led the field with his book *Evidence that Demands a Verdict*. William Lane Craig, a professor of philosophy at Talbot School of Theology, seems to be evangelicalism's current apologetic superstar.[7]

---

6 For many years, Roberta Bondi lived with a "simultaneous attraction and repulsion toward God the Father." When she heard the name "Father" in public prayer, "a sense of inadequacy, helplessness and depression" would overwhelm her. Her heart's unfulfilled longing for her own father was matched by an unfulfilled longing for God.

At a critical point in her graduate studies, she happened on a book of sermons by the Egyptian desert monks who believed in a God whose love knows no bounds. The Father is gentle, they said, and "uninterested" in our sin. God "is always so much more willing than human beings to make allowances for sin, because God alone understands our circumstances, the depths of our temptations and the extent of our sufferings." God does not want us to grovel, but simply to be ourselves, which is the truest meaning of humility: "accepting ourselves and others just as we are, limitations, vulnerabilities and major imperfections included," which frees us to "love and act fearlessly with power and authority." Bondi believes we see this same freedom to love and act fearlessly in Jesus, who shows us what the Father is really like. *Memories*, 23–33.

7 This genre seems to be undergoing a growth spurt, in part in response to the

Why the flurry of activity defending the existence of God or the "absolute truth" of Christianity on philosophical or historical grounds? The usual answer is: in order to convince unbelievers Christianity is true. I sense there may be another answer: to convince ourselves Christianity is true.

In our hearts there lives a God from whom, and for whom, we feel no love. Over time, to dampen the turmoil that such a God generates in us, we go numb. We stop feeling anything at all about God. Our numbness is so effective at putting distance between us and God that God no longer seems real—it's as if there is no God. This makes us feel guilty. We want to reconnect with God. But we cannot go looking for God in the lived experience of our hearts, because there only a demanding, rejecting Father lives. So we go looking for God in the safety of our intellects—we look for "reasons" to believe in God. We hope those reasons will help us find a God we can connect with and feel genuinely good about.

But all this is below the surface. At a conscious level, no doubt, we are building rational arguments to convince unbelievers that there is a God. Why are we disturbed by unbelievers? Perhaps they remind us of who we are, inside.

---

resurgence of atheism propagated through popular tracts by Sam Harris (*The End of Faith*), Richard Dawkins (*The God Delusion*), and Christopher Hitchens (*God Is Not Great*). A small sampling of current evangelical apologetics: William Lane Craig and Walter Sinnott-Armstrong, *God? A Debate Between a Christian and an Atheist*; J. P. Moreland, *Does God Exist? The Debate Between Theists and Atheists*; Lee Strobel, *The Case for a Creator*. Craig's views are succinctly set out in "God Is Not Dead Yet," *Christianity Today* (July 2008), 22–27.

An illustration accompanying this article depicts ten Christian philosophers, most of them identified with evangelicalism, who find belief in God philosophically respectable. I suspect many of them would not wish to be labeled "apologists" and see themselves as elaborating the intellectual contours of a thoughtful Christian faith so that we can speak intelligibly to one another and to outsiders. It strikes one immediately that, among the ten faces depicted, not one is a woman.

• Occasionally, I meet a college student—usually a male—raised an evangelical, but now an atheist. He trots out rational arguments *against* the existence of a God. His clinching argument, typically, is the presence of suffering in the world. Then we begin talking about his life, and gradually his sadness, his hurt or his anger makes its appearance. Suddenly, he is talking as if God *does* exist, but a God who has hurt or disappointed him—has not answered his prayers, did not heal his friend's cancer, has left him victim to an abusive or broken family.[8]

Atheism, it turns out, is the way this student is trying to wash an all-too-present, but harsh and unfeeling God out of his system. It is safer to think God is not there than to take the risk of being angry with God, perhaps even hate God. At the same time, he *needs* a God to be angry with—otherwise he is left with a rage that has no object.

• I team-teach with other professors, one of them a Bible scholar. His lectures are inventive, off-beat and very funny. Usually, he gets rapt attention. But whenever he begins to use the word "God" or asks students to open their Bibles, he notices a few nodding off, as if on cue. Sometimes, they are the ones most consciously angry at God and in rebellion against what they consider a Bible-obsessed tradition. Their slumber is understandable.

Sometimes, however, the sleepers are those who profess

---

8 I interpret the atheism famously represented by Ivan, the "intellectual" among Dostoyevsky's famous "Brothers Karamazov," as Ivan's self-protective response to his frightening experience of abandonment as a young child in a family brutalized by a father the novel takes pains to depict as cruel and sadistic. Ivan's "numbness," displayed in the strangely rational tone he uses to describe the sufferings of children, is a thin veneer beneath which lies a pool of rage. But even as he rages, another part of him is drawn to the Jesus who, in his own parable of "The Grand Inquisitor," kisses him gently (242).

the sincerest love for God and for the Bible. We have watched this pattern for many years, and have come to know students like these quite well. We wonder whether sleep is their passive resistance to the possibility of discovering that at a deeper level, to their dismay, they are at odds with God.

- Evangelicals commonly say the Bible is the supreme authority in life. They also frequently admit—and bemoan the fact—that they are not very conscientious or "disciplined" in their Bible reading. For long periods they don't open the Bible except in church. Why do they have to force themselves to read a life-giving book—unless they really do not find it life-giving?

- Often, evangelicals admit that they are repelled by the Bible. Whenever they try to read it, the experience leaves them feeling scrutinized, accused or condemned, and they end up feeling more guilty or angry than when they started. They might say: "I hear a lot of bad news, not much good news," or "Every time I read it, it's the same old stuff." Reading the Bible is not a liberating experience for many evangelicals. No wonder—the God they bring to their reading is not a liberating God.[9]

---

9 A recent (July, 2008) advertisement for the *Discipleship Journal*, published by an evangelical group called "The Navigators," arrived in an envelope emblazoned with the words. "Where's the Fire?" In smaller print on the cover, the recipient is invited to check off the statements that apply. Included among these: "You feel guilty when you hear people telling what they learned in their quiet time—and hope they don't ask how yours was" and "You read the Bible and pray because you *should*, not because you want to."

I assume some public relations whiz put these on the cover because they would "catch" a majority of evangelical readers. This whiz is probably right: most evangelicals do not feel drawn to the Bible. This advertisement makes the questionable assumption, however, that if the "fire" is missing in your Christian experience, it's your fault, not God's.

- Evangelicals often describe daily personal devotions as the time to get our "marching orders." This is a military metaphor evoking the image of a general issuing the day's commands. It works well enough for people who have *given up* on simply meeting, in the Bible or prayer, a God who is a supporting and nurturing presence, a God who frees people to relax and live their own lives. Such a regime only works for people who need a daily agenda of duties to perform or improvements to make in their character. Perhaps, "marching orders" help evangelicals stay on the surface of life—doing rather than being, avoiding the deeper places where pain resides.

- Two common evangelical prayers are: "Lord, melt the hardness of our hearts" and "Lord, make us love you more." A common "praise and worship" chorus goes like this: "If I am to be whom you desire. . . Lord, I need an undivided heart."[10] Do we experience our hearts as hardened or divided merely because we are rebellious? Or do we have a God who causes such inner pain that we cannot help but feel divided, and must protect ourselves by becoming numb?

- Sometimes anger at God does, reluctantly, break out into the open when tragedy strikes, particularly the loss of a loved one. Listening carefully, one can hear this theme seeping through the anger: "Lord, I've done my best to serve and obey you, even when I didn't feel like it. The least you could do is take better care of me. *You owe me!*"

---

10 The complete lyrics read: "If I am to be whom you desire/ all throughout my life/ a vessel unto honor, Lord/ to thee and before your throne/ to hear you say that I have done my part/ Lord, I need an undivided heart." Dan Marks, "Undivided Heart," copyright Maranatha Praise, 1996.

An important truth is coming to the surface: all these years, this person was not loving, with a free heart, the One who shows himself, on the cross, to be a fellow-sufferer; instead, this person was submitting to a tyrannical Father in order to avoid punishment or—like the Prodigal Son's older brother—to reap the rewards of childlike compliance. Now, when it's time for the tyrannical Father to keep his part of the bargain, he is nowhere to be found. The sense of betrayal fuels deep anger.

Often, when anger like this is expressed in evangelical circles, it meets with great discomfort and disapproval from fellow-evangelicals. They will encourage the person to "get over it" as soon as possible. Why does it cut so deep and seem so dangerous?

- Many evangelicals will admit that they feel almost constantly guilty. Guilt is sometimes described as "angry accusation directed inward." Perhaps we direct it inward because we cannot safely direct it at its true object: the accusing Father.

- A favorite evangelical book and sermon topic is: "How You Can Know That You're Saved."[11] The Billy Graham sermon, "Final Exam," is an example. In it, Graham answers the young man who said to him, "I have done everything I know to do, but I still have no assurance." Graham says "hundreds of young people" have asked him this question.[12] Maybe that's because it's a very *good* question: it reveals how many young evangelicals have met a God they cannot trust.

---

11 A more recent example is John MacArthur, Jr., *Saved Without a Doubt: How to Be Sure of Your Salvation* (Colorado Springs: Chariot Victor Publishing, 1992).
12 *Calling Youth*, 64.

.   .   .

WHY BOTHER?

When I confess, in conversation, that I have encountered a God who actually likes human beings, who is infinitely forgiving, and who will journey with every last human being to the farthest corners of hell itself—during life and after death, until we are softened to God's love—very often, a devout evangelical will respond by saying, "Then why should I bother to be good?" or "Why should I get saved, if we're all going to get to heaven someday?"

These answers lay bare the heart of the evangelical family secret. Here are people who seem passionately dedicated to "living for the Lord," and yet they are implying that being good, or being "saved," has been a burden. Some part of them wishes they hadn't taken the trouble to be "born again" and live according to God's high standards. This part of them resents that others have "gotten away with" profligate living while they have persisted in an onerous, life-deadening goodness.

And it is obvious why they have persisted: not because they love God, since love for God is its own reward, but because they are afraid of God's wrath. If not for that wrath, they would be "out there having fun" with all those carefree sinners. Their response reveals their deep ambivalence about Christian faith. It has not been truly good news for this life—only for the next. Beneath all the talk of God's love for them and their love for God lies their true motive for being good: they are afraid of a tyrannical God.

Sometimes, I've tried to point this out: "Your resistance to the idea that God's love will find its way to every human heart makes me wonder whether your commitment to God isn't a bit grudging. Do you feel forced into it, rather than drawn to it by love? Doesn't a relationship with God, which the Bible says makes everything new, represent the most fulfilling way to live—the way you really want to live—here and now? Why would you envy people who don't have that relationship? Why would you see such people as getting away with something?"

Usually, hearing it put that way, my conversation partner will backpedal: "Oh, no, it's not like that. I do believe God is love, and I wouldn't give up being good or being saved even if I knew I could get away with it." I am never sure this answer is coming from their hearts. I suspect a part of them is trying to keep the evangelical family secret hidden.

To all appearances, most evangelicals have adapted relatively well to living with a "difficult" Father. We are obedient children who have learned to silence the dissonance in our hearts and play by the rules. Many of us have lived with this Father since childhood, so we are used to—and in part protected from—the emotional climate that his personality generates. This God is so well fixed inside us that we cannot conceive of an alternative God. It helps, also, that this Father is symbolic and invisible, not physically present as are our human fathers. With a little practice, God can be ignored or forgotten for long stretches at a time.[13]

When we are not ignoring the evangelical God, we can go for help to the extensive network of evangelical churches, organizations, media outlets, publishers and entertainers. They offer formulaic answers that make sure the family secret will remain a secret. Although they do not consciously intend it, this works to their advantage. If they are successful in helping us keep it a secret, our inner

---

13 An article in a mainstream evangelical magazine puts it this way: "Most Christians I meet feel stuck. They started a journey, but somewhere, somehow, got stranded. They feel like they're living on the border. There they sit, swapping rumors about God. Or they just stop talking about God at all. They can talk about everything else with ease and eloquence, but their tongues thicken, twist, grow mute about naming and proclaiming God. And this: they feel that the most their faith amounts to is just that: mere talk. They've joined a talking cult." Mark Buchanan, "Stuck on the Road to Emmaus," *Christianity Today*, 43:8 (July 12, 1999), 55.

dissonance will deepen, and we will need their help all the more. They usually advise evangelicals to stay away from therapists who are not "biblically-based," since any exploration of our inner worlds that is not guided by other keepers of the family secret might threaten to expose it, and then the market for their services will shrink.

It is likely, in other words, that many evangelicals will not identify the above symptoms as symptoms. Many evangelicals I know personally do not agree with me that evangelicals even have a family secret. They see the world through very different lenses than mine. In some cases, the issue between us may never be settled, although I am eager to continue the dialogue.

• • •

YOU WILL NOT BE A WHOLE PERSON

Therapists who work with dysfunctional families have a name for the kind of father I have been describing. They call him an "impinging parent." They know that people raised by impinging parents find it difficult, even as adults, to attain a sense of themselves as real and alive. They notice that such people find it difficult to forge healthy, fulfilling attachments to other people.[14]

I want to describe here how impinging parents—out of their own inner pain—steal the very souls of their children. I believe evangelicals who live with an impinging "heavenly Father" are as

---

14 My treatment here supplements the insights of Richard Schwartz's Internal Family Systems Therapy with "object relations" and "attachment theory" approaches to family therapy. I have benefited especially from Adam Phillips, *Winnicott* (Cambridge, MA: Harvard University Press, 1988); Maggie Scarf, *Intimate Worlds: How Families Thrive and Why They Fail* (New York: Ballantine Books, 1995); Deborah Anna Luepnitz, *The Family Interpreted: Psychoanalysis, Feminism, and Family Therapy* (New York: Basic Books, 1988); Robert Karen, *Becoming Attached: First Relationships and How They Shape Our Capacity to Love* (New York: Oxford University Press, 1998).

susceptible to this soul theft as are children who live with impinging earthly fathers or mothers.

What do we need, as children, to attain the sense of ourselves as real and alive—to experience a freedom to be ourselves and to forge healthy, fulfilling relationships? We need primary care-givers who are aware enough of their own needs and feelings—their own internal parts—to relax those needs and feelings while they tune in and attend to ours. This attunement helps the infant learn that the world is a safe place in which to feel exactly what she feels and need exactly what she needs. In the presence of an attuned and responsive parent, an infant learns that her needs are important, that they can be expressed, that they will in some rough sense be received and met. This generalized trust will later make it possible for an adult to take the risks necessary for growth and fulfillment.

As the infant develops, she will learn that reality cannot in every case be trusted to meet her needs and that other people have important needs too. She will learn not to expect immediate gratification and she will learn, largely by watching, how to be responsive to others. But ideally, she will learn to do so without disowning the parts of her that live inside her.

As the child grows, he thrives to the degree that he receives "the unconditional love of the care-giving parent—a free-flowing, spontaneous, and genuine commitment to the child that is proffered with no inappropriate strings attached." Unconditional love conveys to the child that he is meeting the parent's needs *just by existing*—what a remarkable gift!—not by becoming the kind of person the parent wants or by taking care of the parent's emotional needs.

If abandonment is not persistently experienced as a real possibility, the child will feel a freedom to own his inner reality in all its seeming disorder. Within the limits of broken human existence, he will fight to hold on to a sense of his own truth and bring that truth, and all parts of himself, to his human relationships. The presence of that freedom in two people is what makes relationships—in the family, in love and marriage, in friendship—genuine and secure.

Impinging parents cannot offer this kind of love. They cannot see their child as a separate self, but treat her as an extension of themselves, instruments for soothing their own feelings and meeting their own needs. Although they believe, often rightly, that they love their child, the message the child receives is "I love you so long as. . ." or "I will love you if. . ." The word "unless" is always attached to their expression of love, and what follows it, often, is some version of abandonment. This can leave a child living as "on the edge of a precipice. . . filled with dread of some nameless but terrible happening. . . [S]he could do something utterly intolerable, make a fatal misstep that brings about the loss of the [parent's] affection, caring, and protection."[15]

One therapist who works with troubled young adults has compiled a list of the "commands" an impinging parent communicates to his or her children, directly or indirectly, throughout childhood.[16] They are eerily similar to the commands the evangelical God issues to his followers:

> You will not be a whole, separate person, but remain a part of myself. I am perfect—you will not question that. You will obey all my commands. If you deviate, you will feel bad and, emotionally, I will banish you.
>
> You must not dare to need anyone or love anyone but me. I will provide everything you need. You will not leave me physically or emotionally. If you do, I will withdraw from you. You will be attuned to my needs and respond by validating and calming me. If you don't, you will feel terrible emptiness, anxiety and guilt.

---

15 Scarf, *Intimate Worlds*, 384–390.
16 Dorothea S. McArthur, *Birth of a Self in Adulthood* (Northvale, NJ: Jason Aronson, 1988), 1–37.

I will give you gifts to show you my love, but they will actually be intended to tie you more tightly to me. You and I will keep foremost in our minds your failures as a way to affirm your dependence on me. You will not attempt to achieve or master anything unless I specifically direct it. You will see badness in yourself and in others who take you away from me.

Our relationship is more important than any other. You may not express any negative feelings about our relationship to me or to anyone else. If you do, you will feel guilty. You cannot be angry with me, but I can be angry with you. If I am angry with you, I will threaten to abandon you. Whatever goes wrong in our relationship is your fault.

You will never outgrow this dependent relationship because I need you to be this way. You will try to love me, but you will never feel you are loving me enough.

Neither of us must ever come to understand or admit the manipulativeness of these commands or the lack of permission they give you to be yourself.

Commands like these may "work" to tie a child to a parent, but that bond will not be secure, trusting or satisfying. The child will not be able to be herself with the parent, and will never come to know who the parent really is. The child will always be a *child*, never an adult, and the relationship forged will be one of dependence, deceit and mutual manipulation.

Under the sway of such a parent, a child will also have difficulty forging a truly secure attachment to his or her own self. The child "is not at liberty to be who he really is. . . It is his never-ending task to shape himself into someone who will be found acceptable and worthy of love. . . In this kind of emotional framework. . . the dependent youngster is always tirelessly performing." The child will learn to ignore whatever is inside that might threaten the relationship

—must try constantly to be thinking and feeling "good, loving thoughts" that are "acceptable in the parent's eyes." The child will believe the all-seeing parent knows what is going on inside and will use internal gymnastics to banish unacceptable thoughts from conscious awareness.

This means the child's feelings will be tightly controlled. Her own thoughts will seem dangerous. The insecurely attached child spends a lot of energy learning "not to know."[17] In the shadow of an impinging parent, she learns to be rigid, mistrustful and joyless. She chokes off spontaneity. She "must remain in a state of constant alert about what is wanted by the parent. . ." She will not feel free to explore, to follow her questions, to range widely in the surrounding environment, but will have to stay within relatively narrow boundaries, working hard to follow the rules—as unreliable as they may seem.

What the child of an impinging, *conditionally loving* parent is learning, day after day, is to become what many therapists call a "false self." If the child must always be attuned to the parent's feelings, wishes and needs, and respond in a way that makes the parent happy, he does not learn to acknowledge, welcome or understand his own feelings, wishes and needs.

In order to avoid emotional abandonment, he becomes compliant. "Tell me how to keep you loving me," a part of him says, "and I will be sure to do it. It is you that really matters, not me." Under the control of this protective part, people cannot feel alive and real. They cannot become truly themselves.

•   •   •

---

17 Scarf, *Intimate Worlds*, 389–390.

ARE WE FOR REAL?

It is not much of a reach to hear in the "commands" of the impinging parent the "commands" often communicated or implied by the stony-hearted—and, I trust, false—God of authoritarian religious traditions like evangelicalism. They are toxic, twisted, manipulative *counterfeits* of the Ten Commandments and other biblical texts, whispered deep into the human spirit by a voice one's conscious ears are trained not to hear.

The last command—"Neither of us must ever come to understand or admit the manipulativeness of these commands or the lack of permission they give you to be yourself"—makes it hard even to identify them as commands. This helps account for their continuing power, and for the fact that they remain a secret.

Unless we do identify and free ourselves from them, we may never rest in the love of God and feel the freedom to be the vulnerable and beautifully complex human beings we are. Instead, we will try to be "what God wants us to be," interpreting that maxim in ways that do not permit us to be free, alive, flowing and real. We will be under the power of parts of us that, understandably, are determined to protect us from a tyrannical divine parent. These fearful parts will make us seem false: submissive, obsequious and compliant.

But when we speak with other Christians, we will have to *claim* to feel truly alive and real, *claim* to be freely ourselves, and behave in ways that give support to these claims—because that is what pleases the impinging God. We will sing songs about being "happy all the time"[18] and insist on smiling placidly at funerals. We will "practice"

---

18 A Sunday school song from my childhood:

> "Since Jesus Christ came in and saved my life from sin,
> I'm in-right, out-right, up-right, down-right happy all the time."

The factual inaccuracy of these lines never crossed my mind at the time.

warmth and friendliness because the impinging God requires that we show others how much we love them. We will scrupulously follow all the rules, avoiding what we interpret to be "the appearance of evil." We will unwittingly become "false selves" for God.

But others from outside the evangelical fold may look at us and ask: "Are they for real?" They may be impressed by our moral discipline without being attracted to us as persons—unless they, too, wish to be paragons of virtue instead of simply themselves. They may find us hard to get to know "down deep" and leave our company feeling unsatisfied and unconnected. If they join us for a while, they may discover that our relationships with one another do not live up to their billing—they seem shallow, superficial, contrived. They may sense that our "love" for them is intermixed with duty and is easily distracted. They may discover that, beneath our placid exterior and bland smiles, lurk repressed anger, hatred, intolerance.

The phrase "plastic people" might come to their minds when evangelicals are mentioned.

Outsiders, especially the non-religious, are quite adept at noticing the "false selves" of American evangelicals. But teenagers on the inside have an eye for it too. A college student once told me this story from his teenage years:

> My parents were respected lay leaders in an evangelical church. They showed up at church every Sunday morning, and my three younger brothers and I had to go with them.
>
> My older brother and I had usually been out carousing until the wee hours of the morning, so we were in a foul mood when our parents came to wake us up. Actually, all four of us hated getting up for church. Mom and Dad had to nag us out of bed, badger us into wearing something "presentable," and plead with us to wolf down some breakfast. They'd almost *physically push* us out of the house and into the car.

All the way to church, we'd sit in the back bitching and moaning and scrapping with one another while our parents yelled at us to straighten up. We always got to church a couple minutes late. Mom would herd us up the front steps, still grousing at each other. But the minute we stepped inside the door, we turned into perfect angels. The only pews still empty were usually at the front of the sanctuary. Everybody's eyes would follow us. I knew exactly what they were thinking, because I'd hear them saying it to our folks after church: "What a fine family you have! Such good Christian boys!"

I would sit there in the pew and look around me. Here were all these fine Christian families, all decked out in their Sunday best, smiling their Sunday smiles, just like us. I knew a lot of those kids. They had been out all night, too—drugs, sex, alcohol, general mischief. I knew their families were as messed up as my family was. But there we sat, singing our hymns and praying and looking for all the world like perfect little Christian families.

I remember one Sunday having this sudden urge to do something really crazy. I wanted to get up and walk to the front and stand there on the platform and open my pants and piss on the carpet. And then I wanted to look around at the whole bunch of them and say: "See this? This is me. This down here on the carpet? This is *real*."

I never did it, of course. But sometimes I wish I had.

•   •   •

ANOTHER "SECOND COMING"

Often, at the beginning of a semester, I'll take a long walk with one of my students. We usually warm up by telling each other about ourselves. My student will describe his family in ways that are either very positive or very bland. Sometimes, I'll hear a slight hint that there is more beneath the surface, but I don't usually probe for details. The student will rarely say anything to imply that he doesn't have perfect parents and a happy family life.

And then I'll take a walk with this same student two or three months later. In the meantime, he's gotten to know me as a receptive person who welcomes the truth, who doesn't expect people to be perfect, who doesn't condemn. He's begun to trust me with his secrets. As we round a bend, he'll say: "Remember when we were walking right here in August, and I was telling you about my wonderful family? Now you know they aren't so wonderful." The student has been carrying a family secret, and he's decided it's not important to carry it any longer. By telling it to me, he's practicing telling it to himself. Sometimes, he'll say it feels like a load has been lifted from his shoulders.

In part, I believe, such students have found the courage to tell the truth because they have discovered that there are many selves inside them, and who they "really" are isn't any single one of them. So the part of them that is critical of their parents—even sometimes quite angry—is only one of many parts. There are other parts in there—like the one they first let me see, the one that defends their parents as perfect individuals. They have a part that feels guilty and disloyal when it criticizes their parents. They have a part that treasures their parents. They have a part, usually hidden quite deeply, that feels sad, hurt, abandoned by their parents and yearns for reconnection. These diverse parts jockey constantly for primacy in their inner system, which leaves them feeling emotionally confused—even, as they might say, "messed up."

As we talk, I try to listen to all these parts with openness and respect. I search for the right time, the right words, to let the student know that each part, no matter how disturbing, is attempting to play some positive role, even though it may take a while to understand exactly how.[19] Each part has an important story to tell, a story that makes sense once we hear it out. I suggest they consider the possibility that, buried beneath all these parts, there is a real self that is calm and clear, compassionate and curious.[20]

This real self can be trusted to receive every part of them with warmth and understanding. It can be trusted to know what is best for them. It can be trusted to know the difference between a false God and a true God, and it will always be drawn by the true God.[21]

If there is a part in many of us, as evangelicals or religious people generally, that is angry at, hurt by, or even hates the God we have been taught about since childhood, I believe it is for good reason. If we keep our anger and hurt a secret, I believe it is because other parts live in us, parts that are afraid of God or parts that feel guilty. None of these parts is the whole of us. But it is important that we welcome, respect and listen to them all. Until we do that, it will be harder to

---

19 I believe the same about every voice—or every part—that has had a role in shaping an unhealthy and harmful evangelical theology: the part of Billy Graham that warns us of eternal damnation, the part of Carl Henry that purveyed a coldly, rational "Tetragrammaton," the part of Stephen Paine's father that impressed on his son a God who might throw him away, the part of John Stott that allows holy love to obscure the meaning of love, the part of the Baptist pastor that speaks for an alienating and punitive "Lord," the part of my father that believes there is a limit to God's forgiveness, the part of the impinging parent that impinges.

Each of these parts, although caught up in a web of fear and without perspective on itself and its own true needs, intends a good, protective purpose. They give us help in avoiding the wrath of a God whose punitive nature is fixed in the substratum of our guts; or they offer rational explanations to medicate the painful emotional dissonance we might otherwise feel in the presence of the wrathful God; or they keep us from expressing outright our discomfort with this God—a discomfort which, all by itself, is enough to activate God's seemingly vengeful spirit. Each of them, in other words, helps us find ways to live with a God whose wrath we cannot afford to question. Each needs to be acknowledged, understood and loved. That is the only way these different parts will find healing within a transformed inner world, find ways to express themselves less self-destructively, and move the person toward wholeness.

20 Schwartz describes this "true" self beautifully in his *Introduction to the Internal Family Systems Model* (Oak Park, IL: Trailheads Publications, 2001), 43–58.

21 As Jesus said: ". . . when I am lifted up from the earth, [I] will draw all people to myself" (John 12:32).

hear from our real self. Our real self knows God is all good. Our real self is drawn to the good God by a genuine love, a love that looks and feels nothing like the "love" that our "false" or protective evangelical parts strive so earnestly and tirelessly to feel.

So I want to say a few words in favor of these so-called "false selves."[22]

"False selves" are not consciously trying to deceive anybody. They are just trying to be, and do, what is expected of them. They are trying to protect us from abandonment, by God or by others. They are a plea for love.

A religiously-motivated "false self" serves an important adaptive function—protecting other parts of us, exiled deep inside, from being further injured by an impinging, stony-hearted God. To leave the softer, needy, scared or lonely parts of us at the mercy of a stony-hearted God (not to mention the censure of stony-hearted religious people) is to risk a deeper wounding.

The evangelical "false self" gives us the best protection it can in an environment that is not truly nurturing. It reflects a primitive awareness that, at an emotional level, God is not taking care of us, so we had better take care of ourselves. It resembles the "self-sufficiency" that Carl Henry and Edward Carnell projected onto God, but it is utilized as a defensive maneuver to protect us from this very God.

I want to be very clear about this: I am not launching a moral crusade against "false selves," calling in the False-Self Police, urging

---

22 Schwartz uses the word "part" instead of "false self." I use the term "false self" with misgivings. It sounds pejorative—to be "false" seems to be "bad." I don't mean it that way. I use it, in part, because it is ubiquitous in both therapeutic and contemplative language and because, when we meet it in another, it does seem to us as if something "false" is happening. I think of a "false self" as a part of us that's not telling the whole truth. It *is* a part of us, but it parades as the whole of us, or the deepest part of us. It isn't "the Self" as Schwartz describes it. Adam Phillips offers one take on the "false self" in *Winnicott*, 133–134. Thomas Merton, in *New Seeds of Contemplation* (New York: New Directions Books, 1961), 21–34, has a specifically Christian understanding of the term.

evangelicals to identify and squelch their "false selves" and "just get real" with one another. Moral crusades do not produce freedom or wholeness—they just produce even falser selves. Genuine growth toward authenticity and the freedom of Jesus does not come in response to a new list of "shoulds." "False selves" will not go away, but they will lose much of their power, and perhaps find more construc- tive roles to play, when the purpose for which they were constructed is no longer necessary.

I believe the evangelical "false self" camouflages, beneath its surface of sunny compliance, another part of us that holds a well- founded anger at a stony-hearted and impinging God. Under the guise of protecting the heavenly "parent" from criticism, the "false self" protects us in the only way it knows. But it is only biding its time. The evangelical "false self" is waiting for the "blessed appearance" of a God whose love is the genuine article—not impinging, but liber- ating; not "holy" and punitive, but freely forgiving.

Evangelicals are known for eagerly awaiting the "second coming of Christ." Perhaps, we are a people crying out of the depths for the dawning of some *really* good news: the coming of a real God, a God who will show us God's genuine humanity, revealing to us One who is closer to us than we are to ourselves.

Even so come, Lord Jesus.

PART TWO

IN THE COMPANY OF
THE HUMAN JESUS

*"I understand Jesus' love, but God is another story.
I don't find them to be alike at all."*

"Maybe your understanding of God is wrong."
William P. Young*

---

* *The Shack: Where Tragedy Confronts Eternity* (Los Angeles: Windblown Media, 2007), 163–164.

CHAPTER 6

The Human Jesus
Meeting a God who comes in weakness

**If Christ is weak and humble on earth,
then God is weak and humble in heaven.**
Jurgen Moltmann[1]

AT THE OUTSET OF THIS BOOK, I confessed that I have come to love Jesus with all my heart. Now I would like to tell you about that Jesus, and invite you to listen for the good news he brings—good news about God, and also about you and me.[2]

---

1   *The Trinity and the Kingdom: The Doctrine of God* (Minneapolis: Fortress Press, 1993), 31. Moltmann is paraphrasing the view of British scholar C. E. Rolt in a 1913 book, *The World's Redemption*, (London: Longmans, Green and Co., 1913), 27. It was Martin Luther who first enticed me to begin imagining God through the lens offered by the human Jesus. I did not read the German Lutheran theologian, Jurgen Moltmann, until I had completed what I thought would be the final draft of this book. I was surprised at how closely my own thinking paralleled Moltmann's. I have gone back and added some of his insights and inserted occasional references to his work for readers seeking more detailed and comprehensive theological explorations of the themes I pursue in these chapters.

2   Jesus' story is told in the four Gospels. The Gospels do not present a seamless argument for the kind of Jesus—or God—I will describe in these pages. Each Gospel writer brings his own interests and sensibilities to his story-telling, and each reader brings the same to his or her reading. Story-tellers cannot foresee the way their readers will read them. I leave open the question of whether the Gospel writers consciously intended their stories to be interpreted as I am interpreting them. I am hopeful, however, that they did.

I will focus on the stories in which I hear the good news of a genuinely human, genuinely loving God. Many more stories are available to make the same point. At the same time, the

Hearing fresh words about Jesus is not as simple as it seems. In our "Christian" cultures, Jesus has long been deep-frozen as a cultural icon. Stories about him have been told and retold for two thousand years, each retelling further obscuring this mysterious person within a cloud of toxic familiarity. Jesus' name is used reflexively in curses and blessings. His face inspires mountains of art objects, the kind hung in fancy museums and the kind sold by street-corner vendors. He has his own line of jewelry.

Jesus' birthday celebration occupies a full month of every year. In his name, we go to shopping malls blaring with songs about a baby in a manger and his charming sidekick, Rudolph. We buy whatever shop-owners decide to display this year and give it all to our family and friends in Jesus' name. A few months later, when Easter arrives, we color eggs and eat marshmallow bunnies for Jesus. We cannot escape Jesus. He is *everywhere*. Which very often means that the real Jesus is nowhere.

It seems almost unbelievable that, when the actual Jesus first emerged from obscurity as a young man in first century Palestine,

---

Bible tells stories that seem, at first glance, to point in a different direction. First glances are often heavily influenced by previous interpretive models; second and third glances may produce new insights. But after many glances, some texts still rub harshly against the God I see in Jesus. This frustrates me, but it also stimulates me. The Bible's resistance to simplification is a constant invitation to something wild and unpredictable just beyond my reach.

My trust for a genuinely human, loving God is not the result of an "objective" or "scientific" study of the Bible or a comprehensive review of Bible scholarship. It grew in me, rather, in the aftermath of a singular event in my life, a very brief, unanticipated moment in which a naked, dying God became strangely present to me. I will tell this story in chapter 8. I have not before or since encountered anything so real. If I express myself with urgency or seeming certitude in these pages, it is not because my ideas are based on incontrovertible evidence or because I have special access to ultimate truth. It is simply the result of a unique moment in which my life was cast in a new light and I was thrust forward in a new direction. I respect the paths that others have taken. But as Martin Luther said, "Here I stand, I cannot do otherwise." (Quoted in Roland H. Bainton, *Here I Stand: A Life of Martin Luther* (New York: New American Library, 1950), 144.

he was not the fully-credentialed messiah—born to a virgin, away in a manger, surrounded by shell-shocked shepherds and road-weary wise men—who inspires today's Christmas pageantry. He was probably just another unknown seeker—a bit more earnest than the rest, drawn to the Jordan River by some vaguely-felt inner hunger, enchanted by a sharp-tongued prophet named John. Once he had talked John into baptizing him, he disappeared again, this time into the Judean wilderness. The Judean wilderness was not a hospitable place. John's disciples might have wondered whether he was gone for good.

But he wasn't. After a couple months he returned, and he brought with him a new sense of urgency. He had something on his mind, and he needed to say it. Sometimes that "something" is described as a "message" or "word" (Mark 1:14); other times it's "the gospel" or "the good news of God" (Mark 1:14). Often, the texts simply say Jesus preached, with no attempt to tell us what he said (Mark 1:38). He seemed to be wandering without a clear destination, stopping to share his message wherever a crowd gathered or an individual called out.

Early on in Jesus' travels, a strange man spotted him in a synagogue and shrieked: "The Holy One of God!" (Mark 1:24) Jesus asked him to be silent and dismissed the frenzied spirit that had seized him. The man convulsed and shouted—and suddenly everything was back to normal. Onlookers didn't know what to make of this. For all his oddness, there was something compelling about this Jesus—an air of authority, some said.

Where did he get it? Where was he from?

•   •   •

"WATCH OUT: YOU'RE BEING FOOLED!"

If we place ourselves into Mark's stories as spectators of the unfolding drama, we might catch a fresh glimpse of this man we know as Jesus. Putting ourselves there, for a moment, what do we see?

A wandering teacher, perhaps; a bit weather-beaten from too many days in the sun, too many nights under the stars. He roams the countryside, enters a town and leaves it almost as quickly. A little clutch of friends shuffles along behind him. Curious crowds run out to see him. The sick and the mad clamor for his attention.

He speaks to people, or simply touches them, and with amazement and gratitude, they testify to being healed. Jesus asks them please not to talk about it. His ears seem to hear what other ears don't, especially the silent cries of human need. He cannot resist faces lined by suffering. His reputation as a miracle worker spreads, the crowds swell, and all this disturbs him. From time to time, he steals away without warning. His friends lose track of him, get worried and go looking for him.

He's got an urgent message—that's clear. But what is it? He doesn't spell it out. He seems reluctant to make too much sense. Often, he answers questions with anecdotes, puzzles or questions. He asks his followers to love their enemies, but then he tells stories that seem to approve of people who condemn or destroy their enemies (Matthew 21:33; 22:13). He teaches infinite forgiveness, but then tells stories about the torments of hell. He tells his disciples to carry a sword, and then chastises one of them for using it in his defense (Luke 22:36, Matthew 26:51–52). He's obviously not a systematic expositor and, aside from some mysterious tracings in the dirt, he never writes a single word for posterity.

The late French writer, Jean Sulivan, has eyes for this man's strangeness:

He captivates crowds, but not in the manner of political leaders who need crowds in order to exist. He. . . simultaneously wants to show himself and to hide. He has a powerful understanding of propaganda, but ultimately uses it to bring individuals to act for themselves. Imagine a public relations genius, who successfully launches a product and suddenly declares, "Watch out: you're being fooled! It has nothing to do with miracles—it's something else." Or better, imagine a powerful political leader who breaks the illusion, stops using his talent for deception, reverses the supposed order of priorities, and talks directly to the men and women of today. He'd be shouted down, eliminated.[3]

Even Jesus' closest friends consider him an enigma. Sometimes, surrounded by a crowd, he seems strangely alone. His silence can speak more loudly than any words. His befuddled followers trail him down dusty roads, arguing in hushed tones about his latest epigram. He is at once serious and relaxed, intense and spontaneous, preoccupied and startlingly present to the aching hearts of humans in trouble. Sometimes, he seems to be brooding, his spirit troubled. Occasionally, he gets angry and shows it. He weeps in public. He spits on eyes, kneels in the dust, walks on water.

He seems to enjoy the company of losers and knaves, and they like him in return.[4] He says he is fishing for human beings, but he does it by talking in riddles. He seems to understand and even approve when his listeners go away annoyed, confused or sorrowful.

He is not always tactful or pleasant. No writer records him as laughing. He can be acerbic, difficult, argumentative. He's not

---

3 *Morning Light: The Spiritual Journal of Jean Sulivan* (New York: Paulist Press, 1988), 42–43. Sulivan's journal is in a class by itself—a spiritual meditation that is theologically provocative, intellectually challenging and personally nourishing.

4 The relationship Jesus had with "sinners," if we take it seriously, may say all we need to know about God: that God *likes* us, and once we really "get" that, we will like God in return.

afraid—sometimes he seems almost eager—to offend religious people. When he breaks rules, he does it in the presence of the people it will most disturb. Sometimes, he goes out of his way to shock. Within earshot of his mother he asks: "Who is my mother?" (Mark 3:33). The most enthusiastic of his disciples he calls "Satan" (Mark 8:33).

Jesus is hard to pin down. His descriptions of his exact relationship to God vary widely depending on the occasion or the audience. In the very same breath, he can call people bad names—hypocrites, fools, snakes—and then assure them they are his "little chicks" whom he would like to gather under his wing (Matthew 23:37).

A peace-loving man, he says he comes to bring a sword (Matthew 10:34). In the end, it is a Roman sword that draws his blood. He stands bound and mute before his accusers. He goes to the slaughter like a lamb. As he hangs dying, he asks God to forgive his killers, even though they haven't asked for forgiveness, nor shown the slightest interest in it. Although his enemies act like they know exactly what they are doing, he tells the world, in his dying breath, that they don't. Then he asks God, with whom he claims the deepest intimacy, why he has abandoned him (Luke 23:34, Mark 15:34).

Does this odd fellow look like someone we'd want to call "God"?

•　　•　　•

AN AWESOME GOD?

Here I am, using that word "God." I wish I could avoid it. It has become such a problematic word.

"*God*," writes Martin Buber, "is the most heavy laden of all human words. None has become so soiled, so mutilated."[5]

"How to *unsay* the ponderousness we humans attribute to this

---

5 Quoted in Nicholas Lash, *Easter in Ordinary*, 203.

word, 'God'?" asks David James Duncan. "How to strip the man-added dreck from the word that the Being may be loved for Who the Being is?"[6]

Is it possible that some of this soiling, this "man-added dreck," appears in our imagining of a God who is not too small, but rather too big?

Listen to it. *God.* Doesn't it just *feel* big?

Powerful orators tend to draw it out: *Gaaahd.* Can you hear it erupting out of the mouth of James Earl Jones or Laurence Olivier, echoing into the silence of a cavernous stone cathedral? The word just *tastes* big. It *feels* weighty, all-encompassing, super-sized. It insists on sharing its aura with us: we levitate just a bit if we say it with the right inflection. It begs to be written large and bold: GOD![7]

Typically, we capitalize the word when it refers to *our* God. Other people's gods do not deserve this honor. Compared to *our* God, other gods seem *small, weak, ineffectual.* We find it hard to believe that people actually worship these false gods. Stories illustrating their supernatural powers are obvious fabrications. Our own miracle stories are not fabrications, but literal truth. In praise-chorus language, *our* God is an *awesome* God—and he's the *only* awesome God out there.

Like every human word, but perhaps more than most, the word "God" drags behind it the accumulated baggage of its journeys through time and culture. Stored securely in its Christian baggage are these assertions:

---

6   *God Laughs and Plays* (Great Barrington, MA: Triad Books, 2006), 24.

7   Nancy Mairs adds a slightly different emphasis: "Whenever one speaks of God, God goes stiff as a corpse. . . [A]t the moment of utterance the potentiality of God coalesces and freezes into Something That She Is but not All That She Is." *Ordinary Time: Cycles in Marriage, Faith, and Renewal* (Boston: Beacon Press, 1993), 11–12.

Some people have more extreme responses to the word "God." Film-maker Oliver Stone embraced Buddhism as a way to "get out from under the monstrously oppressive God the Father." Quoted in Orville Schell, "Searching for the Dalai Lama," *The Nation* (April 3, 2000), 18.

- God created the world out of nothing.
- God destroyed the world in a flood.
- God parted the Red Sea.
- God destroyed Jericho.
- God used the Babylonians to punish the Hebrews.
- God destroyed the Babylonians for punishing the Hebrews.
- God raised Jesus from the dead.
- God sits on a throne in heaven.
- God will destroy the wicked.

The most memorable stories seem to be about creating, controlling, destroying.[8] They seem, if we read them on the surface, to call for great size and great power. The moment my tongue begins to form the word "God," my mind activates its stock of God-stories to filter out anything that might be less than super-human in size and power.[9]

Evangelical theology condenses the long biblical and post-biblical conversation into a few lofty metaphors that leave no doubt about God's overweening size and power: Heavenly Father, Sovereign Lord, Mighty Creator, Wise Lawgiver, Supreme Judge, Coming King. Carl Henry's God is in good company with these inflated images.

Evangelicals, drawing on the work of scholars like Henry and his numerous spiritual descendants, like to compile lists of God's

---

8 It isn't within the scope of this book to offer an overall reinterpretation of these stories. But I believe it is an urgent Christian task, and a stimulating and edifying opportunity, to reread each of them through the lens offered by the person and words of Jesus. How would the one portrayed in weakness on the cross read these texts?

9 One of my students answered the college application question that asked, "What are you thinking and feeling about Christianity these days?" by writing: "I think I am small and God is big." John Caputo asks: "Has not the name of God from time out of mind been associated with unlimited power so that 'God Almighty' is practically a redundant expression?" Caputo's *The Weakness of God: A Theology of the Event* offers a philosophically serious, but playfully-written companion volume to this chapter.

"attributes." The most common entries are omnipotence, omniscience, omnipresence, holiness, justice.[10] Love, of course, usually appears, but often at the bottom of the pile. The labels at the top don't remind us of a wandering, enigmatic storyteller who gets lynched, and loves the lynchers.

When evangelical Christians speak of God, the actual flesh-and-blood Jesus—to whom the church gives second shrift in the Trinity—takes a back seat to "God the Father."[11] This replicates the priorities of patriarchal culture, which had an even tighter grip on the church in ancient culture than it has on the church today. But "the Father" is an invisible entity, a "spirit," while Jesus was an

---

10 Grace M. Jantzen, in *Becoming Divine: Towards a Feminist Philosophy of Religion* (Bloomington, IN: Indiana University Press, 1999), calls him "the omni-everything God of classical theism" (74).

11 Christian teaching that the Son is "begotten of" and "sent by" the Father gives plausibility to calling the Father the "first" person of the Trinity. But the centrality of the Son in revealing what kind of Father the Bible is pointing to—someone Jesus addresses in intimate terms as "Abba"—and the belief that in Jesus we see the fullest portrait of real humanity might justify calling the Son the "first" person. Of course, this usage is subversive of the authority of fathers in the patriarchal society in which the trinitarian formula was first worked out.

Jurgen Moltmann emphasizes the Father's warm relational bonds with the Son: "A father who both begets and bears his son is not merely a father in the male sense. He is a motherly father, too. . . He has to be understood as the fatherly Mother of his only begotten Son." This Father has nothing to do with the patriarchal hierarchies that have dominated the Christian West, giving credence to such images as "father of the church," "father of his country," "father of the family" or "father of the universe." *The Trinity and the Kingdom: The Doctrine of God* (Minneapolis: Fortress Press, 1993), 162–164.

Moltmann is probably the leading "theologian of the cross" today—a "thin tradition," according to Douglas John Hall, which winds like a frail thread through the history of Christian theology. *Lighten Our Darkness: Toward an Indigenous Theology of the Cross* (Philadelphia: Westminster Press, 1976), 115ff.

Hall's *God and Human Suffering: An Exercise in the Theology of the Cross* (Minneapolis: Augsburg Publishing House, 1986) is a helpful introduction to the theology of the cross in accessible language. Another recent—and Reformed—voice in this tradition is William C. Placher, *Narratives of a Vulnerable God: Christ, Theology, and Scripture* (Louisville KY: Westminster John Knox Press, 1994).

historically verifiable figure about whom we have extensive eyewitness accounts.

Evangelicals like to quote the text in John's prologue: "No one has ever seen God; the only Son, who is in the bosom of the Father, he has made him known" (John 1:18). If Christians believe Jesus uniquely reveals the invisible God, why don't we pay more attention to the visible fellow from Nazareth when we set out to describe God?[12] Our tendency to default to the more abstract, invisible "Father" suggests, again, that we have imported into Christianity the uncritical association of the term "God" with super-human size and super-human power. An invisible God invites us to project our human assumptions about God more freely.

Informally, evangelicals use what often seem like nicknames for their God: "the Lord," they call him—although this can also refer to Jesus—or "the Almighty." In the following pages, I will follow their lead and refer to the super-human, evangelical God—a false God, I submit, whose character I explored in *Part One*—as "the Almighty." That nickname nicely distinguishes him from the smaller God I glimpse in Jesus.[13]

I wonder if Jesus wasn't offering a critique of "the Almighty" when he called himself "the human son"?[14]

---

12 In many ways, evangelicals do pay attention to Jesus, but the Jesus they have in mind is the triumphant risen Lord and King.

13 Many biblical texts encourage me to take seriously the human Jesus as an "incarnation" of and reliable guide to the character of God. For example: "He is the. . . exact imprint of God's very being" (Hebrews 1:3). "No one has ever seen God. The only Son, who is close to the Father's heart, has made him known" (John 1:18). "For in him all the fullness of God was pleased to dwell. . . For in him the whole fullness of deity dwells bodily" (Colossians 1:19, 2:9).

14 Usually, I will use the term "human son" as a way to "freshen up" and de-masculinize the familiar phrase "Son of Man," which the Gospels identify as Jesus' self-description. The phrase has a long exegetical history and there is little scholarly consensus about its origin and meaning. For a guide to the relevant scholarship, see Delbert Burkett, *The Son of Man Debate: A History and Evaluation* (Cambridge: Cambridge University Press, 1999). Walter Wink's interpretation of this phrase, in *The Human Being: Jesus and the Enigma of*

. . .

DEVIL WORSHIP

Martin Luther, that stubborn sixteenth-century monk-turned-reformer, had the right instincts about this human son, in my opinion. Although I am not a Lutheran, and am appalled by some aspects of Luther's life and thought, I do feel drawn to this uncouth, temperamental man. His struggles with a super-sized, super-oppressive God remind me of my own.

Luther owed his own moment of truth—the turning point of his life—to an encounter with a human Jesus. As a young monk celebrating his first mass, he had cringed in the presence of God the Father. For him, this Father was a harsh and condemning judge whose "righteousness" required him to punish evildoers. Luther was honest enough to admit he couldn't feel any love issuing from this God. He was sure God hated him—and he had the temerity to hate God in return! What refreshing honesty!

Because, under the church's influence, Luther's picture of God reflected a just and holy Father, and because Jesus had claimed identity with the Father, Luther assumed that Jesus was hateful, too. "From childhood on," he wrote, "I knew I had to turn pale and be terror-stricken when I heard the name of Christ; for I was taught only to perceive him as a strict and wrathful judge."[15]

This image of Jesus as the Almighty crumbled for him during his study of the Psalms. He began to suspect that the Old Testament's God of righteousness is really a warmly loving, suffering Father revealed in a small, "weak" and most unmajestic place: the bleeding flesh of a naked, dying Jesus. A trusted mentor encouraged him:

---

the Son of the Man (Minneapolis: Augsburg Fortress, 2002), is not far from my own.

15 Quoted in Erik H. Erikson, Young Man Luther: A Study in Psychoanalysis and History (New York: W. W. Norton and Company, Inc., 1958), 71.

"Take a fresh look at Jesus," he said. "He is a human being who doesn't terrorize, but comforts."

These experiences alerted Luther to the dangers of projecting onto Jesus our already-formed mental image of God. He urged Christians to pay special attention to the stories of the human Jesus—that's where God tells us what God is truly like! Avoid thinking of God in any other way than through the prism provided by the human Jesus, he wrote.[16]

Luther believed our speculations about the "majesty" of God only led us astray.[17] "You must not climb *up* to God," he wrote, "but *begin* where [God] began—in his mother's womb, he became human— and deny yourself the spirit of speculation. If you wish to be certain in your conscience and beyond danger from the devil, then you should know no God at all apart from this human [Jesus], and depend upon this, his humanity. . . Hasten to the crib and to

---

16 Luther was not denying the Christian doctrine of the Trinity—that God is in some very important sense three as well as one. Rather, he was questioning the assumption, common in his day as well as in our own, that the three have essentially varying types of "personality."

Lutheran theologian, Jurgen Moltmann, insists that the crucified Jesus must be the beginning and center of Christian thinking about the Trinity. This will shift the focus of that doctrine from sovereignty to relationality and from domination to love: "If a person once feels the infinite passion of God's love. . . then he understands the mystery of the triune God. God suffers with us—God suffers from us—God suffers for us: it is this experience of God that reveals the triune God." *The Trinity and the Kingdom,* 4. See also *The Crucified God* (New York: Harper and Row, Publishers, 1974).

Catholic theologian Catherine Mowry Lacugna's approach to the Trinity is compatible with Moltmann's. See *God for Us: The Trinity and Christian Life* (New York: HarperCollins Publishers, 1993). When I speak about Jesus as the one in whom I have glimpsed the Father, I am not implying that Jesus is identical with the Father or that the Father is nothing besides Jesus. But it is my conviction that what *can* be known about the *kind* of God the Father is must be harmonious with what we glimpse in Jesus.

17 Common descriptors like "majesty" and "glory" are so associated with the Almighty that they can seem useless in identifying the God glimpsed in the dying Jesus. Moltmann suggests they be used carefully and paradoxically: "God is nowhere greater than in his humiliation. God is not more glorious than in his impotence. God is nowhere more divine than when he becomes man." *Trinity,* 119.

his mother's bosom and see him, an infant, a growing child, a dying man. Then you will be able to escape all fear and errors. This vision will keep you on the right way."[18]

Luther had a warning for Christian philosophers and theologians: when you start speculating about God, unleashing your common sense or reason instead of beginning with Jesus, you're making friends with the devil. As Luther saw it, the devil knows that Christians like to repeat, mindlessly, hoary old formulas like "Christ is truly God." When the devil hears them chanting these formulas, he goes to work "to prevent the heart from joining Christ and the Father so closely and solidly together" that they appear to have "one and the same word, heart and will."

According to Luther, the devil knows he has successfully prevented Christians from merging God and Jesus closely together when he hears them say: "Yes, I certainly hear the friendly and comforting words which Christ speaks to the troubled conscience; who knows, however, how I stand with God in heaven?" By "fabricating," under the devil's influence, "one kind of Christ" and a different kind of God, Luther says, we "miss the true God" who "*does not will to be found and grasped any place else than in this Christ.*"[19]

When I first read these words, I was astounded. Luther accused the church of doing the devil's work! What gall! I warmed to Luther's confidence that true comfort can be found only in a fully human Jesus, and that this Jesus is the only reliable source for knowledge about the Father. It gave me hope that my heart could be weaned from its self-destructive allegiance to a big, unsatisfying God.

Many evangelicals—who "know" theoretically that God is

---

18 Quoted in Gerhard Ebeling, *Luther: An Introduction to His Thought* (Philadelphia: Fortress Press, 1972), 234–235. Italics added. These lines originally appeared in Luther's *Galatians* (1535) as a commentary on Galatians 1:3.

19 Quoted in Paul Althaus, *The Theology of Martin Luther* (Philadelphia: Fortress Press, 1966), 189–190. Italics added. Luther did not consistently follow his own admonition, illustrating how difficult it is to exorcise this sort of devil.

infinitely loving—feel secretly oppressed by the "majestic," powerful, harsh and condemning "Father" who lived in Luther's heart—just as I have. Luther has a simple explanation for this feeling: when we worship *this* kind of Father, we inadvertently worship the devil.[20]

•   •   •

YOU DO NOT KNOW MY FATHER

In Jesus' culture, the "scribes and Pharisees" were the most vigorous champions of the Almighty. Today, they might be known in evangelical circles as "men of God" or "the godly". They were deeply earnest and pious men who fancied themselves the last of the old-time believers. They took the scriptures seriously and tried to follow its precepts as exactly as any modern-day evangelical. They seemed invested in their reputation as those who had a special relationship with the Almighty. And they were quite certain that the Almighty looked nothing at all like Jesus.

Jesus and the godly locked horns constantly. Watching their jousts was one of the more entertaining spectator sports available in small-town Palestine.

John's Gospel records a series of encounters between Jesus and the godly. Often, these interactions get triggered by a few words from Jesus that leave the godly flabbergasted. For example, Jesus says: "I am the bread that came down from heaven" (John 6:41). To the godly, Jesus doesn't look all that heavenly—nor particularly tasty. He looks like an ordinary peasant who has stumbled out of the Galilean hills with a quick tongue, an uncertain ancestry and no religious credentials. He has a knack for healing, but so do a lot of charismatic preachers.

---

20 "The cross of Jesus marks a divide between the human God who is freedom and love and the 'counter-God' who keeps men under his sway and dominated by fear, like demons. . ." Moltmann, *The Crucified God*, 196.

Besides, he's a local boy, isn't he? We know his mother and father—isn't this Jesus the son of Joseph? Everybody has heard the rumors about Joseph and Mary. Nothing "almighty" going on in *that* corner of Nazareth.[21]

Jesus baits them again: "I am the light of the world." He tells them "the Father" has sent him. The godly feel their temperatures rising. To the godly, "Father" means "Almighty," and this fellow, for all his magic tricks, doesn't qualify. "Your testimony is not valid!" they shout. "Where is your Father? And who are *you?*"

Jesus knows they can't recognize him, and he knows why: "You do not know me, and you do not know my Father. . . If God were your Father, you would love me. You are from your father the devil. He is a murderer and a liar and you are his faithful servants." These words whip the godly into a frenzy. They accuse Jesus of "having a demon"—the equivalent of schoolyard boys shouting "same to you!" They're about to stone him, when Jesus slips away (John 8). Martyrdom is coming, but not quite yet.

Why the fury? No doubt the godly feel threatened by Jesus' popularity among the ordinary people. His authority threatens their authority. But the godly also seem mesmerized by Jesus. Their exchanges bristle with emotional energy, suggesting that, although he infuriates and appalls them, he also captivates and intrigues them. What is the hold Jesus has on their imaginations?

Perhaps the godly of Jesus' day, like the godly of our own, are divided within themselves. One part of these godly men—the part they put on public display—loves the Almighty; another part—a part they hate to show, even to themselves—chafes under the tyranny of this same Almighty. That scared, hurt part of them—so

---

21 Moltmann says Jesus' conflict with "the devout and the ruling class and their laws. . . was provoked not by his incomprehensible claim to authority as such, but by the discrepancy between a claim which arrogated to itself the righteousness of God and his unprotected and therefore vulnerable humanity. . ." *The Crucified God*, 130.

different from their public personas—is tantalized by the possibility that "the Father" may actually look like this human son.

That part of them longs for a smaller, kinder God—a God who, instead of making infinite demands on them, offers their weary spirits safe haven. A God who embraces, and invites them to embrace, their own humble humanity, just as it is; invites them to release their humble humanity from its inner prison, constructed by fear and self-hatred—a prison into which their vaunted "Almighty" has consigned it.

That would explain their fascination, but also their fury: it's directed at the part of *themselves* that *yearns* to taste the bread come down from heaven.

·   ·   ·

A HUMAN SABBATH

Of the four Gospels, Mark's seems the one least tempted to portray Jesus in a superhuman light. The early Christian church, like any human institution in its situation, must have felt irresistible pressure to make a hero of its dead Savior. That's what we do with martyred leaders. If Jesus' self-understanding was grounded, as I am arguing, in a humanity that he shared with every other human being, his followers would have had to struggle mightily to resist "infinitizing" him and to reflect his self-understanding accurately when they told stories about him.

Mark's Gospel seems to make the effort. Its Jesus appears quite determined to distinguish himself from the Almighty. Perhaps, as the earliest of the Gospel narratives, it was a bit less susceptible to the pressures of a professional clergy and institutional worship.

Mark's Gospel opens its story, however, on what can easily strike us as a most conventional note. He tells us that Jesus is God's son. If we read this with our habitual lenses, we assume Mark is trying to give weight to his narrative by assuring us its main character is associated with a big, powerful deity—"he's the Son of the Almighty!" But I think Mark has the opposite strategy in mind: instead of using a big "God" to burnish a little Jesus' credentials, he's using a little Jesus to bring a big "God" down to size. He is getting us ready for a surprise: God is someone small and human, like Jesus!

Our own eyes, if we are Christian readers, have been conditioned by two thousand years of church power-seeking, which has "almightified" Jesus to enhance its own reputation and give it some extra pull in the world. Christian eyes may not see, at first, how human Mark's Jesus is. But Mark's original readers, without two-thousand-year-old lenses, may have had the opposite problem: Jesus may have seemed strangely *unlike* the Almighty to them.

That's what I think Mark intended. Right at the start of his narrative, he named Jesus the Son of God in order to heighten rather than settle the mystery of his character (Mark 1:1). Only later did he revert to Jesus' own self-understanding: the human son. He hoped his readers would scratch their heads and say: This *human* is the Son of *God*? That's not any God *I'm* familiar with!

Early in Mark's Gospel, a disabled man is lowered by his friends through a roof and into Jesus' presence (Mark 2:3). He wants Jesus to heal him. Instead of healing him—I'll bet there's a twinkle in Jesus' eye—Jesus forgives the man's sins. The godly are outraged. This is blasphemy! Only God can forgive sins! Jesus simply says: "The human son has authority on earth to forgive sins"—and tells the man to get up and walk home.

What is Jesus getting at?

If your God is big and strong—let's say he's an evangelical God—you will think: Jesus agrees with the godly about God's lofty prerogatives. Only God can forgive sins. Jesus wants to show that he's lofty, too, just like the Almighty, so he forgives some sins.

But what if Jesus wants to wean the godly from their big, lofty

God? Then he might *collapse* the distance between what is God-like and what is human, knocking the props out from under the godly's conveniently sharp distinctions. If a *human* son can forgive sins, then maybe the godly have a wrongly inflated view of the Almighty.[22] God and humans—at least humans at their "most human"—*share* the authority to forgive sins. It's a truly *human* thing to forgive. This interpretation would prepare the reader for later episodes when Mark reveals that ordinary humans—Jesus' disciples—can also cast out demons and heal sicknesses, just as Jesus did.

In the second story, the godly chide Jesus' disciples for gathering grain on the sabbath (Mark 2:23ff). Jesus tells them David and his companions broke similar rules. "The sabbath was made for humans," he says, "and not humans for the sabbath; so the *human* son is lord even of the sabbath."[23] It seems odd that Jesus does not defend himself by claiming "divinity," as in "I'm the Almighty, so I can break these rules." Instead, Jesus says he's like David—a human being. Again, he erases the walls built by the godly between human beings and their exalted God. Not only is the human son lord of the sabbath, but David is also lord of the sabbath. And so is humanity at large, since the sabbath was explicitly made for them. Jesus disturbs the self-aggrandizing religious categories of the godly, blurring the neat lines they have drawn between humanity and their "mightier-than-thou, holier-than-thou" God.

Through lenses like these, it is possible to see Jesus opting for humanity in his miracle-working as well. There is no doubt that extraordinary events happen in Jesus' presence. But he seems reluctant to make them happen, as if they are sending the wrong message. It disturbs him that people press him for miracles. When he raises

---

22 In his *An Essay on Criticism* (1711), Alexander Pope expressed a similarly inflated view of God: "To err is human, to forgive divine."

23 In this context, one could read "lord" less as designation of divinity than as a synonym for "superior to."

a girl from the dead, he downplays the event, telling the relieved parents she has just been sleeping. "Give her something to eat," he says, as if she had merely fainted from hunger.[24] As a rule, he deflects credit: "*your* faith has healed you," he says. He orders people to keep his miracles secret. When his disciples manage to perform similar miracles, Jesus promises that they will do *greater* works than he.

And we need to notice that, on the one occasion when a miracle seems most in order, Jesus performs none: he dies just like every human being who has ever been crucified. Once again, he surprises those for whom "Son of God" suggests the Almighty. In coming as God to be with us, he comes as a God very like us, raising questions about what it means to be God, and what it means to be human.[25]

* * *

THINKING "LITTLE"

In Mark's Gospel, Jesus likes small things. He says the reign of God is like a mustard seed, "the smallest of all the seeds on earth"

---

24 Of course, it is possible she *has* just been sleeping, or has fallen into a sleep-like state or coma.

25 John Caputo alerts us to the possible misuse of Jesus' miracles: "Dead bodies rise, substances are transmuted, impermeable walls are permeated. But none of this is to be confused with a strong force, with the power of a super-being or a super-hero to bend natural forces to his almighty will with a display of awe-inspiring power. In such deadening literalism, God becomes the ultimate laser show at Disneyworld, an exercise in world-weary fantasizing that, when we awake from our reveries, leaves us face to face with the grim visage of ineluctable reality, with the dead bodies of the tsunami or the victims of ethnic cleansing. . . The power of the kingdom is the powerless power to melt hearts that have hardened, to keep hope alive when life is hopeless, to revive the spirits of the dispirited and the despairing. . . Death is turned into life, not by a power that overpowers things, like the God of omnipotence-theology, but by the power of powerlessness. The kingdom is a field of weak forces, like forgiveness, which does not trade force for force and thereby feed the cycle of retaliation, or like the kiss with which Jesus subdues the Grand Inquisitor after the Cardinal makes a great show of how much power he has over Jesus in *The Brothers Karamazov*." *The Weakness of God*, 16.

(Mark 4:31). The biggest offering, he says, is the "two small copper coins" given by the poor widow (Mark 12:42). When his disciples notice the temple's "large stones" and "large buildings," Jesus predicts they all "will be thrown down" (Mark 13:1–2). When Jesus enters Jerusalem to the cries of "Hosanna!" he takes pains to ride an animal smaller than himself (Mark 11:7).

The male disciples, whom Mark consistently portrays as missing the point, do not like small things.[26] Jesus sees them talking out of earshot. He asks what they're talking about. They seem embarrassed. Finally, they admit they're arguing about which of them is "the greatest." Like Muhammad Ali—though with less warrant—they want to be "the greatest," to thump their chests and cry with the sports fan, "We're number one!" Jesus draws their attention to something small: a child. "Whoever welcomes one such child in my name welcomes me," he says, "and whoever welcomes me welcomes not me, but the one who sent me." One could read this text as indicating that children, Jesus and God are all similar—perhaps even identical.

James and John don't seem to get it. A little later, they try to trick Jesus into supporting their delusions of grandeur: "Give us whatever we ask you for, will you?" Jesus doesn't agree—instead, he asks them what they want. "Grant us to sit, one at your right hand and one at your left, in your glory," they say.

"You do not know what you are asking," Jesus replies. He knows they're confused about the word "glory." To them, "glory" feels superhuman; it connotes something shiny, impressive and strong. But Jesus knows that to see a person's "glory" is simply to see his or her true nature. Jesus' "glory" will be revealed when his littleness and his weakness are finally seen—specifically, when he suffers and dies. He broadens the point for the other disciples: "Whoever wishes

---

26 Remainder of this section refers to Mark 9:33–37 and Mark 10:35–45.

to become great among you must be your servant, and whoever wishes to be first among you must be slave of all. For the human son came not to be served but to serve, and to give his life a ransom for many."[27] This is not the kind of "glory" James and John have in mind.

Again and again in Mark's Gospel, I hear Jesus saying: "Let me tell you what God is like. God is *not* the Almighty. Does 'Almighty' sound humble? Does 'Almighty' sound like 'servant'? Or 'child'? God is not 'the greatest.' God is not 'number one.' God is not 'glorious.' You've got God dead wrong. So next time you hear the word 'God,' try noticing the big majestic images that first come into your head. Take those images and place them into a mental box marked 'questionable.' Then play for a few minutes with these ideas: God is 'little.' God is a 'child.' God is a 'servant.' God is a 'human son.' Imagine a naked body on a cross, and think: 'God is defenseless.' Notice how different that feels. Notice how it makes you feel."[28]

---

27 "Ransom" imagery is often used to support views of the atonement that make God out to be an ogre. It has been used to support the "penal substitutionary" view of atonement. The view of atonement I suggest in Chapter 7 interprets this language not as meaning "my suffering is to free you from the penalties for sin dictated by a holy God," but as "my suffering is the price I must pay to bring people back to themselves."

28 Annie Dillard quotes Simone Weil and Rabbi Isaac Luria to the effect that "God's hands are tied. . . Nature works out its complexities. God suffers the world's necessities along with us, and suffers our turning away, and joins us in exile. Christians might add that Christ hangs, as it were, on the cross forever, always incarnate, and always nailed." *For the Time Being*, 168–169.

Christians have added exactly this: "[A]nyone who owes his salvation to the delivering up of the Son to death on the cross can never think of God in the abstract, apart from the cross of Christ. For him, God is from eternity to eternity 'the crucified God'." Moltmann, *The Trinity and the Kingdom*, 159.

Karl Barth expresses a similar idea: "He is the Lamb slain, and the Lamb slain from the foundation of the world. For this reason, the *crucified* Jesus is the 'image of the invisible God'." *Church Dogmatics*, II/2, "The Doctrine of God" (Edinburgh: T. & T. Clark, 1957), 123.

When I told a friend that I see in Jesus a God whose hands are tied, she was appalled: "That's a God who is *no* God. . . That's not God at all!" I understand what she was feeling.

• • •

GOD HELP ME!

The two occasions on which the disciples expressed their desire to be "the greatest" and to sit next to Jesus in his "glory" both immediately follow Jesus' prediction that he will soon suffer and die. So I assume the disciples' visions of grandeur were functioning unconsciously as self-protective mechanisms of denial. To imagine that the Almighty would make them "great" was a way to diminish the dark cloud of suffering that now loomed on their horizon. It was a way to calm their deepest anxieties.

I'm quite familiar with this mechanism of denial. Many times, I have involuntarily breathed a prayer to the Almighty, seeking rescue from danger, illness, failure, or the awkward consequences of my own stupidity.[29] Even since reading Luther and embracing a smaller God in Jesus, and letting go any expectation that the Almighty stood by to extract me from difficulty, I have been susceptible to sudden pangs of fear that trigger old mental habits.

One memorable morning, as the commercial aircraft I was riding in suddenly shuddered violently and began losing altitude, I said to myself: "Jesus may not have believed in an Almighty, but right now I do!" I was frightened enough to send more than a few desperate words heavenward. I know I am not alone in conjuring, in times of trouble, a magical friend. "God help me" may be one of the most commonly uttered human expressions on the planet.

Such a God defies the very meaning of the word "God." No wonder the godly were confused.

29 Like many Christians, I have, since childhood, operated on the assumption that the Almighty and I have struck a deal: if I try my best to obey his commands, he'll take care of me. The deal assumes that God has the necessary power to act forthrightly in my defense. A defenseless God leaves me feeling betrayed and a bit resentful: if he's not the Almighty, and can't protect me, why should I go to the bother of obeying his commands? So coming to terms with the humanity of Jesus can reveal hidden aspects of our own motivations.

To believe in this kind of God, however, we must try hard to forget most of what we know about life. Although my flight sputtered to its destination, many others have not. Tens of thousands of lives have been lost in fiery crashes. News clips of such accidents often feature interviews with the few survivors, who give God credit for saving their lives; they don't say, and we don't say, that the Almighty chose to ignore the pleas of the dozens, or hundreds, sitting in the seats next to them. I may be cured of an illness, and may thank God, but I know that many people, including dear friends and relatives, have called on God and have not been cured of their illnesses. The Almighty's track record, in this game of rescue that we have assigned him, is dismal. That's something else we must forget.

And what if we lift our eyes to the wider texture of life on this planet throughout time? If God is the Almighty Fixer, how do we explain the screaming tragedy of human history? In our century, as in every century, human beings wantonly slaughter one another while it seems the Almighty, at best, stands idly by. Or worse— zealots from virtually every religious tradition, Christians included, quote the Almighty as justifying, endorsing, even celebrating the most appalling brutalities.

Among the slaughtered, of course, there are always plenty of children—children starving in Ethiopia, children dismembered in Sierra Leone, children burned in churches in Rwanda[30] and Mississippi, women and children raped and slaughtered in the Congo, children abused in every nation by adults who were themselves abused as children. There are children being abused at this

---

30 Nora Gallagher writes in her memoir of faith: "My husband, who is not a Christian, says to me in the midst of an argument, 'In Rwanda, 50% of the people were Catholic.' His words stop mine on my lips: if religious faith cannot stop genocide, of what use is it at all?" *Things Seen and Unseen: A Year Lived in Faith* (New York: Alfred A. Knopf, 1998), 4.

Philip Gourevitch has written a thoughtful and stunning account of the Rwanda genocide. *We Wish to Inform You that Tomorrow We Will Be Killed with Our Families* (New York: Farrar, Straus and Giroux, 1998).

very moment, perhaps within a mile of the room where I write these words, or the room where you read them. Where is the Almighty, in his celebrated omnipotence? Enough of this![31]

It is almost too much to bear. I try to forget it so I can greet the sunrise with a smile.

Occasionally, I am shaken out of my determined forgetfulness and reach feebly for a theodicy—some kind of explanation for or defense of the ways of God. I have not yet found one that seems persuasive. Sooner or later, they all force me to choose among five dubious alternatives: "there is no God"; "the Almighty is not good"; "the Almighty could prevent evil, but it would cost us our freedom"; "Satan causes evil"; or "trust God, his ways are unfathomable."

An answer that makes more sense to me is: God is small—a child, like Jesus said. God simply does not have the kind of power we ourselves crave and project onto him—the power that could fix our lives by tinkering with the laws of the universe. In that sense, God is a child.[32]

---

31 "The suffering of a single innocent child is an irrefutable rebuttal of the notion of the almighty and kindly God in heaven. For a God who lets the innocent suffer and who permits senseless death is not worthy to be called God at all. Wherever the suffering of the living in all its manifold forms pierces our consciousness with its pain, we lose our childish primal confidence and our trust in God." Moltmann, *The Trinity and the Kingdom*, 47. John Caputo concurs: "The massive omnipresence of natural destruction in this world as well as of unjust death and innocent suffering—violence too often committed in the name of God, or in the name of someone else's God, or lamented to have transpired 'in the absence of God'—is testimony against this omnipotence. It is not a mystery, but a mystification and a conceptual mistake. It is, moreover, an unworthy way to treat God; it is unworthy to think of God in terms of his power to deliver the goods, which is like loving a cow for its milk, as Meister Eckhart says. . . Divine omnipotence is a concept fulfilled in fantasy, spinning wildly in ideal space, with absolute velocity, while the brutal course of the real world proceeds at a slower, bloodier pace." *Weakness of God*, 79–80.

Evangelicals explain the genie's absence by suggesting that the Almighty holds back his power in order to guard human freedom. The butchery of six million Jews, or fifty million Russians, seems a large price to pay for human freedom.

32 There is one other possibility: to keep forgetting most of what we know, and keep believing in our magical deity, just because it makes us feel good. Karl Marx thought this

Which does not mean that the God whom Jesus is revealing to us does nothing at all, fiddling while Rome burns, averting "his" eyes while blood flows in the streets. Such a God would not only be powerless, but unresponsive and uncaring. No—God acts, but in the only way that pure love can act: God is continually present in the world, a living spirit that invades reality at every moment and at every place, that speaks as love does—in whispers, unceasingly— into each and every human heart. God's whisper may be heard in our dreams, in the voices of our friends and enemies, in the cries of our hearts, in deep silence. When we are listening, and when we are not.

In the most brutal episodes of human history, God has been present—not in power, the kind that we understand or reach for, but as the humble whisper of love into the hearts both of the butchers and the butchered. God cannot force us to listen to this "still, small voice" of love, this tender touch of love, much less to answer the call of love in our daily actions. When we ignore the call of love, God can do nothing at all about it—except, of course, continue to whisper, continue to call, continue to touch, continue to be present in the silence.[33] This is the meaning of "God is love."

---

was the way it mostly worked, which is why he called religion "the opium of the people." "Contributions to the Critique of Hegel's Philosophy of Right: Introduction," in Eugene kamenka, ed., *The Portable Marx* New York: Penguin Books, 1983, 115.

Marx did not belittle the suffering that cried out for such opium—he, more than most, was aware of the cruelty of life under capitalism in mid-nineteenth-century Britain. He said religion is the "expression of real suffering," and wrote movingly of religious yearning as "the sigh of the oppressed creature, the heart of a heartless world, and the soul of soulless conditions" (115). But he did not believe a false god offered real relief.

33 Melissa Raphael argues that God was present in Auschwitz in the small human gestures that women made, to show care to themselves and others. She suggests that theologies describing God as "hidden" or "absent" in Auschwitz demonstrate a masculinist bias. My interpretation, in Chapter 2, of the "big, powerful, sovereign" God as a surrogate father to the men who did evangelical theology at the turn of the century is consistent with Raphael's thesis. See *The Feminine Face of God in Auschwitz: A Jewish Feminist Theology of the Holocaust* (London: Routledge, 2003).

If God cannot straightforwardly micro-manage human events so as to rescue the abused child, the tortured prisoner, the cancer victim, neither can God rescue God's very own self, incarnated in Jesus. God can and will continue to whisper—to the killers as well as the killed, to the mourners as well as the mockers. God can and will hang on the gibbet in utter solidarity with the son, helplessly receiving the cruel blows rained down on the naked, dying flesh of the beloved.[34]

There is a kind of power in God's whispers. But it is the power of powerlessness. It changes things, but invisibly, unpredictably, unaccountably and, from our point of view, unreliably. It is not the kind of power we imagine, or wish, God to have.[35]

*   *   *

---

[34] "The Bible directs man to God's powerlessness and suffering; only the suffering God can help." Dietrich Bonhoeffer, *Letters and Papers from Prison*, ed. Eberhard Bethge (New York: Macmillan, 1972), 361.

[35] My portrait of God begs the question: "Didn't the creation of the world require power?" John Caputo (drawing on a close reading of Genesis 1 and on Catherine Keller's *Face of the Deep: A Theology of Becoming*) offers one helpful possibility. He suggests that God did not create from nothing, but from "a barren earth, lifeless waters, and a sweeping wind." God spoke to these pre-existing elements, "by addressing them to *bring them to life*, to awaken life in them, to make life stir through their massive limbs the way one calls a sleeper to awake. *He calls them into life; he does not bring them into being*, for the whole point is that they were there all along, from time out of mind, in a somnolence deeper and more dreamless than any sleep we can imagine. Genesis is not about being, but about life."

I suggest it is no more difficult for a small God to call creation into life than it is for a weak and dying man, in his last moments on a cross, to call somnolent human beings into life. Caputo implies as much: "So the word must keep on calling, *re*-calling, again and again, what things were called to be—alive and not dead, fruitful not barren, filled not empty. Creation is not a finished deed, but an ongoing process of re-creation." *Weakness of God*, 55–58.

TELL NO ONE

If Jesus was indeed interested in revealing a smaller, less powerful God, thereby freeing people from their captivity to the Almighty, I am convinced he did so out of a heart of compassion. He was not a debunker who took sadistic pleasure in tearing away from people the meager protections offered by the illusion of an almighty God. He was not an academic philosopher, trying to win an argument for the sake of some abstract truth. He invited people to imagine a smaller, "weaker" God for one reason only: because a God like that is the only God who promises genuine healing.

That's what I believe accounts for Jesus' diffidence about miracle cures—his tendency to ask people he cured to "tell no one" (Luke 5:14). He knew a miracle cure didn't guarantee genuine healing. Although physical suffering touched him deeply, and he sought to relieve it whenever possible, he knew the deepest scars were not physical, but emotional and spiritual. Healing for those scars was not readily visible to the naked eye.

If we listen closely to Mark's Gospel, we can hear Jesus trying to connect with the spirits of the sick even as he healed their bodies. Jesus says to the man whose friends are lowering him through the roof, "Your sins are forgiven" (Mark 2:5). Jesus calls the woman who touches him in a crowd "daughter," and says *"Your* faith has made you well" (Mark 5:34). Jesus says to Jairus, whose daughter lies at the point of death, "Do not be afraid, continue to trust" (Mark 5:36).

In each of these situations, and in many others throughout the Gospel narratives, Jesus reaches for something interior to the person. Sometimes he does it with words, sometimes with a touch, sometimes, I imagine, with a look in the eye or a tone of voice. He is looking to heal the deeper wounds, whose pains destroy the spirit.

Crowds don't tend to notice such subtleties. They love the spectacular. Jesus knew the spectacular was misleading and harmful. It associated him with size and power, and with a God of size and power. Jesus knew that an oversized God—the Almighty—cannot touch the deepest wounds. He cannot heal what really ails us. He cannot save us from ourselves.

•   •   •

RESCUING THE EXILES

Why does the big, powerful God have such a hold on us? I think it's because a part of us feels very small and very weak.[36] That part is born in childhood, when we are in fact very small and very weak. Though we "forget" about it, it continues to live inside us. When it bubbles unexpectedly to the surface, we feel like little children again. Sometimes, this feels good, but at other times it feels terrible. This part carries both the carefree delight and the confusing hurt we felt when we were small and weak.

As we grow, in order to protect ourselves from future pain, we try to make sense of whatever has hurt us—particularly when we are hurt by those we love. As children, we never make sense of our hurts by blaming the loved ones who hurt us. We always blame ourselves: I deserve to be hurt because. . . I'm bad, I'm not lovable, I'm not important, I don't exist, I'm small and weak, I'm dirty, I'm a failure, I'm stupid, I'm defective, I'll never amount to anything. Internal voices like these serve as warning signals to help us avoid doing things that will result in further hurt. But they also shape our

---

36 Richard C. Schwartz's therapeutic model has offered me tools for thinking about what it means to be a "real human being" and what it might mean for broken human beings to be "saved." I will follow his lead by describing our internal alienation (another word for the Bible's term "sin") as the enmity between our various "parts."

I deliberately avoid the use of the word "sin" in these pages, since it has been so contaminated by moralistic associations and its very sound (replicating the ominous "hiss" of the serpent) can provoke self-condemnation and images of a punitive God. But when I describe the human tendency to estrange ourselves from that which is deepest in us and in God, and when I describe (in Chapter 8) how I think humans become haters and killers of Jesus, I am exploring what I understand the Bible to be designating by the term "sin."

self-understanding. We go through life listening to voices like these repeating—for our own "good"—that we are "no good." An automatic, silent self-scapegoating distorts our behaviors and poisons our relationships with others.

To quiet these voices—or parts of us—and give us relief from their accusations, we unconsciously create other parts that try to manage our lives to keep us from being hurt. We may cultivate a public persona: an efficient organizer or a careful planner, a manager of appearances or a social climber, someone who laughs at hardship or a rigid moralist, someone with a strong will-power or a rational filter that dismisses feelings. These "parts" strive to keep the small, weak parts of us hidden, from ourselves as much as others. The skills they represent can be quite useful in everyday life. But they also leave the small, weak, childlike parts of us—the parts of us that look most like Jesus—feeling alone and desperate for healing.

Jesus knew that healing—another word for salvation—would mean rescuing those childlike parts from their exile, embracing them with compassion, and making them fully welcome members of our inner world. He knew that, for that kind of salvation, an "Almighty God" is no help at all.[37]

*   *   *

AN "ALMIGHTY" MANAGER

But why not?

Because the Almighty is just one more of those "managers" that tries to help us forget the small, weak person living inside. The

---

[37] Erik H. Erikson writes: "Every adult, whether he is a follower or a leader, a member of a mass or of an elite, was once a child. He was once small. A sense of smallness forms a substratum in his mind, ineradicably. His triumphs will be measured against this smallness, his defeats will substantiate it." *Childhood and Society,* rev. ed. (NY: W. W. Norton, 1963), 404. Because Jesus, in his supreme self-awareness, understood this dynamic, he could escape its drivenness and turn it to our salvation.

Almighty—a false God erected in a corner of our internal lives—is the trump card that the religious part of us plays, in difficult circumstances, to promise us relief from pain.

The Almighty starts out, benignly enough, as a way for children to calm the terrors of their own vulnerability in a frightening universe.[38] Children imagine God as a bigger version of their "omnipotent" parents. With a little help from these same parents, children learn to project a similar omnipotence onto God, so they can feel protected wherever they go. Their comfort is illusory, but it does help establish a necessary foundation of trust in the spirit of the young child.[39]

But if, as we grow into adulthood, we continue to see the Almighty as a protector from failure or suffering, we'll be tempted to begin waging an internal war on unwanted parts of our being. In the name of the Almighty, we'll demonize and try to expel the "unholy" parts of us; we'll repress the parts of us that are afraid and don't trust; we'll minimize the parts of us that hurt and are unhappy; we'll turn our backs on the parts of us that feel weak and small. The Almighty will have become the functional equivalent of an internal "manager," keeping vast areas of our inner world in darkness.[40] The part of us which speaks for the Almighty means us well—it wants

---

38 "[E]ach child grounds himself in some power that transcends him." Ernest Becker, *The Denial of Death* (New York: The Free Press, 1973), 89.

39 Heinz Kohut suggests that children project their infantile grandiosity (their imagined "mightiness" or invulnerability) onto the parent. Maggie Scarf summarizes this in *Intimate Worlds* (New York: Ballantine Books, 1995), 350–351. She believes this is a developmental imperative that can translate into a healthy self-esteem in later years.

40 Luther is perceptive to call this deity "the devil." The Almighty is an imposter who masquerades as a God of love while keeping us from loving all that is ourselves. To paraphrase 1 Peter 5:8, the devil—in the guise of the Almighty—walks about as a mighty lion, seeking someone to devour—and what he seems hungriest for is the most vulnerable part of us, where we feel small and insignificant. The serpent in Genesis 3 may have been appealing to the felt smallness of the first woman and man by tantalizing them with the possibility of being "like God" (Genesis 3:5).

us not to suffer. But it "protects" us by dividing us from ourselves. It despises our weak and childlike parts and buries them deep in an inner dungeon.[41]

Sooner or later, this system of self-protection wears thin. The small, weak, hurt parts of us, isolated from the rest of us, feel ever needier and find ways to break out into the light of day, hoping to be healed. As these "exiles" build pressure for release, or show themselves in unguarded moments, the Almighty in us must work all the harder. For many Christians, this is a self-defeating cycle: we use the Almighty to keep a tight lid on our needy, weaker, more scared or sorrowful parts, giving them so little love or attention that they try all the harder to break through. In their desperation they can do great damage, expressing themselves in addictive behaviors or destructive relationships. Then we apply another dose of the Almighty to condemn them and chase them back into hiding.

I believe Jesus understood all this instinctively. He knew the Pharisees were using the Almighty as a protective mechanism, to buffer them from parts of themselves that they feared and hated: their felt weakness, smallness, defenselessness, woundedness. Jesus knew the disciples were doing the same: aspiring to power, aspiring to greatness, to quiet the voices inside that told them they were weak, vulnerable, insignificant, and therefore somehow bad. Jesus knew those who thought of the Almighty as a handy Fixer, as a magical Healer, as their special possession, as guarantor of their significance or purity were only building thicker internal walls against their own suffering.

Behind these walls, the tender, wounded parts of them lived, despised and alone.

Jesus knew our salvation depends on a small God, a seemingly incapable God, a wounded God. And he seemed to know that such

---

41 Of course, shame and suffering are exactly the path to salvation to which Jesus invites us in his death on the cross.

a God would have to become dramatically visible before our protective parts would feel safe enough to turn toward their inner enemies in understanding and compassion, and make all things new.

.   .   .

WHERE IS GOD?

The Jewish writer Elie Wiesel, who survived the hell of Auschwitz as a teenage boy, knows the mystery of a God whose hands are tied.[42] He tells of the day he and thousands of inmates were made to watch as a young boy and two adults were hanged.

"Where is God? Where is he?" a man behind him cried as the silent boy's chair was tipped and he swung from his neck. The inmates were then marched past the gallows. Wiesel writes:

> The two adults were no longer alive. Their tongues hung swollen, blue-tinged. But the third rope was still moving; being so light, the child was still alive. . . For more than half an hour he stayed there, struggling between life and death, dying in slow agony under our eyes. And we had to look him full in the face.
>
> He was still alive when I passed in front of him. His tongue was still red; his eyes were not yet glazed.
>
> Behind me, I heard the same man asking: "Where is God now?"
>
> And I heard a voice within me answer him: "Where is he? Here he is—he is hanging here on this gallows. . ."[43]

---

[42] Walter Brueggeman writes: "Claims for Yahweh's sovereignty and fidelity must now be made quite provisionally, and in light of the burning flesh of Auschwitz." The holocaust must make us suspicious toward "the triumphalist story of faith that is too easily recited on the basis of the Bible. Any triumph is made thin by this event, and every triumph is made unstable by this reality." *Theology of the Old Testament* (St. Paul, MN: Augsburg Fortress Publishers, 1997), 329.

[43] Elie Wiesel, *Night* (New York: Bantam Books, 1960), 61–62. Wiesel wrestles with the

Jesus, too, hung on a gallows, crushed by the madness of human history. His death was foreshadowed in the prophet Isaiah's portrait of the suffering servant: "He was oppressed, and he was afflicted, yet he opened not his mouth; like a lamb that is led to the slaughter, and like a sheep that before its shearers is dumb, so opened he not his mouth" (Isaiah 53:7).

If in the human son we catch a glimpse of the invisible God, it is in the guise of a lamb who, in his manifest weakness, joins every suffering child in history's seemingly interminable slaughterhouse.

---

implications of this and other stories from his death camp experience in his memoir, *All Rivers Run to the Sea: Memoirs* (New York: Alfred A. Knopf, 1995). Of particular poignancy are three rich, soulful pages (103–105) titled "God's Suffering: A Commentary," where he writes: "Nothing justifies Auschwitz . . .The barbed-wire kingdom will forever remain an immense question mark on the scale of both humanity and its Creator. . ."

Unlike myself, Wiesel seems to assume that God was powerful enough to prevent Auschwitz: "By allowing this to happen, God was telling humanity something, and we don't know what it was." But Wiesel also believes God suffers with God's people, and so we can "pity" God, "who witnesses the massacre of his children by his other children" and weeps.

CHAPTER 7

Born Again from Above
Becoming a real human being

This being human is a guest house.
Every morning a new arrival.
A joy, a depression, a meanness,
some momentary awareness comes
as an unexpected visitor.
Welcome and entertain them all!
Even if they are a crowd of sorrows,
who violently sweep your house
empty of its furniture,
still, treat each guest honorably.
He may be clearing you out
for some new delight.
The dark thought, the shame, the malice,
meet them at the door laughing,
and invite them in.
Be grateful for whoever comes,
because each has been sent
as a guide from beyond.
Rumi[1]

JESUS SEEMS MAGNETIC. A word or two and the disciples abruptly
leave their nets and follow him. The crowds cannot stay away from

---

1 *The Essential Rumi*, Coleman Barks, translator (New York: HarperCollins Publishers, 1995), 109.

him. He has a "presence" that seems to flow from something mysterious in him, internal to him.

I imagine the people around him felt it, but did not know how to name it. The Gospel writers don't know how to name it either. They may hope their stories will make his presence real so we can feel it ourselves and draw our own conclusions. But that isn't easy. The Jesus stories are set pieces, repeated endlessly, frozen into hoary old meanings. We've read or heard them so often that we know the end of the story before we get there, and we know exactly what it "means". Our minds shut off, our imaginations go dead, and poor Jesus turns bland before our eyes.

I yearn for one moment of time travel—to stand on first-century soil, see this odd figure kneel in the dirt in front of a woman accused of adultery, hear him say he does not condemn her. To see her face, his face. To see the faces of the godly as they turn, silently, and go away (John 8:2–11).

•   •   •

A COMPLICATED MAN

Jesus' magnetism isn't about being nice. Often, he breaks the rules of social behavior. He eats and drinks with ne'er-do-wells whom the godly avoid. He mocks authority. He resists his family's attempts to manipulate him, and often acts coldly toward them (John 2:4). Even toward needy people he can show an almost rude directness (Mark 7:27).

He doesn't let his followers dictate to him when or whether he will be available to others. He speaks his mind even at the risk of seeming arrogant. He lets strong feelings flow through him, and come out into the open. He excoriates inanimate objects, sometimes seeming petty—as when he curses a fig tree for not fruiting out of season—

other times seeming reckless, as when he overturns the money-changers' tables in the temple (Matthew 21:19 and 12).

Jean Sulivan writes: "The one who speaks to me through the Gospels can't be summed up by labels like sweet, humble, and wise, so useful in fitting him into the clerical vision of things."[2] Jesus is a very complicated man. At times, he seems a bit of a loose cannon. But he's never self-indulgent, undisciplined or careless. He doesn't have to express every idea or feeling that comes into his head. He is not a rebel simply for its own sake, and he does not play childish games—even though he writes in the dirt (John 8:6)!

Jesus simply seems to be who he really *wants* to be—one human being responding to other human beings in an honesty grounded in love.

. . .

A REAL HUMAN BEING

What is the hold Jesus has on people? Why his hold on me? I believe it is because he is a real human being.[3]

I admit this is an imprecise phrase. Still, I would like to use it as my theme in this chapter. The words feel intuitively right to me. As I read the Gospel accounts, I place myself imaginatively into the skin of one of the disciples and follow Jesus from place to place, watching. He is never boring. One moment I'm shocked, the next melting in tears. I chuckle, I get confused, I'm irritated. Sometimes, I'm scared—for me, for him, for anyone associated with him. Often,

---

2 *Morning Light*, 55.

3 "Christ is the 'true man' in this perverted and inhumane world. . . He becomes *the human God*." Moltmann, *The Trinity and the Kingdom*, 116, 118. Marcus Borg sees Jesus as "a remarkably free person." *Jesus: A New Vision* (New York: HarperCollins Publishers, 1987), 191.

in the aftermath of the latest outlandish event, I ask myself: "Who *is* this man?"

But as soon as I put this question into words, the spell of his presence is broken and I land with a thud back in the twenty-first century. My evangelical training kicks in, reminding me that this is a theological question, so there's one approved answer: "He's the 'Son of God!' Of *course*, he's magnetic!"

But when the question first comes to mind—"Who is this man?"—it isn't theological. It's personal. What is this man *about*? What is going on inside him? Why am I so fascinated with him? The approved theological answer doesn't speak to those questions. Yes, of course he's the Son of God. But that doesn't capture what I am feeling in his presence. My heart isn't flashing: "Divinity! Divinity!" It's sensing a different, perhaps equally rare, kind of authority.

I think it's the authority of a *real human being*.[4]

In this chapter, I want to follow the thread of those tantalizing words. I believe they point to the kind of healing that Jesus wished for his followers, for the Pharisees, for us. Jesus' story embodies the good news that to be grasped by a small God—a God revealed, in St. Paul's words, "in the likeness of sinful flesh"—is to be drawn toward transformation—toward the possibility of becoming what we most want to become: real human beings, just like Jesus (Romans 8:3).

*   *   *

NOT AS THE WORLD GIVES

As he talks with his disciples, just before his betrayal and crucifixion, Jesus reveals—a bit obliquely—what is going on inside him. He says: "I'm giving my peace to you. I'm not giving it to you as the world

---

4 The ancient Chalcedonian Creed affirms that Jesus was fully God and fully human. The last part of the formulation does not, unfortunately, receive the attention it deserves.

gives it. Don't let your hearts be troubled or afraid" (John 14:27). He's letting the disciples know that a peculiar kind of peace pervades the inner world of a real human being. It can somehow exist even amidst anticipation of a terrible ordeal. Jesus wants to pass this peace on to his disciples—given its context, he may be thinking of this peace as his primary legacy to them. What kind of peace is he talking about?

On the night Jesus speaks these words, the disciples' inner worlds are far from peaceful. A sense of foreboding fills the room. The godly have publicly accused Jesus of demon possession and blasphemy, and threatened to stone him for claiming to be somehow identical with the Father.

At this moment, in another room not far from where this little band is gathered, Jesus' enemies are plotting to kill him. Who knows what they'll do to his disciples? The authorities could arrive at any moment to arrest the lot of them. Meanwhile, Jesus is talking about suffering and dying—like a grain of wheat when it falls into the ground (John 12:24). He drops a little bombshell: two of the people sitting here will turn against him—Judas in betrayal, Peter in denial (John 13:21 and 38). The room is alive with tension.[5] What kind of peace can the disciples possibly feel at a time like this?

Spiritual models that revolve around the Almighty, instead of the human son, tend to approach the inner world in terms of conflict and struggle, defeat and victory. The "ungodly" voices that disturb our inner peace—unbelief, worry, confusion, doubt—are depicted as evil adversaries. Through prayer, will power and other spiritual techniques, they can be forcibly silenced and obliterated from our conscious awareness. We just call on the power of the Almighty, who removes them from our lives and imposes a miraculous inner calm by spiritual fiat.

---

5   See John chapters 12–13.

If the disciples bring this "almightified" spiritual understanding to Jesus' words about peace, they will (mistakenly) hear him saying something like this: "Do you disciples notice how many fearful parts of you are speaking up right now, fighting for primacy inside you— voices of worry and anger, doubt and unbelief? You know these aren't godly voices, don't you? They make you a mess inside. They show that you're scared and weak, faithless and irresolute. Shame on you! Call on the Almighty to help you get rid of all those voices, and then you'll experience 'my' peace."

If Jesus means this, however, he's preaching tired old news. This is how most of us learn to handle inner conflict: with the help of God, we pull a gun on it. We clench our jaws, conjure up our reserves of will power and imitate the Almighty, stomping out everything weak and evil inside us. But Jesus isn't thinking like the Almighty. He has a different "peace" in mind. He emphasizes its uniqueness: "I'm giving you *my* peace," he says. "It's *not* what the world understands as peace."

•   •   •

A WELCOME TO ALL

The days and hours just before Jesus' farewell speech to his disciples offer plenty of evidence that Jesus' spirit is not what we might ordinarily call "peaceful." An intensely complicated mix of internal voices seems to inhabit him. The text names a few of them.

In a prayer just before his farewell address to his disciples, Jesus says, "My soul is troubled now." Then he gives examples of the warring voices inside him: one says "Father, save me from this hour," while the other says "Father glorify thy name" (John 12:27–28).[6] A short time later, as he realizes that Judas is about to betray him, he

---

6 A similar mixture of voices is found in Jesus' words from the cross. Compare Mark 15:34 and Luke 23:46.

tells his disciples he is "troubled in spirit" (John 13:21). But it is in this very context that he gives the disciples his peace, and invites them not to be troubled. Is Jesus preaching a double standard: it's fine for him to be troubled, but not for his disciples? Or does he know a kind of "peace" that continues to dwell inside even when we're troubled?

I believe it is this paradoxical kind of peace Jesus is giving his disciples. I would describe it as a "climate of hospitality" that characterizes Jesus' inner world. Jesus knows humans carry many different parts within them. Some of those parts are at odds with other ones. Even now, a part of Jesus is saying: "You're headed for disaster—ask the Father to save you from it, or do something heroic to avoid it." Another part of him responds: "No, you need to be yourself—be small and accept your suffering—if you're going to be 'glorified'—that is, if you're going to reveal your true nature and the true nature of the Father."

In his prayer, Jesus doesn't try to annihilate one of these, or combine them into one voice. He welcomes both of them—and perhaps others not recorded—into the flowing dialogue that constitutes his spirit. He does not deny the existence of, or try to squelch, the varied moods and voices of his interior world. He does not set one part of himself up as a judge or censor over the other parts, allowing it to label the others "good" or "bad," "godly" or "ungodly." He welcomes *every* part.[7]

This means that Jesus is the rarest of creatures: a human being who is not at war with himself. Because a warm hospitality reigns in his inner life, he can afford to be uniquely self-aware. He can pay attention, without self-accusation or shame, to everything that is in

---

7 This doesn't mean, of course, that Jesus is ignorant of the great harm that some parts of us can do when they exert dominance. But I believe he understands that the parts burst into dominance and do their harm when they are not accorded full dignity and made welcome inside us. When we are willing to hear from all of them—even, as Jesus' prayer illustrates, the part that seems to question the will of the Father—they relax and permit our deepest selves to act. And our deepest selves will always act in love.

him. He can embrace the multiple parts that make up every human personality.

Some of them the world counts respectable—parts that try to manage our lives efficiently and shape the good impressions others have of us. Others the world counts disrespectable: volatile, impulsive parts that seek to protect us by doing damage to others or even, ironically, ourselves; secret, childlike parts that are sad or hurt or broken.

Jesus is familiar with each of these inside himself. He meets them, as they arise to the surface of his awareness, with genuine curiosity and compassion. He extends hospitality even to the seemingly unattractive, the troublesome, the sinister, the childish. Even to those parts whom Luther might have called "the devil."

In this climate of inner hospitality, Jesus' varied parts need not compete with one another, shouting louder and louder for Jesus' attention, shouting louder and louder for other people's attention. Each is permitted its own dignity, each gets a hearing. So each—even the "disrespectable" ones—gradually finds its proper and constructive part to play in Jesus' inner world. This dynamic internal process of friendly relationships between the varied parts of Jesus' spirit is clearly the kind of peace the world doesn't give. It's not the rigid or artificial peace of the godly or the fearful or the dead. It's a deeply authentic, alive and flowing peace that opens Jesus to the entire range of human subjectivity.[8]

---

8 I don't believe it is an accident that Jesus reconnected with this "unworldly" peace in the practice of prayer. In the Christian tradition, contemplative prayer—particularly its "kataphatic" formulation prominently identified with Ignatius of Loyola—has represented a time-tested spiritual path to the full recognition and acceptance of every part of one's inner world. It knows that "presence" is the entire secret of healing.

A simple, practical expression of this form of prayer—the "Compassion Practice"—has been developed by Frank Rogers at Claremont School of Theology, in association with Mark Yaconelli and Andrew Dreitcer, under the auspices of the Triptykos School of Spiritual Formation. Their website: www.triptykos.com.

So Jesus embraces all that he is. He is fully, and *really*, human. With a zone of hospitality at his center, and a unique freedom to be aware of what is inside him, he is naturally aware of what is inside other people. He isn't surprised by anything he senses inside others—he understands all of it as normal and natural. For someone living in this zone of hospitality, it is no great feat to exude compassion for others even when he speaks hard truths quite straightforwardly. He knows and accepts what is in the human heart, because he knows and accepts what is in his own heart. He is unsurprised by anything human.[9]

If we were able to receive this peace at Jesus' hands, the war we wage against ourselves would be over. We would know what it means to befriend ourselves—dare I say to love ourselves? And since friendship with ourselves—meaning acceptance of and compassion for all that is in us—lies at the heart of genuine friendship with others—even our enemies—the violence that soaks our world in blood would soon be at an end.

If such a "peace" had dawned in Jesus' day, the crucifixion would not have happened.

Of course, "crucifixions," large and small, continue to happen daily in our world. So this "peace" must not be easily learned.

•   •   •

LIKE LITTLE CHILDREN

It's surprising how often children appear in the stories about Jesus.[10]

---

9 "Now when he was in Jerusalem at the Passover festival, many believed in his name because they saw the signs that he was doing. But Jesus on his part would not entrust himself to them, because he knew all people and needed no one to testify about anyone; for he himself knew what was in everyone" (John 2:23–25).

10 The key texts are: Mark 9:33–37, 9:42, 10:13–16, 10:24; Matthew 18:4, 19:13. John Miller, in *Jesus at Thirty: A Psychological and Historical Portrait* (Minneapolis: Fortress Press, 1997), 39–41, lists the many additional texts where Jesus references fathers and

He stops to talk with them, and sits them on his lap. He heals them. He refers to them often in his parables and teachings. He says they are the most genuine citizens of heaven. He depicts adults endearingly as children. He issues dire warnings against harming the "little ones." He calls himself a human son and claims to be one with children. He tells his disciples they need to be more like little children.

As we have seen, he implies that God resembles a little child. Perhaps Jesus is fascinated with children because they are parables of what it means to be a "real human being."[11]

When the disciples want Jesus to tell them which one of them will be "the greatest" in the "kingdom of heaven," Jesus calls a little child to him and says: "Unless you turn and become like children, you will never enter the kingdom of heaven" (Matthew 18:1–5). In the "kingdom of heaven"—a spiritual state in which everyone is a "real human being"—there seem *only* to be children.

Is this because we ourselves are never more "real human beings" than during those first, vulnerable days of our lives? As we emerge from the womb, we are remarkably spontaneous—remarkably "ourselves." We are instinctively available to the entire range of human subjectivity. When our parents first hold us in their arms, they expect nothing of us except to be whatever we are at the moment. We can fidget, shriek, wiggle, pummel the air—it's all fine with them. When

---

father-son relationships.

11 Fyodor Dostoyevsky shows a similar fascination with children as real human beings in *The Brothers Karamazov* (New York: New American Library, 1957). Even if one has read it before, to reread it with special attention to the role of children—noticing, for example, the characters who are children, what is said about children (for example, in Ivan's terrifying monologue titled "Rebellion" and his story about "The Grand Inquisitor"), and what is in view when, countless times, the words "childlike" and "childish" are used—is almost to be reading a brand new novel.

My friend, Jim Titus, was the first person to bring this to my attention. An excellent treatment of this theme is William Woodin Rowe, *Dostoyevsky: Child and Man in His Works* (New York: New York University Press, 1968).

we expel a bit of gas, or something worse, no one takes offense. We can express freely whatever is coursing through us, without judgment, blame or shame—without self-criticism or self-condemnation of any kind. We are in some fashion real human beings, at peace—in an "ignorance is bliss" fashion—with all that we are.

In normal human development, this peace cannot last. Inevitably, "the knowledge of good and evil" invades our awareness.[12] We begin receiving messages from the world around us that much of what is inside us is not welcome—in fact, some of it will get in the way of our being loved. These messages vary widely. Some are gentle, offered in a climate of safety; others harsh, punitive, even violent. Some condemn us wholesale; others attempt to draw fine distinctions— mostly lost on children—such as "love the sinner, hate the sin."

Whatever the variations, the result is nearly always the universal disease of shame. We come to believe, in varying degrees, of course, that much of what is in us is not good, and if we make it visible, we will not be loved. Secretly we turn "the knowledge of good and evil" back upon ourselves, becoming our own worst enemies.

Which means we do not remain *real* for very long. As the internal war deepens, various parts of us go to work fashioning a different self than the one we are—an attractive, approved and ultimately unreal self. We trade authenticity for approval, which feels to us, superficially, like love. An image of what it means to be "perfect" forms in our brains. We try to live up to that image by extinguishing all that seems inimical to it. We work to make ourselves—on the inside as well as on the outside—a package that looks smoother, shinier, more contained and rigidly controlled than a real human being can actually be. We lose touch with who we really are.[13]

---

12 See Genesis 2:16–17; 3:1–7. Jacques Ellul shows how disastrous this so-called "knowledge" has been for human beings in *To Will and To Do: An Ethical Research for Christians* (Philadelphia: Pilgrim Press, 1969).

13 Two moral development researchers find that young American girls often stop being

Jesus is drawn to children because they are closer to being real human beings than they will ever be as adults. Instinctively—at least, until they learn otherwise—they accept the ever-changing kaleidoscope of their own being. Jesus invites us to do the same. He says it's the key to entering the kingdom of heaven.

* * *

ONE WITH THE FATHER

What gives babies the freedom to embrace, without judgment, all that is within them? They do it naturally, of course. They are reflecting an unconscious, primal form of trust. They come into this world naively trusting reality. They do not expect censure for being who they are. They seem, in some elemental way, to embody the naïve belief that life will welcome and gently hold them. This is another way of saying: they know they are loved.

This is Jesus' secret as well: he can permit himself to be a real human being because, like the newborn infant—or like Adam and Eve in the primal garden before they "knew" good and evil—Jesus trusts reality. For him, the ground of reality is a divine Spirit he calls "Father." He trusts the Father. He knows the Father loves him without condition, and he trusts that love. Jesus knows the Father is turned toward him, is radically *for* and *with* him. He knows

---

themselves as they approach puberty. They learn that if they express their true thoughts or feelings, they lose friends and jeopardize the approval of important adults. If they keep quiet about what's inside them and conform, they keep these relationships, but also find them unsatisfying because they're based on pretense.

Only a minority of young women go through their teen years with their unique voices intact. Many conform so well that they "forget," or feel confused about, what they actually think or feel. They "become" whatever is required of them. They fall prey to "the tyranny of nice and kind." Lyn Mikel Brown and Carol Gilligan, *Meeting at the Crossroads: Women's Psychology and Girls' Development* (Cambridge, MA: Harvard University Press, 1992), 53–62.

the Father is pleased with him, just as he is. He knows the Father welcomes and gently holds him.

Although it sometimes appears so, human beings are not isolated individual units who can make it on their own. We wither in the absence of love. At the core, we are hard-wired for connection with others. We spend the first nine months of our existence in the most literal and intimate connection with another human being. We are born helpless and depend on others to nourish and protect us. We cannot survive, physically or emotionally, as isolated beings— something in us wants to be seen, known, cherished and needed by other human beings. If we express a desire to live without relationships, it is typically a sign that we have been badly damaged by genetic accident or by trauma early in our lives. We are not fully human, not fully ourselves, unless our deep relationality finds fulfillment— unless we are securely held by the love of another, and trust that that love will not permanently abandon us.

Jesus seems absolutely certain of his connection with the one he calls Father.[14] He trusts this Father's love, and knows that nothing inside him can jeopardize it.[15] Jesus has internalized this love so deeply that he can say, "I am in the Father and the Father [is] in me" (John 14:10).[16] At the deepest place inside him, it seems, this Father's self has joined with his self in an unbreakable connection of mutual love. So Jesus' being is permeated by trust, a trust not narrowly focused outside himself, nor inside himself, but diffusely felt in all

14 When he told the disciples they didn't need to be troubled, he followed those words with these: "Believe in God" (John 14:1).

15 St. Paul had the same experience, it seems. He says that "neither death, nor life, nor angels, nor principalities, nor things present, nor things to come, nor powers, nor height, nor depth, nor anything else in all creation" would ever be able to separate him from the love of the Father (Romans 8:38–39). St. Paul indicates that trust is more important than life itself by writing, in this same context, "As it is written, 'For thy sake we are being killed all the day long; we are regarded as sheep to be slaughtered'" (Romans 8:36).

16 He also said "I and the Father are one" and "Believe in God; believe also in me" (John 10:30, 14:1).

parts of his being and in the very atmosphere of the world. His trust for himself and God are so intermixed as to be indistinguishable. He trusts "reality." He trusts "life." He trusts something deep inside him. Like St. Paul, he "lives and moves and has his being" in this medium of trust (Acts 17:28).[17]

So there is nothing to censure him, nothing to threaten him, nothing to condemn him. He experiences "the peace that passes understanding" (Philippians 4:7). We cannot know all that is within him, of course, but we can allow ourselves to surmise that, whatever is there, he welcomes. He is a real human being.

·   ·   ·

BORN-AGAIN JESUS

How does this happen? How does Jesus come to experience this radical trust? Perhaps it washes over him in a moment so sudden, so unexpected, that he thinks of it as a kind of re-birth, a moment of coming alive, an experience creating something so new in him that he feels like a newborn baby. That would explain the metaphors he uses in his talk with Nicodemus.

Nicodemus is one of the few Pharisees we know by name because he takes the risk of coming alone in the night to talk with Jesus (John 3). Maybe he senses that Jesus is a real human being, and is beginning to trust him. Maybe he wants to be a real human being, too.

But Nicodemus seems a bit nervous, so he starts off with a little flattery: "We know you come from God because you do marvelous things." Jesus knows the question that is in Nicodemus' heart, so he cuts to the chase: "Unless you are born anew, you won't see

---

17 A beautiful example of the sustaining power of this trusting connection is the Holocaust memoir of Etty Hillesum: *An Interrupted Life: The Diaries of Etty Hillesum, 1941–1943* (New York: Pantheon Books, 1983).

the kingdom of God." Jesus thinks of this "kingdom" as a spiritual reality where only babies—the most real of human beings—dwell.[18]

Now the question hangs in the air between them: "Nicodemus, are you ready to be a baby again?" Nicodemus seems baffled: "How can an old man like me be born anew?" Jesus answers: "We've all been born of flesh; now we must be re-born of the Spirit." He teases Nicodemus gently: "Are you a teacher of Israel, and yet you do not understand these things?"

I think Jesus knows that being re-born of the Spirit is very difficult to understand—unless it has *happened* to you.[19] Even then it's not easy to talk about. You can't adequately describe it, or put it in a formula. It's an event.[20] It comes when you least expect it—Jesus tells Nicodemus it breaks in "from above." When it breaks in, it sets us off in a whole new direction. We look around and see we're on an unfamiliar road, and don't quite know how we got there. We feel like babies again.

I believe something like this happens to Jesus when he's baptized in the Jordan River. At about the age of thirty, as the tradition has it, he becomes a follower of a wild-eyed, austere-living, "fire-and-brimstone" preacher named John the Baptist. Since we know next to nothing about the so-called "hidden years" of Jesus life to that

---

18 Cynthia Bourgeault says evangelicals think of the kingdom of God as "a place you go when you die—if you've been good." She thinks, rather, that it's "not later but lighter—some more subtle quality or dimension of experience accessible to you right in the moment. You don't die into it; you awaken into it." *The Wisdom Jesus* (Boston: Shambhala Publications, 2008), 30.

19 Although evangelical soul-winning mechanisms, like Campus Crusade's "four spiritual laws," make it seem quite easy, almost mechanical—as though we can make it happen whenever we want.

20 John Caputo describes an event as a "wispy and willowy thing, a whisper or a promise, a breath or a spirit, not a mundane force." He says it "cannot be clocked by the tick-tock of ordinary time but has to do with a transforming moment that releases us from the grip of the present and opens up the future in a way that makes possible a new birth, a new beginning. . ." *Weakness of God*, 7, 6.

point, we cannot be sure what draws Jesus to John. But we do know that John advocates a strict ethical code (Luke 3:10–14), preaches the need for "repentance for the forgiveness of sins" (Mark 1:4) and warns of "the wrath to come" (Matthew 3:7). Something in the spirit of this message awakens Jesus' curiosity, enticing him to join the crowds listening to John on the banks of the Jordan.

Luke's Gospel tells us that, as a child, Jesus was "strong" and "filled with wisdom" (Luke 2:40). Perhaps this indicates a precocious interest in the realm of the spirit, encouraged by his mother's hope that, as the heavenly visitor had promised, her first-born would be "the Son of the Most High" (Luke 1:32) The Gospels record only one story that hints at Jesus' youthful religious experience: his encounter, at age twelve, with the teachers in the Jerusalem temple. He spends several days in theological conversation with his elders, and leaves them "amazed at his understanding and his answers" (Luke 2:47).

Given this performance, it is likely that Jesus knows "the law and the prophets" and, under the influence of the godly of his day, has sought to satisfy his spiritual yearnings by submitting to their strict ethical demands. Perhaps some part of him believes that ethical perfection is the only way to please the Father. If this were the case, then a part of him does not trust that, without attaining perfection, he will be loved by the Father.[21] In this, he would only be human.

Of course, it is impossible to perfectly fulfill a rigid ethical code. The stricter the code, the greater the burden of the failure and guilt in its wake—and the deeper the fear that one is not worthy of love,

---

21 Recent scholarship offers a number of intriguing attempts to reconstruct Jesus' hidden early years and assess their influence on his religious perspective. Donald Capps, *Jesus: A Psychological Biography* (St. Louis: Chalice Press, 2000) reviews the best of these and offers its own analysis, which leans on the hypothesis that Jesus' birth was illegitimate.

To me, a more believable treatment is John W. Miller's, *Jesus at Thirty.* Miller thinks that Jesus' unique understanding of God is explicable if we hypothesize that he lost his own very caring father (Joseph) at a young age. I have not leaned on either hypothesis for my far more modest reconstruction of Jesus' youthful development.

cannot be loved, and will not be loved. Perhaps it is this burden that brings Jesus to the Jordan River. He may have fallen under the spell of John the Baptist, a substitute father figure who seems willing, at first with misgivings, to hear Jesus' repentance, wash him clean, and start him on a new path toward perfection. Perhaps he hopes his encounter with John will earn him John's—and ultimately God's—love.

If this is what Jesus takes down with him into the waters of the Jordan, it is not what he brings up out of them. Mark's Gospel tells us that "just as he was coming up out of the water, he saw the heavens torn apart and the Spirit descending like a dove on him. And a voice came from heaven, 'You are my Son, the Beloved; with you I am well pleased'" (Mark 1:10–11).

In a flash, I believe, the landscape shifts inside Jesus. His years of anxious exertions suddenly fall away, and the picture of the Father that has heretofore animated and perhaps tortured him dissolves into thin air. In that moment, as I imagine it, he realizes these are not the words he expected to hear—words like: "Now that you have repented, and been dipped in the Jordan, you are clean and quali-fied to be my beloved. Continue to be clean, and I will continue to call you beloved."

Instead, he hears the words he has—without completely knowing it—most yearned to hear: "Just as you are, I am pleased with you; just as you are, you are my beloved; nothing you can do, or not do, will ever shake this love." He knows it is not his strict obedience to "the law" that his Father loves—it's him, just as he is.[22] He is his

---

22 One could say Jesus has heard, perhaps for the first time, that God actually "likes" him. James Alison explores, very creatively, the difference between saying "God loves us" and "God likes us" in *On Being Liked* (New York: The Crossroad Publishing Company, 2003), 15.

heavenly parent's beloved child. [23] He can lay down his "heavy burdens" and rest.[24]

I would contend, on the basis of his recorded ministry, that there is something else that he now knows, and knows for sure: that this good news is meant not just for him, but for every human being on God's good earth. *Each of us* is God's beloved. This is the "good news of God" that he proclaims when he returns to Galilee after John is arrested and begins to preach: "Now is the time; the reign of God is right here! Repent! Believe the good news!" (Mark 1:14–15).[25]

---

23 It appears that this "moment of truth" does not go unchallenged for Jesus. "Immediately," Mark tells us, Jesus is compelled "by the Spirit" to go to the wilderness, where he spends forty days being "tempted by Satan" and "waited on" by angels (Mark 1:12–13). I interpret this story as an important (because Spirit-initiated) battle between competing parts of Jesus that arise in the aftermath of his vision—parts that attest to the truth and utter sufficiency of his vision and parts that cannot believe it or do not trust it.

In this light, the first temptation—"If you are the Son of God, command these stones to become loaves of bread"—might be interpreted as a suggestion from the doubting part of Jesus that God's love is not enough to satisfy his spiritual hunger, but that he must act autonomously to feed himself.

The second temptation—"If you are the Son of God, throw yourself down" [from "the pinnacle of the temple"] and "his angels. . . will bear you up, so that you will not dash your foot against a stone"—seems to indicate that Jesus wants the Father to prove his love by a magical rescue operation.

The third temptation—"All [the kingdoms of the world] will I give you, if you will fall down and worship me"—shows Jesus wrestling with a part of him that is aware that the one who calls him Beloved is not the Almighty of conventional religion, but a smaller, gentler Father who offers him not earthly power, but suffering and defeat, buffered only by a love that will not let him go. Does he want to trust this love (Matthew 4:1–11)?

24 "Come to me, all you that are weary and are carrying heavy burdens, and I will give you rest" (Matthew 11:28).

25 Bob Ekblad, in A *New Christian Manifesto: Pledging Allegiance to the Kingdom of God* (Louisville: Westminster John Knox Press, 2008) interprets Jesus' baptism as his identification with the "bad guys" in the Exodus story: "Pharaoh, his army, chariots, horses and riders" who drowned in the Red Sea. It is thus a preview of Jesus' core message: that we are called to love our enemies.

Ekblad writes: "The waters are the place of God's defeat of the enemies of the kingdom of God—the principalities and powers. . . All distinctions between insiders and outsiders, the saved and the damned, perpetrators and victims, the righteous and the unrighteous, clean and unclean, Israel and the nations are leveled when insiders go under water. . .

The word "repent," of course, because of its use by evangelists who preach the "bad news," has the power to throw us back into the arms of a moralistic, demanding God. But Jesus is using this tired and troublesome word in an altogether new way. He's not saying: "Name all your sins and say you're sorry you're such a bad person; say you'll never do those things again!" He's saying: "You need to turn your picture of God around. You've got God wrong. God isn't the demanding taskmaster who will love you and fix your life if you strictly obey his commands. God is the still small voice, speaking deep inside you, naming you God's beloved.

"God isn't out there on a throne controlling world events; God is in here, right now, one with you, whispering love to you. God isn't the punishing judge you hear about from John the Baptist and your local Pharisees. God isn't your enemy, and God doesn't want you to be your own enemy. God likes you just as you are. God is a lover, through and through, and you are God's beloved.

"Isn't this good news? Can you hear it, somewhere deep inside yourself? Can you believe it? Can you see how it puts you in a brand new world?

"Don't you want to go in this altogether new direction?"

•   •   •

Under water we all die totally. Under water, God's chosen people join the damned."

Ekblad suggests that illegal immigrants along the southern border of the U.S., often called "wetbacks," are "a near perfect metaphor describing the immigrant status of all who are baptized in Jesus and become his followers" (34–37). Ekblad's deep engagement with the Bible and his long experience with marginalized peoples, enable him to speak passionately and convincingly to privileged Americans about Jesus' solidarity with the poor. I agree with Ekblad that this solidarity is a natural outworking of the "good news" Jesus heard as he came up out of the water.

WHY ARE YOU SO AFRAID?

I've offered this imaginative retelling of Jesus' experience of being "born again" because I want to take his humanity seriously, and allow it to inform the way I understand my own humanity. If Jesus was fully human—"like his brothers and sisters in every respect" (Hebrews 2:17)—then to some unknown degree he must have shared the propensity of human beings to be governed by fear. If his experience in the river turned him completely around, it had to speak to his fears. It had to alter, in a surprising, life-changing way, the deep human anxiety that we are not good enough for God; that God is not absolutely and unremittingly good enough to be called "love"; and that this love will not be sufficient to meet our needs in times of trouble.

Fear—of emotional even more than physical danger—seems to be the engine of our millennia-long survival as a biological species on a dangerous planet. A keen attunement to fear has stimulated our species' remarkable creativity; in large part, we have our fears to thank for most of the material, technological and social developments that we associate with "civilization."

Our fear sensors have thus evolved into finely-tuned instruments. Pangs of fear, great and small, too familiar to notice and too numerous to name, daily, hourly, nudge each human being toward one or another internal or external protective device and the safety that it promises. The most basic fear, I would suggest, beneath every other, is the fear that we are alone and unloved.

The opposite of fear is trust—the deep sense that we are not alone, and we are loved. I suspect that these two "existential" states are the bedrock of our human condition, the two basic orientations toward the world from which all others derive. Once we have named fear and trust, we may have inadvertently named every primary interior state that it is possible for a person to experience.

Countless times, the Bible reminds us of the ubiquity of fear and the possibility of trust. [26] When angels appear, their first words tend to be: "there's no need to be afraid." Jesus seems supremely attuned to fear, seems to understand how it can distort reality if it is given free reign, and often calls it to the attention of people around him. Mark's Gospel offers an example (Mark 4:35–41).

Jesus and the disciples are caught in a "great windstorm," and they're about to go under. As they hang on for dear life, and struggle to keep their boat afloat, Jesus takes a nap on a cushion. In a panic, they wake him up. He quiets the wind and the sea so completely that the text says there is a "dead calm"—a beautiful way to describe the surreal and pregnant quality of this moment.

I suspect the disciples are sitting in a stunned silence. Finally, Jesus breaks the silence by confronting the disciples with what may be life's biggest question: "Why are you afraid? Are you still unable to trust?" Perhaps Jesus means: "Why can't you trust that your lives will be physically preserved?" I prefer to think he means: "Why can't you trust that, in life or in death, you are the beloved children of your heavenly parent?"

The disciples appear to ignore the question. They are unwilling to take the inward journey—a journey toward self-understanding,

---

26 In his study of the Psalms, Patrick D. Miller writes: "The heart of the oracle of salvation and its effective and performative word is the simple assurance, 'Do not fear.' It occurs in most of the salvation oracles and is the most characteristic single feature of this divine word." *They Cried Unto the Lord: The Form and Theology of Biblical Prayer* (Minneapolis: Fortress Press, 1994), 144. The words "do not fear" appear several hundred times in the Bible. Jesus uses them (e.g. Mark 6:50, Matthew 14:27).

It is not much of a stretch to imagine that these words are one way to encapsulate "the good news of God" Jesus brought back from his experiences in the wilderness. I do not believe the best way to understand these words is "you shall under no circumstances be afraid," but rather "despite your fears, you will one day discover that there was nothing ultimately to be afraid of—you could have trusted all along."

In a very helpful exegesis of Old Testament admonitions to "fear God," Paul Borgman makes "fear not" and "fear God" virtually synonymous. He suggests the "fear of God" is "trust," and not "trembling." *Genesis: The Story We Haven't Heard* (Downers Grove, IL: InterVarsity Press, 2001).

toward a new kind of realness or wholeness—that Jesus' question invites. We know from other texts that Jesus thinks there are two paths for us to walk in our lives—a broad way and a narrow way, a way that smacks of death and a way that shimmers with life (Matthew 7:13–14). His question suggests that to take the broad way—the way we normally take—is to follow the lead of our fears: the primary human fear that we are not truly loved and the countless, nameless fears, springing from that primary fear, that poke their heads up almost without pause in the dim recesses of our awareness, keeping us in a mildly defensive mode, nudging us in ways to which we're often blind.[27]

We travel this broad way most resolutely when we avert our eyes, resist naming our fears, try to ignore them as they whisper or howl constantly within us, and—in ignoring them—paradoxically, give them control of our lives. On the narrow way, where we know we are loved, we can feel our fears, welcome their voices, understand their good intentions, and ask them to relax even as we listen for another voice, the voice of our trust.

Jesus' question to the disciples in the boat invites them to pay attention—to notice these two voices within them. But the disciples can't hear Jesus' question because they're too busy with their own: "Who then is this, that even wind and sea obey him?" The disciples are caught up in the miracle that Jesus has performed by calming the seas. Without the certainty that they are loved, they reach for magic and power. They imagine that Jesus enjoys a special relationship with the Almighty that permits him to do such deeds. Perhaps they hope their association with Jesus will give them some hold on magic or power, so that they can become something more smooth and shiny, something more contained and rigidly controlled, than they feel themselves to be.

---

27 Most Americans, coaxed by their fear-obsessed government, followed that broad way after the terrorist attack on 9/11/01.

Perhaps magic and power—precisely the glittering possibilities offered Jesus by the tempter in the wilderness—will help these poor bedraggled disciples be approved, and thus protected, by the Almighty.

This means only that the disciples do not yet trust the Father whom Jesus trusts. They don't trust that the Father is radically *for* them, radically *with* them, regardless of external circumstances. When their fears come calling, they are abjectly vulnerable to them. They either grant them full sway over their feelings and actions or they declare war on them and try to make them go away.

When Jesus' fears come calling, they enter a hospitable inner world fashioned by Jesus' trust in the Father's love. Jesus welcomes his fears, attends to them, understands how hard they are working to protect him, is grateful for them. With this welcome, Jesus' fears don't have to fight so hard to be heard. They can relax and permit the part of Jesus that trusts the love of the Father—not really a "part," but his deepest, "realest" self—to govern Jesus' actions in the world. And those actions will always bear some trace of the hospitality from which they sprang.

●　　●　　●

THE LAST WORD

It is possible to hear in certain of the stories about Jesus' last days a hint of this interior process at work. On the night he is arrested, shortly after he promises the disciples his "peace," he takes a few of them to a place called Gethsemane to pray. Mark's version of the story goes like this:

> And he took with him Peter and James and John, and began to be greatly distressed and troubled. And he said to them, "My soul is very sorrowful, even to death; remain here, and watch." And

going a little farther, he fell on the ground and prayed that, if it were possible, the hour might pass from him. And he said, "Abba, Father, all things are possible to you; remove this cup from me; yet not what I will, but what you will" (Mark 14:32–36).

Matthew's version is almost identical to Mark's, but Luke adds these words:

And there appeared to him an angel from heaven, strengthening him. And being in agony he prayed more earnestly; and his sweat became like great drops of blood falling down upon the ground (Luke 22:43–44).

I think it's remarkable that these ancient texts, which usually content themselves with a word or two at most about Jesus' interior state, offer such detail when they narrate this story. They want to make sure we know that Jesus is hearing from the same inner voices any of us would hear from were we in his situation. Instead of censoring them in the name of some heroic ideal, Jesus trusts the Father with all of them, including the unheroic. In other words, he trusts the Father to welcome and hold even the voice that does not trust the Father—the voice of fear. This is the paradox of a truly radical trust in the Father: it opens the way for us to confess aloud our *lack* of trust in the Father.

Once Jesus chooses to give both fear and trust their place inside him, his trust grows. He finds himself drawn to love. He reconnects with the one from whom he heard the word "Beloved," the one who now holds him. And in this love, his fears can dissipate, and he can act and speak in love.

A similar inner dialogue may be going on as Jesus dies. The only words from the cross that Mark records are: "My God, my God, why have you forsaken me?" (Mark 15:34). This most human of cries gives voice to the pain and fear and loss—and perhaps even some trace of anger—that burn inside Jesus.[28] They testify to the existence in Jesus' spirit of a desperate, untrusting voice: "God is utterly gone. You are utterly alone." And yet Jesus directs these very words *to* the Father, as if to say: "There is another voice in me, another part of me, that knows you are still here, and trusts you." Even in his deepest suffering, Jesus embraces the full range of human subjectivity. The voice of trust and the voice of doubt live side by side within him.

Mark describes Jesus' death this way: "And Jesus uttered a loud cry, and breathed his last" (Mark 15:37). Luke, perhaps giving words to this loud cry, writes: "Then Jesus, crying with a loud voice, said, 'Father, into your hands I commit my spirit!'" (Luke 23:46). Is it possible that, once one has become a real human being, trust will always have the last word?

·   ·   ·

MY BURDEN IS LIGHT

I am slowly working my way toward an understanding of the "inwardness" that dawns when a real human being is born. I'm taking pains with this because I believe conventional spirituality so often falsifies it. Evangelical spirituality, in particular, tends to falsify it. Evangelical spirituality adopts the "born-again" metaphor quite eagerly—even excessively—but it tends to use it in a way that I believe resists the inwardness that is born anew of the Spirit.

For many evangelicals, the new birth inaugurates (at least temporarily) friendly relationships with God and others. But I have not seen it, very often or for very long, give rise to friendly relationships with themselves. The "judgmental" parts of them that aim

---

28 A contrary point of view is offered by an early church father, Cyril, who refused to believe that Jesus felt fear and weakness. He believed Jesus felt forsaken for humanity at large, but not for himself. Moltmann, *Crucified God*, 229.

for moral perfection—the perceived goal of born-again persons—almost immediately go back to their old jobs of spotting the "bad" parts of them and battling to extinguish them. Because these persons mistakenly perceive the "bad" parts as "selfish," they launch spiritual crusades to liquidate "self."[29] They activate internal parts that promise to control the inner world so that it will reflect the Almighty's "ideal" for a truly Christian temperament.

In evangelical spirituality, in other words, "making peace with God" doesn't imply making peace with oneself. It is as if Jesus said: "Come to me, all who labor and are heavy-laden, and I will help you get your act together—and that will take some work."

What Jesus actually said is: "Come to me, all you that are weary and are carrying heavy burdens, and I will give you *rest*." He speaks of himself as "gentle and lowly in heart"—just like the one he called Father, who proclaimed him "Beloved"—and promises that his "yoke is easy" and his "burden is light" (Matthew 11:28–30). He does not mean that the journey toward wholeness is pain-free. There may even be a crucifixion in store for the one who trusts in the love of this Father. But even the pain of crucifixion can be endured, and our souls find rest, when we trust this love. It is this state of inner rest, of "peace," that characterizes those who have experienced the joyful freedom to become a real human being.

This freedom begins for us, as it began for Jesus, the moment we meet a Father who calls us "beloved" in a way that we absolutely trust.

If Jesus had put this freedom into words for Nicodemus, he might

---

29 "Selfishness" is often misunderstood, I think. Selfish acts don't arise—as we seem to think—from some part of us that's just by nature greedy, grasping and intolerant of other people's needs. It's also never an expression of our deepest self. It's always a defensive measure initiated by a part of us that is trying to protect us from emotional harm. Every selfish gesture comes from fear. It doesn't mean harm to another, but the avoidance of harm to us. We cannot force our selfish parts to go away. We can only love them, and watch them melt.

have said: "You are beloved of God, just as you are—and you will always be. So why not hearken to the voice in you that invites you to relax, just like a new-born baby. You know, you don't have to work so hard to be *good*. Get real! Open yourself to everything that is in you. Feel the warm glow of hospitality. It's okay to be something of a mess from time to time! Don't worry—inviting the voice of self-judgment to relax won't make you more 'selfish.' Actually, you'll be surprised at how connected you will feel to your neighbors. And to your enemies. And even to yourself."

This peace among our inward parts, a peace that is accepting of all that is in us and all that is in others, inaugurates an entirely new spiritual reality. It is a place of freedom and a place of rest. Jesus called it the "kingdom of God." It is what being "born again" is really all about.

CHAPTER 8

Despised and Rejected
Meeting myself at the cross

I myself am the enemy most in need of love.
Carl Jung[1]

THE NEWS THAT A HEALTHY human being has been born into this world brings great joy to our hearts.[2] We break into smiles, pass out the cigars, congratulate anyone whose genes have contributed to this grand event, and toast the tiny bundle we hold in our arms. And then each year, as this baby makes its way toward adulthood—and finally old age—we light candles in memory of the promise and the thrill of that first day, the day on which this human being came into the world.

What if that tiny baby is the "real human being" who turns out to be God among us, the hope of the world? Then what you get is "Christmas." Of course, consumer capitalism, drunk on the good cheer emanating from the merry jingle of coins bouncing into the till, has lately shaped our celebration of Christmas. But the malls are

---

1 Quoted in Brennan Manning, *Abba's Child: The Cry of the Heart for Intimate Belonging* (Colorado Springs: NavPress Publishing Group, 1994), 41.
2 In the words of Jesus, "When a woman is in labor, she has pain, because her hour has come. But when her child is born, she no longer remembers the anguish because of the joy of having brought a human being into the world" (John 16:21). In this chapter I describe the kind of "birth" in which each of us is both mother and child.

right to advertise "JOY" on their Christmas banners and fill our ears with canned versions of "Joy to the World."

Joy is rightfully an expression of the Christmas spirit. The angels in Luke's Gospel, after issuing their standard greeting "No need to be afraid," assured the shepherds that they brought "good news of great joy for all the people." The wise men, seeing the star over Bethlehem, "were overwhelmed with joy" (Luke 2:10, Matthew 2:10).

But joy and sorrow are often intermixed in human life. Mary, the mother of this newborn child, may have sensed this from the start. When an angel, announcing the birth of Jesus, told her the Lord was with her, she felt "much perplexed by his words," so the angel had to tell her she need not be afraid (Luke 1:29–30). In the hours after Jesus' birth, when the shepherds told her that heavenly beings had announced a Savior, she "pondered" these words "in her heart" (Luke 2:19). And when Mary and Joseph took Jesus to the temple, old Simeon's "blessing" must have stricken terror: "Behold, this child is set for the fall and rising of many in Israel, and for a sign that is spoken against (and a sword will pierce your soul also), that the thoughts out of many hearts may be revealed" (Luke 2:25–35). Mary learned early, as she held the squirming infant in her arms, that it is not an unmixed blessing to give birth to a Savior.

It is never an unmixed blessing to give birth to any human being. Each tiny infant embodies a surreal contradiction of hope and dread. In the moment of birth, feelings of relief and hope usually edge out the fear. We gather around an exhausted mother and celebrate the promise of love that this compact bundle of warm human flesh symbolizes. Very soon, however, our ears hear the first tiny cry of distress pushing through our euphoria, warning us that pain will be this child's portion as surely as it has been ours.

And we ourselves may sometimes be the source this child's pain. Who has not caused pain to a child? Often the pain is accidental—but sometimes, it is not. Are there humans who have never spoken an unkind word to a child, even when the child is one they also fiercely protect? Never felt anger toward a child—perhaps their very own child, a child they also deeply love? Mary, pondering, surely knows this is a world in which children suffer at the hands of those who love them as well as those who don't.

It is not without significance that each year, just a few months after we have celebrated the birth of this real human being, we must commemorate his death. The cuddly baby in the manger becomes the grisly corpse on the cross. How is it possible that these two are the same? And what can it mean for our salvation?

●   ●   ●

WHY DID HE HAVE TO DIE?

Novelist Tim Winton was not a churchgoer.[3] But he had heard many Bible stories as a child, and when he became a father, he told them to his son, Jesse. Most of the stories were about Jesus, but they were always about Jesus' life, never his death. Tim didn't tell Jesse that Jesus had been crucified. When Jesse was seven, Tim decided it was time.

Tim and Jesse lived in a small, cold house in "a windswept lonely place." On Good Friday, they climbed into Jesse's bunk to get warm. Jesse asked for a Jesus story. Tim took a deep breath and launched into the tale of Jesus' crucifixion. He told Jesse how Jesus walked to Golgotha, how men drove nails through him. It surprised Tim how many details he remembered. He realized he had heard this story "so many—almost too many—times."

---

3 Winton, a masterful novelist (*That Eye, the Sky, The Riders, Shallows, Cloudstreet, Breath*), is regarded as one of Australia's most gifted writers. He told this story in "A Conversation with Tim Winton," conducted by Michael McGirr in *Image: A Journal of the Arts and Religion*, Issue #10 (Summer 1995), 43–58.

But telling it to his son, Tim felt the shock afresh. "I was in a complete state of nakedness psychologically," he says. "I couldn't get through the story without being torn. . ." As for Jesse, he couldn't believe his ears. Winton writes: "Before I got to the end, [Jesse] was already there. The very idea that his Jesus could have this happen to him was absolutely heartbreaking. . . We [lay] there on this little narrow bed and howled for. . . twenty minutes."

In some ways, Jesse's story resembles Stephen Paine's bedroom encounter with his father and the story of the cross. No doubt, both little boys wondered the same thing: why would someone kill Jesus? For Stephen Paine, the answer came ready-made: Jesus had to die because only a brutal punishment can convince the Almighty not to discard bad human beings like pieces of trash. To Stephen's ears, the Almighty must have seemed hard-hearted—not only toward human beings, but also toward his son Jesus. There is no sign that Stephen and his father howled in heartbreak, like Tim and Jesse did when they heard the story of Jesus' death.

In this chapter, I want to answer Jesse's and Stephen's unspoken question rather differently than Stephen's father did. I will propose a less hard-hearted alternative to evangelicalism's "defining story." In my view, there *is* something wrong with us—badly wrong—that needs fixing. But what's wrong isn't that we have angered God by offending his holiness or rebelling against his law. What's wrong is a deep sickness of soul that moves God with compassion.[4]

When God looks on us with kindly eyes of love, he sees what the father in Jesus' parable about the "prodigal son" would have seen had he trailed his son to the far country and observed his lonely

---

4 Marcus Borg depicts Jesus as radically criticizing holiness as a paradigm for governing the social world and, instead, advocating compassion as the basis for social relations. Instead of saying, "be holy as God is holy," Jesus said, "be compassionate as God is compassionate." *Conflict, Holiness and Politics in the Teachings of Jesus* (Harrisburg, PA: Trinity Press International, 1998), 139. I suggest we permit compassion rather than holiness to restructure our understanding of the atonement as well.

habitation among the pigs. God sees beloved children, sick of soul, trapped in a nightmare we have unwittingly created, without a clue as to what we need for true healing. And God wants to do what the prodigal's father wanted to do: invite these lost children home, bringing healing and peace to their souls. God wants to find a way to transform floundering, suffering children into real human beings. Because God understands what's wrong with us, such a transformation will have to grow out of God's own suffering.

In the previous chapter, I offered my understanding of what was "right" about Jesus. He was able to be a real human being because his internal war had ceased. He was no longer at enmity with any part of himself. He knew the Father loved all of who he was, so he could love it all, too. And he could love all of everyone he met. He embodied, inside and out, "the peace that passes all understanding."

The disciples did not—at least, before the resurrection—experience that peace. Until we have been awakened and transformed by an experience of love, we *can't* experience that peace. Internal warfare is our normal state.[5] Because our warfare splashes out into the surrounding world, creating enemies among people we know personally as well as people in distant places, the body count is very high.

But the first victim is ourselves—a truth we manage to "forget" in our compulsion to find and fix the problem "out there." This self-victimization and its inevitable fruit—the victimization of others—is what is wrong with us. If we can understand how it works, we may see more clearly why Jesus had to die to save us from it.

·   ·   ·

---

5 Paul, the apostle, seems to suggest that this enslavement to internal warfare is one meaning of the term "sin," when it is used to designate not a specific act, but a general condition (Romans 7:14–20).

SUFFERING AT SIX

I want to tell three stories that illustrate this internal warfare in life's most ordinary events. I'll begin very close to home.

I am six years old, sitting in the front row of my father's church during the annual revival services. A visiting preacher is working hard to save our souls, and it's taking longer than usual. I'm suffering, but not at this moment for my soul. It's my bladder that's in great pain. I need a bathroom—right *now*. But I can't bring myself to stand up and walk that long central aisle to the rear exit. All those heads turned my way, all those gazes fixed on me. I can't bear the thought.

I sit as still as I can and tense the appropriate muscles. The preacher tells his last few stories and invites sinners to the altar. If I'm lucky, the service will end in a few minutes. But sinners are not responding, so the preacher persists. We sing multiple stanzas of an invitation hymn. A few sinners step forward. The preacher is encouraged. We sing a few more. My heart is sinking. My legs are trembling. I wonder whether it's possible for bladders to burst under pressure. Sinners are gathering right in front of me, at the altar, cutting off my escape route. I've waited too long; I've passed the point of no return.

My six-year-old mind makes a desperate decision. I will let just a little out. That will relieve the pressure and get me through the benediction. Nobody will notice just a little. So I do, and I feel sudden relief. But not for long—the pressure is building again. The preacher has found his second wind. I let a little more out. In a few minutes, a little more. Finally, in an exhilarating rush, I let go. What a wonderful feeling.

But the relief is short-lived. I notice an odor, and I'm sure the sinners kneeling on the carpet just in front of me notice it, too. My tan trousers are turning to dusky brown. The service is ending, the congregation is rising. I'm glued to my seat. I can hardly breathe.

The aftermath is less catastrophic than I imagine it will be. I whisper to my mother. She hustles me out a side door, takes me home and helps me into dry clothes. Mercifully, she says it's all right and gives no speeches.

But I am full of dread. I imagine that everyone in church knows what happened to the preacher's oldest kid. I'll not be able to show my face again without seeing the laughter in people's eyes and hearing the taunts from the lips of my peers. And I'm angry: angry at my father for being the pastor of this church; at my mother for making the family sit up front with him during revival services; at the church people for the shame I expect to feel from them the next time I see their faces. My anger says: "It's all their fault. The enemy is out there."

But this voice is purely reactive, a part of me rising to protect me from the unbearable intensity of another voice. This voice says: "It's your own fault. You're six years old—and you're wetting your pants in church? You don't have the courage to do a simple thing like go to the bathroom? You actually imagined you could let a little out and nobody would notice? What were you thinking! Now everybody has seen what a little baby you really are. You *deserve* whatever ridicule you get." This voice turns my enmity inward. I hate the small, weak, scared, easily hurt person I am inside. I would like to obliterate that person from the planet.

Can a dying man save me from this brutal disconnection with myself—a disconnection from which flows all that the Bible calls "sin"—and make me whole?[6]

* * *

6 It is likely that, in his dying moments, Jesus lost control of his bladder in full public view. If so, the argument of this chapter will be that it was for my salvation.

I'M SCUM

In David James Duncan's novel, *The Brothers K*, a teenage girl struggles with a similar disconnection. [7] Bet's older brother Irwin has been emotionally broken by his experience in combat. He has been moved into his family's home and lies virtually comatose in an upstairs bedroom. Bet cannot keep herself from spying on Irwin at night, watching and listening as Irwin's wife Linda works out her own sorrow and anger as she tries to bring Irwin back to life.

What Bet hears appalls and fascinates her. She confesses her secret in a letter to her older brother, Everett:

> [Linda] goes in with Irwin. She takes off her clothes. Then she takes off Irwin's clothes. And she does things. Whispers to him, like lovers do, or just cries and cries, while she rubs him, every-where. Rubs him and slaps him. "Wake up, wake up, come out of this! You can hear me, liar! You hear, you fucker! Look at me. You feel this. Look at your penis. You couldn't do this if you were so dead! Wake up, you lying bastard!'

Bet's voyeurism shames and mortifies her. She tells Everett:

> I'm sick in the head. . . I sneak around, Everett, and listen at doors. I've been doing it for years. I can't stand myself for doing it, I hate myself. . . I'm a worm. I'm scum. . .

Bet's self-enmity and her enmity for Linda cycle in an endless feedback loop. "[Linda's] crazy," she tells Everett. "I really think she's ill. . . I'm sick too, sicker than her. But I'm starting to hate her for it. I shouldn't. I shouldn't even know. But I can't sleep knowing

---

7   (New York: Doubleday, 1992), 606–610.

they're down there, and she's doing this. . . I hate me. I hate her. . . Linda's sick. I'm sicker."

Everett's response to Bet displays a wisdom born of his own difficult journey toward wholeness. He helps Bet see that the part of her that is fascinated with Linda's behavior is nothing to be ashamed of:

> I would guess their bodies are beautiful when you watch. . . So maybe you get off on watching, feel aroused yourself? I just want to say that those are normal feelings, Bet, healthy sexual feelings, there's nothing sick about them, or about you. So don't revel in some imaginary darkness, don't puff it all up into something deeply and majestically wrong.

He does not condone her surreptitious behavior—in fact, he helps her see that her intrusion into the mystery of Linda's and Irwin's relationship is a kind of theft. But the one it's really hurting, he tells her, is herself. He helps her understand that a part of her already knows this, or else she would not feel sick. He lets her know she is not alone in her obsession: "I've done things as strange, we all do strange things." He assures her that she will someday have a part in a similar mystery, a beautiful mystery all her own.

Behind every word he speaks to Bet is Everett's awareness of the terror we feel, and the self-hatred that can issue from it, when we touch the edges of our own neediness and feel the shame wash over us. Can a naked man on a cross give us fresh eyes for our own neediness, draw its sting, and heal our enmity with ourselves and others?

•　　•　　•

MY HUMBLE SELF

Writer Lewis Nordan offers another glimpse of "what's wrong with us" in this story from his memoir.[8]

A boy of fifteen mows lawns in Mississippi, dreaming of faraway places. It is the 1950s, and New York City, he hears, is full of beatniks. He decides his place is with them—sitting in coffee houses, listening to jazz. He takes a Greyhound to Grand Central Station and checks into a tiny, dirty room in a shabby hotel. He lies on the bed naked, sipping from the half-pint of whiskey he brought with him from Mississippi. Despair and loneliness settle in. He wishes he had never left home.

Drunk and still naked, he slips down the empty hallway and into the bathroom. When he returns to his room, his door has swung shut and he is locked out. He retreats to the bathroom and slaps enough wet toilet paper on portions of his body to provide the thinnest semblance of modesty. He pushes the elevator call button and soon the elevator door swings open.

The elevator has an operator—an abnormally small man. This "midget" wears a faded, dirty uniform and a pillbox hat. He is sullen and unfriendly. For a price he agrees to go to the lobby and bring the boy a key.

The sight of the elevator operator puts the boy into a terrible depression. He feels himself condemned by cosmic powers. He sees in the elevator operator "a freak": a tiny man, "wrinkled, dirty, alcoholic," his voice "a bitter squeak." In that small man, in other words, the boy sees himself. Years later, he writes:

> In a sense, the [little man] was me, tragedy and comedy locked
> in a single human form. He was the hidden part of myself that,

8 "My Humble Self," from *Boy with Loaded Gun* (Chapel Hill: Algonquin Books, 2000) in *Harper's Magazine* (December 1999), 39–42.

before I could become an adult, I had to accept as my own—solitary, lonely, deformed, drunk, costumed in ways that least spoke of myself, small, out of proportion to what I wanted out of life, but me in any case, the inner self that has nothing to do with the inner child we hear so much about these days. This was the inner midget, my humble self.

If Nordan had been an angrier boy, more heavily scarred inside—or perhaps in the company of drunken friends rather than standing alone in a dank hallway—he might have projected his shame outward into violence toward this small man who looked too much like "the hidden part" of himself.

Instead, Nordan says, "This midget was my salvation." Somehow he had the grace—if not at that moment, then in ensuing years—to put his arm around this little man inside him and accept it as an important part of himself, in need of comfort. He was able to make peace with it and to welcome it home.

Is this a metaphor of the wholeness Jesus offers us by substituting himself for those parts of us we are tempted to despise—our small, solitary, lonely, humble selves—when he hangs, for all to see, on the cross?

•   •   •

THE REVENGE OF THE WEAK

I'm asking "what's wrong with us" as a way of moving toward a fresh understanding of the meaning of the crucifixion. I've begun with examples from the ordinary lives of young people—because most readers will remember experiences like these, and because it's during those early years of our lives that our internal enmity gets underway.[9] But if we think on a larger scale, "what's wrong with us" goes far beyond the torments of a little boy in church or a teenager in a hotel hallway.

What's wrong with human beings is not just that we hate ourselves, but that we try to diminish the intensity of our self-hate by hating one another. We fly into rages and hurt one another, we launch crusades against one another, we persecute and slaughter whole races of people. What's wrong with us when we do unspeakable violence to one another?

James Gilligan, a medical doctor, spent years as director of a hospital for the criminally insane and as director of mental health for the Massachusetts prison system. He had daily contact with brutal murderers, spoke with them at length about their lives, came to know their hearts. In his book, *Violence*, he tells some of their stories.[10] Although I will spare the reader the most disturbing details, the following stories still deserve a "parental advisory." They are hard to read without revulsion and a breaking heart.

Ralph W, father and husband, Sunday-school teacher and choir director, murdered a fourteen-year-old girl and buried her body in his backyard. Later, he reported feeling no remorse—in fact, he said, "I've never shown feelings because I haven't had them." He remembered one exception, however: as a child, he was "filled with rage" when his mother humiliated him by telling his friends

---

9 Both of these examples, and most of the succeeding examples, describe self-enmity in men. Gershen Kaufman, in *Shame: The Power of Caring,* observes that while the same internal dynamic is at work in men and women, women may be "shame-averse" while men are "shame-phobic," implying shame is felt more intensely in men than in women.

It has often been observed, however, that the effects of men's self-enmity is more visible—men turn their shame more quickly into violence against others, while women turn it more often against themselves. Below, I will tell the story of Dostoyevsky's Lise, who turns her self-enmity toward others in her imagination, but also toward her own body in reality.

10 James Gilligan, *Violence: Reflections on a National Epidemic* (New York: Vintage Books, 1996). Stories in this section can be found on pages 34–35, 60–64, 78–82.

he had a "crush" on a girl at school. He knew that, as an inadequate and unattractive person, he would be publicly ridiculed, now that his secret was out. He never expressed the rage he felt—toward his mother, toward himself—until the moment when he took the life of an innocent, vulnerable teenage girl.

Ross L, twenty years old, killed a former high school class-mate who offered him a ride home on a cold winter night. He stabbed and mutilated her, and threw her body out of the car. He told Gilligan that other people had always treated him unfairly, disrespected and picked on him, perceiving him as a weakling and not a "real man." He said he "didn't like the way [the girl] was looking at me" and "didn't want her talking about me."

As a high school student, although he had been unsuccessful in love, he had bragged of being the local "Don Juan." He had also boasted of his "mechanical expertise with cars." After his crime, he said that by accepting a ride from this girl, "he had been forced to admit that he lacked both the money and the mechanical skills to have a car of his own, and he had to depend on her for help."

Dennis X, aged nineteen, killed a neighbor whom he hardly knew, accusing him of being the devil and planting unwanted sexual desires inside him. He felt ashamed of these desires, but also of his wish to be taken care of, like a baby, by his mother and sister. Gilligan observes that "feelings of worthlessness, failure, embarrass-ment, weakness, and being less than a man were central to Dennis X's experience of himself." Immediately after the murder, he felt less shame because he had proven himself to be a man.

These are only a few of the horrible case studies Gilligan recounts. He writes:

> I have yet to see a serious act of violence that was not provoked
> by the experience of feeling shamed and humiliated, disrespected
> and ridiculed, and that did not represent the attempt to prevent

or undo this "loss of face."[11] In each of these cases, the murder victim was barely known by the murderer, and had done nothing disrespectful to provoke the murderer's violent acts. Clearly, the feelings of shame and disrespect were coming from inside, from a part of the murderer that was hating itself—was accusing the murderer of being weak, inadequate, worthless, baby-like. These murders occurred because an innocent external party got caught in the crossfire between *internal* enemies.[12]

The person each of these men murdered was in every case the killer's *second* victim. The first was the murderer himself. Can a bloodied body on a cross bring healing to this kind of enmity?[13]

*   *   *

NO REFUGE AND NO APPEAL

The question, "what's wrong with us," can take us into still deeper waters. The truth is that for human beings, although not for *real* human beings, there is nothing imaginable, or perhaps unimaginable, that cannot be enacted—that *has* not been enacted.[14]

---

11 Gilligan, *Violence*, 110.

12 Gilligan says that killing doesn't actually take the shame away because "one is left still knowing one's own shameful secrets" (85).

13 Gilligan reminds us that the first recorded account of the "genesis" of shame is in the book of Genesis, when Adam and Eve discover they are naked. Their experience of self-enmity begins when they cover themselves, to hide their nakedness from a God whom, under the influence of the serpent, they misapprehend as "the Almighty" (83).

14 It would not be difficult to trace the genesis of the worst outbreaks of mass violence in human history to the very same internal dynamic of self-enmity and self-victimization. Gilligan interprets the Holocaust as the result of the Nazis' sense of self-enmity or shame. The "collective murder of the Jews can be seen as a symbolic representation of the thought: 'If we destroy the Jews, we will destroy shame—we cannot be shamed'." (69) Philip Gourevitch describes how mass shame resulted in the murder of a million Rwandans in *We Wish to Inform You that Tomorrow We Will Be Killed with Our Families* (New York:

High on the list of the imaginable yet unimaginable is the abuse of children. We turn away in disgust from such stories. Even in our penitentiaries, child abusers symbolize the most heinous of criminals, and their fellow-inmates make them pay.[15]

Stories of child abuse figure significantly in what many consider to be the world's greatest work of literature, Fyodor Dostoyevsky's *The Brothers Karamazov*. Ivan, the family "intellectual," uses gruesome accounts of child abuse to counter his brother Alyosha's belief in a loving God.[16] Ivan describes true stories, taken from his newspaper, of soldiers cutting fetuses from their mothers' wombs, tossing them into the air and catching them on the points of bayonets. The soldiers surround one mother, entertain her baby, make it laugh, put a pistol to its face—and pull the trigger. These men, Ivan adds sardonically, "are particularly fond of sweet things."

Ivan offers many stories matching these in horror. In some, it's the children's own parents who commit the most heartless atrocities. One example only: A "well-educated, cultured" father beat his child with a birch rod covered with twigs because "it stings more." Ivan comments: "I know for a fact that there are people who at every

---

Picador, 1998). Ernest Becker explores a similar dynamic in *Escape from Evil* (New York: The Free Press, 1975).

Is it possible that George W. Bush went to war against Iraqi leader Saddam Hussein because he and his vice-president didn't know how to become friends with the voice inside them that accused them of being weaklings?

15 It seems that prisoners who persecute imprisoned child abusers are working out a kind of crude justice. Gilligan writes: "The violent criminals I have known have been objects of violence from early childhood. They have seen their closest relatives—their fathers and mothers and sisters and brothers—murdered in front of their eyes, often by other family members. As children, these men were shot, axed, scalded, beaten, strangled, tortured, drugged, starved, suffocated, set on fire, thrown out of windows, raped, or prostituted by mothers who were their 'pimps'; their bones have been broken; they have been locked in closets or attics for extended periods, and one man I know was deliberately locked by his parents in an empty icebox until he suffered brain damage from oxygen deprivation before he was let out" (45–46).

16 Material in this section is taken from 220–223.

blow are worked up to sensuality. . . which increases progressively at every blow they inflict." He believes "it is a peculiar characteristic of many people—this love of torturing children, and children only."

Ivan casts his net as widely as possible: "In every man a demon lies hidden—the demon of rage, the demon of lustful heat at the screams of the tortured victim." Ivan believes there is a more or less sadistic part living—although perhaps deeply hidden—in every human being.

But why is sadism so often attracted to children? In Ivan's view, "it's just their defenselessness that tempts the tormentor." The child "has no refuge and no appeal" and this "sets the tormentor's vile blood on fire." But what exactly is it about sheer vulnerability that evokes rage? Is it not true that those who abuse children have most often themselves been abused? Are they compulsively repeating the abuse done to them, compulsively turning their rage against the object who looks exactly like the part of them that has been wounded—a naked, suffering part whose weakness is so painful, so shameful, that only rage directed outward can relieve the self-hatred and self-punishment that it evokes?

Is it possible that a suffering Jesus, hanging naked and helpless on a cross, might awaken memories of the helpless child inside each of us? If so, then in those who have suffered abuse, he might have the potential *both* to set his tormentors' blood on fire *and*—in a moment of salvation—to heal the parts of them that look just like that body on the cross.

Adults who abuse children in unconscious repetition of the abuse they suffered as children betray a tragic distortion of their humanity. The compulsiveness of this behavior illustrates well how twisted can be the expressions of our internal warfare. I find it easy to agree with Dostoyevsky when he suggests that a "demon of rage" lies behind this behavior.

Dostoyevsky's novel also offers us the portrait of a teenage girl who is disturbed enough to merit the label "a little demon." Lise is one of Dostoyevsky's most intriguing characters. She trusts Alyosha, a gentle and sensitive young man, more than anyone else in her life. In a burst of honest confession, she tells him that she wants to do evil things—like setting fire to her house, marrying someone just to beat him, committing murder. She tells the story of a man who crucified a four-year-old on a wall, admitting she imagines watching the child die, enjoying his pain. At fourteen, Lise is a world-class sadist.

But there is also a masochist in her—her cruel intent toward others is matched by a cruel intent toward herself. After Alyosha leaves, she unbolts the door, puts her finger into the crack, and slams the door, leaving her finger crushed and bloody. What causes this kind of internal enmity? Lise has a mother who raves hysterically, who cannot listen, who cannot be present to her daughter, who fantasizes leaving her daughter and traveling to a distant land to be a "sister of mercy."

Lise's sadism towards children is an outward projection of a sadism towards herself, which punishes herself for being a person her mother cannot love. There is a childlike part in Lise who feels utterly alone, uncared-for, rejected; and another part in Lise who hates herself for being, as she sees it, inherently unlovable.[17]

What can Jesus possibly do to heal Lise's enmity with herself?

•   •   •

THE "DEMON" OF GODLINESS

Demons—sometimes called "unclean spirits"—figure frequently in the stories about Jesus. They do seem, in most cases, to be demons of rage, and they do turn their rage against their host, giving us graphic examples of self-enmity. Those who are demon-possessed

---

17 References to Lise's story are taken from Dostoyevsky, *Karamazov*, 191, 51, 529–531, 60.

pummel their own bodies with rocks and chains or throw themselves into fires.[18] Is the real object of their hatred the helpless child inside them? Are they threatened by Jesus *precisely because* he awakens their own childlike parts that hurt and want to be welcomed; that are lonely and yearn to be loved rather than exiled into the darkness?

The writer of Mark's Gospel brings demons into his narrative at exactly the same moment he brings the godly into his narrative. Maybe he wants us to notice that the devout and the mad are related species. They're both good examples of "what's wrong with us"— they're divided against themselves. Perhaps this, in part, explains their hostility to Jesus: they see in Jesus a person *not* divided against himself, whose childlike wholeness is so inviting to one part of them that it takes the strongest possible response from another part to resist that invitation.

Jesus takes on the godly as directly as he does the demon-possessed. He notices that they're keen on having a good reputation. "They do their deeds to be seen by others," "they love to have the place of honor at banquets," and "to be greeted with respect in the marketplaces, and to have people call them rabbi." He calls them hypocrites: "You are like whitewashed tombs, which on the outside look beautiful, but inside they are full of the bones of the dead and all kinds of filth" (Matthew 23:5–7, 27–28). That's what becomes of the weak and helpless and hurting parts of us that we hate and exile into darkness: instead of joining the other parts of us in a hospitable inner world, they fester and become diseased.

Jesus knows the godly are not aware that they have made enemies of themselves. After he gives sight to a blind man, Jesus says in the presence of the godly: "I came into this world. . . so that those who do not see may see and those who do see may become blind." The godly seem offended: "Surely we are not blind, are we?" Jesus replies

---

18 See, for example, Mark 5:3 and 9:22.

cryptically: "If you were blind, you would not have sin. But now that you say 'we see,' your sin remains" (John 9:39–41).

Jesus is saying: if you could admit you are blind, you would be seeing clearly for the first time, and that insight would inaugurate a more honest relationship with yourself, with others—and with God. But since you cannot admit that you are blind, you're trapped in your self-alienation and self-enmity. Your enmity with yourself—which you "medicate" by being pious—splashes out into enmity towards others, particularly those who resemble the vulnerable self inside you that you have made an enemy.

Two stories in Mark illustrate this self-enmity "turned outward." In the first, Jesus heals a man's withered hand on the sabbath. The godly, watching from the sidelines, accuse Jesus of violating the sabbath (Mark 3:1–6). In the second, the godly try to trap Jesus into approving what, in the context, seems a cavalier permission to divorce one's wife (Mark 10:2–9).

In each story, the godly exhibit an astounding lack of compassion for vulnerable or childlike human beings. In both cases, Mark says the godly's hearts are "hardened." What's wrong with us when we cannot feel compassion toward helpless, childlike persons? It's likely they remind us of helpless, childlike persons inside ourselves toward whom we feel enmity, not compassion.[19]

It's the godly who crucify Jesus—another helpless, childlike

---

[19] Matthew's Gospel (2:1–18) offers a similar story of a heart without compassion—in this case, for actual children. King Herod is "troubled" by a star that announces the birth of a king, works himself into "a furious rage," and orders every male child under two to be killed.

Why so indiscriminate and heartless a slaughter? When the wise men do not return to tell him the whereabouts of the baby Jesus, do they awaken his felt smallness, his impotence, exposing the ridiculous frailty hidden under royal robes? Was this his logic: "I will kill those who awaken my deepest fears, reminding me that within me there is a vulnerable infant, 'without refuge or appeal'?"

Thanks to this story of Herod, the torture of helpless children runs as a dark undercurrent beneath the joyful account of the birth of the helpless Christ-child.

person who may actually resemble someone very close to themselves, although a self they cannot love. Can this crucifixion become for these unwitting "child-abusers" a painful, liberating moment of truth?[20]

*   *   *

THE DUST OF DEATH

If the crucifixion is meant to be a moment of truth, what truth will it need to tell? It will need to show us that our own worst enemy is *not* God. Our own worst enemy is ourselves. And if it is to be a healing moment, in which we experience compassion toward those parts of us that we have despised and rejected, it will have to be much more than a moment of truth. It will have to be a moment of love.

The narrative of the cross invites this moment to occur. The Gospel writers give inordinate attention to the last week of Jesus' life leading up to his crucifixion. "Here is where you will meet Jesus," they seem to say. They don't contrast the events of his death with the events of his life. They imply rather that his manner of death is a continuation of his manner of life as a real human being. They say: here is how a real human being—a human being no longer at

---

20 Dostoyevsky's *The Brothers Karamazov* (272–273) offers a beautiful example of such a self-revelation. When the saintly elder, Father Zossima, is a young man, he is spurned by the woman he loves. This leaves him feeling powerless, shamed and "filled with sudden irrepressible fury." In the aftermath, he beats his servant ferociously.

Waking the next morning, he feels "vile and shameful" and remembers what he has done: "It all rose before my mind. . . he stood before me and I was beating him straight on the face and he was holding his arms stiffly down, his head erect, his eyes fixed upon me as though on parade. He staggered at every blow and did not even dare to raise his hands to protect himself. This is what a man has been brought to, and that was a man beating a fellow creature!. . . It was as though a sharp dagger had pierced me."

Young Zossima falls on his bed and weeps. "In truth," he thinks, "perhaps I am more than all others responsible for all, a greater sinner than all men in the world." This becomes for Zossima a transforming moment, the commencement of his journey of salvation.

enmity with himself—dies at the hands of those whose self-enmity has gone ballistic.

Can we allow our eyes to linger on the dying Jesus, ugly and disturbing as he is? If so, what might we see?

A naked human being has been drilled to a wooden post. Ragged figures hang on either side of him. Though they cry out to one another, each is utterly, unfathomably alone. The crowds reserve their cruelest jeers for the one in the center.

His body is splayed like a carcass awaiting the butcher's knife. Gaunt pelvic bones protrude. Ribs can be numbered. The head hangs forward, eyes opaque with pain. A human being, barely alive.

His lips are moving, almost imperceptibly forming the first words of an old poem, a memory from his eager youth, now so far away. Those ancient words are now his: "My God, my God, why have you forsaken me?" (Psalm 22:1). A timeless human cry, straining from a black abyss toward a silent God.

As death's fog envelopes his failing flesh, he hears the tortured lines of this ancient poet. Do we have ears that can really hear them?

> Why are you so far from helping me,
> from the words of my groaning?
> O my God, I cry by day, but you do not answer;
> and by night, but find no rest.
> I am poured out like water,
> and all my bones are out of joint;
> my heart is like wax;
> it is melted within my breast;
> my mouth is dried up like a potsherd,
> and my tongue sticks to my jaws;
> you lay me in the dust of death.

This is a cry of abjection from the dust of death.[21]

What salvation could possibly sprout from such unpromising dust? This stricken form offers no guided tour of bliss, musters no triumphant army, composes no organized body of religious answers. He is simply and purely human flesh in its moment of extremity. He is the bruised and wounded creature at its most frightened, its most despairing, its most vulnerable. How can this grotesque image, a human being in hopeless abjection, become our salvation?

There is a well-conditioned evangelical inside me who knows the answer. This part of me jumps out of his seat, frantically waving his hand in the air. He wants to dampen my identification with the suffering Jesus by reminding me of evangelicalism's "defining story." He says:

> This dying man is God's Son, sent here by the almighty Father to pay the penalty for my sins. Jesus says he's forsaken because his Father is up in heaven awaiting the consummation of his justice. God's eyes—too holy to look upon sin—must be turned away from his precious son. The Father is allowing his wrath to flow until the very moment Jesus breathes his last. Then, the Father will be free to open his arms to his errant children—the ones, at least, who confess their sins and admit that their sins killed Jesus. Toward all the rest, God will continue to nurse his wrath, even while beckoning them to accept his love.'[22]

---

21 Psalm 22 gradually segues into tones of praise: "He has not despised or abhorred the affliction of the afflicted. . . Posterity shall serve him. . . and proclaim his deliverance. . ." Perhaps this tone is faintly echoed in Jesus words from the cross, "Father, into thy hands I commit my spirit" (Mark 23:46). But if we rush too quickly away from the "eternal now" of Jesus' torment in order to breathe the air of triumph, we desert Jesus in his suffering—as we desert ourselves in our suffering—and cannot experience the saving meaning of the cross.

22 "We have made the bitterness of the cross. . . tolerable to ourselves by learning to understand it as a necessity for the process of salvation." Moltmann, quoting H. J. Iwand in *The Crucified God*, 41.

This "evangelical" part of me deserves a hearing. His fears need to be understood. His yearning for salvation needs to be recognized and honored. He is doing his best to protect me from touching the painful edges of my own suffering. I want to meet him compassionately, so he will relax a bit and allow me some openness to hear a different story.

Luther invites me to that different story. This crucified human being, he says, is not the object of a hard-hearted Father's wrath. He *is* the "Father," present in human flesh. He is "Emmanuel"—God with us.[23] He bears our mutilation without accusing or condemning us. In Jesus' life, we have seen the Father's love in action—welcoming the adulterous woman, raising Lazarus, giving sight to Bartimaeus, speaking respectfully with the five-times-married Samaritan woman, sorrowing over the uncomprehending young lawyer, socializing with prostitutes and tax collectors and sinners, engaging tenderly with children, gently accepting Judas the betrayer and Peter the denier. In the person of Jesus, we have seen a Father who can be trusted to deal gently with us and love us at our worst.

This Father, present to us in that abject figure, tells us we are forgiven even when we set ourselves resolutely against love. We are forgiven because the Father knows that, when we resist love, we cannot possibly know what we are doing. In dying helplessly, the Father shows us that our enmity will *not* provoke his enmity. The Father *will continue* to love us, to look warmly on us, even to "like" us—because the Father knows that the "real" us, hidden beneath the parts of us that battle constantly with one another, is beautiful, and gentle and as deeply compassionate as the One who first created us.

---

23 I am taking Martin Luther's advice, as quoted in Chapter 6: "The true God. . . does not will to be found and grasped any place else than in Jesus." We must *join the Father with Jesus*—"so closely and solidly together" that they share "one and the same word, heart, and will."

This God, without a trace of "almightiness," evokes our trust and our love. When we *meet* this un-"Godly" God on the cross, and *experience* this moment of healing love, we will have taken the first step in the journey toward salvation. We will, in fact, have "repented" —we will have new eyes for God. We will know beyond a doubt that God is not our worst enemy. We will know that God is not an enemy at all.

And we will be prepared for the second movement of our salvation—if anything, more difficult than the first.

.   .   .

YOUR SINS PUT HIM THERE!

Evangelicalism's defining story tells me I am emphatically *not* the figure on the cross. Jesus is "divine"—the "Son of the Almighty"— and I am human, the opposite of divine, a limited earthly being. Jesus is morally perfect and I am a willful, inveterate sinner.

This radical distinction between Jesus and me is precisely what permits him to die in my place—it qualifies him to be my "substitute" as a "sacrifice" to the Father's wrath. In many evangelical sermons, that radical distinction is accentuated: "Your sins put him there! Your fists nailed him to the cross! Your rebellion crucified the blessed Son of God! His blood is on your hands!" Guilt and shame are wielded skillfully to place the widest possible chasm between myself and the figure on the cross.[24]

---

24 This dis-identification with Jesus has, arguably, made it easier for white Christians to participate in the lynching of African Americans. Lynchings often paralleled Jesus' crucifixion. As Jesus died on a "tree," lynching victims were often hung from or tied to trees for gruesome tortures, and sometimes victims cried out to the tortured Jesus as they died.

Because evangelical atonement theology has buffered Christian sensibility with "sacrifice" imagery, trading on the "penal substitutionary" atonement theory, and identified Jesus as "other" than ourselves, Christians could re-enact the crucifixion scene—even

The tragedy—indeed, the cruelty—of this preaching is that it mires me more deeply in my "lostness." It *accentuates* my enmity with myself. It follows the logic of guilt and shame: to bring people to God, you have to make them run away from themselves. So it tells me my sin should disgust me just as it disgusts God. It raises the decibel level of the part of me that stands in judgment over the rest of me. It heightens the contempt I already feel for the voices inside me that I label "bad." It fuels an inner climate of fear instead of trust, of hostility instead of hospitality.[25] So its promise of salvation is a cruel hoax. It deepens my wounds instead of healing them. It cannot give birth to a real human being.

If there is to be salvation in this cross, it must help me see myself as more *like* than *unlike* the figure on the cross. It must give me eyes for *myself* in this naked, dying human.

* * *

THERE IS NO ONE TO HELP

I suggest we read Psalm 22 again, but not with evangelicalism's "defining story" ringing in our ears. Let us imagine that it is perhaps not about the divine Son whom God chose to punish in our place.

Let's read it slowly, pausing after each line, "holding" the words gently as they offer themselves to us. Let's listen from the inside, attending to the captives in our inner prison—the parts of us we

---

make a burning cross the symbol of their righteousness—without feeling humanly identified with or connected to the victim who symbolically filled the place of Jesus.

This ground is explored provocatively by Orlando Patterson in *Rituals of Blood: Consequences of Slavery in Two American Centuries* (New York: Basic Civitas, 1998), 171–232.

25 Conventional religion, as one of the "principalities and powers" described by St. Paul in Colossians 2:8–19 and other texts, depends on the continuing reign of fear instead of trust.

never mention aloud, voices we hear only during long nights of wakefulness, in fleeting dreams, or in ephemeral daytime images.

> My God, my God, why have you forsaken me?
> Why are you so far from helping me,
>> from the words of my groaning?
> O my God, I cry by day, but you do not answer;
>> and by night, but I find no rest. . .
> O Lord, do not be far away!
>> O my help, come quickly to my aid!

Something in me wants to shout: "No, no, this isn't me. This is much too dramatic, too sentimental! I've never felt *this* forsaken— not *really*. . . I've never *really* suffered, not like this victim on the cross. I don't feel *really* alone. I've got friends who love me. I *know* God is with me."

I know this voice very well. It works overtime to protect me from the frightening upsurges of a yawning loneliness; from the flashes of despair that tell me God does not exist, that nothing means anything, that the universe is black and cold and empty; from the panic that overtakes me, momentarily, when I see a challenge ahead of me that I know I can't meet, and I see no source of help.[26]

Can I ask this protective part of me, gently and appreciatively, to trust the presence of the Spirit in this psalm? To soften its hold for just a moment, so I can connect with the feelings I exile so effectively

---

[26] John Caputo—the most poetic of contemporary philosophers of religion—suggests in many places in his writings that authentic religious faith is always in dialogue with the voice of doubt. One example: "I do not think that we know whether we believe in God or not, not if we face the cold truth. On the contrary, I think we spend a good deal of time slipping back and forth between the two, between Abraham and Zarathustra, Augustine and Nietzsche, trying to find out what we think." *Radical Hermeneutics: Repetition, Deconstruction, and the Hermeneutic Project* (Bloomington, IN: Indiana University Press, 1987), 288.

from my awareness? Can I ask it to grant me just a few moments of freedom as I listen?

> I am a worm, and not human;
>> scorned by others. . .
> All who see me mock at me. . .
>> they shake their heads. . .

That self-protective voice returns: "Come on, now. Don't be so dramatic. You sound paranoid. You don't have *real* enemies. No one is plotting against you. Where is this self-pity coming from?" This part of me has helped me keep my equanimity by locking the "worm" away, out of sight and out of mind. It wants to help me forget the shame I often feel—my painful self-consciousness around strangers; my need to manage the impressions of others, to appear to them something more whole and shiny and all-competent than I really am; my unfounded suspicions that I am being laughed at.

Can I once again gently ask this protective part of me to trust the presence of a Father who is never ashamed of me, and to soften its hold for just a moment while I let myself connect with the part of me that feels the shame I've buried so deeply inside myself?

> Yet it was you who took me from the womb;
>> you kept me safe on my mother's breast.
> On you I was cast from birth,
>> and since my mother bore me
>> you have been my God.
> Do not be far from me, for trouble is near
>> and there is no one to help.

"No one to help"—the words soften something in me. The cries of a baby, the suffering eyes of a child—somehow they always move me. I try to hold back tears when I see pictures of children in hunger and pain with "no one to help." But my tears flow anyway. My heart hurts for the child crying in its crib, wet and cold in the night, hungry for milk or afraid of the dark, terrified that it has been abandoned forever. When I weep for these children, am I also weeping for a part of myself?[27]

A memory surfaces from childhood. It has flashed into my mind many times during my adult years, as if it is calling out to me. A part of me has consigned it to the category of the comical. But what is funny about it?

My parents left me to care for my younger brothers while they went to a midweek church meeting. I was perhaps eight. I took these "adult" responsibilities seriously. My two brothers also took their freedom from parental authority seriously. All hell broke loose. My brothers tore through the house, paying no attention to my frantic disciplinary measures. A feeling of abject helplessness welled up in me. Dark panic gripped me as the chaos rose like floodwaters around me. I needed help—desperately. I needed my parents. Where were they?

The time for their return was long past. Suddenly, it dawned on me: they had left me alone forever. Something, someone, had taken them. I would never see them again. I sank to the floor in the front hallway, slumped against the door and sobbed helplessly.

Are Jesus' tortured words calling me back to this moment? Do they want to remind me how my "carefree" childhood was actually punctured by moments of terror and forsakenness—moments I have mostly forgotten? Beneath the often-placid surface of our memories, aren't there lurking numerous forgotten brushes with helplessness or

---

27 "The pain hardest to bear is your own." Henri J. M. Nouwen, *The Inner Voice of Love: A Journey through Anguish to Freedom* (New York: Image Books, 1999), 88.

terror? With hurts that were not comforted? With petty but deeply wounding persecution? With seemingly incurable loneliness?

Is there anyone without at least one memory of such an experience, lurking behind the walls we build to distance ourselves from a yawning emotional abyss? Is a helpless child not still huddled somewhere in our inner world?[28] Does he or she not call for our attention during the difficult moments that come to every adult, and do we not most often turn our backs and look away?

If we relaxed the tight grip we have on our fears and our tears and listened to the psalm that reminded the dying Jesus of himself—if we imagined the desperate human being who uttered these words as the light died within him—might the suffering child inside us finally glimpse itself in the forlorn figure on the cross? Might that recognition constitute salvation?

* * *

VISITATION

The picture I have been painting in this chapter—of the melding together of the person I am on the inside with the person we see on the cross—is my attempt to describe what Christians call the "new birth." I would not write about it with such passion if it were not my own experience.[29]

---

28 "There is no present identity of a man without continuity with his past. Only then is a man present with all the strata of his life, for his childhood is a part of his present form. . . If a man develops himself in the *pathos* of God towards *sympatheia*, and *sympatheia* means openness, then in the situation of the crucified God man can develop openness backwards. There is no merely present or future authority before which he must separate himself from himself or deny his childhood. . . Openness to the future is conditioned by openness to the past." Moltmann, *Crucified God*, 311–313.

29 I have never been eager to share this story, lest it lose its immediacy for me and become a set piece in a canned narrative. I have only mentioned it aloud in three or four personal conversations, and have not written it down until prodded by friends who read this book in manuscript and said: "You must tell your own story." In retrospect, it seems a very small

It happened when I was in my late forties, on an average Sunday morning at the end of an average church service. I was sitting in a small armchair near the fireplace in the lounge that served as our meeting place. I have no recollection of which other "regulars" were in attendance, except for my brother-in-law, Jim, who was sitting nearby.

We had just sung a closing hymn, and the people around me were beginning to rise and greet one another. Small, quiet conversations had broken out in the room. I lingered in my chair and gazed absent-mindedly at the flowers on the hearth. My mind drifted. . . and then "something happened," the room and the people disappeared, and I was in another place and time. . .

And just as quickly I was back in the room, and I was on my feet, and Jim was looking at me: "Are you okay? You look a little dazed." I stared at him blankly for a few seconds, then shrugged "I'm okay" and left the room.

It was a dream-like state, except that I was fully conscious. A kind of vision. Alyosha, the third of the Karamazov brothers, had a mystical experience at his mentor's wake. Afterwards, he said: "Someone visited my soul in that hour." When I read this line, months after my own experience, I thought: "That's what it was—a visitation."

Against a dark, empty background, I saw a cross with a figure hanging on it. I knew the figure was Jesus. His eyes were downcast. He was in great pain. But then he wasn't Jesus any longer. He was my father, Walter Frank—same torn body as Jesus, but a different face, my father's face. And then he wasn't my father any more. He

---

thing, occupying the briefest moment in time, almost nothing at all; and yet it constitutes a pivotal moment in my life.

How does one speak rightly of such a paradox? Or should one speak at all? And yet, I have benefited from the willingness of others, some of whom I cite below, to tell their stories. So I offer mine in gratitude.

was me. He had my face. I was there, eyes downcast, hanging on a cross. And then it all faded and I was hearing Jim's voice.

For days, this visitation stayed with me. At first, I dismissed it as trivial, a funny trick my unconscious had played on me. But it didn't gradually dissolve—instead, it grew more solid. It seemed to be saying, "Pay attention." So I began to notice myself turning toward it with curiosity.

I felt sure of what it meant: that Jesus and my father and I were not three, but one. In our wounded humanity, we were not different, but the same. As time elapsed, I also noticed new feelings, a new awareness inside me. I felt all sense of enmity between Jesus and me, my father and me, myself and me was melting away. Somewhere beneath my skin I felt indissolubly connected to Jesus and to my father and to myself. The three of us seemed blended into one, washed in a sweet and tender love.

It was the moment Jesus came alive for me. My father came alive for me as well. And something in me came alive that is still alive today.

•   •   •

CHRIST CAME DOWN

The salvation event—we could call it a "new birth"—comes in many shapes and sizes, as many perhaps as there are human beings.

For Anne Lamott, the salvation event comes when she is "in a rather desperate situation, clearly alcoholic, suicidal, going down the tubes." She's just had an abortion, and is lying in bed, bleeding and drinking and smoking dope. She writes:

> I became aware of someone with me, hunkered down in the corner, and I just assumed it was my father, whose presence I had felt over the years when I was frightened and alone. The feeling was so

strong that I actually turned on the light for a moment to make sure no one was there—of course, there wasn't. But after a while, in the dark again, I knew beyond a doubt that it was Jesus. I felt him as surely as I feel my dog lying nearby as I write this. . . I felt him just sitting there on his haunches in the corner of my sleeping loft, watching me with patience and love.[30]

For Irwin Chance, the broken American soldier in David James Duncan's novel, *The Brothers K*, the salvation event comes in bits and pieces over the course of a life, but reaches a crescendo when he looks into the eyes of a Viet Cong boy who is about to be executed and sees the boy looking back at him with pure curiosity. A Bible verse floods back into him, one he had memorized in Sunday school as a kid: *"Whosoever shall humble himself as this little child something something, whoso shall help, or maybe receive, or anyhow shall stick up for one such child in My Name, receiveths, or sticks up for, or anyhow stands by Me*. Yeah."[31]

For a nameless little girl in Lydia Davis' story, "The Liminal Man," the salvation event comes as she lies in the dark "crying hopelessly":

Someone is angry; she has done some final thing for which there is no forgiveness tonight. No one will come in, and she can't go out. The finality of it terrifies her. It is a feeling close to a feeling she will die of it.

Then a figure comes in, "almost of its own accord," "small, soft, self-effacing," and "his presence tells her that all is well and she is good, and she has done her best though others may not think so."[32]

---

30 *Traveling Mercies: Some Thoughts on Faith* (New York: Anchor Books, 2000), 42, 49.
31 Irwin Chance is a fictional character in David James Duncan, *The Brothers K* (New York: Doubleday, 1992), 449.
32 *Break It Down* (Knopf: New York, 1986), 18–19.

For Mitsuko, the tortured, self-hating woman in Shusaku Endo's novel, *Deep River*, the salvation event happens on a tour of India. During her college days in Japan, she had been repulsed by the grotesque crucifix displayed in a little campus chapel. But now she finds herself deeply touched as she descends into an Indian grotto to view the Hindu goddess Chamunda. Chamunda lives in a graveyard, surrounded by human corpses.

> Her breasts droop like those of an old woman. And yet she offers milk from her withered breasts to the children who line up before her. Can you see how her right leg has festered as though afflicted with leprosy? Her belly has caved from hunger, and scorpions have stung her there. Enduring all these ills and pains, she offers milk from her sagging breasts to mankind.

The stone image of Chamunda pierces Mitsuko's heart. In her mind's eye, Chamunda appears superimposed over the crucified Jesus she had once despised. Mitsuko steps into the muddy Ganges. Flowers float by, and the ashes of the dead, and a puppy's carcass. Light sparkles over the river, "as though it were eternity itself." Embarrassed that she is actually praying, she says:

> There is a river of humanity. Though I still don't know what lies at the end of that flowing river. But I feel as though I've started to understand what I was yearning for through all the many mistakes of my past. . . What I can believe in now is the sight of all these people, each carrying his or her own individual burdens, praying at this deep river. . . I believe that the river embraces these people and carries them away. A river of humanity. The sorrows of this deep river of humanity. And I am a part of it.[33]

---

33 Endo, *Deep River*, 139–140, 175, 209–211.

For nineteen-year-old Immaculée Ilibagiza, it came while she was hiding with six other women for three months in a tiny bathroom, listening in horror to the sounds of the Rwandan genocide just beyond her walls—long-time neighbors gleefully torturing and murdering other long-time neighbors, childhood acquaintances drunk on bloodlust searching the house, calling her name, bent on her slaughter. She writes:

> I sat stone-still on that dirty floor for hours on end, contemplating the purity of his energy while the force of his love flowed through me like a sacred river, cleansing my soul and easing my mind. Sometimes I felt as though I were floating above my body, cradled in God's mighty palm, safe in his loving hand... In the midst of the genocide, I'd found my salvation... I'd been born again in the bathroom and was now the loving daughter of God, my Father.

When Jesus comes to Immaculée in a dream, she notices how thin he is, how his ribs protrude and his cheeks are "lean and hollow." It is this human Jesus who tells her there is no need to be afraid.[34]

For Dmitri, the oldest of the Karamazov brothers, the salvation event comes in a dream shortly after he has been stripped naked, interrogated, and falsely accused of murdering his father. In his dream, he is riding in a cart on a snowy steppe past a ruined village. A ragged woman stands by the road, holding a hungry baby, crying, holding out its bare arms, "its little fists blue from cold."

"Why is it crying?" Dmitri asks desperately, and the driver says, "The babe's cold. Its little clothes are frozen... they're poor people, burned out. They've no bread."

Dmitri cannot understand: "Tell me why it is those poor mothers stand there? Why are people poor? Why is the babe poor? Why is the

---

34 Immaculée Ilibagiza with Steve Erwin, *Left to Tell: Discovering God Amidst the Rwandan Holocaust* (Carlsbad, CA: Hay House, Inc., 2006), 107, 110–111.

steppe barren? Why don't they hug each other and kiss? Why don't they feed the babe?"

A "passion of pity" rises in Dmitri's heart; he wants to cry, and to do something "so that the babe should cry no more, so that the dark-faced, dried up mother should not weep, that no one should shed tears again from that moment." He awakens and his heart glows, and he feels as if he is moving "forward toward the light," and he longs "to live, to live, to go on and on, toward the new beckoning light, and to hurry, hurry, now, at once!" There is "a new light, as of joy, in his face."[35]

For Simone Weil, the salvation event comes as she recites a George Herbert poem. Suddenly, she says, "Christ came down and took possession of me." She "had never foreseen the possibility. . . of a real contact, person to person, here below, between a human being and God." When it happened to her, she writes, "neither my senses nor my imagination had any part; I only felt in the midst of my suffering the presence of a love, like that which one can read in the smile on a beloved face."[36]

The Spirit of God is wildly profligate in the manner in which it intersects with and begins its transforming process in the lives of human beings. It is not picky about religious labels. The stranger from Nazareth who walked a small patch of earth two millennia ago—his name and face, his death on a hill called Golgotha—may or may not, by name, constitute the narrative context for the salvation event.

I am presently inclined to believe, however, that if it is a genuine salvation event, it will share, if only fragmentarily or symbolically, the texture of the experiences I have explored in this chapter: it will re-connect us with the hidden and rejected parts of our own being; it will let us know we are not alone in our brokenness; and it will immerse us

---

35 *The Brothers Karamazov*, 463–465.
36 "Spiritual Autobiography" in *The Simone Weil Reader* (Mt. Kisco, NY: Moyer Bell Ltd., 1977), 15–16.

in a deepening pool of compassion that joins us—in ways we will find hard to describe, but not to feel—to ourselves, to one another, and to the divine spirit who lives in and through and around us.

Whether or not Jesus is explicitly named, this event will be mediated by the Spirit and in the name of Jesus.

*   *   *

THE PERSON IN THE MIRROR

Each of us comes from the womb naked and bloody, in a deeper resemblance to the one on the cross than we might readily admit. By the time we are returned to the ground, we are likely to be naked and bloody again. Between those defining moments, we scurry to protect ourselves from the truth—the pain—of our own inner experience.

We dress up in garments both real and symbolic. We dignify ourselves with credentials, titles, accomplishments. We cultivate character, display our virtues, emulate heroes. We practice the appropriate presentation of ourselves in daily life, and hide the inner tumult behind shiny surfaces without visible cracks. We try to suffer little and lack nothing. Like the prodigal son in his confident autonomy, we are often very far from ourselves. In fact, we are enemies of ourselves.

This is my story, at least.

Because he knows my story, Jesus can only work my "salvation" by bringing me very close to myself.[37] Gently, by his willingness to be openly who he is—a real human being—Jesus invites me to

---

37 Was Paul referring to this self-revelation in Galatians 1:15–16: "God. . . was pleased to reveal his Son in me. . ."? Henri J. M. Nouwen: "Where you are most human, most yourself, weakest, there Jesus lives. . . Bringing your fearful self home is bringing Jesus home." *Inner Voice*, 49.

meet *myself* in nakedness.[38] The cross becomes a kind of mirror, in which I see reflected my own shabby, sometimes tortured, but beautifully tender humanity. As I hear in the psalmist's words my own cries, and see in this mirror the truth of my own human being, the compassion that I feel for the dying Jesus gives birth to compassion for my own dying self. I find myself "repenting"—that is, turning over completely the way I see and relate to myself, the way I see and relate to others and to God. The war I wage against myself—a conflict that has poisoned so much of my life, so many of my relationships—begins to wane in its intensity.

Once I have seen with eyes of compassion the hurt, vulnerable part of me that lies just below the surface, why would I wish to do it further violence? I find that, in moments of stillness, a wave of trust and of peace washes over me as I realize how good it feels for my protective weapons to relax, how whole I feel when I am at one with myself. How beautiful it is to begin to taste that inner climate of total self-acceptance, of welcoming hospitality, that allowed Jesus to be a real human being.

As I rest in this hospitality, it becomes quite natural to trust that the figure on the cross, who reveals myself to me, also reveals true God to me. This moment of truth—that God and I become one in the dying Jesus—will never be forgotten. Wellsprings of compassion can begin to open and flow from my own precious humanity to the vulnerable human Jesus, then naturally to the graciously

---

38 Moltmann: In the crucified Jesus, God "brings back to [humanity its] despised and abandoned humanness." Moltmann rephrases the Athanasian Creed this way: "God became human that dehumanized humans might become true humans. We become true humans in the community of the incarnate, the suffering and loving, the human God."

Moltmann quotes Luther approvingly: "Through the regime of his humanity and his flesh, in which we live by faith, he makes us of the same form as himself and crucifies us by making us true humans instead of unhappy and proud gods: humans, that is, in their misery and their sin. . . He thus restores the despised weakness of the flesh which we have perversely abandoned." *Crucified God,* 212, 231, 212–213. (In these quotes, I have substituted "human" for "man.")

human God, and from there back once again to the most beautifully human me and to everyone I know. I am connected to the One who calls me "beloved." It feels like being born again—as a real human being.

CHAPTER 9

To Hell with Jesus
Getting salted in a saving fire

*Bread and stone both come from Christ and, penetrating to
our inward being, bring Christ into us. Bread and stone are love.
We must eat the bread and lay ourselves open to the stone,
so that it may sink as deeply as possible into our flesh.
If we have any armor able to protect our soul from the stones
thrown by Christ, we should take it off and cast it away.*
Simone Weil[1]

DURING HIS SHORT LIFE as a wandering prophet, Jesus often characterized the human problem as a peculiar kind of blindness. He spoke
most directly about this spiritual disability in his regular jousts with
the religious leaders of his day—the godly.

"You think you are uniquely clear-sighted," he seemed to be
saying, "but in fact you are utterly blind. You are in the dark as to
what is truly going on inside you and who you really are." He urged
his disciples to become "children of light" (John 12:36).

As he hung on the cross, life draining out of him, he drew attention, one last time, to human blindness: "Father, forgive them,"
he said of his killers. "They don't know what they're doing"
(Luke 23:34). He seemed certain that his murderers were not innately

---

1 *Waiting for God* (New York: Harper and Row, 1973), 157.

malicious. They were a mob of ignorant people, stumbling around in the dark, doing a great deal of damage in the process.

In the previous chapter, I proposed a narrative of the crucifixion as a moment in which we might become aware of our blindness and receive our sight.[2] Before the naked, dying Jesus, our eyes may be opened to the presence of a small, weak, suffering God. Before the naked, dying Jesus, our eyes may be opened to the presence inside us, beneath our glittering but fragile protective devices, of a small, weak, suffering human being. In Jesus—"the light of all people," according to John's Gospel (John 1:4 and 9)—we may see both God and ourselves with new clarity, because we now see both with a deep sense of identification and compassion. As we embrace that which is small, weak and suffering in God and in ourselves, we may find that our alienation dissolves, enmity ceases, and we begin a healing journey.

But what of those whose blindness persists? What about those with cold hearts and broken consciences who stand at the foot of the cross jeering and scoffing? What about those who, in their blind allegiance to the Almighty, wield the cross like a magical weapon to declare their superiority to the "unsaved," while refusing any conscious identification with this dying man? Will these ever relax their protective defenses so that a healing journey can begin?

I believe Jesus' answer is "Yes—but only by fire."[3] Jesus knows those who persist in their blindness are on their way to hell.

●　　●　　●

---

2 My account, of course, in no way exhausts the meaning of the cross and the possibilities for understanding the atonement. See Baker, *Proclaiming the Scandal of the Cross* and Jersak and Hardin, eds., *Stricken by God?* for creative, biblically-grounded alternatives.

3 These are St. Paul's words in I Corinthians 3:15.

BROUGHT DOWN TO HADES

To many minds, hell is Christianity's most reprehensible teaching. Non-believers notice readily what Christians often ignore: there is something unhinged about a God who tells people to love their enemies while he promises to torment his own enemies without mercy—and for eternity.

Literature abounds with examples of hell's ability to cool people towards God. A century ago, William Dean Howells described the relief he felt on realizing he had lost his faith in God—it meant he need no longer fear going to hell if he died in the night.[4] My friend Bev began moving away from the church when her brother died in a motorcycle crash and a Christian told her: "You know, Bev, your brother went to hell."[5]

Novelist Mary Gaitskill is thankful she did not grow up religious. She remembers a childhood encounter with two little girls who, "on hearing that [she] didn't believe that Jesus was the Son of God, screamed, 'There's a sin on your soul! You're going to hell!'" She ran home to her mother, who said to her: "God is love and there is no hell."[6]

I honor these skeptics, and all who know in their hearts that the conventional view of hell as eternal punishment for our sins makes God a monster and mocks the meaning of the word "love." Those who reject such a hell have taken the word "love" far more seriously than have most Christians. Those who reject such a God bear witness to the human yearning for a better God than the one many Christians worship. I take the existence of this yearning as a sign that a truer, better God can be found.

---

4 "Eighty Years and After," reprinted from *Harper's Magazine* (December 1919) in *Harper's Magazine* (March 2000), 81.

5 Bev Laird, "Faith Autobiography." Used by permission.

6 "Revelation," in David Rosenberg, ed., *Communion: Contemporary Writers Reveal the Bible in Their Lives* (New York: Anchor Books, 1996), 115–116.

And yet, despite its reprehensible misuse by organized religion throughout much of Christianity's history, I want to take the risk of treating the reality of hell quite seriously.[7] The defenders of a punitive hell are *correct* in noticing that Jesus gives them plenty of ammunition for their sordid crusade. Jesus uses the term "hell" and related images more often than any other biblical figure or writer. If you call your brother a fool, he says, you are "liable to the hell of fire." Make peace with him or you will land in "prison" until you have "paid the last penny" (Matthew 5:22, 26). If your eye "causes you to sin," he says, your whole body is destined for hell (Matthew 5:29–30).

Jesus warns his disciples to "fear the one who can destroy both soul and body in hell" (Matthew 10:28). He tells the godly—a "brood of vipers"—that they are in danger of hell, and anyone who listens to them is "twice as much a child of hell" as they are (Matthew 23:15). A servant who hides his master's money instead of investing it, Jesus says, ends up in "outer darkness" to weep and gnash his teeth (Matthew 25:30). Jesus warns a town that rejected him that it will be "brought down to Hades" (Matthew 11:23).[8]

That Jesus uses these images so often in the Gospel accounts convinces me that he considered hell a useful spiritual truth. But the Jesus whose life and teachings—and whose heart—I have been exploring in this book is not a Mafia don who rubs out his enemies. He's a real human being who loves out of his weakness and opens himself, nakedly, to our enmity. The hell that preachers use to scare sinners into a quick and easy salvation resembles neither weakness, nor love. So I am intrigued that Jesus is not squeamish about the imagery of hell.

---

7 Evangelical Protestants don't have a lock on reprehensible misuses of this teaching. Jean Delumeau chronicles many colorful instances of the use of hell as a terror tactic by the medieval and early modern church in *Sin and Fear: The Emergence of a Western Guilt Culture, 13th–18th Centuries* (New York: St. Martin's Press, 1991).

8 See also Luke 9:43–47; 12:5; 10:15.

●   ●   ●

HOPE FOR THE GOATS

For those raised within the dogmatic confines of evangelicalism, a little interpretive breathing room on the topic of hell does not come easily. What hell looks and feels like is burned deeply into our childhood brains, leaving no uncertainty about its "literal" meaning.

As my trust grew in a God who shows up as a vulnerable human being, however, the conventional meaning of hell gradually lost its hold on me. In light of Jesus' forgiveness for his enemies, such a hell is simply not believable. If the doctrine of hell is not simply to be dismissed as a harmful holdover from Egyptian or Greek antiquity, its meaning must somehow reflect the universal compassion embodied in the naked, dying Jesus.[9]

Matthew's Gospel records Jesus telling a story that seems to be about both compassion and hell. It is one of Jesus' most sustained sayings, often quoted on the subject of eternal punishment: the famous story of "the sheep and the goats" (Matthew 25:31–46). It is set in a mysterious future, where the human son appears "as a shepherd" and calls "the nations" together. When they have gathered, he separates the sheep from the goats, and addresses each group separately. He tells the sheep they have inherited the kingdom because they took care of him when he was a stranger and a prisoner—when he was sick, hungry and naked.

The sheep are puzzled—they seem to have forgotten about their own charitable activity. So the human son explains that whenever they took care of "one of the least" of the members of his human family—whom he calls his "brothers and sisters"—they

---

9 My teaching colleague at the Oregon Extension, Dr. John Linton, first convinced me of this by his unsurpassed insight into and creative interpretation of many of the New Testament's references to hell. This chapter, particularly its approach to the story of Lazarus and the rich man, borrows heavily from John's lectures.

were actually taking care of him. He rewards the sheep with "eternal life."

Then the human son turns toward the goats. They failed to take care of him, he says. Like the sheep, the goats seem surprised, and ask for an explanation. The son reminds the goats about all the times they refused care to the stranger and the prisoner, the sick, the hungry and the naked. In neglecting these suffering ones, he says, they were neglecting him, too. He sends the goats to "eternal punishment" in an "eternal fire prepared for the devil and his angels."

At first glance, and in most sermons, this story is about showing compassion for those in need. The son seems deadly serious about caring for the world's "least" fortunate. So the story heartens Christians who support progressive social causes. The fate of the goats adds an extra bite to their humanitarian appeals: if you don't give your money to help the poor, you may end up in hell. Preachers on this side of the political spectrum may not linger on the threat of hell, or even quite believe in a conventional hell, but they're tempted to trade on it for the sake of their agenda.

Implicitly, perhaps without noticing, they use a story about compassion to warn that compassion has an outer limit: those who show no compassion will receive no compassion.

This seeming shift in the story's sensibility—first compassion, then no compassion—makes it useful to other Christians as well, those interested in defending a harshly punitive understanding of hell. A recent evangelical spokesperson names this story "the single most important [biblical] passage" for understanding the doctrine of hell. He seems to savor the fact that the word "punishment" in early Christian literature always means "long-continued torture," while "eternal fire" denotes "never-ending suffering." He doesn't want us to soft-pedal the horrible fate of the lost, since it comes on "the authority of the Son of God."[10]

In my view, neither interpretation takes the deeper character of Jesus' life and message very seriously. Both assume Jesus cared deeply about the fate of some people, but not a whit about the fate of others. Both turn a story about compassion into a story about condemnation. At best, they imply that Jesus was a sloppy thinker. At worst, they depict him as teaching that compassion has its limits. Neither one respects Jesus as a careful but subtle theological thinker who persisted to the very end in understanding God not as the condemner, but as the condemned.

A more respectful reading begins by noticing that, contrary to the view expressed by our evangelical theologian, it is the "human son" and not explicitly the "Son of God" who appears in Jesus' story. This smaller, weaker son comes "in his glory" and "sits on the throne of his glory."

Jesus has already taught his disciples that *his* peculiar glory—his true identity—is not the glory of the Almighty. We know, although

10 Robert A. Peterson in Edward William Fudge and Robert A. Peterson, *Two Views of Hell: A Biblical and Theological Dialogue* (Downer's Grove, IL: InterVarsity Press, 2000), 140–145. An alternative view, "conditionalism," has recently gained ground among evangelicals. It teaches that the wicked will not be kept alive and tormented, but will be summarily destroyed.

A spokesperson for that view believes that by "punishment" Jesus means not torture, but a penalty. In our judicial system, for example, the most extreme penalty is execution, which is what Jesus has in mind. He calls it "eternal" because "once destroyed, [the wicked] will be gone *forever*." Edward William Fudge in Fudge and Peterson, *Two Views of Hell*, 44–46.

Another representative of this position is Clark Pinnock and Robert C. Brow, *Unbounded Love: A Good News Theology for the 21st Century* (Downer's Grove, IL: InterVarsity Press, 1994). See chapter VIII, "Hell: Rejecting Love." It seems a healthy development that the conditionalist approach has been permitted any voice at all in the evangelical dialogue. My misgiving about it is that it embodies, at best, a truncated form of compassion in which the "goats" are exterminated instead of tortured forever. The Nazis displayed this form of "compassion," in which death had the final say over life.

I believe the resurrection of Jesus permits us to hope that life will ultimately be victorious over death.

it took the disciples a while to catch on, that Jesus' "glory" was revealed in his vulnerability, his suffering and death at the hands of his enemies. So by the "throne of his glory," Jesus—a sly and paradoxical thinker—may well have had an old rugged cross in mind.

If so, this story, to paraphrase our evangelical spokesperson, comes not on the authority of a regal representative of an almighty potentate, but on the authority of a weak and dying man who forgave his executioners. Such a story *cannot* end in a compassion that refuses to extend itself to goats.

By twice mentioning his paradoxical "glory," I believe Jesus is helping us understand the first group he introduces us to—the sheep. Sheep are those who have been transformed by their twin encounters with the sufferer within them and the suffering Jesus. Quite naturally and without conscious effort—which explains their surprise at Jesus' depiction of them—they recognize themselves in the lonely and hurting of the world and care for those neglected ones as they would care for the lonely, hurting parts of their own spirits. Their unselfconscious love ripples out into an ocean of compassion, touching the neglected of the world—including the neglected parts of those who seem un-neglected—as well as the neglected human son and the suffering spirit of the God revealed on the cross.[11]

---

11 Father Zossima, the mystic in *The Brothers Karamazov*, says "all is like an ocean" (295). Once we have been dipped by suffering into the ocean of love, and feel ourselves immersed in its healing waters, we begin to feel the suffering of all people, everywhere, even those who are as yet unaware of their own suffering. It is as if the water, the medium that surrounds and holds us, brings the ripples and currents of every human suffering, everywhere, to lap against our bodies.

This may be the cause of Jesus' melancholy. Observing Jesus' response to suffering people, however, also encourages us to drain any hint of perfectionism out of our thinking about suffering. Jesus carried the suffering of every human, but he also permitted himself to be finite. He did not make it his agenda to heal every person whose suffering he felt. He took time away from suffering people to care for his own spiritual needs. He held his gift for empathy in tension with his awareness of the tragedy of the human condition and his trust in the Father, who he knew would someday wipe the tears from every eye.

Goats have not had this transformative experience, so while they have perhaps felt pangs of pity, or performed token acts of charity, they have not committed themselves to the neglected in a way that signifies compassion.[12] When they meet suffering people, they don't see themselves, because they have not yet really seen the suffering parts of themselves, hidden so deeply from their own and others' view. Their sentence is harsh: "eternal fire." The human son, by all appearances, does not much care for goats.

But how can this be? What genuine herdsman would not also care about his goats? They are his, after all, since he's the one who called them together, and they have come to him as if they know him. And this is the kind of shepherd who forgives the very ones who kill him—who, in their lack of compassion, are certainly "goats." If the human son in this story is one in spirit with the human son who dies on the cross, he understands the tragedy inherent in the goats' lack of compassion: the goats *don't know what they are doing!*

Will he reward their ignorance with anything less than the forgiveness he extends to his executioners? Or will he repay their lack of compassion by showing them no compassion? Wouldn't that mean he, also, does not know what he is doing? Such a human son is himself a "goat"! Could Jesus possibly have intended for his story to have concluded in such a blatant contradiction?

---

12 I may be a bit too hard on the goats here, and a bit simplistic about compassion. I do believe that genuine compassion is always given its impetus inside us by the part of us that is broken and suffering and finds itself embraced by another part of us. We show compassion because we know compassion. But I don't believe that being "in touch" with that broken and suffering part must be conscious, nor do I think that a conscious transformation or conscious awareness of the "event" of the cross is required before compassion can begin. The part of us that is broken and suffering can recognize its counterpart in another person at *any* time, and make its feelings known in instinctive responses like tears or anger.

The sheep *listen* to those feelings, and follow their lead. The goats allow a part of themselves to *hide* those feelings away from their own awareness because they are afraid of what it says about their own impoverished or helpless state.

If the character of Jesus as the image of an ever-compassionate God makes any sense at all, these goats will have to be invited to salvation—every last one of them, over and over again, until their eyes are opened. They will have to meet themselves in the naked one on the cross. They will have to discover, to their horror, what exactly they have been doing.

If we trust our story, and the one who tells it, this journey will feel like a punishment, like a passage through "eternal fire."[13] But it will also be the path to re-connection—with themselves, with the suffering ones they formerly ignored, and with the suffering God.

---

13 I am aware that many of the judgment passages in the Bible can be interpreted as directed against impersonal structures like ideologies, economic systems, governments and other corporate entities. Paul calls them "principalities and powers" and, with other biblical writers, speaks of them as living entities. They draw "life" from the humans under their sway, causing social collectivities to do things individual humans might resist doing, enslaving the very people they pretend to serve.

In the story of the sheep and the goats, a "powers" approach notices that the human son gathers nations, not individuals, for blessing or judgment. Matthew tells the story in the context of apocalyptic happenings—"wars and rumors of wars" among the nations. In this view, Jesus is expressing his outrage at the way powerful social and political entities treat the naked and the needy with whom he—as a naked, needy God—identifies. This approach also notices that the eternal fire to which Jesus sends the goats is "prepared for the devil and his angels"—another way of representing non-human entities (internal psychic structures or external social structures) that alienate humans from themselves, others and God.

Jacques Ellul draws on this approach for his biblical exegesis in *Apocalypse: The Book of Revelation* (New York: The Seabury Press, 1977). The foremost representative of this position in contemporary Lutheran thought is Walter Wink in his trilogy *Naming the Powers, Unmasking the Powers,* and *Engaging the Powers* (Minneapolis: Fortress Press, 1984, 1986, 1992 respectively). A typically eloquent, dense and passionate survey of the work of the powers is Karl Barth, *The Christian Life* (Grand Rapids, MI: William B. Eerdmans Publishing Company, 1981), 213–233.

This approach is not entirely incompatible with the one I offer above—for example, the goats may be under the sway of a fear-motivated internal "protective mechanism" that (in Chapters 6 and 7) I named as the "devil" that Jesus confronted in his wilderness temptation. I am less comfortable with the "powers" approach when it envisions *annihilating* rather than redeeming the cause of our alienation, although the treatment of Babylon in Revelation 18 gives me pause.

*   *   *

YOU ARE IN AGONY

As it turns out, Jesus tells another story—the New Testament's most well-elaborated portrait of hell—that hints at the saving purposes of "eternal fire." It's the story of Lazarus, a poor, sick, starving man who begs for a living (Luke 16:19–31). The dogs that lick his sores seem to be his only friends. He spends his miserable life at the gate of a rich man, yearning to eat the scraps of food falling from his table. The rich man wears expensive clothes and feasts "sumptuously" every day. The story gives no indication that the rich man ever shares a single scrap with his poor neighbor Lazarus.

Lazarus dies and finds himself in a place of great comfort: Abraham's bosom. The rich man dies and finds himself in hell. In his "torment," he calls for help. "Father Abraham," he cries, "send Lazarus to dip the end of his finger in water and cool my tongue; for I am in anguish in this flame."

Abraham's answer has far-reaching theological implications. "Child," he says, "remember that during your lifetime you received your good things, and Lazarus in like manner evil things; but now he is comforted here, and you are in agony." An existential equation: good things in life, bad things in death; bad things in life, good things in death. Does Jesus think it's as simple as that?

It helps us unpack this story if we think of the rich man as a "goat." He has lived his life without compassion. Daily, a starving man sat at his gate and he never thought to offer him the crumbs from his table. Why has he not shown compassion? Because he has not met the naked Jesus, so his eyes have not been opened to his own nakedness.

If we take Abraham's equation seriously, the rich man's "good things" have acted as blinders. A part of the rich man has used riches as a kind of internal "protector," separating him from aware-ness of the poor man inside him, keeping that poor man's pain at bay. Maybe his fine clothing has been so important to him because it has disguised the poverty of his nakedness. Maybe his good fortune has convinced him he's a superior human being, countering another voice inside him that says: "You're the lowest of the low." Maybe his protective voices have whispered in his ear: "You're rich! You're handsome. You're healthy. You're not like Lazarus."

Surrounded by "good things," the rich man has been able to exile into a deeply hidden place the suffering that is common to human beings. Without an experience of the crucifixion, connecting him compassionately with his own hidden nakedness, how could the rich man recognize empathically, or feel one with, the poor man on his doorstep? How could he possibly know what he's been doing?

Lazarus, on the other hand, has had only "evil things," and that seems to have given him a non-stop ticket to Abraham's bosom. Jesus gives no indication that Lazarus got to this wonderful place by being morally superior to the rich man, or by virtue of a stellar religious faith.[14] The only hint of what qualifies a person for Abraham's bosom is the fact that there Lazarus is "comforted."

Perhaps, we get to Abraham's bosom merely by being truly miserable and admitting that we need comfort. The rich man, blind to whatever cross-like experience may have come his way—perhaps, ironically, the very appearance of miserable Lazarus at his gate—is out of touch with his own neediness. So he has no use for comfort.

Lazarus does not have the rich man's protective mechanisms, like

---

14 "Let us be careful not to smuggle into the character of Lazarus some hidden virtue. He is absolutely a needy one, a poorest Lazarus. His plight may strike our ears as embarrassing, but the fact cannot be altered that Luther included in the diseases of Lazarus. . . syphilis! Whoever wants to make him out bad. . . let him make him out as bad as he likes. He will have cause enough. But let him also realize, it is *not* a question of the goodness or badness of Lazarus that we are dealing with. . . God is love . . . that kind of love which seeks a person because he is needy and because it can and will help . . ." "Miserable Lazarus" in Karl Barth and Eduard Thurneysen, *God's Search for Man* (New York: Round Table Press, 1935), 89.

wealth and fine clothing. He bears in his desperate daily experience the deepest meaning of the cross. Lazarus has met himself as naked, wounded and needy—like Jesus. He's *exactly* the kind of person the sheep will care for because, of course, they know they are Lazarus, too. Abraham certainly knows he is Lazarus, since he welcomes Lazarus into his bosom. So the "Abraham" in this story is a "sheep." He represents all those who have experienced themselves, and overcome their blindness and self-enmity, in the cross. And he represents the one Jesus called Father, whose suffering, sheep-like compassion undergirds the world.

By offering us Abraham's existential equation, Jesus seems to be saying: "Sooner or later, if we are to enjoy the bliss of Abraham's bosom, we will all, every one of us, need to have our internal protective parts transformed by fire. Before we can be comforted, we will have to recognize our self-enmity and know ourselves, with compassion, as naked and needy."

Lazarus' life was a kind of hell, bringing him painfully to the knowledge of his neediness. Perhaps in Abraham's bosom he learns a deeper compassion for that neediness. The rich man does not come to know his neediness until death. He is in another version of the hell Lazarus endured in life. Perhaps no human being finally arrives in Abraham's bosom unscorched by the fires of hell—suffering in this life or in the next. To be scorched is to have our protective parts transformed by fire, to have our nakedness revealed to our own eyes. Unless that nakedness is revealed, and then embraced with compassion, we do not know ourselves as human or truly whole. Fire is a healing gift for the goats.

In the story of the sheep and the goats, Jesus uses the word "punishment" to describe this gift. The scorching of our protectors cannot but feel like punishment—a punishment in which we participate; indeed, in which we may be our own worst punishers. In the emotional pain even of a cleansing fire, we realize we are reaping the consequences of the many years we invested in building protective walls against the naked truth of ourselves.

Our evangelical spokesperson believes "punishment" means "long-continued torture," which does appear to be what the rich man is experiencing in hell. But in Jesus' mind, whatever else "punishment" means, it does *not* mean "condemnation." It describes a necessary process in a journey of salvation.

Hell, then, is a metaphor for the *kindness of God*, who cannot bring us to ourselves except through suffering. Each person's suffering is unique, an incalculable mixture of the hidden and the visible, the emotional and the physical, the "felt" and the "unfelt." Jesus adds another helpful distinction: the suffering in this life, and the suffering in the next. No instrument of measurement is available for calibrating the workings of Abraham's equation.

Jesus seems to want to make a simple point: suffering is the portal through which everyone must pass to become a real human being. No one evades the fire. It comes in life, or it comes in death. As Jesus taught his disciples, "everyone will be salted with fire" (Mark 9:49).

·   ·   ·

I'LL DRINK TO THAT

I have a friend who daily endures the fires of hell.[15] Leo is eighty-five-years-old, although he tells me proudly he can still split firewood like a man of fifty. He spent a rough childhood in the Kentucky coal country, dropped out of school, ran away to the Navy, and fought on a destroyer in the Pacific.

When he was mustered out in 1946, Leo drifted onto an Indian reservation in Nevada. He fell for a young Native American woman and fathered several children. He eagerly adopted Native ways,

---

15 Leo is not his real name, and I've altered a few other identifying references.

doing bead- and featherwork, making his own buckskin clothes, learning the language from one of its last fluent speakers. He worked on the railroad, then in the woods as a lumberjack, then on a ranch as a cowboy. For a while, short on money, he was a prize-fighter in the small towns strung along California's eastern Sierra.

Leo lived recklessly. He took pride in his prowess with women, flirted with other men's partners, claimed to have fathered quite a few children who are still unknown to him. He drank heavily and brawled in numerous off-reservation bars, occasionally spending a night or two in jail. In part because of his winning sense of humor and his deep respect for tribal culture, and also because he could legally purchase alcohol when Native Americans couldn't, he was a fixture at the 'round-the-clock drinking bouts that comprised the social life of many young tribal men and women. He still packs a loaded six-shooter. He quotes Shakespeare. He shares his scant resources with any stray dog, cat or goose that comes to the door of his tiny shack.

I've spent many hours listening to Leo's life stories tumble out in intriguing fragments, mostly without chronological reference. His memory, although random, is astounding. He can tell stories of Saul, Jonathan and David, which he heard as a boy in Sunday school, although he has not read the Old Testament or darkened the door of a church in seventy-five years. His memory for the jobs he has held, jokes he has told, trees he has felled, log cabins he has built, animals he has husbanded, men he has fought, and women he has wooed—or failed to woo—is prodigious. But now and then, he will mention the name of one woman of whom he is reluctant to say more. Just the mention of her brings tears to his eyes.

One day, with a little prodding, he told me about her. They met and fell in love in a bar. He was in his fifties. She was a widower. He built a log cabin for her, and they moved in. She loved and cared for him with a gentleness and warmth he had never experienced. He remembers these years as the happiest of his life.

But the years were too few. After a short hiatus, he began drinking again. He neglected her for his friends. He treated her spitefully. He could not remain faithful. She endured it, and then resisted it, and then warned him that he was driving her away. He responded defensively, with hostility and bravado and more drinking. So she left him. She kept in touch with him, let him know that she would always care deeply for him, but that she would never come back to him. As Leo told me this, his tears flowed freely, tracing a pattern down his leathery face. He said he thinks of her every day.

On one of my visits, Leo and I talked about God. He said he knew there would be a "judgment" when he died. He would have a lot to answer for, but nothing so dastardly as his treatment of the woman he most deeply loved—the woman who most deeply loved him. He figured he deserved whatever punishment God gave him. I could see that he had been feeling this woman's suffering and silently punishing himself for many years.

I asked Leo what he thought about Jesus' prayer on the cross to his Father, begging that the lynch mob be forgiven because they didn't know what they were doing.

"Does that mean you don't think there's a place called hell?" he asked. To Leo, hell is built into the structure of the universe, more certain to exist than even heaven.

"No," I said, "Jesus believed in hell. So I do, too. But if Jesus' killers ever really come to understand that they're forgiven, *when* do you think they'll most feel like they're in hell?"

"When they realize what they did," Leo said, looking up at me. We sat in silence for a very long time while Leo's eyes filled with tears.

After a while I said: "Maybe God's not punishing you, Leo. Maybe you're punishing yourself."

Leo said what he always says at times like these: "I'll drink to that."

We sat in silence. I wasn't quite ready to change the subject.

"You're already in hell, Leo," I said.

"That's what it feels like," he said. We were quiet again.

Although my time with Leo is spent mostly listening to him tell his stories, I took a chance on a quick "story" of my own.

"Leo, I think of God as someone who wants to take you out of hell, not put you in it. The only way God can do this is by forgiving the part of you that hardened itself against the one you loved, the part that treated her so badly. But God doesn't just forgive it. God understands why that part of you was doing what it was, how it was hardening you, too—possibly against something really painful deep inside yourself. God knows you didn't know what you were doing. God feels your pain, and loves all of you—*all* the parts of you, just as they are."

I wasn't sure Leo was feeling any real love from God at the moment, but I hoped he could feel a little bit from me.

"That's not the God they taught me in Sunday school," Leo said, smiling.

"Yeah, I know. But that was a long time ago, Leo. You're an old geezer now. You know a few things about life. You could try this kind of God on for size."

Another small silence—and then Leo changed the subject.

<ul><li></li></ul>

●   ●   ●

ABRAHAM'S CHILD

Jesus' story about Lazarus and the rich man offers clues to more subtle aspects of hell's operation, aspects that seem to go beyond Abraham's existential equation. The story seems to hint that the fires of hell burn every one of us *both* in this life *and* in death. In life, riches protect the rich man from any awareness of his nakedness. But beneath this armor, we can be sure, lives an anxious, lonely man.

Our psychological "protectors" can keep us from recognizing and fully embracing our own nakedness, but they can't make us happy or help us feel an inner connection with ourselves or others. Emotionally, we pay a price for our distance from ourselves. We live in a state of internal enmity, which poisons our spirit and ruins our relationships.

So we can be sure the rich man's life is also a kind of hell—a low-intensity hell, perhaps, from which his riches distract him. From time to time, certainly, life's exigencies evade his management tools, his internal protective parts fall down on the job, and his neediness slips through. He tries to plaster over these cracks with purple and fine linen, with sumptuous food and drink—who knows with what else. He holds hell at bay. Now, in death, the fires are burning away his protection and he is coming to himself. He is "in agony." He feels the full intensity of the pain stored up beneath the riches of his life. This is good news—he is on the path to salvation.

Lazarus, conversely, is in hell in this life. He is not able to escape the painful awareness of his own nakedness. He *lives* his nakedness. The story offers graphic details of his condition, as if to say: life for Lazarus is a high-intensity hell. Now, in death, he is safe and comforted in Abraham's bosom. But in a sense, he still suffers. When the rich man asks that Lazarus be sent to cool his tongue with a drop of water, Abraham tells him that "a great chasm has been fixed, so that those who *might want* to pass from here to you cannot do so." If Lazarus knows his naked neediness and has learned self-compassion, as the story suggests, then we know he is a "sheep."

The rich man in hell is now the very kind of man Jesus indicated the sheep would want to care for—so, perhaps, Lazarus feels in his own spirit the rich man's suffering. If so, then Lazarus has taken the rich man's hell into himself, even in Abraham's bosom. Would he hesitate to visit the flames with a drop of water for his poor neighbor? Perhaps the "great chasm" operates, for a time, just as much to keep

Lazarus in heaven as to keep the rich man in hell. Lazarus is the very kind of person who *might want* to go to hell for the rich man.[16]

Will the rich man be healed by the gracious fires of hell? His call for comfort—a sign of his neediness—is cause for hope, since it was Lazarus' sheer neediness that qualified him for Abraham's bosom. But there is nothing easy or automatic about salvation. A chasm blocks the rich man's path. Jesus does not say who put the chasm there. Does it represent the unfinished nature of the rich man's journey? Has love not yet found a way to relax the parts of the rich man that are protecting him, so that he can come to himself?

But the story does imply that the rich man has at least begun his journey toward wholeness. In torment, he thinks of his five brothers.[17] He asks Abraham to send Lazarus with warnings about the fire awaiting them. His compassion is coming to birth. He senses his brothers need the ministrations of a starving beggar. He hopes the beggar will inaugurate, for his brothers, an experience of the crucifixion.

When Abraham addresses the rich man, he calls him "child." The rich man may be a "goat," but in Jesus' mind he's still Abraham's child. Will Abraham abandon his child? No more than Jesus would abandon a child, whom he considered "the greatest in the kingdom" (Matthew 18:4). At this moment, perhaps, a chasm separates the rich man from the source of comfort and love. But intimate words, like "child," can be whispered across this chasm. So heaven must not be very far away from hell. Perhaps Abraham's presence to his child in hell is the beginning of the rich man's comfort.

Our most successful evangelical soul-winners may not have it

---

16 I am implying here that I believe God and "the saints in heaven" will in some sense also be in "hell" until the last human being is brought to eternal life. How could love not suffer so long as one human being is suffering? If there are no tears in heaven (Revelation 21:4), perhaps this is because there are no sufferers left in hell.

17 A reminder of Jesus' words in the story of the sheep and the goats: "the least of these my brothers and sisters" (Matthew 25:40).

quite right. The chasm between "heaven" and "hell" in this story does not seem truly infinite. The rich man, though dead, is not beyond the reach of love. All he needs is for someone naked and alone to seek him out in hell—a loving emissary of the naked God, come to liberate him from his own internal prison.

●   ●   ●

TO HELL AND BACK

If Jesus knew that hell is a liberation and a healing, why would he tell us the fires of hell are eternal? Jonah, one of the Hebrew Bible's most picturesque characters, may help us here.

Jonah's story is familiar. He hears a call from God, telling him to go to Ninevah to preach repentance. Instead, he goes to sea, thinking to get "away from the presence of the Lord." In the middle of his voyage, God churns up "a great wind" that quickly becomes a fierce storm (Jonah 1:3–4). The story doesn't tell us what God has in mind. If God is the Almighty, perhaps he's just showing Jonah who's boss. But if God is the one revealed in the naked Jesus, the storm may be the beginning of Jonah's descent into a gracious hell.

As the storm howls, Jonah hides away in "the inner part of the ship." Like the disciples on the eve of their own spiritual transformations, Jonah's protective parts are hard at work. They put him fast asleep. The captain seems annoyed that Jonah can be so out of touch. "What are you doing sound asleep," he shouts. "Get up! Call on your God! Perhaps the god will spare us a thought so that we do not perish!" (Jonah 1:5–6).

Whether or not Jonah humors the captain and prays to God, the story doesn't say. As I picture it, Jonah is the only person on deck not praying. Even though he's been dragged out of his hiding place, he's still hoping God hasn't noticed him. Praying threatens to bring him to God's attention.

The storm worsens and the ship founders, so the sailors hold a quick lottery to find who is at fault. The lot falls on Jonah, which makes one suspect it was rigged from the start—as most choices of scapegoat are—to finger the odd man out. In this case, the odd man is the sleepy Hebrew who isn't praying. A bit lamely, Jonah defends himself: "I worship the Lord, the God of heaven, who made the sea and the dry land" (Jonah 1:9). Perhaps it's dawning on him that, since he's on the sea, God is in the vicinity.

This might help explain what happens next. After telling his shipmates he's "fleeing from the presence of the Lord," and watching them grow more frantic and the sea more tempestuous, Jonah asks his mates to throw him into the drink. His mates go to heroic lengths to avoid sacrificing Jonah, to no avail. In the end, with prayers for mercy, they toss Jonah overboard and a large fish swallows him up.

And now the text shifts abruptly from narrative to poetry. It gives us no information about the three days and nights Jonah spends in the belly of this large fish, as if he's gone to a liminal place where all attempts at description fail. What we get instead is Jonah's prayer. Its language leaves no doubt that the fish's belly is a metaphor for hell.

> I called to the Lord out of my distress,
>> and he answered me;
> out of the belly of Sheol I cried,
>> and you heard my voice.[18]
> You cast me into the deep, into the heart of the seas,
>> and the flood surrounded me;
> all your waves and your billows passed over me.

---

18 "Sheol" is the closest Old Testament equivalent to the New Testament's "hell." It depicts a deep, dark and silent place that receives the dead. One Old Testament text suggests a parallel with these words: "For a fire is kindled by my anger, and it burns to the depths of Sheol, devours the earth and its increase, and sets on fire the foundations of the mountains" (Deuteronomy 32:22). I interpret Sheol and hell as related metaphors.

> Then I said, "I am driven away from your sight;
>> how shall I look again upon your holy temple?"
> The waters closed in over me; the deep surrounded me;
>> weeds were wrapped around my head
>> at the roots of the mountains.
> I went down to the land whose bars
>> closed upon me forever;
> yet you brought up my life from the Pit,
>> O Lord my God (Jonah 2:2–6).

Sheol, the Pit, the deep, wrath, prison, the sea, Hades, Gehenna, fire, hell—the Bible is wonderfully profligate in constant reconfiguration of this transformative experience. Perhaps, the Bible wants to warn us against getting caught up in rigid labels and naïve literalism, so we won't allow our sermons to get too graphic. Instead, it wants us to feel, in our guts, the existential experience it is pointing to—an experience common to all of us, if we could only see it.[19]

A close reading of Jonah's prayer offers broad hints that his experience of hell does not quite conform to evangelical doctrine. Two seeming contradictions disturb the picture.

First, Jonah is in a place where God both *is* and *is not.* "I am driven away from your sight," Jonah says, not long after uttering these words: "You heard my voice." Jonah stands in the tradition of the psalmist: "Where can I go from your spirit? Or where can I flee from your presence? If I ascend to heaven, you are there; if I make my bed in Sheol, you are there" (Psalm 139:7–8).

Second, Jonah's song declares emphatically, on the one hand,

---

19 Brueggeman has a helpful discussion of the Pit. He writes: "The core narrative of human life and human destiny is 'into the Pit' of trouble and 'out of the Pit' by the power of Yahweh. . . The truth of human personhood vis-à-vis Yahweh is that the human person is not helplessly and hopelessly consigned to the Pit, because the power of Yahweh can break the grip of the Pit." *Theology of the Old Testament,* 483, 553–554.

that he will never escape from this place of darkness. Its "bars," he writes, "closed upon me *forever*." But it turns out that the opposite is also true. As the story continues, Jonah *will* escape Sheol, and he'll go on to further adventures in Ninevah. Evidently, *forever* is not literally a period of time extending infinitely far into the future. As a spiritual reality, *forever ends*. When we enter the biblical world, words like "forever," "eternal" and "everlasting" are not quantitative, but qualitative measures—connoting a peculiar existential experience whose intensity, if only for a moment, feels infinite. Emerging from such an intensity can feel like nothing short of resurrection.[20]

Which is what happens to Jonah. After a wrenching encounter with himself and God in the darkness of the deep, Jonah is "spewed" onto dry land. When he finally heads for Ninevah, it will be as one whom Sheol has vomited up. Jonah has been to hell and back.

* * *

GOD FORBID IT

Jesus' disciple, Peter, seems to have a little "Jonah" in him. He's rash, like Jonah, and he seems drawn to deep waters. Twice, impulsively, he jumps out of a boat and into the sea (Matthew 14:29, John 21:7).

---

20 Another well-known biblical story offers a similar portrait, only rarely remarked on by evangelical preachers. Sodom's destruction by fire and brimstone is often used to emphasize hell's eternal results. Both the traditionalist and conditionalist scholars I cited above use Sodom in this way. One says hell's torture lasts forever and the other says hell's destruction lasts forever (Fudge and Peterson, *Two Views of Hell*, 70–71, 153–156). Both also quote Jude 7: "Likewise Sodom and Gomorrah. . . serve as an example by undergoing a punishment of eternal fire." Although they quote prolifically from obscure texts, neither scholar notices that the prophet Ezekiel puts words in God's mouth starkly contradicting the finality of Sodom's fate: "I will restore. . . the fortunes of Sodom and her daughters. . . Sodom and her daughters shall return to their former state" (Ezekiel 16:53–55).

If there is resurrection for Sodom, a virtual synonym for unforgivable sin, how can there not be resurrection for all who feel the flames of fire?

He fishes for a living, so this may be normal behavior. Or is it an indication that something in Peter wants to be baptized?

Peter's first dunking occurs during a stormy sea crossing (Matthew 14). The boat is laboring in a storm. A ghost materializes off the port bow. The disciples shrink in terror until the ghost says something that sounds like Jesus: "Take heart, it is I; do not be afraid."

Perhaps Peter is terrorized like the others. If so, he doesn't show it. I imagine him playing tough, looking relaxed, chuckling at his weak-kneed friends. Maybe they're too terrorized to notice his panache, so he raises the ante: "Lord, if it is you, bid me come to you on the water." Jesus says "Come"—one word only, not revealing what Jesus is actually thinking about Peter's idea.

So Peter jumps overboard and the wind catches him, and he panics and begins to sink. "Lord, save me!" he shouts. For just one moment, as an earnest of things to come, Peter is in hell. Then Jesus grabs his flailing hand and hauls him into the boat.

So Peter is safe, for now. But then Jesus asks him one of his patented, unsettling questions. He draws attention to Peter's "little faith" and asks: "Why did you doubt?" Jesus is inviting Peter to a cross-like experience—to meet himself in nakedness as the small, scared human being he is on the inside. But Peter—like the Pharisees—has a powerful internal part that protects him from his nakedness, a kind of "false self" that fancies itself a giant of faith. This part of him intends to risk all for Jesus. Peter probably doesn't get it when Jesus names him "the Rock," likening him to a dense, sinking object. He won't live the truth of his own suffering, and love his fellow human beings without condescension, until he meets his inner sinker. There will need to be heavy seas—or scorching fires—before the "real Peter" can be born.

A short time after his near-drowning, Peter is back to form. Jesus asks his disciples who they think he is (Matthew 16:13–25). Like a precocious fifth-grader, Peter jumps up first, hand waving in the air. "You are the messiah, the son of the living God."

For the moment, Jesus affirms Peter's answer, and Peter must feel pretty satisfied with himself. But it turns out that Jesus has so forthrightly accepted this title only because he wants to disrupt the meaning, in the disciples' minds, of the very word "messiah." He tells his disciples great suffering is ahead, and that he will be killed. This is an unbearable challenge to Peter's triumphant self-image, as well as his triumphant image of Jesus and the almighty "Father" who stands behind him.

Instantly, Peter scolds Jesus: "God forbid it," he says, appealing to his image of a "Father" who doesn't suffer, and who doesn't allow his loyal followers to suffer. In the name of this God, Peter is emphatic: "This must never happen to you!" And Jesus scolds him right back: "Get behind me, Satan! You are a stumbling block to me!"

Here Jesus spells out the deepest meaning of his life. His journey will take him to hell, and Peter's self-protective mechanisms cannot stop this. But more: Jesus invites Peter to relax his self-protection and take the journey with him. Immediately after rebuking Peter, he says: "If any want to become my followers, let them deny themselves and take up their cross and follow me. For those who save their life will lose it, and those who lose their life for my sake will find it" (Matthew 16:24–25). To follow this Savior is to walk into a fire.[21]

But Peter, like most of us, is dense. Soon thereafter, on a high mountain, Jesus' face and clothes begin to glow (Matthew 17:1–8).

---

21 Moltmann believes that Jesus "experiences a hell of rejection and loneliness on the cross" in a way that believers do not need to experience. He writes: "Christ experiences death and hell in solitude. His followers experience it in his company." *Crucified God*, 263. If this is true, it may be too simply expressed. Many Christians have testified to feeling a "dark night of the soul" in which God's absence is, paradoxically, a painful manifestation of God's presence. A helpful meditation on this subject is Gerald G. May, *The Dark Night of the Soul: A Psychiatrist Explores the Connection Between Darkness and Spiritual Growth* (New York: HarperSanFrancisco, 2004). I comment further on this in Chapter 10.

Peter is naturally afraid, but instead of honestly confessing his fear, he leaps into action. He forgets the stormy sea and the predicted cross. "Lord, it is good for us to be here," he says, a whole new future taking shape before his eyes. "If you wish, I will make three dwellings, one for you, one for Moses, and one for Elijah."

At that moment, a cloud drifts by and a voice says, "This is my Son, the Beloved. . . listen to him!" Someone wants Peter to know he's not listening.

All of Peter's protective mechanisms finally come to crisis on the eve of Jesus' death (Matthew 26:31–35 and 74). Once more, he shows how captive he is to a false sense of himself. Jesus is informing his disciples that, in the turmoil to come, they will all desert him.

Peter's "false self" pipes up: "Everyone else will, but not I," he says. "Even though I must die with you, I will not deny you." But just a few hours later, after Jesus has been taken into custody and Peter is warming himself by a fire, a stranger questions him about his relationship to the would-be messiah. He hears a very different protective voice inside saying: "I do not know the man."

And now the dam breaks inside Peter. He finally catches a glimpse of the scared, weak, doubting, naked Peter inside, and goes into the darkness weeping bitter tears. Peter has descended into hell, a painful but hopeful place where he can finally meet the "sorrowful one" whose sorrows he has never been prepared to accept. His encounter with his own broken humanity, and the brokenness of the "almighty" image he has of God, opens him to the possibility of healing.[22]

---

22 This surprisingly hopeful outcome is hinted at in John's account. After Jesus predicts Peter's triple denial, he says: "Let not your hearts be troubled; believe in God, believe also in me." He knows God's faithfulness will ultimately burn away our denials (John 13:36–14:1).

Hell, it seems, is only—albeit painfully—a way-station on the journey to salvation.[23]

*   *   *

HE DESCENDED INTO HADES

Jesus once treated a crowd that had gathered around him to these cryptic words: "This generation is an evil generation; it asks for a sign, but no sign will be given to it except the sign of Jonah. For just as Jonah became a sign to the people of Ninevah, so the human son will be to this generation" (Luke 11:29–30).

How does Jonah point to Jesus? Perhaps by spending three days in Sheol and then returning—a human son who goes to hell and back.[24] When Jonah finally meets the Ninevites and warns them about God's judgment, he speaks with the conviction of one who has experienced

---

23 To my mind, if you will permit me a crude anachronism, Peter is the quintessential evangelical Christian. He is the disciple most outspoken about his "faith." He is most eager to answer the questions right. His plan for the "three tabernacles" shows the keen entrepreneurial ambition that evangelicals have brought to the free market of American religion for at least two centuries. We might even credit him with envisioning the first evangelical theme park!

Peter has all the lovable sincerity of a Billy Graham, all the astounding energy of a Rick Warren, all the easy answers of a Pat Robertson, all the slick assurance of a James Dobson and all the self-deception of a Ted Haggard. I wonder: does Peter's experience point the way to a special form of hell reserved for American evangelicals, an "outer darkness" where bitter tears become the necessary doorway to salvation?

24 Canadian songwriter, Leonard Cohen, works this metaphor beautifully in one stanza of his song "Suzanne Takes You Down," in *Parasites of Heaven* (McClelland and Stuart, 1966):

Now Jesus was a sailor and he sailed upon the water;
He spent a long time watching from his lonely wooden tower.
And when he knew for certain only drowning men would see him,
He said, "All men will be sailors then until the sea shall free them."
But he himself was broken long before the sky would open.
Forsaken, almost human, he sank beneath your wisdom like a stone.

that judgment—not as condemnation, but as salvation. He knows that hell's eternity is not literally eternal, and that those who find themselves alone in their sufferings there are not literally alone.

It will perhaps be a cold day in hell before evangelical preachers use the story of Jonah to explain that "eternal" flames are *not* without end and that Jesus is *present* in hell. But large sectors of the Christian church have kept alive the strange idea that Jesus went to hell to put an end to its tortures.

Peter's Epistle depicts Jesus, in his death, going to preach "to the spirits in prison, who in former times did not obey" (1 Peter 3:18–20). He knew what he was talking about. The Apostles' Creed states boldly, of Jesus: "He descended into Hades." The Apostle Paul follows up a stirring hymn to the "Father of us all, who is above all and through all and in all" with the tantalizing vision of Jesus completing and cementing this cosmic unity by descending "into the lower parts of the earth" where he "made captivity itself a captive" (Ephesians 4:8–10). These are the poetic notes struck by a sometimes-too-prosaic Paul, dramatizing what his letters tell us again and again: in Jesus, we are set free—and not we only, but every human being, living and dead!

Paul can be still more explicit about the universal nature of his hope. In his letter to the Philippians, he envisions a time when "at the name of Jesus every knee shall bend, in heaven and on earth and under the earth, and every tongue confess that Jesus Christ is Lord, to the glory of God the Father." This confession appears in the context of his eloquent hymn to the crucified Jesus, who appeared in "the form of a slave, being born in human likeness" and "humbled himself" to the point of "death on a cross" (Philippians 2:10–11 and 7–8).

There is little doubt that, for Paul, the Jesus who descended to "the lower parts of the earth" and "made captivity captive" was the human son, crucified and risen again so that all humans could encounter, in the cross, the revelation of their own crucifixion and the experience of their own resurrection. As he himself had, when he met the crucified one in the midst of his own hell on the road to Damascus. Perhaps during the succeeding three days, as his own blindness was being revealed to him and finding a cure, Paul heard from Jesus' own lips the promise Jesus had made to his disciples that, when he hung on a cross, he would draw every last person to himself.[25]

•　　•　　•

YOU CANNOT HELP US

Just before Jesus predicts Peter's denials, he promises Peter that, when the time is right, Peter too will suffer. "Where I am going you cannot follow me now," he says, "but you shall follow afterward." Since Jesus is moving intentionally toward the hell of his own suffering, he may be implying that, once Peter is transformed by an encounter with his own nakedness, he too will, of his own accord, like his master, "take up his cross" and follow Jesus into hell.

For Jesus, and eventually for Peter, the life of faith may be constituted by a willing solidarity in suffering with the stranger and the prisoner, the sick, the hungry and the naked, as well as with the "goats" who do not recognize their kinship with the needy. When he told his disciples they would all be "salted with fire," he also urged them to cultivate an awareness of this "fire" of suffering within them as a way of finding genuine connection with other people: "Have salt in yourselves," he said, "and be at peace with one another."[26]

I know no clearer example of someone taking the salt of suffering into herself than Etty Hillesum. In 1943, this young Jewish woman arrives in the barracks at Westerbork, a Nazi transit camp in the

---

25 St. Paul's conversion story is told in Acts 9 and again in Acts 22 and 26. Jesus' words are recorded in John 12:32, and are followed by an explanation: "He said this to indicate the kind of death he was to die" (verse 33).
26 Mark 9:50.

eastern Netherlands.[27] Although her position in the Jewish Council of Amsterdam could exempt her, she joins her family as they await an inexorable fate: to be herded into boxcars and shipped like cattle to the killing grounds at Auschwitz. She embraces the journey into hell.

While Etty waits, she offers her feeble assistance to the miserable souls chosen to precede her. "We dress them and escort them to the bare cattle trucks," she writes in the final pages of her diary, "and if they can't walk, we carry them on stretchers." She visits patients in the camp's hospital, wondering which ones will be shipped eastward the next day to certain death.

From one of the beds, a partially paralyzed young girl with "thin wrists and a peaky little face" calls to her.

"Have you heard?" the girl says. "I have to go."

"We look at each other for a long moment," Etty writes. "It is as if her face has disappeared, she is all eyes. Then she says in a level, grey little voice, "Such a pity, isn't it? That everything you have learned in life goes for nothing. . . How hard it is to die."

Hovering near the paralyzed girl sits "a little hunchbacked Russian woman. . . spun in a web of sorrow."

"She looks at me for a long time in silence," writes Etty, "and then says, 'I would like, oh, I really would like, to be able to swim away in my tears'. . . She asks me with her strange accent in the voice of a child that begs for forgiveness, 'Surely God will be able to understand my doubts in a world like this, won't he?' Then she turns away from me, in an almost loving gesture of infinite sadness. . ."

"What is going on?" Etty asks. "What mysteries are these, in what sort of fatal mechanism have we become enmeshed?. . . God Almighty, what are you doing to us?"

Etty is living in hell. Her diaries graphically portray the gradual

27 *An Interrupted Life: The Diaries of Etty Hillesum, 1941–1943* (New York: Pantheon Books, 1983), 146, 149, 151, 209, 211, 212. Her story is told again in Patrick Woodhouse, *Etty Hillesum: A Life Transformed* (New York: Continuum, 2009).

process by which she fights her false comforts, evasions and denials—fights even the instinct to hate those who hate her and her people—and takes the hell of her own and her neighbors' suffering more deeply into herself. As she does so, God becomes more and more real to her, more and more intimate with her.

But the God she meets is not "the Almighty," the conventional "omni-everything" divinity left over from her childhood religious training. The God who bleeds onto her pages in the darkest days of the Holocaust is very near and very small. She prays:

> I shall try to help you, God, to stop my strength ebbing away, though I cannot vouch for it in advance. But one thing is becoming increasingly clear to me: that you cannot help us, that we must help you to help ourselves. And that is all we can manage these days and also all that really matters: that we safeguard that little piece of you, God, in ourselves. And perhaps in others as well. Alas, there doesn't seem to be much you yourself can do about our circumstances, about our lives. Neither do I hold you responsible. You cannot help us, but we must help you and defend your dwelling place inside us to the last.

In the hell of the Holocaust, Etty gradually becomes alive to a God who draws her irresistibly into the most intimate of relationships.[28] This God is small, utterly helpless to change the circumstances of her life or the lives of millions of fellow-sufferers. But this One is *present* with her in hell, permitting her to confess her nakedness, embrace God's nakedness, and find comfort. In the presence of a God who cannot help, she finds help and healing.

"I don't feel I'm in their clutches," she writes. "I feel safe in God's arms. . ."

---

28 Henri J. M. Nouwen's *The Inner Voice of Love* is a primer in the journey of a Christian into hell, where he or she is met by Jesus. Moltmann quotes Pascal: "in [Jesus] we find both God and our misery" (*Crucified God*, 281).

CHAPTER 10

Breaking the Almighty's spell

*Learning compassion in
the school of sorrow*

> *Were it possible, we might look beyond the reach
> of our knowing. . . Then perhaps we would endure
> our griefs with even greater trust than our joys.
> For they are the moments when something new
> has entered into us, something unfamiliar. . .
> Everything within us steps back; a silence ensues,
> and something new. . . stands in the center
> and is silent.*
> Rainer Maria Rilke[1]

GOATS COME IN EVERY SHAPE and size, of course. They inhabit every religious—and every non-religious—tradition. I suspect a "goat" can be found somewhere inside every person. There is a small herd of goats inside me, toward whom I try to extend my love when they seem to be getting frisky. Goats can only be quieted, and eventually transformed into sheep, by love.

Evangelical Christianity breeds a special category of goat: the kind whose lack of compassion seems to grow out of, and is often

---

1 *Letters to a Young Poet,* Joan M Burnham, transl. (Novato, CA: New World Library, 2000), 74.

supported by, a supercharged loyalty to the Almighty.[2] In times of trouble, these evangelical goats do not let sorrow, anger or confusion come close enough to touch them. "It must have been the Lord's will," they might say. "We don't know the Lord's mind. . . Sometimes things like this are hard to fathom. . . but we must learn to trust the Lord. . ."

You can sometimes hear "goats" speaking up at funerals: "There's no need to be sad. We can rejoice because our loved one has gone to be with Jesus." When disaster strikes, a goat might say: "The Lord must be trying to teach us something." Goats aren't trying to be callous in these situations—in fact, their conscious intent is to comfort. But their inability to allow human suffering into themselves, to "hold" it inside themselves without trying to "fix" it, often means that the people they are trying to console don't feel consoled. They feel even more alone in their sorrow.

Sometimes this "goaty" callousness is so blatant that it gets headlines. After the World Trade Center attacks in 2001, a prominent American evangelical, Pat Robertson, put these words on his website:

> The focus of many in America has been on the pursuit of health, wealth, material pleasures and sexuality. . . We have allowed rampant pornography on the Internet, and rampant secularism and the occult, etc. to be broadcast on television. We have permitted somewhere in the neighborhood of thirty-five to forty million unborn babies to be slaughtered by our society. . . We have a court that has essentially stuck its finger in God's eye and said, "We are going to legislate you out of the schools and take your

---

2 Evangelicals are no more tempted to resist mourning than anyone else. Arguably, however, our loyalty to (and fear of) the Almighty means we are more deeply practiced at it, and institutionally committed to it, than many other subcultures—particularly those which, in ritualistic ways, invite the tears to flow.

commandments from the courthouses. . ." We have insulted God at the highest level of our government. Then, we say, "Why does this happen?" It is happening because God Almighty is lifting his protection from us. [3]

Aware that his readers might get the wrong impression, Robertson added:

Now, I am filled with compassion. It just tears my heart when I think of the families of these suffering. But I want to say as surely as I am sitting here today, this is only a foretaste, a little warning, of what is going to happen. We have not seen the massive destruction of life in our urban centers that can take place with sarin gas and with the biological and chemical warfare that is available to these rogue people, not to mention, suitcase nuclear bombs that they probably have available as well. We must come back to God as a people.

The outcry that followed these remarks suggested that, for Americans who suffered loss on 9/11, or who shared the torment of those who did, Robertson's claim of compassion had a hollow ring.[4]

Robertson's remarks are only one example among many. Prominent evangelical ministers issued similar remarks after 9/11, after the earthquake and tsunami in the Indian Ocean in 2004, and

---

3 *Robertson's Statement Regarding Terrorist Attack on America* at The Official Site of Pat Robertson (www.PatRobertson.com), 2008.

4 Hanna Rosin offers another example of the unconsciously mixed messages for which evangelicals are famous. Michael Farris, founder and president of Patrick Henry College, seemed compassionate when he criticized St. Augustine because "he burned people at the stake." He said that he had "problems with people who burn people at the stake." In the same conversation, however, he said: "Augustine is roasting in hell." Rosin, *God's Harvard*, 258–259.

after Hurricane Katrina's devastating impact in 2005.[5] For many Americans, these responses are grotesque. They cement evangelical Christianity in the popular mind as an emotionally immature faith, a faith that confines itself to the "head" and permits no access to "heart" or "soul."

But even for evangelical Christians who continue to think of God as the "Almighty," such responses must evoke mixed feelings. One voice inside says: "Yes, that seems right, the Almighty is in control of world events, so this trouble must have come either by God's direct decision or God's permissive will." But another voice whispers: "There's something wrong here."

What's wrong, I believe, is not that Robertson and those like him are hard-hearted people. They are speaking in a way that they believe to be sympathetic and caring. But that way of speaking, I will suggest in this chapter, reflects an unconscious resistance to mourning.

The biblical symbol of this resistance is the city of Babylon. "I rule as a queen," she said. "I am no widow, and I will never see grief."

---

5 On September 13, 2001, in an on-air conversation with Pat Robertson, Baptist minister Jerry Falwell said: "The ACLU has got to take a lot of blame for this. . . throwing God out of the public square, out of the schools, the abortionists have got to bear some burden for this because God will not be mocked and when we destroy 40 million little innocent babies, we make God mad."

In the same interview, he addressed pagans, feminists, gays and lesbians, saying, "You helped this happen." The next day, Falwell apologized to feminists, gays and lesbians, but added that organizations that seek to secularize America "created an environment which possibly has caused God to lift the veil of protection which has allowed no one to attack America on our soil since 1812" (www.CNN.com, 9/14/01).

On September 12, 2005, prominent evangelical Charles Colson said: "*Did God have anything to do with Katrina?* people ask. My answer is, he allowed it and perhaps he allowed it to get our attention so that we don't delude ourselves into thinking that all we have to do is put things back the way they were and life will be normal again" (www. mediammatters.org, September 13, 2005).

Similar diagnoses of the causes of the tsunami were offered by Christian, Muslim and Jewish spokespersons (www.religioustolerance.org), indicating that evangelicals are not alone in worshipping a wrathful, almighty deity.

Babylon believed her spiritual powers protected her from the help-lessness, the abject despair, of loss (Revelation 18:7–8).[6] Are evangelicals the current embodiment of Babylon?

If we are, then we have become the institutional equivalent of a goat. We can offer token pity or easy fixes to those who hurt, but we cannot as easily be present in naked compassion to them. Perhaps, it is not America that will suffer God's "wrath," as Robertson and others would have it, but American *evangelicals*. Perhaps we will need to share the fate of Babylon—"pestilence and mourning and famine," and burning in a healing fire—before we will admit the depth of our own losses and touch the sorrow that already lives within us.

This would be a kind of hell, no doubt, but it is in hell that goats can be transformed into the sheep they really want to be—the sheep that, in some secret place within them, they already are.

• • •

SOMEONE LOSES
Mourning is a prototypically human experience. It follows in the wake of loss, and loss leaves its mark indelibly on every human life. "There may be just one universal story," one writer has said. "Someone loses something."[7] And when we lose, if we respond truthfully, we mourn.

Does their special relationship with the Almighty mean that evangelical Christians are exempt from loss? A foolish question, of course. As human beings, evangelicals are no more exempt from

6   The text notices that Babylon trades in "slaves—and human lives" (Revelation 18:13), suggesting that, if we resist the process of mourning, we will bring serious damage to those around us. I believe we do this damage every time we blithely proclaim bromides about the will of God or prescribe the happiness of Jesus to a suffering world.

7   Ken Foster, "Introduction," *The KGB Bar Reader* (New York: William Morrow and Company, 1998), xii.

life's exigencies than are the adherents of any religious tradition—or the followers of no tradition at all. I have seen this most concretely in church.

For about twenty-five years, I participated with my neighbors in a small country church. Each Sunday morning, a score of us sat in a circle, sang a hymn or two, read a psalm or a Gospel story, and then—as a form of prayer—talked informally about our lives. Each week, some would speak—offering a line or two, or a longer narrative—while others remained silent. Over the years, we entrusted a great deal of our lives to one another.

The stories we told one another in church were mostly stories of loss. A man whose mother had Alzheimer's worried about the strain on his father. One woman's brother-in-law suffered from a degenerative syndrome, while another's brother-in-law was dying of heart disease. A young woman recounted a painful visit with her parents, who could not hide their disapproval of her. A man battled his ex-wife over custody of their six-year-old, who accompanied her father to church wearing on her face the strain of her parents' tug-of-war. A man reported that his job application had been rejected. Another asked us to pray for his nephew, a drug addict. A woman joined our fellowship after her husband died in a collision with a train, leaving her with three small children. A man and his two daughters lost wife and mother to leukemia. A woman's sister suffered from chronic fatigue. A long-time member died after enduring debilitating pain for two decades.

All this suffering entered the room with us each Sunday morning. Our joys came into the room with us as well, and our services were often punctuated by laughter and celebration. But the more serious, and the more persistent, business of the group was our pain. In this respect, we were in no way different from our non-Christian neighbors: we had many reasons to mourn.

•   •   •

LOSS UPON LOSS

But evangelicalism's losses are not restricted to the daily lives of its individual adherents. It has also endured losses as an identifiable social and religious movement for at least the past century. The evangelical God—the Almighty—has been dethroned in a country once thought "Christian." In that dethronement, there is plenty of reason to mourn.

In earlier chapters, I described evangelicalism's fall from social respectability.[8] The new gods—modernism, capitalism, secularism, consumerism, skepticism, technical and scientific rationality—seemed to have no use for the Almighty. Religious people were assumed to be ignorant—and pathetically so. As we have seen, these losses were painfully felt by the young scholars who strived to separate themselves from fundamentalism and regain evangelicalism's power—and the world's respect—in the post-war period. These losses are still at least implicitly felt by many evangelicals who idealize an earlier time and yearn to return America to its "godly" roots.[9]

Beginning in the Reagan years of the 1980s, some evangelical voices began to sense the tide beginning to turn. Reagan claimed to be "born again." Religion received growing interest among scholars and earned a grudging respect in the public square. The rise of the megachurch, as a symbol of evangelicalism's vitality,

---

8 I ploughed this ground in great detail in my earlier book, *Less Than Conquerors: The Evangelical Quest for Power in the Early Twentieth Century*.

9 This loss hovers in the background of many of the interviews in Christian Smith et al., *American Evangelicalism* (131–142). A sampling: "We're almost a persecuted group"; "I certainly don't think our society any longer has the Bible as a standard"; when "they took the Bible out of schools," America started going "downhill. . . It is gradually getting worse and worse and worse." The study offers no evidence that evangelicals are tempted to rethink their depiction of the Almighty in light of these observations.

became legendary. But questions were raised as to whether religion's "respectability" was less an achievement of evangelical striving than of modernity's own self-criticism. And the diversity of the new religiosity—a wild, eclectic pluralism with little respect for traditional orthodoxy—seems to have merely energized a new generation of evangelical doomsayers.

Some still hope for the re-birth of a truly Christian society. But the new life temporarily breathed into such hopes by a surge of Christian political activism has dissipated in light of the incompetence and unpopularity of the Bush presidency—and the association of evangelicals with that administration has merely heightened the reputation of religious persons as ignorant, right-wing bigots.[10] Most Americans say they believe in God and churches may be booming, but evangelicalism seems as far from regaining leadership in American society as ever.

Meanwhile the tenacious hold of "godless" media and hedonistic consumer capitalism has only tightened. A television drama willing to take God seriously, like *Touched by an Angel*, does nothing to alter an entertainment milieu feeding—and feeding off of—a public taste for violence and sex. Pornography proliferates like a wildly metastasizing cancer. Divorce tears families apart. Teens cycle downward into depression and addiction. Evangelicals who feel the pain of individuals in confusion and a society that seems to have lost its way—or

---

10 As of this writing, the assumption that evangelicalism is simply "the Republican Party at prayer" is being challenged by a smattering of so-called "new" evangelical voices staking out a more "progressive" Christian social ethic (concern for the poor, human rights, peace, the heath of the planet).

One of its spokespersons, Joel Hunter, a megachurch pastor from Orlando, Florida, says: "What has passed for an 'evangelical' up to now is a stereotype created by the people with the loudest voices. But there's a whole constituency out there that it doesn't apply to. Now something is happening. You can feel it like the force of a tsunami under the water." Quoted in Frances Fitzgerald, "The New Evangelicals: A Growing Challenge to the Religious Right" in *The New Yorker* (June 30, 2008), 30.

who simply like to bemoan America's "moral decline"—are not without the constant invitation to mourn.

Those evangelicals who lift their eyes beyond their own or evangelicalism's fortunes to events transpiring on a broader world stage will also find—as humans do everywhere—plenty of reason to mourn. The immeasurable human suffering that will forever stain the reputation of the twentieth century now lacerates the twenty-first. This reality screams for recognition, but defies summarization.

Its paradigmatic symbols must be allowed to speak for themselves: the mass carnage of Flanders in World War I, the gulags of Siberia, the Spanish Civil War so grippingly celebrated in Picasso's "Guernica," the Warsaw Ghetto, the bombing of Dresden, the death camps of Auschwitz and Dachau, the mindless slaughters of D-Day and Hiroshima.

Unspeakable tragedies, mass insanities, now summarized in a gruesome nomenclature: Selma, My Lai, Pol Pot, apartheid, Jonestown, Ethiopia, "the disappeared," Idi Amin, North Korea, Bosnia, Sierra Leone, Rwanda, 9/11, the Gaza strip, the Taliban, Abu Graib, Guantanamo, Darfur. And these are only the most obvious. One century of the dying and the dead fast bequeathing its legacy to the next.

How can evangelicals bear to read the news without bursting into tears? And yet, it seems, we can. Somehow, we followers of the "Sorrowful One" hang onto our smiles and retain our equanimity in the face of abysmal suffering. And often, we go further: we justify or explain that suffering, just as we explain the dashed evangelical hopes and the day-by-day human losses we and those around us suffer, by recourse to the will of Almighty God. Surrounded by loss upon loss, we stubbornly refuse to mourn.

•   •   •

DISORDERED GRIEVING

That is not to say we have no sadness in us. I believe we have vast pools of sadness in us. The losses we have suffered, individually and collectively, are real, and I believe that they have lodged themselves in the depths of our spirits. But something blocks our tears and keeps our sorrows impounded deep inside us, far away from our own conscious awareness. Too often, something keeps us offering explanations and false consolations instead of simply weeping helpless tears with those who weep. What could that be?

The process of mourning has been studied in great detail by psychological thinkers over the past century. No one has mapped its landscape more thoroughly than the British scholar, John Bowlby. He was a pioneer in charting the relatively uniform stages that healthy individuals traverse as they mourn their losses. He noticed that some individuals seem thwarted in that normal development, and he wondered why. He helps us understand the evangelical refusal to mourn.

When people sustain a major loss, Bowlby says, their first response is "shock and denial."[11] They feel numb, and are unable to assimilate the event. They may display an unreal calm, as if nothing serious has happened—although this calm can be punctuated by angry or tearful outbursts. In time, however, they enter the second stage of mourning, which may last months or even years. Their emotions swing wildly: sobbing, wailing, groaning, guilty and self-reproachful feelings, rages against those "responsible" for the loss, bitterness toward the lost loved one, hostile feelings toward family members and well-meaning friends. Brief periods of denial may return, and mourners imagine they will soon wake up from this bad dream to find that their loved one has returned.

---

11 John Bowlby, *Attachment and Loss* (3 volumes), (New York: Basic Books, 1969, 1973, 1980). The stages of mourning are treated in Volume III: *Loss* (1980), 85–111.

As mourning proceeds, the reality of the loss settles in and denial fades. The mourner realizes that life will have to be lived—in some new, unimaginable way—without the loved one. This begins the third phase of mourning: intense sadness alternating with periods of depression and apathy. The loss is more and more fully accepted—its pains experienced, its sorrows embraced. These can be hopeless times of deep loneliness. Tears flow freely. The sun doesn't seem to shine and reasons for getting out of bed in the morning seem scarce. This is mourning in its purest form, and it may go on for years.

And then one day, to his or her surprise, the mourner begins thinking about the future again. A redefinition of oneself takes hold: no longer is the mourner "husband" or "wife," but now "widower" or "widow"; no longer child of a parent, but now orphan; no longer "with" someone, but alone. The sorrow does not disappear, but it is gradually joined by other more hopeful voices in the mourner's internal chorus. Gradually, the mourner mixes back into the stream of life as a quietly transformed person, begins to embrace life with growing enthusiasm, and begins to trust human relationships again.

By enduring this journey through pain and sorrow, Bowlby believes, most people integrate loss into their lives in healthy ways, and experience a healing—not the kind that makes sorrow go away, but the kind that makes sorrow a friend rather than an enemy, and gradually integrates it into a life of hope, joy and compassion.

But Bowlby knows this doesn't always happen. Sometimes, he says, the grieving process is derailed and mourning cannot run its proper course. Most commonly this occurs, he writes, when people get stalled in the first stage of mourning: shock and denial. Some part of them steps forward to block awareness of their loss and help them avoid the disintegrating pain that the grieving process represents. This part keeps them permanently numb. These people—"disordered" grievers—cultivate a calm spirit, paste on an artificial smile, and deny that anything really important has happened.

Bowlby calls this condition "the prolonged absence of conscious grieving."[12] I believe he is describing twenty-first-century evangelical Christians.

·   ·   ·

SAYING "NO" TO SORROW

In his scholarly book on mourning in modern culture, Peter Homans helps us see how "the prolonged absence of conscious grieving" might have some very serious side-effects, and how these, in turn, shed light on a common evangelical character-structure.

Homans suggests that our ability to mourn is only one aspect of a larger, and critically important, human capacity: the ability to grow in self-awareness. When we allow mourning to touch us deeply, he says, we find ourselves naturally opening up to a non-judgmental exploration of our inner worlds. Mourning awakens our need to understand how we function at deeper, unconscious levels of our being.

A truly non-judgmental access to our deeper self, he writes, is not generally available to individuals in traditional or authoritarian cultures. In those cultures, powerful leaders and rigid teachings grab hold of and shape the individual's inner world according to strict understandings of what is true and right and good. Authoritarian leaders prize the cohesion and obedience of the group more than they do the individual's needs or wants. Leaders know that internal exploration and self-discovery are inherently destabilizing to the group because they alert people to individual needs or idiosyncratic desires. Such leaders work to keep their adherents from looking inward at all.

Of course, one way to keep them from being open to, or curious

---

12 Bowlby explores this "disordered grieving" at length in *Loss,* 137–262.

about, what is going on inside them is to keep them blissfully ignorant of their sorrows. Leaders who want pliable followers, Homans writes, work hard to keep them emotionally numb.

They do this in many ways. They might greet human suffering with theological formulas that "explain" why bad things happen and why, therefore, we need not be surprised—or perhaps even very sorry—that they happened. They might assure their followers, after tragic events, that God is still in control. They might condemn people who represent a part of us that we hate (say, the feminist, the homosexual or the Muslim terrorist) so that followers will immediately shut off any access to a part of themselves that resembles the "other" or recognizes the "other" as a fellow human being.

They might warn people against the pitfalls of "godless psychotherapy" and funnel them into church-supported, "biblically-based" counseling programs where, too often, telling the truth about one's own inner world is sacrificed to the imperatives of believing and behaving in "godly" ways. They might emphasize, in sermon after sermon, that we cannot trust our feelings, that they lead us astray unless we discipline them by sheer force of will.

In all these ways, and more, evangelical leaders encourage their followers to see their inner worlds as the devil's playground, where strict controls must be used to shape a godly temperament, and honest exploration must be shunned. The natural consequence, for many sincere and well-meaning evangelical Christians, is a "prolonged absence of conscious grieving"—an inability to mourn.

Homans says the "mere thought" of inner self-discovery "terrifies those in power by consciously calling attention to their own unconscious worlds and to the separateness which such attention facilitates."[13] Moreover, he observes, the closer you are to the centers

---

13 Peter Homans, *The Ability to Mourn: Disillusionment and the Social Origins of Psychoanalysis* (Chicago: University of Chicago Press, 1989), 126.

of power in a culture or social group, the more likely you yourself are to be psychologically closed and emotionally numb.

Perhaps this helps us understand why such otherwise pleasant and kind-spirited folks as Pat Robertson and Jerry Falwell can say such cruel and thoughtless things. There is a part of them that is very afraid, not only of what their followers might think and feel if they allowed tragedy to take them inward, but what they themselves might think and feel.

·   ·   ·

THE ALMIGHTY DOESN'T WEEP

Bowlby was interested in the question of why certain people, and not others, might be susceptible to disordered mourning. His discovery, like Homans', singled out the influence of "authoritarian leaders," but he found those "leaders" very close to home.

People who refuse to mourn consciously, Bowlby writes, are invariably carrying physical or emotional injuries with them from their childhood. Their parents—the cause of these injuries—were either absent or were cold, judgmental and demanding. These parents were uncomfortable with their children's softer or more vulnerable feelings—their tears, their fears, their expressed needs for love or attention. Feelings like these were not met with sympathy or acceptance. In such an un-nurturing atmosphere, these children became ashamed of their feelings, and of their yearning for loving attachment. They considered these to be signs of inadequacy or weakness.

To protect themselves from feeling weak, children in these circumstances learned to block awareness of their feelings, not admitting them to themselves and certainly never showing them to others. They became emotionally distant adults who aspired to cool rationality, "strength of character," self-sufficiency and self-control. In Bowlby's words, children like these "come, like [their] parents, to

327

view [their] yearning for love as a weakness, [their] anger as a sin and [their] grief as childish." In times of loss, they feel an instinctive terror of the emotions that begin to swirl inside them. They hide their sorrow, even from themselves, behind a smiling façade, and resist the descent into the abyss of mourning.

I suspect that many evangelical parents, sincerely attempting to help their children become "godly" adults, discourage their children's self-awareness and the open expression of needs or feelings. But I am particularly interested in the divine parent that hovers over evangelical religious practice—a divine parent, who resembles the human parents Bowlby identifies as shaping the temperament of people who cannot mourn.

I described this divine parent in *Part One* of this book: a harsh and demanding father who impinges on the selfhood of his children, controlling their inner worlds as effectively as their outer, and whose threats of eternal abandonment effectively prevent his children from honestly saying what they feel about him.

For many evangelicals, this moratorium on honest expression applies to a whole range of doubts and conflicted feelings. In times of hardship and loss, it is a natural human instinct to raise questions about the role of the divine in shaping events—particularly a divine like the Almighty, whose power is limitless. Did God do this? Could God have prevented this? Is God punishing us? Could a loving God have permitted this?

Deep emotions accompany such questions: confusion, worry, sadness, anger, disappointment, reproach. Many of these feelings are directed, quite naturally, at God. If we live in the shadow of a judgmental, demanding and potentially abandoning God, we will not have permission to voice those doubts or permit ourselves to feel those feelings. We will need to cultivate denial ("No, I'm sure the Lord is still in control") and stay numb ("No, I'm not sad or angry; I know there's a reason for this").

Evangelicalism's divine "Father" gives every incentive to his children to deceive both him and themselves about their feelings. Many of them learn to shun the awareness or expression of feelings altogether, lest the long-repressed swirl of conflicting emotions explodes into the light of day. The result, I argued in Chapter 5, is a peculiarly evangelical variant of a "false self."[14] Under the protection of that false self, evangelicals cannot give themselves permission to mourn. But that "false self" is, in large part, a consequence of living with the Almighty. Unless we can escape the "spell" of the Almighty, we will never convincingly weep with those who weep.

*   *   *

OFF THE PEDESTAL

As deeply driven into our bones as this "almighty" God appears to be, the prospects for escaping his spell might seem slim—particularly if we are not allowed to voice, either to ourselves or to God, our conflicted feelings and our honest doubts. But in normal human development, there is an intriguing parallel that suggests a way forward: the process by which, sooner or later, we must all escape the spell of our parents if we are to live our own lives.

To our childhood eyes, our parents are larger-than-life. They are gigantic in stature, possessing all-power, all-wisdom, all-knowledge. They are our magical protectors and healers. But they cannot remain so, without fixing us in permanent dependency and damaging our ability to become fully ourselves. So gradually, and in some cases suddenly or with violent force, life conspires to make us face up to the disappointing truth that our parents are finite human beings.

---

14 Following D. W. Winnicott, Bowlby uses the same words—"false self"—to describe the mask worn by those whose mourning process is stalled at the stage of shock and denial. If you are unable to mourn, he implies, you are unable to become fully yourself. Bowlby, *Loss*, 224–225.

Inside, they are a jumble of tangled emotions and loose ends. They are often hasty or mistaken in their judgment. They can be unintentionally cruel. They are insecure and sometimes defensive. They are not altogether comfortable in their own skin. They are often puzzled, confused, blind-sided by life's exigencies. They are not all-powerful or all-wise. In fact, they are something of a "mess"—just like us.

The discovery of a parent's humanity can be deeply disturbing. Just to entertain thoughts of a parent's limitations can make children feel guilty and disloyal. Our parents' humanity threatens our own sense of safety and power. It destabilizes our own project of shaping a smooth, shiny internal and external persona. So it can be a difficult transition. We experience it as disillusionment—a kind of loss—and respond to this "crisis of faith" by mourning in the ways that Bowlby has described.

Some people move quickly through this disillusionment. Others remain trapped in denial, and cling to illusions that their parents are superhuman. Some seem more open than others to the anger one naturally feels during grief. Nurturing parents, who understand what their child is going through, and graciously receive all the feelings that the child expresses during this mourning process, are helping the child build internal resources useful in later experiences of loss.

For me, this process of disillusionment was drawn out over many years. My father's role as pastor—thus spokesperson for God—along with the seamless admiration my mother expressed for him, and the high esteem in which he was held by everybody I knew, all heightened his aura for me, so that it was not easy for me to glimpse his humanity. I think of an incident in my childhood as marking a kind of beginning in that process.

On a summer evening when I was twelve, I came home later than usual from roaming the neighborhood with a friend. My father was uncharacteristically suspicious, accusing me of staying out after dark in order to participate in some unspecified, but probably nefarious behavior. I had not been misbehaving, but I did feel guilty and defensive about coming home late. For the first time in my life, I yelled angrily at my father. In a storm of tears and curses, I let him know he was a rotten father, and if he tried to control me like this, I would teach him a lesson by running away from home.

My father was as shocked by my outburst as I was. A few minutes after I slammed my bedroom door to make my point, he knocked, came in and apologized. He said he was sorry for accusing me falsely. He said he loved me and trusted me more than I knew. I was surprised, and greatly relieved that I didn't have to follow through on an entirely hollow threat. We hugged, and the episode was over.

Over the ensuing days, I carried with me a vague sense that something important had happened—I had stood up for myself, and this had felt good. To my surprise, it had turned out well. I had no way to know the larger meaning, of course—I was beginning to admit that my father was not all-knowing or all-wise, and my outburst was a sign that a healthy disillusionment was underway.

My childhood family was one of those—common in the 1950s, particularly among evangelicals—that did not encourage self-disclosure or self-awareness. Both my parents came from childhood families marked by marital discord and emotional pain, and both, as teenagers, found in the Almighty a rescue from that pain and the promise of a life of happiness. The recipe for happiness was to "give" any and all unwanted feelings to God—and not to mention them to any other human being, particularly one's own children.

My father and mother were very good at displaying for their children—and approving *in* their children—only the feelings the Almighty approved. Anger, sadness, discouragement and worry were not among those feelings. As a result, my relationship with my family members was a meeting of surfaces. With very little access to my father at all—he was preoccupied with church business during my entire childhood—and given his guardedness about the "messier" human landscape within him, I had little opportunity to work out a more realistic picture of who he really was and to consciously mourn the loss of the ideal parent. In Bowlby's perspective, I was stalled in the stage of numbness.

Since my father was unable to help me along in this process, I was forced to draw on my own slowly-dawning self-understanding for a more illusion-free picture of my father. A turning point occurred on my thirty-ninth birthday when—seemingly out of the blue—I remembered my angry twelve-year-old encounter with my father. I puzzled over why it had suddenly come to mind, and then I realized that on this birthday I had reached the age my father had been when *I* was twelve!

It struck me, forcefully, that at the age of thirty-nine, I was nothing like the person my father had seemed to be when I was twelve. He had seemed big and wise, powerful and serene, and I had been the hurt and confused little kid. But as I approached forty, I experienced myself as a bundle of insecurities and hurts. And I knew that a part of me had learned to manage impressions well enough so that those insecurities remained hidden behind a serene and masterful surface. Instantly, I had a different father—as if the "old" father had simply walked out the door and passed an entirely "new" father walking in.

I now understand that the father who had first accused and then apologized to me had been at that moment a scared, confused man, just as I am in adulthood. His apology had been a sign, not only of his humility, but also of his imperfection and insufficiency—truths I had not known how to assimilate until much later. When, as an adult, I gained this new perspective on my father, I felt a surge of love for him that was unlike any I had felt before—a genuine compassion, accompanied by a deep curiosity to know more about this "new," intriguingly "strange" father.

The experience was a turning point in my relationship with my father. It inaugurated a journey toward a more natural, adult connection with him, a connection in which both of us could finally become more fully ourselves in each other's presence, sharing with one another the angers and hurts that lay beneath the surface, but also our mutual admiration and our gratitude for each other's care.

If we all, sooner or later, must mourn the loss of our "all-powerful" parents, is it not just as likely that we must mourn the loss of the "all-powerful" Almighty? Would the fruit of that mourning be a genuine curiosity about the strange new divine parent who takes his place—a pure curiosity, undistorted by our stale, evangelical agendas? Would a burst of genuine curiosity not revolutionize our prayer practices and our experience of reading the Bible?

I believe the mission of the cross is to set this mourning in motion. It unmasks the Almighty to reveal a smaller, more vulnerable, more "foolish-looking" God. This human God—like our real human parents—looks very much like ourselves, like the selves we really are. This God is no better able to manage the events of history, to guarantee our success or protect us from injury, than we are. This God is no more the Almighty than we are.

But this God, revealed in the sorrowful one on the cross, *is* a warm, accepting, emotionally real "parent" who, as one who knows trouble, promises to be *with* us in times of trouble. This God's essence is not holiness, but love, and God's promises are about relationship, not about reward. This God invites us, in times of trouble, to mourn fully, to "groan inwardly," as the Apostle Paul puts it, clinging to the hope that "neither death, nor life, nor angels, nor rulers, nor things present, nor things to come, nor powers, nor height, nor depth, nor anything else in all creation" will separate us from the love of a divine parent who holds us, who will suffer and die with us, who will bring us to life eternal (Romans 8:23 and 38–39).

This smaller human God—the One revealed by a dying figure on a cross—knows from personal experience the pain we feel when we lose the consolations of the "almighty" God, and dissolve in bitter tears.

●　　　●　　　●

A GOD WHO HIDES

Bringing our human parents down to human size, so that we can have a more human and intimate relationship with them, is not something we consciously plan. We are not in control of that transition. The exigencies of real life simply conspire to make it happen.

It is the exigencies of life that conspire to bring the big, almighty God down to human size as well. For many people, these exigencies seem relatively gentle. The human Jesus may come, and the Almighty lose his power, in a riveting sermon or in the reading of a Gospel text; or in works of literature[15] or theology; or in a vision or a conversation or a song. The human Jesus may come in a jail cell or out among the lilies of the field. These "comings" can be quiet events, opening us to a process of mourning that is almost invisible to those around us. Our suffering seems bearable, the transition relatively smooth.

But for others, the exigencies of real life are sudden and cruel. They unleash chaotic inner forces that threaten to tear us apart. They rip off the Almighty's mask before our eyes, violently, forcing us to ask the questions we have so long evaded, compelling us to consider answers we find unbearable. We don't know that we will make it through. And if we do, we know that it was not our doing. We were carried along on a mysterious grace.

One of the most eloquent narratives of this forced march to a more

---

15 I know of people who have met the human Jesus, for example, in Shusaku Endo's novels, *Deep River* and *Silence*, J.D.Salinger's *Franny and Zooey*, Cormac McCarthy's *The Crossing*, Etty Hillesum's *An Interrupted Life*, Fyodor Dostoyevsky's *The Brothers Karamazov* and *Crime and Punishment*—to name only a few.

human God is the memoir written by Nicholas Wolterstorff after his son Eric died in a mountain-climbing accident.[16] Wolterstorff reveals his seething despair, the "cold burning pain," the months of "indescribably painful" torment, his haunting regrets over words of love and forgiveness not spoken, the searing finality of Eric's absence. Images of darkness recur: he finds himself trapped in "a place of cold inky blackness"; in burying Eric, he writes, "it was me on whom we shoveled dirt."

From this bitter soil, watered by his tears, questions burst forth. At first, they are about Eric, about loss, love, life and death. "How can I bury my son, my future. . . ? Why did he climb that mountain?. . . Why did he climb it alone?. . . Must we all be swept forever on, away, beyond, beauty lost, and love. . . ? What does it mean, Eric dead. . . ?"

But as sorrow settles deeper into his soul, Wolterstorff's questions turn their searchlight on God. Did God shake the mountain and thereby *cause* his son's death? "No!" he answers quickly. But then, why did God not *prevent* his son's death? "I do not know why God would watch him fall," he writes. "I do not know why God would watch me wounded. I cannot even guess."

In these questions, I hear Wolterstorff wrestling with the remnants of an Almighty lodged in the deeper wells of his consciousness.[17] The God he questions, in his grief, seems to be the all-powerful sovereign who could have caused Eric's death and could have saved him, had he wished to do so. Because Wolterstorff cannot let go of the magical, omnipotent God, he cannot evade the painful questions

---

16 *Lament for a Son* (Grand Rapids, MI: William B. Eerdmans Publishing Company, 1987). I have drawn on 13, 15–16, 19, 23, 26, 33, 42–43, 46, 54, 57, 63, 65, 68–69, 71–72, 79, 80–82, 85–86, 92, 96–97.

17 What follows is my interpretation of Wolterstorff's memoir. I do not mean to imply that Wolterstorff would necessarily assent to this interpretation in whole or in part.

about why a God who loves him, and loves his son, did not use his almighty power to prevent this unbearable loss.

In the midst of these questions, in a place of deep darkness, Wolterstorff calls out for the "almighty" God. But he cannot find him. He echoes Psalm 42: "Why have you forgotten me? Why must I go about mourning, oppressed by the enemy?" He quotes Isaiah: "Truly, you are a God who hides yourself. . ."

His lament rises to a crescendo: "How is faith to endure, O God, when you allow all this scraping and tearing on us? You have allowed rivers of blood to flow, mountains of suffering to pile up, sobs to become humanity's song—all without lifting a finger that we could see. . . If you have not abandoned us, explain yourself."

In Wolterstorff's telling, God never offers an explanation. Instead, it seems, God *comes*. But it is not the old almighty God who comes— the regal mastermind, the magical, omnipotent protector. Instead, almost by surprise, "we catch sight of God himself scraped and torn. Through our tears we see the tears of God."

This is a revelatory moment for which Wolterstorff does not prepare his readers. And rightly: he was not prepared for it himself. "For a long time," he writes, "I knew that God is not the impassive, unresponsive, unchanging Being portrayed by the classical theologians. . . But strangely, his suffering I never saw before. . . Though I confessed that the man of sorrows was God himself, I never saw the God of sorrows. Though I confessed that the man bleeding on the cross was the redeeming God, I never saw God himself on the cross, blood from sword and thorn and nail dripping healing into the world's wounds."

Wolterstorff's memoir points to a God who neither shook the mountain that took his son's life, nor prevented its shaking. Its author doesn't seem to wonder whether such an Almighty God—the kind who literally shakes mountains—has *ever* existed, or whether, on the contrary, God has always been a smaller, more vulnerable, more warmly human presence, "slaughtered from the foundation of the world" (Revelation 13:8). But his account, by my reading, lends itself to the latter. It portrays a "weak" God who could not do more than to be present to Eric in his death, and who in its aftermath appropriated and inhabited the fires of hell with Wolterstorff, drawing him deep into the heart of suffering—God's suffering, and his own.

Wolterstorff, in the end, said "Yes" to this journey. He gave himself to mourning. He did not seek comfort in false pieties, put on a happy face, try to "get over it." He moved in with his sorrowing self, set up housekeeping with his own hurt. The events of his life virtually forced him to enter the darkness, where he allowed himself to experience the weeping and the gnashing of teeth which Jesus used as a metaphor for hell. And he emerged both a more sorrowful and—as I read his story—a more authentic human being.[18]

* * *

---

[18] Buddhist voices speak of a similar journey. One of those who speak to my heart is Pema Chodron. In *Comfortable with Uncertainty* (Boston: Shambhala Publications, Inc., 2002), she writes: "Spiritual awakening is frequently described as a journey to the top of a mountain. We leave our attachments and our worldliness behind and slowly make our way to the top. At the peak we have transcended all pain." The path of a truer spiritual awakening, she says, "goes down, not up, as if the mountain pointed toward the earth instead of the sky. Instead of transcending the suffering of all creatures, we move toward turbulence and doubt however we can. We explore the reality and unpredictability of insecurity and pain, and we try not to push it away. . . At our own pace, without speed or aggression, we move down and down and down. With us move millions of others, our companions in awakening from fear. At the bottom we discover water, the healing water of bodhichitta. Bodhichitta is our heart—our wounded, softened heart. Right down there in the thick of things, we discover the love that will not die" (1–2).

Anne Lamott relates a Hasidic tale illustrating, similarly, that the way "up" is down. A certain rabbi "always told his people that if they studied the Torah, it would put Scripture on their hearts. One of them asked, 'why *on* our hearts and not *in* them?' The rabbi answered, 'Only God can put Scripture inside. But reading sacred texts can put it on your hearts, and then when your hearts break, the holy words will fall inside.'" *Plan B: Further Thoughts on Faith* (New York: Riverhead Books, 2005), 73.

BLOATED CHILD, BLOATED GOD

Nicholas Wolterstorff also emerged a more compassionate human being. His memoir affords only brief glimpses of this journey, but those glimpses suggest that in Wolterstorff's encounter with grief we can see how goats are slowly transformed into sheep.

When we begin to have different eyes for God, Wolterstorff writes, we begin to have different eyes for *the world*. As the conventional God—I would call him the "Almighty"—gives way in our imagination to the image of a sorrowful, bleeding Jesus, we notice we are seeing the presence of God in places we might have previously overlooked. God's image appears, for example, "not in the rich and powerful of the earth," but in "the face of that woman with soup tin in hand and bloated child at side."

It follows, although Wolterstorff does not spell this out, that having different eyes for God gives us different eyes for ourselves. In the presence of a broken God, we meet afresh our own brokenness. We are less tempted to imitate the "rich and powerful of the earth" by cultivating a false self that looks shiny, impressive, and superficially whole. We see not just God but also *ourselves* in the beggar woman and the bloated child. We don't work as hard at hiding our weakness, our neediness, our suffering. Our false selves join a false God in retirement.

Wolterstorff implies that mourning has wrought these kinds of changes in his self-understanding. He seems less inclined to identify with the Almighty, more likely to see himself in the broken man from Nazareth. "The wounds of Christ are his identity," he writes. "They tell us who he is." And, I would add, they tell us who we are as well.

These changes—in our image of God, of others and of ourselves—are gifts that come to us only as we allow our experiences of deep loss to enroll us in the school of suffering. In that school, we learn to become ourselves. "The valley of suffering," Wolterstorff writes, "is the vale of soul-making."

Wolterstorff finds that a new radiance "emerges from acquaintance with grief."[19] But sorrow continues to live in him as well—he thinks it lives in all those who participate in God's kingdom. That sorrow fuels a deep compassion for the sorrow of others wherever we see it. "The suffering of the world has worked its way deeper inside me," he writes. It has left him "open to the wounds of the world."

I believe Nicholas Wolterstorff's experience charts the path toward "sheephood"—toward the embodiment of genuine compassion —that every "goat," evangelical or otherwise, will finally take in this life or in the next. It is the path of the cross. On that path, we meet a different God—bruised, bloodied and broken. We discover that we ourselves are like that God—bruised, bloodied and broken. And in this discovery, we will find that every *other* human being is like that God—bruised, bloodied and broken.[20]

Transformed by these discoveries, we may be surprised at how readily our hearts will overflow with compassion. In times of trouble, we will no longer take false comfort in hollow assurances about an omnipotent deity. We will know the presence of a weeping deity, and weep with those who weep.

●　　　●　　　●

19 Etty Hillesum learns a similar radiance in the school of suffering: We must "open ourselves up to cosmic sadness," she writes. "Clear a decent shelter for your sorrow. . . And if you have given sorrow the space its gentle origins demand, then you may truly say: life is beautiful and so rich. So beautiful and so rich that it makes you want to believe in God" (*An Interrupted Life*, 81–82).

20 James Alison calls this compassion "a shepherd's heart which is deeply moved by humans and human waywardness." He says a shepherd's heart "means being able to look at wolves in their sheepliness" and "love them as such." Alison depicts Jesus as experiencing just this "deep commotion of the entrails," and suggests that Christian "saints" are those who feel a similar "inexplicable visceral commotion toward humanity." See *Raising Abel: The Recovery of the Eschatological Imagination* (New York: The Crossroad Publishing Company, 1996), 188. Reading Alison's work has occasioned deep shifts in my theological paradigm and in my understanding of Jesus.

SALVATION FOR THE FALSE GOD

In Chapter 5, I offered a few words in defense of the evangelical "false self." Here, I want to offer a few words in defense of the evangelical "false God."

Although I think it is time we lose our illusions about the Almighty, and mourn his loss, I have avoided using language that suggests we utterly obliterate or "kill" the Almighty. I don't believe hatred for, or destructive impulses toward, the Almighty are the path to freedom. They may be "natural" responses to an Almighty who has, perhaps since childhood, hovered over us, imprisoned us in fear, and stifled our journey toward a healthy freedom. So such feelings may be important way-stations on the journey toward healing. But to let them run rampant within us won't get us the freedom we want.

If we allow the part of us that hates the Almighty to control us, instead of understanding where it is coming from and learning to love it along with the rest of our parts, we immerse ourselves in emotional venom, and we are the only real victims.[21]

I also doubt that the Almighty *can* be killed. When we try to kill the Almighty—a campaign that seems to preoccupy currently popular atheists like Christopher Hitchens, Sam Harris and Richard Dawkins[22]—we are trying to rid our inner world of a part of us that came into existence inside us, perhaps when we were very young children, in order to protect us. This part plays a similar role as the "omnipotent parent," who also lives inside us. It offers the small and often scared child a modicum of safety, comfort and peace of mind. It helps us negotiate a dangerous world. We owe it our thanks.

But, as with every protective part of us, the inner voice of the Almighty exacts a price. It warns us that, in order to get safety,

---

21 Nursing our hatred, in Anne Lamott's words, "is like drinking rat poison and then waiting for the rat to die." *Traveling Mercies: Some Thoughts on Faith* (New York: Anchor Books, 1999), 134.
22 Their books are referenced in Chapter 5, footnote 7 (page 164).

comfort and peace of mind, we must conform to certain rules and precepts. It assures us that the consequences of not conforming are grim. This, of course, is objectively true in human life: if we do not conform, we are likely to suffer at the hands of the "authorities" in our lives—parents, teachers, playground monitors, camp counselors, juvenile courts, and so on—who require conformity. A distorted version of the "wrath of God," in other words, is objectively grounded in everyday life: society at large makes us reap what we sow.

The part of us that speaks for the Almighty tries to protect little boys and girls from sowing hardship for themselves, by giving conformity a divine blessing. Like every protective part of us, it means us well. But in fact, carrying with it so much primitive fear, it does its job "too well," and ends up harming us and distorting our relationship with God.

Once it is "born" in us, no protective part ever goes away. Trying to obliterate the punitive Almighty from our inner lives simply chases it into hiding. It will return—and often with a vengeance. This is why many atheists continue to argue vociferously with the God they hate, bearing that God quite a huge animus, even though they believe such a God doesn't objectively exist. It seems he does exist, inside them, just as he exists inside evangelical Christians—and to some degree inside most humans. He resides in a part of us that we will never be able to expunge.

For any human to be free of the Almighty's spell, the "Almighty" in us does not need to be destroyed. It needs to be transformed. In a manner of speaking, it needs to die, and rise again, as it did for Nicholas Wolterstorff when he was plunged into mourning the loss of his beloved son.

For both atheist and evangelical Christian, the death of the Almighty and the resurrection of a better God can take many routes. Every one of them enrolls us in the school of mourning; every one constitutes a kind of journey through hell. These experiences soften us toward the world inside us, leading us toward compassion for all the parts of us—including the part of us that carries the energy of the almighty God. Once we are opened to a non-accusing engagement with all that is inside us, and feel true curiosity toward our inner world, we will come to understand the protective role that this part—the almighty God—has played in our early lives. We will also likely find that this part is weary of its role and would like to retire to less active, less poisonous duties.

And it can and will do so, as we give up both our earnest defenses of it and our bitter diatribes against it. As this "Almighty" part of us trusts that we have a core self to lead us on life's path—a self shaped by the image of the crucified Savior—it will lose its fear, let go of its weapons of coercion, and join the more hospitable conversation that true spiritual transformation makes possible inside us.

In that conversation, instead of playing the role of hostile divine accuser or fearful doomsayer, perhaps it will speak with the voice of a friendly realist. For the follower of Jesus, it might remind us where our words or our behavior might run into opposition in the world, let us know the costs of non-conformity, or call us to an eternal perspective—except now, this perspective will not be shaped by a regal potentate, but by our experience of the One dying on a cross. The voice of God will no longer sound shrill or angry. It will not issue threats. It will offer its gifts freely, and trust our truest self to know how to receive and use them. The Almighty in us will, in other words, be "born again."

Evangelicalism's "official narrative"—its "defining story" of "penal substitution"—cannot work such a healing transformation. The story of a God who punishes his son in order to satisfy his sense of justice can only re-energize the part inside us that represents the voice of a cold and heartless Almighty—an "awesome God," whom it is impossible to love. It must then, invariably, awaken its polar opposite: the part of us—often well hidden—that feels hostility towards the Almighty.

Evangelicalism's "official narrative," in other words, is itself the cause of—and never the solution for—the "divided heart" that the evangelical praise chorus so deeply yearns to overcome. It is a sufficient explanation for the deep emotional ambivalence that evangelicals feel toward the God they met in childhood or at the moment of "salvation."

We can and will experience true transformation if, in the cross, we meet the broken God and our suffering broken selves. There, as our hearts flood with compassion, the Almighty who lives inside us will die a natural death and be raised again as one who truly loves us. And although our face is stained with tears, everything inside us will shout for joy.

CHAPTER 11
The Freedom to Be a Mess
Stumbling into genuine wholeness

> *One must abandon every attempt to make
> something of oneself—even to make
> of oneself a righteous person.*
> Dietrich Bonhoeffer[1]

WHEN I LOOK INTO A MIRROR, there appears to be only one person looking back at me. But the mirror lies. I am, in fact, many people. A vengeful person lives inside me next door to a forgiving person. I am calm, confident and knowing. I am scared, self-doubting and ignorant. I am an angry cynic. I am a tender-hearted sentimentalist. I am sure death will triumph over love. I know love will conquer all.

An "atheist" inside me knows that I am an accident of chemistry granted a few short breaths and an illusion of significance before I melt into the soil of a cold, silent planet. A "believer" in me knows that a warm heart of flesh beats at the center of the universe. I am all these people, all these voices—an ongoing conversation that degenerates, occasionally, into cacophony.

One of the voices clamoring for my attention is a part of me I call "the Housekeeper." He is the would-be manager of my personality. The Housekeeper appears in my imagination as a prim, middle-

---

1 Quoted in Annie Dillard, *For the Time Being* (New York: Alfred A. Knopf, 1999), 171.

aged man in a light blue shirt, with a sensible striped tie and neatly-pressed navy slacks. He is tireless in his vigilance and his attention to detail, and he seems to be everywhere at once. He is obsessed with tidiness and good order, and he is painfully sensitive to appearances—he worries constantly about how other people are assessing my character.

If the Housekeeper thinks I am listening to him and following his guidance, he is all sweetness and light, a male version of June Cleaver smiling benignly as she whisks away the very last dust bunny in a sunlit living-room. But when he is nervous—and he is usually nervous—he turns into the "Housekeeper from Hell," a Hannibal Lector who has insinuated himself into the ownership of my house and governs it ruthlessly. It is no longer I, but he, who is in charge.

Whenever I look into a mirror, it is the Housekeeper's eyes by which I examine myself. He is checking to make sure that everyone I meet—family, friends, strangers—will see that there is only one of me. That one must be the wise, serene individual who has his act together. The Housekeeper doesn't like the interior cacophony—all those voices inside me, pulling and tugging in different directions. The spontaneous ebb and flow of my emotional world gives him heartburn. He is terrified that others will see the disorder of my inner life. He works hard to keep the mess I am from becoming too obvious.

Naturally, the Housekeeper is upset that I'm sharing this information with you!

Very often, when I'm alone with my thoughts, the Housekeeper goes to work on the mess that is me. He pummels me with *shoulds* and *oughts*. I should be a paragon of virtue. I should display the fruits of the Spirit. I should have unwavering faith and zero doubt. I should never get angry. I should not have sexual thoughts. I ought to be the perfect husband, the perfect father, the perfect friend, the perfect professor. I ought to emulate Christians who are doing important things in the world—whose inner and outer lives do not seem to be a mess, who show integrity and courage and live, emotionally, in neat, well-ordered rooms. I ought to be "happy all the time."[2]

The Housekeeper himself, ironically, is rarely happy. It frustrates him that he cannot make my inner and outer demeanor as respectable as I look in a well-posed photograph.[3] I am never quite right in his eyes. So he is never without an agenda for me. Today, I need to rouse the lazy part of me out of bed. Tomorrow, I'll need to stifle the whiner and the complainer. Next week, I'll need to get rid of that lustful person. Even when I accomplish something admirable, the Housekeeper does not let me rest. He worries that I will become proud, and of course, "pride goes before a fall." He urges me to keep my nose to the grindstone—and do even better next time. To the Housekeeper, I am *never* good enough, just as I am.

But the Housekeeper dreams big. He expects, someday, to finally achieve full control of my inner world. Then he will strangle all the parts of me that don't fit his model of a unified and orderly personality. If strangulation fails, he will banish unwanted parts of me to a dank dungeon in my unconscious, where he hopes they will starve to death. Then he will have achieved his goal: an inner world where nothing much happens, a world as quiet as death itself. No strong feelings bursting up out of the dungeon to raise dust or jostle the knick-knacks. No deep needs rising to leave broken dishes on the floor or cigarette burns on the coffee table. Nothing untoward, unpredictable, unmanageable.

A sterile, silent, perfectly-ordered house. This is the Housekeeper's idea of what it means to be whole.

*   *   *

2 See Chapter 5, footnote 18 (page 176).

3 Although I notice that, if you give him just a little time, he can find something wrong with virtually every photograph.

WE ARE ALL BEGGARS

The penchant for interior housekeeping is a common human trait. But it is evangelical Christianity's specialty. Lately, as threats of hell yield diminishing returns (thank God), good housekeeping has become evangelical Christianity's claim to fame. Come to Jesus and he will clean you up and put everything in order. He will fix your addiction, repair your marriage, bolster your work-ethic, make you healthy and wealthy, discipline your children, give you moral backbone and tell you how to vote. Jesus will fix your *life*.

Of course, the Jesus who promises to do all this for evangelicals doesn't sound much like the unpredictable Jesus of the Gospel stories. The tidy, evangelical Jesus is less a friend of the disreputable, more a champion of respectability; less the insistent rule-breaker, more a nagging rule-enforcer; less the disturber of order, more a paragon of internal tidiness. The Jesus described in the Gospel stories does not seem to be in the running for the Good Housekeeping award.

But the Bible does give such an award—it goes to the scribes and Pharisees, the godly folks of Jesus' day. These are the biblical characters that we evangelicals most resemble. These are also the people who kill Jesus. You would think that dubious achievement might give excessive tidiness a bad name.

In the Gospel narratives, the godly seem obsessed with appearances. Unceasingly, they cultivate their ideal selves— resplendent in virtue, cleansed of vice, pleasing to God. They're busy little beavers, always dusting and straightening and taking out the trash. If the Almighty ever comes knocking, they want to greet him in their "sabbath best"—hair combed, nails clipped, smiles plastered firmly in place. They want their carpets spotless and their air fresheners strategically placed. They hope the Almighty won't hear all that noise coming from the dungeon.

We get a wonderful glimpse of these godly housekeepers in the story of Jesus' encounter with a blind beggar (John 9). Jesus has just smeared some mud on the beggar's dead eyes—a messy start, to be sure—and told him to go wash it off. The beggar washes and his sight is restored. His neighbors can't believe it—he's been blind forever. They interrogate him, but he doesn't give them the answers they want. So they take the beggar to the godly, who interrogate him further, and then interrogate his parents, and then interrogate him again. The godly are annoyed with Jesus for healing beggars on the sabbath—the Big Housekeeper in the Sky would never approve. Since they can't make the beggar blind again, they want him to confess that his healing is the work of a sinner.

As the story continues, it becomes apparent that the godly, like most compulsive housekeepers, have a "hearing disability." They're so flooded with fear that they can't really *listen*. They need to have the right answers—the ones that support the agenda of the Housekeeper inside them. They are uninterested in the beggar's messy truth. So they try to shut the beggar up—which simply replicates what they are constantly doing to their own internal beggars.

But the blind beggar won't be shut up. Under their questioning, he begins to emerge as an individual—a real human being—showing that Jesus has touched not only his eyes, but also his soul. When the godly keep nagging at him, he shows his spunk: "I have told you already, and you would not listen. Why do you want to hear it again?" He tries a little joke: "Do you also want to become his disciples?"

His answers get progressively fuller and more confident as he finds his voice. But the godly do not want a beggar to actually express opinions—to have a real self—so they abruptly and contemptuously end the conversation: "You were born entirely in sins, and are you trying to teach us?" In frustration, they drive him out.

Which is precisely how the godly treat their own inner beggars. Their housekeepers drive them out. And don't many of us do the same? Sitting along some back road inside us all, no doubt, there lives a beggar—untidy, lonely, helpless and stuck, without visible resources, without a voice—hoping someone will come along with a word of love. In some darkened room inside us lives a blind man, more confused and uncomprehending about the meaning of things than we, or the godly, would like to admit. Surely an open, seeking, grateful person also lives inside us, a voice that yearns to discover in the mysterious human Jesus the kind of God that might enter the dungeons with us and take the prisoners out into the fresh air.

That voice of freedom may be calling to the godly, too. But their obsessive housekeepers are too frightened of their interior beggars to listen to the part of them that longs to hear good news. In their anxiety, they cannot give open ears to either voice. It's tidiness they want, so they must drive such voices away. In time, they must drive the untidy Jesus away as well.

"We are all beggars"—these are Martin Luther's last recorded words.[4] Like the blind beggar, Luther met a compassionate Jesus, who taught him to speak in his own voice. That voice so agitated the representatives of the Almighty in his day that they also drove him out. But Luther kept right on speaking.

For the rest of his life, Luther continued to wrestle with a punitive Housekeeper who lived inside of him. He may have been a bit too determined to extinguish it, rather than love it, and that gave it continued power in his life. But his encounter with the human Jesus did grant him the freedom, very often, to ignore the commands of the Housekeeper inside him and speak in his own voice.[5] The God he met in the newborn baby, the growing boy, the dying man taught

---

4 According to Simone Weil, God is a beggar, too. Because God knows love cannot be coerced, God comes to us "like a beggar." "Justice and Human Society" in Eric O. Springsted, ed., *Simone Weil* (Maryknoll, NY: Orbis Books, 1998), 122.

5 "An immovable and apathetic God cannot be understood as the foundation of human freedom. An absolutist sovereign in heaven does not inspire liberty on earth. Only the passionate God, the God who suffers by virtue of his passion for people, calls the freedom of men and women to life." Moltmann, *The Trinity and the Kingdom*, 218.

this "most untidy" of Christendom's great teachers that it was all right for him to be the mess he was.

At times, Luther could be very clear about this. He wrote to a friend: "Always beware of aspiring to such purity that you no longer wish to appear before yourself as a sinner or even to be one anymore. Christ dwells only with sinners."[6]

---

6   Quoted in Eduard Thurneysen, *A Theology of Pastoral Care* (Richmond, VA: John Knox Press, 1962), 162. Henri J. M. Nouwen, in *The Inner Voice of Love* (49), echoes this theme: "Where you are most human, most yourself, there Jesus lives."
In a painfully honest song, folksinger Greg Brown admits he's not sure how he feels about sharing his raw humanity with Jesus:

Oh Lord, I have made you a place in my heart
among the rags and the bones and the dirt.
There's piles of lies, the love gone from her eyes,
and old moving boxes full of hurt.
Pull up a chair by the trouble and care.
I got whiskey—you're welcome to some.
Oh Lord, I have made you a place in my heart,
but I don't reckon you're gonna come.
I've tried to fix up the place, I know it's a disgrace,
you get used to it after a while—
with the flood and the drought and old pals hanging out
with their IOUs and their smiles.
Bare naked women keep coming in
and they dance like you wouldn't believe.
Oh Lord, I have made you a place in my heart,
so take a good look—and then leave.
Oh Lord, why does the fall get colder each year?
Lord, why can't I learn to love?
Lord, if you made me, it's easy to see
that you all make mistakes up above.
But if I open the door, you will know I'm poor
and my secrets are all that I own.
Oh Lord, I have made you a place in my heart
and I hope that you leave it alone.

"Lord, I Have Made You a Place in My Heart," *The Poet Game* (Red House, 1994).

•   •   •

THE FIXER

What is the Housekeeper's problem? He is a stranger to trust. My fears have created him, and they control him. His deepest fear—built on the painful experiences that come in every human life—is that if I am known for the mess I am, I will not be loved. This is a fate—as I have said before—worse than death. So the Housekeeper is consumed with anxiety. He is certain that, at any moment, the unruly parts of me will escape their dungeon, break through the cellar door, and run amok through the house. Those who love me will love me no more. And, of course, *I* will love me no more.

So the Housekeeper is an inveterate "fixer." But his concern is not limited to me. He is easily triggered by other people, who look like the parts of me he wants to banish. He seems to think it will help his cause if he banishes—or fixes—them as well. The Housekeeper wants me to tell such people that Jesus—or the right sermon, book, counselor, support group or exercise gym—can clean up their messy lives. Then they will be more like me—the surface me, the moral me, the me who at that moment has convinced himself that he lives in a neat, tidy house with a tidy little Jesus. If such people accept my help, maybe we can be friends.

Of course, the Housekeeper is not a fan of the real Jesus. Bruce Cockburn sings about the real Jesus: "It isn't to the palace that the Christ child comes, but to shepherds and street people, hookers and bums."[7] Had a commonly-recognized homosexual community existed in his day, I have no doubt Jesus would have come to them as well. The stranger from Nazareth embraced the cast-outs of his day without condescension. He did not come to them as the Almighty-Housekeeper-in-the-Sky looking to fix them up and turn them into

---

7   "Cry of a Tiny Babe," *Nothing But a Burning Light* (Sony, 1991).

solid citizens. He came to them as a ragged vagabond and, eventually, as a disgraced and dying criminal.[8]

The Housekeeper prefers the approach of the Almighty. If the folks I meet who remind me of my hidden beggars won't be fixed, the Housekeeper urges me to condemn and avoid them. The alcoholic, the womanizer, the gossip, the drug addict, the lazy student, the angry friend, the boastful, rebellious, irreverent, slovenly, mournful or depressed—these are bad people who need to change their ways. If they don't, I must keep them at a distance.

I can try to "love" them in an abstract sense—and I can certainly be "nice" to them—but I cannot *like* them. I cannot feel genuinely drawn to them, connected at the deepest levels to them, because that would threaten to connect me at the deepest levels to myself—my poor banished selves—and my self-disdain and anxiety would flood back in. So far as helping me love myself, all that internal scrutiny would have accomplished nothing.

The Housekeeper who lives inside me is very well -intentioned— I tip my hat to him—and he is good at what he does. But he is in the dark when it comes to knowing how a loving embrace of one's self actually works. For example, he doesn't know that I will never truly love myself if I must earn that love by being perfect—not just because I will never be perfect, but also because genuine love is never *conditional* love. We do not learn to love ourselves by making a list of all our strengths and talents and personal charms and then deciding

---

8 Shusaku Endo, the late Japanese Christian novelist, molded his final book, *Deep River*, around the messiness of the crucified Jesus. One of his main characters, Mitsuko, absent-mindedly sits in a chapel pew and opens the Bible in the rack in front of her. She stumbles onto these words: ". . . he hath no form or comeliness; and when we shall see him, there is no beauty that we should desire him." This has no meaning for her, until she glances up and sees a crucifix. On it hangs a "scrawny, naked man." She cannot understand how anyone could believe in this "ugly man."

This man—like Otsu, the bumbling, insecure, disreputable young man in Endo's story, who does believe in this Jesus—is the very embodiment of a mess. *Deep River* (New York: New Directions Books, 1994), 44–45.

that this makes us lovable. Self-love is the warm embrace of all that we actually are.

The Housekeeper is in the dark about relationships with others as well. True friendship isn't built on offering one another only our cleaned-up selves. Relationships between "false selves" are false. The more of me I keep in hiding, the less of me is actually partici-pating in the relationship. That messy, flowing, often unruly internal conversation is actually *me*. If I don't bring *me* to my relationships, I do not experience real connection with others. I'm left vaguely dissatisfied, lonely, yearning. The Housekeeper notices that dis-satisfaction, but takes it as a sign that he's failed to clean up properly. So he goes into a frenzy of tidiness, which only reinforces the same empty cycle.[9]

Jesus befriended people *as they were*. He could not have done so had he not befriended every part of himself. He embraced the "shepherds

---

9 Several years ago, when she was a college student, Heather Hillstrom Starbird sent me this illustration of the psychic costs of having an active internal Housekeeper:

"I just got out of an ancient philosophy class. It was about having an ordered soul as *the* avenue to happiness and virtue and God. Walking out after class, some of us were talking. I mentioned the tight, heavy feeling in my chest—that I felt angry at these Greek guys we were reading. The others felt the same way, which surprised me a little. These words 'ordered', 'rightly', 'proper'—they actually made people angry. Everyone felt like a bad person because inside they were such a mess. And they felt like those ideas robbed them of the ability to connect with each other.

"One said: 'We seem to connect better by admitting our disorder to each other and letting it be okay.' When we were standing in a circle about to part, someone said: 'I'm so glad you guys are like this, too.' She was talking about feeling like she was so below standard—and she just wanted to be able to show it and connect with others through it. She grabbed someone's shoulder and then we were all spontaneously grabbing arms and shoulders in a sort of mock-desperation, and for a second we almost came together in a big hug. We then hesitated, felt ridiculous and went our different ways.

"I think a lot of us are dying to admit that what is most real and true is what has not been crafted to perfection, and is ultimately beyond our ability to tame, construct, control. There's some longing to acknowledge that pretty much everything feels way out of control. And then to be able to say, 'But it will be okay' and live honestly with what the world, and ourselves, really are. Which is kind of a mess'."

and street people, hookers and bums" only because he had learned to embrace, and carry into his relationships, the hookers and bums who lived inside himself.

Paradoxically, this means Jesus had even befriended his own Housekeeper. When I realize the damage the Housekeeper has done to me, the freedom he has stolen from me, the falseness he has enforced on me, my temptation is to expel him once and for all. Of course, that would only shove him down into the dungeon, where he has put so many other parts of me. I'm sure he wouldn't be content to stay there very long.

Before I can get the Housekeeper to calm down and stop trying to out-shout every other voice, I'll need to understand the depths of his anxiety and hear what he has to say.[10] If I listen long enough, and gently enough, he may confess the fears and hurts that animate his vigilance. He may admit he is tired of being so afraid, of working so hard, and wishes he could rest.

If I show the Housekeeper the honor of engaging him as one would a worried child, gently plying him with questions that search out the root causes of his anxiety, I will learn that the Housekeeper is simply the part of me that is not yet convinced there's such a thing as unconditional love.[11] Once the Housekeeper gets a chance to

---

10 Simone Weil says true attentiveness means saying to another: "What are you going through?" This is the heart of any compassionate encounter. Inner healing means bringing that question, in honest curiosity, to every part of us, particularly those that seem most "powerful" inside us, because in fact they are the most fearful and carry the deepest wounds.

I cannot recommend highly enough the short piece in which Weil writes these words: "Reflections on the Right Use of School Studies," in George A. Panichas, ed., *The Simone Weil Reader* (Mt. Kisco, NY: Moyer Bell Limited, 1977), 51.

11 "Think of each wound as you would of a child who has been hurt by a friend. As long as that child is ranting and raving, trying to get back at the friend, one wound leads to another. But when the child can experience the consoling embrace of a parent, she or he can live through the pain, return to the friend, forgive, and build up a new relationship. Be gentle with yourself, and let your heart be your loving parent as you live your wounds through." Nouwen, *Inner Voice*, 109.

unburden himself, and trusts that I am sympathetic to his concerns, I'm sure he will relax. That would feel like freedom.

The freedom to be a mess is the freedom to bring my whole variegated, complicated inner world *into* my relationships with both myself and others. Giving others what is really me—the whole of me—is what it means to love. If I cannot love out of the truth of what I am, I cannot love at all.

*   *   *

A MESS?

I am aware that the word "mess" has negative connotations for many people. It can easily be misunderstood and it invites ready caricature. In earlier drafts of this chapter, I used the less provocative word "real," a functional equivalent which I found useful (in Chapter 7) for describing Jesus. In the end, I came back to "a mess" because it highlights the unruly and sometimes contradictory ebb and flow of the inner life.

I think it is worth the risk, as well, because it resists the perfectionism which plagues the life of the spirit. I can imagine devising a spiritual program to make myself "real," thus fueling the downward spiral of anxious effort and self-judgment. These do not sound to me like freedom. I find it less tempting, although not impossible, to devise a spiritual program for making myself "a mess."

But I also chose "mess," because I have met many Christians who feel exactly that way and are ashamed to admit it. They are not the well-put-together Christians appearing in magazine ads for evangelical colleges and seminaries or life-changing weekend conferences at fancy hotels. They don't resemble the Christian paragons depicted by victorious-sounding preachers and writers. They are guilty, lonely, alternately apathetic about and angry at God, resentful towards loved ones, afraid, unbelieving. They are full of yearnings—for pleasure, alcohol, drugs, sex, adventure and other glittering commodities. They are puzzled by the source and intensity of these yearnings and by their inability, at times, to resist their promptings.

When they measure themselves against the "victorious Christians" set before them as models, they come up failures. They imagine the Almighty berating them, and to save him the trouble, they berate themselves. These are the walking wounded—too often, the *silent wounded*—of American evangelicalism. Their numbers are larger than most evangelicals are prepared to admit. Some have jumped, or hobbled, off the evangelical treadmill—perhaps hearing the good news under other Christian auspices, perhaps finding relief in other religious traditions, or in non-religious support groups, or in nothing at all.

Of the many audiences I hope this book reaches, these walking wounded are the ones I most prize. I hope they will find some encouragement, as I do, in the freedom Jesus offers us to embrace the often messy reality of *who we really are*.[12]

●　　　●　　　●

WHY DO YOU SUBMIT?

The Apostle Paul experienced the birth of this freedom. This was no mean feat, since Paul, before he met Jesus, was one of the champion Housekeepers of his day.

Paul started out his saintly life as Saul, a Pharisee, the godliest of the godly. He had been "educated strictly" according to Jewish

---

12 As an aid in this journey toward freedom, compatible with and in many ways illustrative of the "good news" Jesus brings, is Jay Earley, *Self-Therapy: A Step-By-Step Guide to Creating Inner Wholeness Using IFS, a New, Cutting-Edge Therapy* (Minneapolis: Mill City Press, 2009). Earley's work is a practical, user-friendly guide to the groundbreaking therapeutic model represented by the work of Richard C. Schwartz.

law and was "zealous for God" (Acts 22:3). He was a religious prodigy— perhaps not unlike the youthful Jesus. "I advanced in Judaism beyond many among my people of the same age," he wrote, "for I was far more zealous for the traditions of my ancestors" (Galatians 1:14).[13]

We first meet Saul at the stoning of a young Jesus-follower named Stephen. Stephen has dared to preach—to the godly—that the godly were the ones who murdered the human son, Jesus. For this, he gets stoned to death. Young Saul holds the coats for the godly, and watches approvingly, as they work their vengeance on Stephen (Acts 7:52, 58).

Soon, Saul is a leading Pharisee himself. Zealous for the Almighty, he travels the Damascus road, "breathing threats and murder against the disciples of the Lord" (Acts 9:1). Somewhere along that road, a light from heaven strikes him blind. For three days, he lives without food or drink in total darkness (Acts 9:3–9). Perhaps he remembers Jonah in Sheol, and is not without hope.

After three days, a Jesus-follower named Ananias visits Saul and calls him "brother"—a sign, surely, that Ananias recognizes a "Saul" inside himself—and Saul is born again. He gets new eyes and a new name. Before breaking his fast, he memorializes his encounter with "the sea" in the waters of baptism. Then, to everyone's amazement, he starts talking about Jesus. He says this infamous friend of the ungodly and the untidy is actually the Son of God (Acts 9:17–20). Clearly, this paragon of the godly has met a different God.

Perhaps because he has been in such thrall to his own Housekeeper, Paul speaks often and emphatically about the freedom

---

13 I am not implying that Judaism was, or is, more prone to a housekeeping obsession than any other major religious tradition, including Christianity. Nor am I implying that Paul's conversion was from Judaism to a rival or superior religion: Christianity. Recent scholarship concludes that Paul considered himself a faithful Jew throughout his life. This scholarship is nicely summarized in Paula Fredericksen, *Augustine and the Jews: A Christian Defense of Jews and Judaism* (New York: Doubleday, 2008).

he experiences in Jesus. His own words for scrupulous housekeeping are "confidence in the flesh." He confesses to having plenty of it himself—in fact, he once thought himself "blameless." But now he calls his obsession with personal tidiness sheer "rubbish." Instead of an outward or inward *perfection*, he wants a *relationship*: "I want to know Christ," he writes, "and the power of his resurrection and the sharing of his sufferings by becoming like him in his death" (Philippians 3:6–10).

In pastoral moments, Paul warns against identifying the voice of the Housekeeper with the voice of God: "Do not let anyone condemn you in matters of food and drink or of observing festivals, new moons, or sabbaths," he says. "Do not let anyone disqualify you, insisting on self-abasement. . . Why do you submit to regulations, 'Do not handle, Do not taste, Do not touch'? All these regulations refer to things that perish with use; they are simply human commands and teachings" (Colossians 2:16–22).

As someone with a hyper-active, internal Housekeeper, Paul knows the appeal of regulations. They have "an appearance of wisdom" and seem to promote "self-imposed piety, humility, and severe treatment of the body." But "they are of no value in checking self-indulgence."

Here Paul does a little linguistic sleight of hand, overturning our assumption that self-denial is the opposite of self-indulgence. He thinks self-denial is, in fact, closely related to self-indulgence (Colossians 2:23). Both of these are examples of what Paul calls "the flesh"—ways of thinking and acting we are captive to. Sexual excess is one of these, but religious excess—our rage for perfection—is another. Paul surprises his readers by suggesting that giving ourselves over to the religious part of us is as dangerous as giving ourselves over to the sexual part of us.[14] In both of these, a part of us

---

14 In Colossians 2:16–23, Paul names festivals, new moons, sabbaths, self-abasement, worship of angels, visions, rigor of devotion, severity to the body. In the same context, in

is in control—"the flesh" rather than our true self—which means we are animated by fear rather than trust.[15]

For Paul, the zeal of the flesh—in this context referring to the zeal for compulsive godliness—is not the way to freedom. And it is always "for freedom" that Jesus sets us free, he writes. "Stand firm, therefore, and do not submit again to a yoke of slavery" (Galatians 5:1).

Occasionally, in Paul's letters, we can still catch the scent of a Housekeeper in recovery. Paul has the difficult job of helping a widely scattered collection of young Jesus-followers learn what it means to live in freedom. No doubt his charges, new to this freedom, make plenty of mistakes, stumbling from freedom back into conformity, license or "the flesh," and then rediscovering their freedom again.

Some of them, still tempted by their own internal Housekeepers from time to time, may push Paul to give them firmer guidelines for Christian living than he would like. Perhaps the youthful Pharisee that still lives inside Paul prods him to supply these guidelines, even though their legacy may be an anxious perfectionism.

But Paul seems aware of this danger and takes steps to mitigate it. Most of his instructional passages are actually just general examples of the freedom of a transformed spirit ("love, joy, peace") and leave plenty of room for diverse applications; or else they are meant to give practical guidance in thorny individual circumstances. And taken together, these passages represent a small proportion of Paul's writings. When they do appear, they are usually contextualized by reiterations of the good news of Jesus and the radically new

---

Colossians 3:5, he names fornication, impurity and passion.

15 The term "flesh"—although much misused in evangelical circles, particularly in harangues to pubescent youth—is not a bad word for these excesses. Compulsive housekeeping, like other excesses, is so habitual that it just feels like a natural part of us. When the Housekeeper controls us, he represents himself as who we really are, even though he is only part of us, a kind of "false self" that protects us from both the pain and the joy of being a real human being.

subjectivity that flows out of the heart of those who hear it. The essence of that subjectivity, invariably, is compassion.

Paul's careful distinctions, however, do not prevent evangelical preachers from using Paul's texts to activate their listeners' internal Housekeepers, week after week, while ignoring or explaining away Paul's urgent plea that we take up the freedom that we have received from the dying Jesus. So Christians are continually discouraged from experiencing the liberation Paul experienced when God knocked him off his horse, freeing him from captivity to his religious zeal so he could make friends with the complicated human being he really was.[16]

•   •   •

FALSE PROMISES

"But wait a minute. . . !" (My Housekeeper's hand is waving frantically; he can hardly contain himself.) "Can't you see the trouble you're courting when you encourage people to be a mess? The freedom to be a mess is an invitation to live thoughtlessly and selfishly.[17] We've made a "mess" of our planet by falling for consumerism's

---

16 The persistent misuse of Paul by the preachers of good housekeeping has made him a favorite whipping boy of young people who criticize evangelicalism for its joyless legalism, social conservatism and spiritual poverty. Paul's comments about the role of women in the church, particularly since they are interpreted as timeless edicts rather than understood sensitively in their cultural context—and because they have been shamelessly exploited by Christian male-supremacists—have made it easy for thinking young Christians to distrust Paul and project onto him the anger they feel at the male religious establishment.

One of the most helpful attempts to offer a more sympathetic, but not a white-washing portrait of Paul is Richard Rohr's lecture series, "Great Themes of Paul: Life as Participation," available from St. Anthony Messenger Press at http://catalog.americancatholic.org.

17 The approach to Christian freedom that I explore in this chapter has been most strongly influenced by Jacques Ellul, especially *To Will and to Do: An Ethical Research for Christians* (Philadelphia: Pilgrim Press, 1969) and *The Ethics of Freedom* (Grand Rapids MI: William B. Eerdmans Publishing Company, 1976). I have also greatly profited from John Caputo, *Against Ethics: Contributions to a Poetics of Obligation with Constant Reference*

promise of "freedom" through purchasing power. We've made a "mess" of our families by the "freedom" to be neglectful and thoughtless in our parenting. The freedom to be a mess is exactly what's *wrong* with our world!"

It's true: a sterile and individualistic grasp for "freedom," proffered by capitalism and the modern Enlightenment, plagues contemporary life.[18] The consumer culture wields "freedom" as its magic talisman. Pepsi Cola, Viagra, Las Vegas and Ford Trucks all offer freedom. The advertising industry plays the "freedom" song incessantly. It knows that human beings yearn for freedom.

But the "freedom" that calls from our plasma screens is exactly the opposite of the freedom encountered in the dying Jesus. The advertising media do not truly embrace the variegated beings we inherently are. In fact, they play on our fears of the mess we are. Daily, hourly, they remind us we are not the happy people whose images they flash before our eyes—although for a price they will make us like them. The media stir up a chaotic brew of desire within us—but not so we can better understand and embrace our comparatively shabby selves in the safety of unconditional acceptance. Certainly

---

to Deconstruction (Bloomington IN: Indiana University Press, 1993).

I write this chapter hesitantly. It cannot be adequate to the subject because my words and my understanding are not adequate to the subject. It will inevitably sound more sure of itself than it ought. Nevertheless, I hope it will encourage readers to explore their own experience of this freedom and to take that experience seriously.

18 Christian freedom is not the modern Enlightenment's freedom: the ability of a neutral mind or an autonomous reason to choose what is good. In the Bible's world, no choice is truly autonomous. Human choice is enslaved to human drivenness and the tendency to self-deceit. It serves "the powers." When humans grasp for freedom *from* God, they fall out of the freedom that grows from a secure relationship *with* God. They fall into anxiety, accusation and self-accusation, self-justification, self-condemnation. Hoping to know "good and evil" apart from God, they give up the freedom of spontaneous trust and love. Morality—the presumptive knowledge of good and evil—becomes a tool for self-justification. Humans learn to use morality almost entirely to call themselves good and their enemies bad. They believe morality is the solution to human problems whereas, because it comes from an alienated heart and has little to do with compassion, it is often the cause.

not to assure us that someone equally shabby stands with us in our suffering.

The advertisers and purveyors of the consumer culture—with its brand names, its celebrities, its glamorous images of fortune and fame—stir up the spirits lying dormant in the dungeon of our unconscious solely in order to sell us the latest consumer gimmick for putting those spirits back to sleep. But our sexual desire will not be placated by purchasing a new automobile or vacationing in Cancun. Our self-contempt will not disappear beneath the latest cosmetic disguises. We will not feel more loved or more lovable if we tighten our skin, drink the best espresso, cheer for a winner, lose thirty pounds, have sex in the one hundred and thirty-seven positions discovered by the ancient Egyptians. These commodities cannot deliver what they promise—nor do their purveyors want them to deliver, since if they did the economy would collapse.[19]

When we evangelicals put an almighty Housekeeper in charge—when we "hate" (for Jesus' sake) the "sinful" reality inside us and determine (for Jesus' sake) to be shiny, impressive and seemingly whole—we are actually succumbing to the inner logic of the consumer culture. When evangelical preachers and writers dramatize the "mess" we are in only in order to sell us the latest moral disciplines, spiritual formulas or devotional regimens, they are imitating, not resisting, consumerism's game of "love promised, love denied."[20]

The invitation to a "close personal relationship" with an Almighty whose love is conditional becomes another glitzy come-on promising a happiness—no brokenness, no mourning, no hell—that it cannot deliver. This promise, like any other that skirts the healing pain of

---

19 "Suffering in a superficial, activist, apathetic and therefore dehumanized society can be a sign of spiritual health." Moltmann, *Crucified God*, 315.

20 And they may be doing it for similar reasons: to heighten brand visibility and build brand loyalty.

genuine self-awareness and suffering's transforming descent into hell, will disappoint us even as it keeps us coming back for next year's new and improved model.

•   •   •

LICENTIOUSNESS

St. Paul would label consumerism's reckless self-gratification "licentiousness" or "license."[21] Pious people often believe that a stricter adherence to the wishes of the Almighty will cure us of licentiousness. In fact, however, licentiousness is very often the unintended *consequence* of the Almighty's tyranny.

When we serve the Almighty by indulging our internal Housekeepers, we must say a strict "No" to the disapproved persons that live inside us. So we condemn and suppress "unrighteous" emotions and desires, refusing them the curiosity and patience we would show a child. Behind the wall of "No," these suppressed voices feed on the energy of the forbidden, becoming ever more unruly and threatening. The more power we give to the "No," the more these parts quietly whisper "Yes."[22] When these parts hear the word "freedom," they can only understand it as an immediate release from every sort of "No." They respond like teenagers whose overly-restrictive parents suddenly disappear, leaving them with an empty house, a well-stocked liquor cabinet and a stash of prescription drugs. This isn't freedom to "be" a mess so much as freedom to "make" a mess. It's just another kind of captivity.

In prim evangelical circles, "licentiousness" often connotes sexuality, and for good reason: the sexual voices inside us are the ones evangelicals most fear and repress. But the word actually connotes

---

21 See for example Galatians 5:19 and Ephesians 4:19. See also I Peter 4:3.
22 Richard Schwartz calls this common configuration of our internal parts "polarization." He describes and illustrates it beautifully in *Internal Family Systems Therapy*, 42–44.

many categories of desire. "Licentiousness" describes the person who decides to say cruel things because he or she always felt coerced into being "kind"; or the person who decides to stop paying child support because he or she is now "free" from moral stricture; or the person who stays in bed on Sunday morning simply because he or she was always made to go to church; or the person who vacations in Las Vegas because the preacher told him not to.

I'm not condemning the voices which entice us to these behaviors. If they do express "licentiousness" and not freedom, they are still understandable responses to the injuries of a life lived under the Almighty's harsh gaze. They are expressions of parts of us that are motivated by some (admittedly limited) understanding of the good. They may even be way-stations along a road to true freedom. But they are not yet the freedom to be a mess that I am speaking of—the freedom born in an encounter with the "small God" we glimpse in the suffering Jesus.

The injuries we do to this planet, and to ourselves and one another, are the effects of *not* enjoying the freedom to embrace the mess we are.[23] The "licentiousness" they represent grows from self-condemnation and self-abandonment, not from an experience of unconditional love. It is for a truer freedom that "Christ has set us free," Paul writes. So "do not submit again to a yoke of slavery" by using your freedom as "an opportunity for self-indulgence" (Galatians 5:1, 13). Paul adds these words because he wants to distinguish genuine freedom from the captivity that masquerades as freedom.

In "the flesh," we live out of our panic to be something we are not—something shinier, happier, more impressive and "whole" than

---

23 "Paradoxically, I find that the more you accept the pain and fear inherent in human experience, the greater your compassion can become, until finally it is no longer merely your compassion, but a small part of the greater love epitomized in the Bible as Jesus." Mary Gaitskill, "Revelation" in Rosenberg, *Communion*, 121. Henri J. M. Nouwen puts it this way: "Try to keep your small, fearful self close to you." *Inner Voice*, 50.

the broken and vulnerable-but-beautiful human beings we are. The Housekeeper's stern voice has its rightful place within our inner conversation. It is a valued *part* of the mess we are. But its panic will drain away and it will let go its stranglehold on our inner lives as we recognize and listen to it, and help it trust the deeper place in us that has tasted resurrection in the midst of death.

That voice of trust is calling us to a better kind of freedom and a more genuine wholeness.

·　　·　　·

ALIVE TO THE PRESENT

Gerald Sittser's story is a testimony to this better freedom.

In 1991, Sittser saw three of the women in his family—his wife, four-year-old daughter and mother—die in an automobile accident.[24] This started him on a journey to hell, a "plunge into a darkness" that snatched from him any prospect of living again "as a sane, normal, believing man." He wanted to die.

A Grace Disguised narrates Sittser's journey through the darkness: his deepening anguish and increasing isolation, the "groans" and "scream" of his pain. It enumerates the measures he took to avoid any kind of feeling: denial, busyness, new relationships, binges, rage. It lingers on his daily hopelessness, his soul-threatening sorrow. It shows him resisting comfort and forgiveness, struggling with God, and eventually striving to forge a new identity and purpose in life.

What this journey taught him, Sittser writes, is that "it is possible to live in and be enlarged by loss, even as we continue to experience it." By "enlarged," he doesn't mean becoming something shiny

---

24 Gerald L. Sittser, *A Grace Disguised: How the Soul Grows Through Loss* (Grand Rapids, MI: Zondervan Publishing House, 1996). Material in this section taken from 10–11, 18, 28, 33–35, 37, 39, 44, 51–54, 61, 65, 77, 78, 89–91, 94, 115, 166–167.

and new. He means living from more of himself—and that "more" is invariably messy.

Sittser confesses to broken and manipulative relationships, self-righteousness, excessive ambition, a need to impress. He admits to angry outbursts at his children and impatience when plans go awry. His freedom is not in justifying the harm he does to himself—that would not be freedom, but captivity. His freedom, rather, is in embracing the truth of his life and relaxing about his own short-comings: "I feel little pressure to impress God or prove myself to him," he writes. "[W]e can stop punishing ourselves and live in [God's] grace."

Sittser's experience makes him a credible witness to the "messy" kind of wholeness I am exploring in this chapter. He says he now has room in his soul for "ingratitude," for "anger, depression, despair, and anguish." These are "all natural and legitimate emotions," he writes, and if we feel contempt for them we are more likely to hurt other people than if we accept them with openness and compassion. As we allow ourselves to experience feelings commonly understood as "negative," we will have a greater capacity to experience feelings commonly understood as "positive." Accepting our anger and depression actually paves the way for "greater joy, strength, peace, and love."[25]

In a few deft lines, Gerald Sittser summarizes the condition I am calling "messiness": "What we consider opposites—east and west, night and light, sorrow and joy, weakness and strength, anger and

25 Another witness to this enlargement of the soul is Nora Gallagher. After accompanying her friend Ben as he died of AIDS, she writes: "I learned something about faith, its mucky nature, how it lies down in the mud with the pigs and the rabble. . . I learned that everything is God's: my fucked-up self, my dirty laundry, my harrowing inability to be perfect for Ben. Everything is God's: shame, suicide, assisted death, AIDS. . . God is not too good to hang out with jet-lagged women with cat litter boxes in their dining rooms or men dying of AIDS or, for that matter, someone nailed in humiliation to a cross. God is not too good for anything." *Things Seen and Unseen* (New York: Alfred A. Knopf, 1998), 12–13.

love, despair and hope, death and life—are no more mutually exclusive than winter and sunlight. The soul has the capacity to experience these opposites, even at the same time."

In difficult times, Sittser writes, we seem at the mercy of these opposites:

> We feel pain, anguish, sorrow, and despair, and we experience the ugliness, meanness, and absurdity of life. We brood as well as hope, rage as well as surrender, doubt as well as believe. We are apathetic as often as we are hopeful, and sorrowful before we are joyful. We both mourn deeply and live well. We experience the ambivalence of living simultaneously "in the night and in the light." Once we truly experience this ambivalence, instead of trying to extinguish it, we can live joyfully out of it.

Sittser puts the lie to the often-heard argument that the freedom to attend to what is inside oneself makes one individualistic, narcissistic, selfish or self-obsessed.[26] The freedom to be a mess, he suggests, is actually good for our relationships. Becoming more fully oneself and more fully available to others are two sides of the same coin. Because we do not try to "get past" sorrow, but give it "permanent residence" in our souls, we can be fully present to hurting people.

Sittser admits that, formerly, he "did not listen intently" to hurting people, or let them "penetrate the protective shell" around his heart. "I am more sensitive to the pain now, not as oblivious and selfish as I

26 "The truth of freedom is love. It is only in love that human freedom arrives at its truth. I am free and feel myself to be truly free when I am respected and recognized by others and when I for my part respect and recognize them. I become truly free when I open my life for other people and share with them, and when other people open their lives for me and share them with me. Then the other person is no longer the limitation of my freedom; he is an expansion of it. In mutual participation in life, individual people become free beyond the limits of their individuality, and discover the common room for living which their freedom offers." Moltmann, *The Trinity and the Kingdom*, 216.

used to be. . . Sorrow indicates that people who have suffered loss are living authentically," he writes. "[I]t expresses the emotional anguish of people who feel pain for themselves or for others." He believes "love becomes more authentic when it grows out of brokenness."[27]

Since his loss, Gerald Sittser writes, sorrow and darkness are never entirely absent. They weave the texture of a new world. It is a far messier world than the one he inhabited before the darkness. But it is not a hopeless world. "I learned gradually that the deeper we plunge into suffering, the deeper we can enter into a new, and different, life—a life no worse than before and sometimes better."

"Deep sorrow is good for the soul," he writes. "It can make us more alive to the present moment."

•   •   •

HE IS RISEN

Although I have not used the word often, what I have been exploring throughout *Part Two* of this book is the meaning of the Christian doctrine of resurrection. When life blooms unexpectedly out of death for Gerald Sittser, he experiences resurrection. When "someone" visits Alyosha's soul as he mourns beside a coffin, he is tasting

---

27 It is only our brokenness, and our freedom to be present to our brokenness, that yields the freedom to be present to the brokenness of others. That presence is love—"love" and "presence" are functionally identical. Love is not doing good deeds for hurting people. Good deeds do not sustain true life. Good deeds may be the natural consequence of love, but it is presence, and presence alone, that constitutes love. When another is present to them, sufferers feel loved even though their lives are not fixed.

Simone Weil understands this well. She writes: "Those who are unhappy have no need for anything in this world but people capable of giving them their attention. The capacity to give one's attention to a sufferer is a very rare and difficult thing; it is almost a miracle; it *is* a miracle. Nearly all those who think they have this capacity do not possess it. Warmth of heart, impulsiveness, pity are not enough. . . The love of our neighbor in all its fullness simply means being able to say to him: 'What are you going through?'" ("Reflections on the Right Use of School Studies," *The Simone Weil Reader*, 51).

resurrection. When Christ comes down and takes possession of her, though she has given up on ever meeting God, Simone Weil knows resurrection.

In the "salvation event," the "new birth," the sudden grip of love and the moment of freedom; in the eyes opened to see ourselves in the crucified one, the ears opened to hear the cries of self-enmity within us, the heart opened to meet those cries with compassion—in each of these "events," something comes alive in us that was dead. They are all just ways of saying "resurrection."

For me, therefore, the salvation event is itself the meaning of Easter. For Jesus to be risen, he must come alive here and now, in the heart of this human being or that. To argue over whether or how it "actually happened," two thousand years ago, is worse than fruitless—it can only be the anxious expression of a part of us that has not been gripped by the small, weak God revealed in Jesus. To *meet* that God is to *know* that Jesus is risen.

The biblical texts seem to share this existential understanding of resurrection. Most of them depict Jesus' followers going about their business, not sure what to make of rumors that the tomb is empty, and then quite unexpectedly encountering their crucified teacher— his wounds still visible—and feeling something shift inside them. For them, the resurrection does not occur until the battered body they witnessed on a bloody cross comes alive for them with a transforming word.

"I am here," his presence says. "I am alive, and I will always be alive and you will always be with me." For those who knew Jesus— and they seem to be the only ones to whom Jesus appears—this is the moment of resurrection.

Was the Jesus who encountered them constructed of the same molecules as the corpse in the tomb, now brought back to life? If the disciples ever wondered about that, the Gospel writers didn't think it important enough to record. Instead of trying to understand whether this was a literal or a metaphorical resurrection, the text shows the disciples receiving and responding to the obvious, stunning reality of it.[28] Mary murmurs "Teacher" and Thomas exclaims "My

---

28 John Dominic Crossan, a leading scholar of the "Jesus Seminar," and N. T. Wright, Bishop of Durham in the Church of England, have waged friendly debates in print and in person on these issues. Wright, who has an enthusiastic following among evangelicals, shows that the way early Christians thought about resurrection was a "mutation"—it was not identical to what the ancient world might have thought about resurrection before Christians introduced it. He believes that only the "empty tomb"—implying the empirically verifiable return to physical life of a corpse—can explain that "mutation." Wright believes only literal resurrection can provide the basis for Christian hope that God will bring a fully healed "new heaven and new earth."

Crossan seems to agree that Christian thinking about resurrection was a "mutation" in ancient thought, but he thinks an "apparition" or a "metaphorical resurrection" explains this mutation as well as an empty tomb. He thinks Mark fabricated the story of the empty tomb. Crossan believes we should stop arguing (although he continues to argue) about whether it was an "apparition" or a literal "resurrection" and get on with bringing God's peace and justice to earth.

Wright believes Christian social action is important, but he doesn't believe a metaphorical resurrection, or apparition, is sufficient motivation. Only a literal "resurrection"—and proper biblical teaching about its meaning—provides an adequate grounding for a Christian's hope in the coming of God's kingdom.

I appreciate the spirit and diligence of these scholars. But I am unable to work up much passion for the debate or for its rationalistic premise. Although, on larger doctrinal issues, I am probably closer to Wright, I have a hard time understanding why "literality" or "facticity" would be persuasive as grounds for hope in a person whose life has not been gripped by the *event* of the crucified Jesus in a manner I described in Chapter 8. I also fail to see how such "literality" or "facticity" adds anything at all to the motivation of someone who has been so gripped.

As I understand it, "hope" is an event, not the conclusion of an argument. It is the experience of Jesus' aliveness, here and now, which animates faith, hope and love. I confess that I suspect the parts of us that want to argue about these issues are the parts of us that don't believe and have not tasted resurrection.

For much more on the Crossan-Wright encounter, see Robert B. Stewart, ed., *The Resurrection of Jesus: John Dominic Crossan and N. T. Wright in Dialogue* (Minneapolis: Augsburg Fortress, 2006). For a cogent video presentation of Wright's perspective, see "Resurrection, Featuring N. T. (Tom) Wright," a DVD published by InterVarsity Press.

Early in the video, Wright says: "If the resurrection didn't happen, there's not much point being a Christian." I am puzzled by this line: it seems to want to ground an experience of faith in something more convincing than faith—but are rational cognition or scientific objectivity really more certain than faith? I would assent to Wright's formula, however, if

master and my God" (John 20:16 and 28). The pilgrims traveling to Emmaus report that their hearts burned within them as Jesus broke bread and gave it to them (Luke 24:32). In Mark's account, Jesus' followers are "seized" by "terror and amazement" (Mark 16:8). And Peter, always the most expressive of the lot, jumps into the sea and splashes naked to shore when he realizes who is waiting for him there (John 21:7).

These are instinctive responses to moments of unexpected encounter. They leave no doubt in those who experience them that something indisputably real has taken place. No one stops to ask what "real" might mean in these circumstances. They're too busy being amazed.[29]

I suspect that is the experience of all who come alive in the presence of the crucified Jesus. They know that something has happened—something real, something miraculous, something freeing, something joyful and life-giving. The resurrection of Jesus makes sense to them, not because an ancient witness says there was an empty tomb, or a nervous evangelical apologist proves beyond a

---

worded as follows: "If the resurrection stops happening, there's not much point to being a Christian."

On the relation of resurrection to hope, see N. T. Wright, *Surprised by Hope: Rethinking Heaven, the Resurrection, and the Mission of the Church* (New York: HarperCollins, 2008).

29 Cynthia Bourgeault is more convinced of the importance of making claims about a literal resurrection than I am, and warns against excessive subjectification of the resurrection event. I am continuing to ponder her insights. But she also has a keen sense for the mystery that clings to the risen Jesus and to those events in which people encounter him. She says there's "something a bit strange" about the resurrection appearances.

"Jesus is back, and he is indisputably in the flesh, but it's not exactly the same flesh he left the world in. Nor does he show any indication of planning to remain here for any length of time. He doesn't reappear in Jerusalem, unpack his bags, so to speak, and start rounding up backers to found the Jesus Christ Institute of Spiritual Transformation." His appearances are "fleeting and ephemeral. . . He is no ghost, that's for sure. And yet there is something distinctly ghostlike about his movements. . ." See *The Wisdom Jesus*, 127–137.

reasonable doubt that there was an empty tomb, but because they have experienced it.

And because they have experienced it, and for no other reason at all, they know the one who comes in the guise of a wounded criminal will not cease coming until that resurrection has happened to every one of the precious human beings who have graced this planet, in every time and place.

.   .   .

FREEDOM HAPPENS

I have been exploring the character of the genuine freedom that comes to life in a real human being as the consequence, concretely and specifically, of a lived event. For Christians, and for me personally, this event occurs in the company of a messy human being named Jesus, who hung in ignominy on a rough wooden cross.

It is not sufficient simply to hear *about* this human Jesus. It is only a proper "event" when we hear *from* Jesus—when we feel the ground shake underfoot in the presence of a love that will never let us go; when we feel the balm of a compassion that, momentarily but unmistakably, quiets the warfare within us.

The "new birth" is not the gift of head knowledge, but of heart encounter—an event which transforms clichés like "freedom" and "mess" into joyful fresh realities.[30]

Such an event only takes place in the presence of a divine Spirit whose answer to our question "Are you with me?" is an unconditional "*Yes*, always, even when you are a mess, even when you feel forsaken." It is *never* the gift of an Almighty who answers:

---

30 "Everything old has passed away; see, everything has become new!" (2 Corinthians 5:17).

Yes—but I will be watching you closely and recording every misdeed; *OR*

Yes—but only if you love me; *OR*

Yes—but you need to accept Jesus as your Savior before you die; *OR*

Yes—so long as you are one of the elect; *OR*

Yes—but please keep telling me I am great and you are small; *OR*

Yes—but only because Jesus' death assuaged my wrath over your sinfulness and rescued my holiness which you have insulted; *OR*

Yes, if you follow my guidelines for holy living.[31]

These responses imply abandonment, not love, so they can only generate fear, not trust. Certainly not freedom. *Threats* cannot nurture human growth toward genuine freedom.[32] Only safety can do that.

This genuine freedom is exhilarating because it is what we most deeply *want*. St. Augustine, famously, put it this way: "Love God and do what you will." [33] He knew the secret of freedom: that when

---

31 "An immovable and apathetic God cannot be understood as the foundation of human freedom. An absolutist sovereign in heaven does not inspire liberty on earth. Only the passionate God, the God who suffers by virtue of his passion for people, calls the freedom of men and women to life." Moltmann, *The Trinity and the Kingdom*, 218.

32 I italicize *threat* here to emphasize that God does not use abandonment as a club. Humans do experience God as abandoning them, but this is to see it from the human side, not from God's side.

33 *In epistulam Ioannis ad Parthos:* "Once for all, then, a short precept is given thee: Love, and do what thou wilt: whether thou hold thy peace, through love hold thy peace; whether thou cry out, through love cry out; whether thou correct, through love correct; whether thou spare, through love do thou spare: let the root of love be within, of this root can nothing spring but what is good."

My friend, Sam Alvord, hesitated to use Augustine's famous formula when counseling college students. He says the meaning of "do what you will" is concrete, dramatic and particularly alluring to adolescents raised in a moralistic or authoritarian community, while the phrase "love God" is abstract and weightless, and often not truly experienced. So "love God" quickly fades, leaving only the alluring invitation: "do what you will"! Apart from an event, freedom becomes licentiousness.

we are free, we want precisely what God wants—to love all of each other and all of ourselves. In the press of life, many times each day, we "forget" what we most deeply want.

When that happens, there's no profit in being reminded that we serve an awesome, holy God or being told that God expects us to love one another. What might actually help are friends who, because they embody the safety of unconditional love, feel free to call us back to ourselves. Friends who ask: "Is this who you really are? Is this what you really want?"[34]

The Spirit of God can be such a friend. So can the people around us, of whatever religious conviction, who personify in that moment God's unconditional love. So can the voice of the self that lives at the deepest place in our own being. In each of these "interventions," the event of the cross can be renewed.

So freedom comes and goes. It is not a permanent "possession" or a "steady state." It "happens," again and again, as we hear and inhabit the good news of the cross afresh. It may come when we least expect it. Often it is mediated to us by another human being who becomes for us, in that moment, the truth of the cross. Authentic human life, and the human ability to love, depends on the continual renewal of this event.

Between freedom's unpredictable comings we wait in memory and in hope. We remember moments of freedom and pray for their renewal. We wait expectantly—and sometimes we forget and do not wait at all—for the helpless but ever whispering God to break in once more, embracing us as we are, reminding us that we are free to be who we really are and thus to receive gratefully all that comes to us in the form of another human being.

Augustine seems to have been aware of this potential: he emphasizes and re-emphasizes the "love God" portion of his saying.

34 Or, as Paul asks his friends, "Who has bewitched you?" (Galatians 3:1).

•   •   •

FREE TO SUFFER AND FREE TO BE WHOLE

The freedom to be present to every part of ourselves and to the full reality of our neighbors, according to the testimony of many Christians through the ages, is the freedom to suffer more deeply. It is the freedom to hurt, to feel what we feel when we hurt and what others feel when they hurt. It is the freedom to be in hell with Jesus, whether it be the hell of our own suffering, or the hell of the suffering of the other human beings who have been given to us as bearers of the sufferings of Jesus.

In that hell, if it is truly what the Bible calls "hell," we may feel the presence of the One who went to hell on a cruel cross. Or we may feel an absence like he did, and find solidarity with every forsaken person.[35] At these times, we will speak our doubt, our anger, our despair into the yawning silence of the One who has promised not to forsake us, but who seems to have done so nonetheless. We will feel one with Jesus in the desperate abandonment of his "my God, why have you forsaken me." Perchance, we will be met in that

---

[35] Many Christian saints have called this experience "the ray of darkness" or "the dark night of the soul" and think of it as a dark inflowing of God into the soul. St. John of the Cross experienced it as the soul itself "perishing and melting away. . . in a cruel spiritual death, even as if it had been swallowed by a beast and felt itself being devoured in the darkness of its belly, suffering such anguish as was endured by Jonah in the belly of that beast of the sea"—where we can do nothing but "abide until the spiritual resurrection" for which we hope. St. John of the Cross, *Dark Night of the Soul* (New York: Doubleday, 1959/1990), 104.

Rowan Williams, the Archbishop of Canterbury, writes in a similar vein: "[S]erious Christians throughout the ages. . . interpret the 'dark night' as the experience of the strange and elusive reality of God himself." *A Ray of Darkness: Sermons and Reflections* (Boston: Cowley Publications, 1995), 82.

Thomas Merton: "God, who is everywhere, never leaves us. Yet, he seems sometimes to be present, sometimes absent. If we do not know him well, we do not realize that he may be more present to us when he is absent than when he is present." *No Man Is an Island,* 178.

abandonment by the abandoned one, and our loneliness and despair will find comfort and healing.

The freedom to be a mess—to be accepting of and present to every part of us, no matter how "shabby", "disreputable" or "troublesome"—is the heart of the Christian understanding of "wholeness." It is not the shiny wholeness of the Almighty and his religious denizens, a bright lacquer sealing over the seams in our broken selves. It is rather the shabby, messy wholeness of a real self, a wholeness that gives an honored place to every jagged fragment floating in the flux of our lives.[36]

In this paradoxical wholeness, we experience hope, a hope that welcomes hopelessness into its embrace, that lives between the painful reality of the "not yet" and the renewed encounters with a resurrection already—unmistakably—felt and known.[37]

In this paradoxical wholeness, there is *joy*—the strange joy that shines from faces tracked with tears.

---

[36] "The incarnate God is present, and can be experienced, in the humanity of every man, and in full human corporeality. No one need dissemble and appear other than he is to perceive the fellowship of the human God with him. Rather, he can lay aside all dissembling and sham and become what he truly is in this human God." Moltmann, *The Crucified God*, 276–277.

Philip Yancey offers two illustrations. When an old friend told the monk Thomas Merton that he (Merton) had not changed despite his years in a monastery, Merton replied, "Why would I? Here our duty is to be more ourselves, not less." And a saying of Rabbi Zusya: "In the world to come I shall not be asked: 'Why were you not Moses?' I shall be asked: 'Why were you not Zusya?'" *Reaching for the Invisible God: What Can We Expect to Find?* (Grand Rapids, MI: Zondervan Publishing House, 2000), 163.

[37] Jacques Ellul elaborates on hope's dialectical relationship with hopelessness in *Hope in Time of Abandonment* (New York: The Seabury Press, 1973), 192.

Moltmann writes: "As Paul says in I Corinthians 15, only with the resurrection of the dead, the murdered and the gassed, only with the healing of those in despair who bear lifelong wounds, only with the abolition of all rule and authority, only with the annihilation of death will the Son hand over the kingdom to the Father. Then God will turn his sorrow into eternal joy. This will be the sign of the completion of the trinitarian history of God and the end of world history, the overcoming of the history of man's sorrow and the fulfillment of his history of hope." *The Crucified God*, 278.

BIBLIOGRAPHY

A

Rebecca Adams and Robin Collins, "Understanding Atonement:
A New and Orthodox Theory" (1996), on-line at
http://home.messiah.edu/~ rcollins/AT7.HTM

James Alison, *On Being Liked* (New York: The Crossroad Publishing
Company, 2003).

James Alison, *Raising Abel: The Recovery of the Eschatological Imagination*
(New York: The Crossroad Publishing Company, 1996).

Paul Althaus, *The Theology of Martin Luther* (Philadelphia: Fortress Press, 1966).

B

Roland H. Bainton, *Here I Stand: A Life of Martin Luther*
(New York: New American Library, 1950).

Mark D. Baker, *Proclaiming the Scandal of the Cross: Contemporary Images of the
Atonement* (Grand Rapids, MI: Baker Academic, 2006).

Randall Balmer, *Mine Eyes Have Seen the Glory: A Journey into the Evangelical
Subculture in America* (New York: Oxford University Press, 1989).

Randall Balmer, *Thy Kingdom Come: How the Religious Right Distorts the Faith and
Threatens America* (New York: Basic Books, 2006).

Karl Barth, *The Christian Life* (Grand Rapids, MI: William B. Eerdmans
Publishing Company, 1981).

Karl Barth, *Church Dogmatics*, II/2, "The Doctrine of God"
(Edinburgh: T. & T. Clark, 1957).

Karl Barth, "Miserable Lazarus" in Karl Barth and Eduard Thurneysen,
God's Search for Man (New York: Round Table Press, 1935).

Ernest Becker, *Escape from Evil* (New York: The Free Press, 1975).

Ernest Becker, *The Denial of Death* (New York: The Free Press, 1973).

Gina Bergamino, "In Missouri," *Christian Century*, 107 (#19),
June 13–20, 1990, 588.

Roberta Bondi, *Memories of God: Theological Reflections on a Life*
(Nashville: Abingdon Press, 1995).

Dietrich Bonhoeffer, *Letters and Papers from Prison*, ed. Eberhard Bethge

(New York: Macmillan, 1972).

Marcus Borg, *Conflict, Holiness and Politics in the Teachings of Jesus* (Harrisburg, PA: Trinity Press International, 1998).

Marcus Borg, *Jesus: A New Vision* (New York: HarperCollins Publishers, 1987).

Paul Borgman, *Genesis: The Story We Haven't Heard* (Downers Grove, IL: Intervarsity Press, 2001).

Cynthia Bourgeault, *The Wisdom Jesus* (Boston: Shambhala Publications, 2008).

John Bowlby, *Attachment and Loss* (3 volumes), (New York: Basic Books, 1969, 1973, 1980).

James Breech, *Jesus and Postmodernism* (Minneapolis: Fortress Press, 1989).

Greg Brown, "Lord, I Have Made You a Place in My Heart," *The Poet Game* (Red House, 1994).

Lyn Mikel Brown and Carol Gilligan, *Meeting at the Crossroads: Women's Psychology and Girls' Development* (Cambridge, MA: Harvard University Press, 1992).

Walter Brueggeman, *Theology of the Old Testament* (St. Paul, MN: Augsburg Fortress Publishers, 1997).

Mark Buchanan, "Stuck on the Road to Emmaus," *Christianity Today* 43:8 (July 12, 1999), 55.

Delbert Burkett, *The Son of Man Debate: A History and Evaluation* (Cambridge: Cambridge University Press, 1999).

C

Donald Capps, *Jesus: A Psychological Biography* (St. Louis: Chalice Press, 2000).

John Caputo, *Against Ethics: Contributions to a Poetics of Obligation with Constant Reference to Deconstruction* (Bloomington IN: Indiana University Press, 1993).

John Caputo, *Radical Hermeneutics: Repetition, Deconstruction, and the Hermeneutic Project* (Bloomington, IN: Indiana University Press, 1987).

John Caputo, *The Weakness of God: A Theology of the Event* (Bloomington, IN: Indiana University Press, 2006).

Edward J. Carnell, *Introduction to Christian Apologetics: A Philosophical Defense of Trinitarian-Theistic Faith* (Grand Rapids, MI: Wm. B. Eerdmans Publishing Company, 1948).

Edward John Carnell, *The Case for Biblical Christianity*, ed. Ronald H. Nash (Grand Rapids, MI: Wm. B. Eerdmans Publishing Co., 1969).

Joel Carpenter, *Revive Us Again: The Re-Awakening of American Fundamentalism* (New York: Oxford University Press, 1997).

Pema Chodron, *Comfortable with Uncertainty* (Boston: Shambhala Publications, Inc., 2002).

David Clark, "Why Did Christ Have to Die?" *New England Reformed Journal*, Autumn 1996.

Gordon Clark, "Faith and Reason," *Christianity Today*, February 18, 1957; March 4, 1957.

Bruce Cockburn, "Cry of a Tiny Babe," *Nothing But a Burning Light* (Sony, 1991).

Leonard Cohen, "Suzanne Takes You Down," *Parasites of Heaven* (Toronto: McClelland and Stewart, 1966).

Charles Colson, *Did God have anything to do with Katrina?*" (www.mediammatters.org, September 13, 2005).

Jack Crabtree in McKenzie Study Center newsletter, copyright 1986.

William Lane Craig, "God Is Not Dead Yet," *Christianity Today* (July 2008).

Percy Crawford, *Salvation Full and Free*, (Philadelphia, PA: Young People's Church of the Air, 1943).

Percy Crawford, *Whither Goest Thou: A Series of Radio Messages Preached on 250 Stations over the Mutual Network* (East Stroudsburg, PA: The Pinebrook Book Club, 1946).

D

Lydia Davis, *Break It Down* (Knopf: New York, 1986).

Jean Delumeau, *Sin and Fear: The Emergence of a Western Guilt Culture, 13ᵗʰ-18ᵗʰ Centuries* (New York: St. Martin's Press, 1991).

Annie Dillard, *For the Time Being* (New York: Alfred A. Knopf, 1999).

Francis W. Dixon, "Is Jesus Lord of Your. . . ?" *Decision* 40:6 (June 1999).

Fyodor Dostoyevsky, *The Brothers Karamazov* (New York: New American Library, 1957).

David James Duncan, *God Laughs and Plays* (Great Barrington, MA: Triad Books, 2006).

David James Duncan, *The Brothers K* (New York: Doubleday, 1992).

E

Jay Earley, *Self-Therapy: A Step-By-Step Guide to Creating Inner Wholeness Using IFS, a New, Cutting-Edge Therapy* (Minneapolis: Mill City Press, 2009).

Gerhard Ebeling, *Luther: An Introduction to His Thought* (Philadelphia: Fortress Press, 1972).

Bob Ekblad, A *New Christian Manifesto: Pledging Allegiance to the Kingdom of God* (Louisville: Westminster John Knox Press, 2008).

Elisabeth Elliot, *Through Gates of Splendor* (New York: Harper and Brothers, 1957).

Jacques Ellul, *Apocalypse: The Book of Revelation* (New York: The Seabury Press, 1977).

Jacques Ellul, *Hope in Time of Abandonment* (New York: The Seabury Press, 1973).

Jacques Ellul, *The Ethics of Freedom* (Grand Rapids MI: William B. Eerdmans Publishing Company, 1976).

Jacques Ellul, *To Will and To Do: An Ethical Research for Christians* (Philadelphia: Pilgrim Press, 1969).

Shusaku Endo, *Deep River*, Van C. Gessel, trans. (New York: New Directions Books, 1994).

Shusaku Endo, *Silence*, William Johnston, trans. (New York: Taplinger Publishing Company, 1980).

Erik H. Erikson, *Childhood and Society,* rev. ed. (NY: W. W. Norton, 1963).

Erik H. Erikson, *Young Man Luther: A Study in Psychoanalysis and History* (New York: W. W. Norton and Company, Inc., 1958).

F

James F. Findlay, Jr., *Dwight L. Moody: American Evangelist, 1837–1899* (Chicago: University of Chicago Press, 1969).

Roger Finke and Rodney Stark, *The Churching of America, 1776–1990: Winners and Losers in Our Religious Economy* (Piscataway, NJ: Rutgers University Press, 1992).

Ken Foster, "Introduction," *The KGB Bar Reader* (New York: William Morrow and Company, 1998).

Frances Fitzgerald, "The New Evangelicals: A Growing Challenge to the Religious Right," *The New Yorker* (June 30, 2008).

Michel Foucault, *Discipline and Punish: The Birth of the Prison* (New York: Vintage Books, 1979).

Marshall Frady, *Billy Graham: A Parable of American Righteousness* (New York: Little, Brown, 1979).

Douglas W. Frank, *Less Than Conquerors: The Evangelical Quest for Power in the Early Twentieth Century* (Eugene, OR: Wipf and Stock Publishers, 2009). Originally published as *Less Than Conquerors: How Evangelicals Entered the Twentieth Century* (Grand Rapids, MI: William B. Eerdmans Publishing Company, 1986).

Paula Fredericksen, *Augustine and the Jews: A Christian Defense of Jews and Judaism* (New York: Doubleday, 2008).

Terence E. Fretheim, *The Suffering of God: An Old Testament Perspective* (Philadelphia: Fortress Press, 1984).

Edward William Fudge and Robert A. Peterson, *Two Views of Hell: A Biblical and Theological Dialogue* (Downers Grove, IL: InterVarsity Press, 2000).

G

Mary Gaitskill, "Revelation" in David Rosenberg, *Communion: Contemporary Writers Reveal the Bible in Their Lives* (Garden City, NY: Anchor Books, 1997).

Nora Gallagher, *Things Seen and Unseen: A Year Lived in Faith* (New York: Alfred A. Knopf, 1998).

James Gilligan, *Violence: Reflections on a National Epidemic* (New York: Vintage Books, 1996).

Laurie Goodstein, "Rev. Dr. Carl F. H. Henry, 90, Brain of Evangelical Movement," *The New York Times*, December 13, 2003.

Philip Gourevitch, *We Wish to Inform You that Tomorrow We Will Be Killed with Our Families* (New York: Farrar, Straus and Giroux, 1998).

Billy Graham, *Calling Youth to Christ* (Grand Rapids, MI: Zondervan Publishing House, 1947).

Joel B. Green and Mark D. Baker, *Recovering the Scandal of the Cross: Atonement in New Testament and Contemporary Contexts* (Downers Grove, IL: InterVarsity Press, 2001).

H

Douglas John Hall, *God and Human Suffering: An Exercise in the Theology of the Cross* (Minneapolis: Augsburg Publishing House, 1986).

Douglas John Hall, *Lighten Our Darkness: Toward an Indigenous Theology of the Cross* (Philadelphia: Westminster Press, 1976).

Carl F. H. Henry, *Confessions a Theologian* (Waco, TX: Word Books, 1986).

Carl F. H. Henry, *God, Revelation and Authority*, 6 volumes (Waco: Word, 1976–1983).

Carl F. H. Henry, *Remaking the Modern Mind* (Grand Rapids, MI: Wm. B. Eerdmans Publishing Company, 1946).

Carl F. H. Henry, *The Uneasy Conscience of American Fundamentalism* (Grand Rapids, MI: William B. Eerdmans Publishing Co., 1947).

Etty Hillesum, *An Interrupted Life: The Diaries of Etty Hillesum, 1941–1943* (New York: Pantheon Books, 1983).

Peter Homans, *The Ability to Mourn: Disillusionment and the Social Origins of Psychoanalysis* (Chicago: University of Chicago Press, 1989).

William Dean Howells, "Eighty Years and After," reprinted from *Harper's Magazine* (December 1919) in *Harper's Magazine* (March 2000).

I

Immaculée Ilibagiza with Steve Erwin, *Left to Tell: Discovering God Amidst the Rwandan Holocaust* (Carlsbad, CA: Hay House, Inc., 2006).

J

Douglas and Rhonda Jacobsen, *Scholarship and Christian Faith: Enlarging the Conversation* (New York: Oxford University Press, 2004).

Grace M. Jantzen, *Becoming Divine: Towards a Feminist Philosophy of Religion* (Bloomington: Indiana University Press, 1999).

Brad Jersak and Michael Hardin, eds., *Stricken by God: NonViolent Identification and the Victory of Christ* (Abbotsford, BC: Fresh Wind Press, 2007).

K

Robert Karen, *Becoming Attached: First Relationships and How They Shape Our Capacity to Love* (New York: Oxford University Press, 1998).

Gershen Kaufman, *Shame: The Power of Caring* (Rochester, VT: Schenkman Books, Inc., 1980).

Catherine Keller, *The Face of the Deep: A Theology of Becoming* (London: Routledge, 2003).

Jane Kenyon, *Otherwise: New and Selected Poems* (St. Paul, MN: Graywolf Press, 1996).

L

Catherine Mowry Lacugna, *God for Us: The Trinity and Christian Life* (New York: HarperCollins Publishers, 1993).

Bev Laird, "Faith Autobiography" (in manuscript).

Anne Lamott, *Plan B: Further Thoughts on Faith* (New York: Riverhead Books, 2005).

Anne Lamott, *Traveling Mercies: Some Thoughts on Faith* (New York: Anchor Books, 1999).

Nicholas Lash, *Easter in Ordinary: Reflections on Human Experience and the Knowledge of God* (Charlottesville: University Press of Virginia, 1988).

Miriam Paine Lemcio, *Deo Volente: A Biography of Stephen W. Paine* (Houghton, NY: Houghton College, 1987).

Deborah Anna Luepnitz, *The Family Interpreted: Psychoanalysis, Feminism, and Family Therapy* (New York: Basic Books, 1988).

M

John MacArthur, Jr., *Saved Without a Doubt: How to Be Sure of Your Salvation* (Colorado Springs: Chariot Victor Publishing, 1992).

Dorothea S. McArthur, *Birth of a Self in Adulthood* (Northvale, NJ: Jason Aronson, 1988).

Michael McGirr, "A Conversation with Tim Winton," in *Image: A Journal of the Arts and Religion*, Issue #10 (Summer 1995).

Brian D. McLaren, *Everything Must Change: Jesus, Global Crises, and a Revolution of Hope* (Nashville, TN: Thomas Nelson, 2007).

Brian D. McLaren, *The Last Word and the Word After That: A Tale of Faith, Doubt, and a New Kind of Christianity* (San Francisco: Jossey-Bass, 2005).

Nancy Mairs, *Ordinary Time: Cycles in Marriage, Faith, and Renewal* (Boston: Beacon Press, 1993).

Brennan Manning, *Abba's Child: The Cry of the Heart for Intimate Belonging* (Colorado Springs: NavPress Publishing Group, 1994).

Dan Marks, "Undivided Heart," copyright Maranatha Praise, 1996.

George M. Marsden, *Fundamentalism and American Culture: The Shaping of Twentieth-Century Evangelicalism, 1870–1925* (New York: Oxford University Press, 1980).

George M. Marsden, *Reforming Fundamentalism: Fuller Seminary and the New Evangelicalism* (Grand Rapids, MI: William B. Eerdmans Publishing Company, 1987).

George M. Marsden, *Understanding Fundamentalism and Evangelicalism* (Grand Rapids, MI: William B. Eerdmans Publishing Company, 1991).

William Martin, *A Prophet with Honor: The Billy Graham Story* (New York: William Morrow and Company, Inc., 1991).

Karl Marx, "Contributions to the Critique of Hegel's Philosophy of Right: Introduction," in Eugene Kamenka, ed., *The Portable Marx* (New York: Penguin Books, 1983).

Thomas Matthews, *Under the Influence* (New York: Macmillan, 1977).

Gerald G. May, *The Dark Night of the Soul: A Psychiatrist Explores the Connection Between Darkness and Spiritual Growth* (New York: HarperSanFrancisco, 2004).

Thomas Merton, *New Seeds of Contemplation* (New York: New Directions Books, 1961).

Thomas Merton, *No Man Is an Island* (New York: Image Books, 1967).

John Miller, *Jesus at Thirty: A Psychological and Historical Portrait* (Minneapolis: Fortress Press, 1997).

Patrick D. Miller, *They Cried Unto the Lord: The Form and Theology of Biblical Prayer* (Minneapolis: Fortress Press, 1994).

Jurgen Moltmann, *The Crucified God* (New York: Harper and Row, Publishers, 1973).

Jurgen Moltmann, *The Trinity and the Kingdom: The Doctrine of God* (Minneapolis: Fortress Press, 1993).

N

The Navigators, Circular Advertisement for *Discipleship Journal* (July, 2008).

David Neff, "The Gospel of Jesus Christ: An Evangelical Celebration," *Christianity Today,* June 14, 1999 (Vol. 43, #7).

Rudy Nelson, *The Making and Unmaking of an Evangelical Mind: The Case of Edward Carnell* (Cambridge University Press, 1987).

Lewis Nordan, "My Humble Self," from *Boy with Loaded Gun* (Chapel Hill:

Algonquin Books, 2000) in *Harper's Magazine* (December 1999).

Henri J. M. Nouwen, *The Inner Voice of Love: A Journey through Anguish to Freedom* (New York: Image Books, 1999).

O

Samuel Osherson, *Finding Our Fathers: How a Man's Life Is Shaped by His Relationship with His Father* (New York: Fawcett Columbine, 1986).

P

J. I. Packer, "What Did the Cross Achieve? The Logic of Penal Substitution," *Tyndale Bulletin* 25 (1974).

Orlando Patterson, *Rituals of Blood: Consequences of Slavery in Two American Centuries* (New York: Basic Civitas, 1998).

Adam Phillips, *Winnicott* (Cambridge, MA: Harvard University Press, 1988).

J. B. Phillips, *Ring of Truth: A Translator's Testimony* (London: Hodder & Stoughton, 1967).

J. B. Phillips, *The New Testament in Modern English* (New York: The Macmillan Company, 1960).

J. B. Phillips, *Your God Is Too Small* (New York: The Macmillan Company, 1961).

Clark H. Pinnock, *Most Moved Mover: A Theology of God's Openness* (Grand Rapids, MI: Baker Academic, 2001).

Clark Pinnock and Robert C. Brow, *Unbounded Love: A Good News Theology for the 21st Century* (Downers Grove, IL: InterVarsity Press, 1994).

William C. Placher, *Narratives of a Vulnerable God: Christ, Theology, and Scripture* (Louisville KY: Westminster John Knox Press, 1994).

Jim Plueddeman, "Blanchard Hall Revisited," *Wheaton Alumni*, December 1990/January 1991.

Alexander Pope, *An Essay on Criticism* (1711).

R

Melissa Raphael, *The Feminine Face of God in Auschwitz: A Jewish Feminist Theology of the Holocaust* (London: Routledge, 2003).

John R. Rice, *Bobbed Hair, Bossy Wives, and Women Preachers* (Wheaton, IL: Sword of the Lord Publishers, 1941).

Rainer Maria Rilke, *Letters to a Young Poet,* Joan M Burnham, transl. (Novato, CA: New World Library, 2000).

Richard Rohr, lecture series, "Great Themes of Paul: Life as Participation," St. Anthony Messenger Press at http://catalog.americancatholic.org.

Garth M. Rosell, *The Surprising Work of God: Harold John Ockenga, Billy Graham, and the Rebirth of Evangelicalism* (Grand Rapids, MI: Baker Academic, 2008).

Hanna Rosin, *God's Harvard: A Christian College on a Mission to Save America* (New York: Harcourt, Inc., 2007).

William Woodin Rowe, *Dostoyevsky: Child and Man in His Works (New York: New York University Press, 1968).*

Jalal al-Din Rumi, *The Essential Rumi,* Coleman Barks, translator (New York: HarperCollins Publishers, 1995).

S
St. John of the Cross, *Dark Night of the Soul* (New York: Doubleday, 1959/1990).

John Sanders, *The God Who Risks: A Theology of Providence* (Downers Grove, IL: InterVarsity Press, 1998).

Maggie Scarf, *Intimate Worlds: How Families Thrive and Why They Fail* (New York: Ballantine Books, 1995).

Julia Scheeres, *Jesus Land: A Memoir* (Berkeley, CA: Counterpoint, 2005).

Orville Schell, "Searching for the Dalai Lama," *The Nation* (April 3, 2000).

Richard C. Schwartz, *Internal Family Systems Therapy* (New York: The Guilford Press, 1997).

Gerald L. Sittser, *A Grace Disguised: How the Soul Grows Through Loss* (Grand Rapids, MI: Zondervan Publishing House, 1996).

Christian Smith *et al.*, *American Evangelicalism: Embattled and Thriving* (Chicago: University of Chicago Press, 1998).

Aleksandr I. Solzhenitsyn, *Gulag Archipelago 1918–1956: An Experiment in Literary Investigation* (New York: Harper and Row, 1974).

R. C. Sproul, Jr., *Almighty Over All: Understanding the Sovereignty of God* (Grand Rapids, MI: Baker Books, 1999).

Heather Hillstrom Starbird, letter to the author.

Robert B. Stewart, ed., *The Resurrection of Jesus: John Dominic Crossan and N. T. Wright in Dialogue* (Minneapolis: Augsburg Fortress, 2006).

John Stott, *The Cross of Christ*, (Downers Grove, IL: InterVarsity Press, 1986).

Jean Sulivan, *Morning Light: The Spiritual Journal of Jean Sulivan* (New York: Paulist Press, 1988).

George Sweeting, *The Jack Wyrtzen Story* (Grand Rapids, MI: Zondervan Publishing House, 1960).

T

Henry David Thoreau, "Life without Principle" in Joseph Wood Krutch, ed., *Thoreau: Walden and Other Writings* (New York: Bantam Books, 1962).

Eduard Thurneysen, *A Theology of Pastoral Care* (Richmond, VA: John Knox Press, 1962).

W

Simone Weil, "Justice and Human Society" in Eric O. Springsted, ed., *Simone Weil* (Maryknoll, NY: Orbis Books, 1998).

Simone Weil, "Reflections on the Right Use of School Studies," in George A. Panichas, ed., *The Simone Weil Reader* (Mt. Kisco, NY: Moyer Bell Limited, 1977).

Simone Weil, "Spiritual Autobiography" in *The Simone Weil Reader* (Mt Kisco, NY: Moyer Bell Ltd., 1977).

Simone Weil, *Waiting for God* (New York: Harper and Row, 1973).

David F. Wells, *No Place for Truth: Or Whatever Happened to Evangelical Theology?* (Grand Rapids, MI: Wm. B. Eerdmans Publishing Company, 1993).

Elie Wiesel, *All Rivers Run to the Sea: Memoirs* (New York: Alfred A. Knopf, 1995).

Elie Wiesel, *Night* (New York: Bantam Books, 1960).

Rowan Williams, *A Ray of Darkness: Sermons and Reflections* (Boston: Cowley Publications, 1995).

Walter Wink, *Engaging the Powers* (Minneapolis: Fortress Press, 1992).

Walter Wink, *Naming the Powers* (Minneapolis: Fortress Press, 1984).

Walter Wink, *The Human Being: Jesus and the Enigma of the Son of the Man* (Minneapolis: Augsburg Fortress, 2002).

Walter Wink, *Unmasking the Powers* (Minneapolis: Fortress Press, 1986).

Nicholas Wolterstorff, *Lament for a Son* (Grand Rapids, MI: William B. Eerdmans Publishing Company, 1987).

Patrick Woodhouse, *Etty Hillesum: A Life Transformed* (New York: Continuum, 2009).

N. T. Wright, "Resurrection, Featuring N. T. (Tom) Wright," DVD (Downers Grove, IL: InterVarsity Press, 2006).

N. T. Wright, *Surprised by Hope: Rethinking Heaven, the Resurrection, and the Mission of the Church* (New York: HarperCollins, 2008).

Y

Philip Yancey, *Reaching for the Invisible God: What Can We Expect to Find?* (Grand Rapids, MI: Zondervan Publishing House, 2000).

Philip Yancey, *What's So Amazing About Grace* (Grand Rapids, MI: Zondervan Publishing House, 1997).

William P. Young, *The Shack: Where Tragedy Confronts Eternity* (Los Angeles: Windblown Media, 2007).

WEBSITES:

www.sharperiron.org/attachment.php?attachmentid=176 (ShaperIron)

http://www.desiringgod.org/ResourceLibrary/TopicIndex/43/1582_How_Does_a_Sovereign_God_Love? (John Piper)

http://www.gotquestions.org (Got Questions Ministries)

www.youthspecialties.com (Youth Specialties, Inc.)

www.triptykos.com (Frank Rogers, Mark Yaconelli and Andrew Dreitcer, The Triptykos School of Spiritual Formation)

www.PatRobertson.com (The Official Site of Pat Robertson 2008)

www.CNN.com (9/14/01).

www.religioustolerance.org (Ontario Consultants on Religious Tolerance)

CPSIA information can be obtained
at www.ICGtesting.com
Printed in the USA
LVHW012226060722
722763LV00007B/232